ALTERNATIVE MEDIA IN CANADA

Edited by Kirsten Kozolanka, Patricia Mazepa, and David Skinner

ALTERNATIVE
MEDIA
IN CANADA

UBCPress · Vancouver · Toronto

21 20 19 18 17 16 15 14 13   5 4 3 2

Printed in Canada on FSC-certified ancient-forest-free paper (100% post-consumer recycled) that is processed chlorine- and acid-free.

Library and Archives Canada Cataloguing in Publication

Alternative media in Canada / edited by Kirsten Kozolanka, Patricia Mazepa, and David Skinner.

Includes bibliographical references and index.
Issued also in electronic formats.
ISBN 978-0-7748-2164-3 (bound); ISBN 978-0-7748-2165-0 (pbk.)

1. Alternative mass media – Canada. 2. Alternative mass media – Social aspects – Canada. 3. Alternative mass media – Political aspects – Canada. I. Kozolanka, Kirsten II. Mazepa, Patricia III. Skinner, David, 1956-

P96.A442C3 2012   502.230971   C2011-908022-2

Canada

UBC Press gratefully acknowledges the financial support for our publishing program of the Government of Canada (through the Canada Book Fund), the Canada Council for the Arts, and the British Columbia Arts Council.

This book has been published with the help of a grant from the Canadian Federation for the Humanities and Social Sciences, through the Aid to Scholarly Publications Program, using funds provided by the Social Sciences and Humanities Research Council of Canada.

Printed and bound in Canada by Friesens
Set in Helvetica Condensed and Myriad by Artegraphica Design Co. Ltd.
Copy editor: Deborah Kerr
Proofreader: Jenna Newman
Indexer: Pat Buchanan

UBC Press
The University of British Columbia
2029 West Mall
Vancouver, BC V6T 1Z2
www.ubcpress.ca

Contents

Acknowledgments

As both academics and media activists, we thank those many practitioners of alternative media who labour unceasingly in the trenches, mostly on the margins, for progressive media transformation, democratic communication, and a more democratic society.

We also thank the anonymous peer reviewers for their obvious expertise and scholarly attention in this project. Their thoughtful and knowledgeable comments were appreciated and incorporated into the book's content. Emily Andrew at UBC Press has been a patient and helpful editor throughout the long journey of bringing this volume to life. Our research assistant par excellence, Nicole Cohen, has our gratitude and admiration for her diligence and attention to every detail and especially for keeping us on track organizationally.

We thank the Canadian Media Research Consortium for its financial support, as independent funding for such projects is essential.

ALTERNATIVE MEDIA IN CANADA

Considering Alternative Media in Canada
Structure, Participation, Activism

KIRSTEN KOZOLANKA, PATRICIA MAZEPA, AND DAVID SKINNER

> *Communications and mass culture are not simply receptacles into which content can be put ... The mass media cannot be changed by a mere inversion of the signs of the messages which they transmit. It is this intimate integration of communications into the totality of relations of production and social relations which must be grasped if we are to understand its function in reproducing the everyday legitimacy ... of domination.*
>
> *– Armand Mattelart (1980)*

Mattelart's criteria for democratization remain valid today. As he underscores, grasping the "totality of relations of production and social relations" suggests that developing a more democratic media system must include changes in media structure, participation, and activism together. The challenge here is not to reproduce the everyday legitimacy of domination, as corporate media tend to do, but to confront power in the many modes of production and representation that support its inequalities, wherever they may be.

Although the resources and dominance of Canada's corporate media make alternative media appear small, the continuing growth and diversity of the latter indicate that they offer much greater potential for public participation in media production and decision making than is evident, or ever possible, in the corporate model. Working from this perspective, this book moves away from traditional perceptions of alternative media as encompassing any content that is not mainstream toward a radical rethinking and repositioning of the field in terms of the relations of production and social relations that characterize alternative media.

Drawing from theorists such as Williams (1977), Keane (1991), and Curran (2002), this book illustrates how alternative media play a key role in public debate, the construction of community, and social justice struggles across a range of social dimensions. Taking a critical approach, it employs Couldry and Curran's (2003, 7) general definition of alternative media as "media production that challenges, at least implicitly, actual concentrations of media power." Although this definition is somewhat ambiguous, it draws attention to the fact that these media occupy contested and shifting terrain, and that the views and ideas they contain are not marginal in any larger social sense, but indicate sustained efforts for more democratic media and society as one and the same. Such a starting point also recognizes that dominant corporate media systematically distort, marginalize, or under-represent particular issues, individuals, or groups (see Hackett and Gruneau 2000), and thus contain or impede attempts at reform or change. It also appreciates that these challenges may take many forms such that the range of what is alternative is itself one of negotiation and contest, as illustrated in the breadth of works included here.

Although we appreciate Schudson's (2000, 183) caveat that "it would be a mistake to see large corporations and the media as working hand in glove to stifle dissent or promote a lethargic public acceptance of the existing distribution of power," there is a plethora of evidence that private corporate ownership does significantly affect the content generated by the media that dominate the Canadian mediascape. Studies by NewsWatch Canada, for example, have documented an "apparent unwillingness or inability to adequately cover" issues of labour, social inequality, corporate concentration, and the relationships between them (Hackett and Gruneau 2000, 166). These studies also identified significant blind spots in coverage of a number of important public issues, such as "environmental degradation as a systemic and ongoing problem," "human rights abuses by Canada's 'friends,'" and "gender-related stereotypes" (ibid.). Critical media scholars have also indicated the absence of, or distortions in, corporate media coverage of a range of social topics, including poverty, gender, race, ethnicity, and Aboriginal peoples (Jiwani 2010a, 2010b; Mahtani

2008; Jiwani and Young 2006; Roth 2005; Keung 2004; Alia 1999). The evidence from critical research indicates that these problems stem from a broad set of complex factors, which, taken together, normalize the exercise of corporate power. These include standardized editorial policies, concentrated ownership structures, and limiting codes and practices of professional journalism, among others (see Canada 2006; Hackett and Gruneau 2000; Hackett and Zhao 1996).

In this context, this book loosely deploys Bourdieu's (2005) notion of the journalistic field to frame alternative media as forms of social action specifically designed to address social, political economic, and cultural issues and concerns. Thus, the social relations, issues, and experiences of groups that are often marginalized or excluded in corporate media are both the focus of and the impetus for alternative media. In this view, a key feature of "media power" is the "power to represent the reality of others" (Couldry and Curran 2003, 7). Additionally, as Couldry and Curran (ibid.) note, the way this reality is represented "is an increasingly significant theme of social conflict," such that "the role of alternative media in providing alternative ways of seeing these groups and events is (also) of increasing importance." Although our analysis situates dominant media and media power as playing a centripetal role in civil society and public communication, we do stress that alternative media are also central – albeit very unequally – in the ongoing struggle over meaning. This struggle includes opening up or democratizing media production, advancing media as a public resource (rather than privately owned property), and appreciating that alternative media can be as diverse as the publics they express, bring together, and activate. Alternative media can thus represent possibilities for progressive social change, or counter-hegemonic transformation, and can, at times, be considered both media and social movement, a point made by Canadian communication scholar Raboy (1984) in one of the first studies of alternative media in Québec.

Although alternative media practice generally lies outside leading regulatory frameworks, an environment that is not conducive to public participation has an incalculable impact on the sites and spheres where it takes place, and it is invariably affected by the dominant political economy and larger Canadian mediascape. This includes a global political economic environment that has experienced both selective prosperity and global recession, in which Canada, like other countries (Bagdikian 2000; McChesney 2008b; Chakravartty and Zhao 2008; Castells 2009), has undergone consolidation and corporatization of its culture and communication industries. Bennett's (2003, 18) encapsulation of the paradox this presents within this complex national and global environment is particularly striking. Bennett maintains that corporate media and global networks are indeed the strongest, but networks of resistance have gained ground as well. Although Canada cannot claim to have more powerful webs of resistance, we can reflect, as Bennett does, on the potential for social transformation both within and beyond our national borders through, by, and in alternative media. We also keep in mind that this observation was made decades ago by Raboy (1984, 11), who wrote that traditional media were changing but so too were political movements. It is this very potential for the possibility of social change that encourages alternative media activity.

Alternative media take any number of material forms and genres, including newspapers, radio, television, film, and magazines, as well as web-based media and a wide variety of non-traditional forms such as zines, postering, tagging, street theatre, murals, and culture jamming. The increasing use of web-based media has led some media theorists to argue that contemporary communications systems "create realms of social interaction that render place inconsequential, if not irrelevant" (Howley 2010, 8). Yet, though there are accelerating trends in global communication, migration, and varieties of convergence (economic, technological, ecological), our everyday experience and avenues of action remain rooted in specific geographic locations and in the political economic and cultural institutions that define those places. Media provide key modes of communicating and understanding that sense of place, and when the imperatives that drive corporate media foreclose on those avenues of expression, both our understanding of the social landscape of which we are a part and the avenues of action that it affords are diminished. In this vein, this book offers an opportunity for alternative media students, researchers, and practitioners, in Canada and abroad, to consider some of the unique characteristics of alternative media in Canada in terms of their political economic and historical contexts to advance democratic change.

A Distinctly Canadian Context

Although alternative media in Canada share certain features with their counterparts in other countries, they are characterized by the peculiarities and exigencies of the history and features of the Canadian state and the diversity of its publics, which need to be identified at the outset. First, what is commonly called Canada's two linguistic solitudes (from its English and French heritage) underlie what are, in many ways, two quite dissimilar media systems – systems that reflect not only linguistic differences but also cultural and political distinctions – as well as divergence between provincial and federal policies. In turn, this distinction is reflected in the relatively light representation and discussion of French-language and Québécois media in this collection. Second, though Canada is sometimes celebrated as having particularly strong and vibrant Aboriginal media, the history and structure of this field reflect the tensions between Aboriginal peoples and the Canadian state: at times, these are enabling; at others, they are frustrating and discriminatory. Third, to an arguably lesser degree, this volatile relationship with the state has also affected Canada's diverse immigrant experience. These experiences are reflected in thriving ethnic media and their range of commercially successful counterparts, which enable people to stay in touch with familiar traditions and communities, as well as reach out to create new ones. As a result, the transcendence of borders and the cultural hybridity of these media make them particularly unique. Fourth, the enduring features of place underlie the breadth of the Canadian mediascape. This includes the vast geographical size of Canada, its varying regional characteristics, and its relatively small population, which have all left their mark on these media. In this context, even with the pervasiveness of electronic communication, these media remain largely local and regional, or intensely glocal in flavour. Finally, the proximity of the United States and the interventionist character of the Canadian state that this proximity has animated, particularly in the fields of media and culture, have also affected alternative media in terms of providing avenues for creating policy fields and mechanisms that might support their future development. In many ways, however, as evidenced in certain regions, particularly those outside of Québec, and in areas such as community radio and community television, this promise remains unfulfilled.

These characteristics underpin the historic and hegemonic development of Canada's mixed communication policy system, particularly its use of media and communication to support explicit nation building, national unity, and cultural identity, from the railway of the nineteenth century to radio broadcasting in the twentieth century.[1] By the time television broadcasting arrived on the policy-making scene, the rhetoric and ideal of public broadcasting (derived from the British model and the example of the British Broadcasting Corporation) had already been established. At the same time, however, existing private stations were allowed to continue and were the core of an eventual private media system that co-exists with public broadcasting in Canada to-day (Raboy 1990; Skinner 2005; MacLennan 2005). Over time, as market media proliferated and the post-war Keynesian consensus was shaken up by late-twentieth-century economic crises, the relative policy balance between pub-lic and private media in Canada's mixed system shifted. Federal governments that supported public service broadcasting gave way to market-liberal ideol-ogy such that both Liberal and Conservative administrations severely cut back funding to public broadcasting – the French and English radio and television components of the Canadian Broadcasting Corporation (CBC). The dominance of the commercial model, together with chronic inadequate funding, forced the CBC to rely on other revenue streams (of which the most immediately lu-crative is advertising), thus increasingly compromising its public service prin-ciples. Other public service media are affected by cutbacks; these include the National Film Board and programs, policies, and services supporting maga-zines, community television, local and regional current affairs, and services to remote and First Nations communities. Overall, the lack of reliable financial resources impedes production of culturally specific programming and isolates community and local media that would otherwise find synergies with the CBC. On a provincial level, this shift in the approach to funding extended to the prov-incial public service educational broadcasters (see Chapter 2 in this volume).

Added to the constant instability of resources is the significant political shift that has occurred in the Canadian policy environment over the last few years. Industry priorities have taken centre stage, with the current (2011) pro-market government open to considerable lobbying by private interests.[2] Recent decisions by the Canadian Radio-television and Telecommunications Commission (CRTC), the national regulatory body whose commissioners are appointed by Cabinet, have been varied in terms of their impact on media development with nods toward "the public interest" primarily under the rubric of "what is best for Canadian consumers."[3] The general trend has been toward facilitating the growth of private-sector media, allowing the industry to create national oligarchies, ironically at the same time as these oligarchies are in-creasingly vulnerable to global capitalism. Although it was a Conservative government that first moved to construct a Canadian national culture through public broadcasting in the late 1920s and early 1930s, today's Conservative Party is firmly ensconced within the New Right political project. Even when CRTC decisions are arguably made in the national interest, such as in early 2010, when the commission ruled against a bid by an Egyptian company to become one of Canada's four major cell phone service providers on the grounds that it violated Canadian foreign ownership restrictions, the federal Cabinet overruled it unilaterally. These shifts are critical, given that the chair of the CRTC has stated that the Broadcasting Act and the Telecommunications Act should be merged into one (Marlow 2010), which places public service provisions – currently central in both acts – in considerable jeopardy.

Nevertheless, previous governments must also share responsibility for the current direction in media and communications policies. During the move away from public service, the federal government (regardless of political party) commonly used the rhetoric of public service and the public interest in announcements as well as in international forums, yet it did not follow through with supportive policy domestically (Mosco 1997). Evident as well – in what continues to be a classic struggle between economic and cultural interests – is the contest between two government departments, Industry Canada and Canadian Heritage, for the right to define policy and lead decision making (Barney 2004). This was particularly obvious in the lack of substantive government response to the recommendations from the Lincoln report on broadcasting (Canada 2003), ignoring the "pressing issues" of chain ownership, vertical integration of content producers and carriers, and cross-media ownership (Skinner and Gasher 2005, 71). Similarly, the Senate's Bacon report (Canada 2006) clearly laid out the need for strong public media and advised stringent caps on media ownership. These recommendations, as with those from previous commissions that called for decisive government action (Canada 1970, 1981), were ignored. Instead, as evident by the above example of the federal Cabinet overruling the CRTC decision, the fixation on economic interests often takes priority over the national, and arguably public, interest. Nevertheless, the continuing recommendations to prioritize the public, as made in the Lincoln and Bacon reports noted above, should be seen as clear and repeated indications of the public's preferences and input concerning policy matters related to media, communication, and culture.

It is this market-led policy action that has contributed to the current state of media ownership in Canada. Although the CRTC did formulate a policy governing ownership in 2008, regulations had already been loosened throughout the 1990s and 2000s, resulting in escalating levels of foreign ownership of media enterprises and concentration of ownership, particularly in terms of cross-media ownership. Converged media conglomerates have holdings in several markets and industries, and as Skinner and Gasher (2005, 53) note, "this means they can: aggregate audiences across media and thus increase their media power; reuse programming and editorial content in a number of platforms to increase efficiency; increase their potential ideological clout to decrease diversity and inhibit dissent; and build significant barriers to entry for new enterprises or competitors." In addition, cutbacks in news operations and staff layoffs tend to follow takeovers in a bid to lower corporate debt burden (ibid., 54). All of this has a decisive and negative impact on both the quality and diversity of news (Waddell 2009).

During this period of concentration over the past fifteen years, formal public participation in key areas of policy making involving new media decreased involuntarily as, ironically, those who argue for public communication have not been able to voice their concerns within the policy-making circle, and instead must fight for inclusion in the process (Moll and Shade 2004). In the period since 1994, examples in which the public was excluded from government-initiated committees and boards addressing new media include the Canadian Network for the Advancement of Research, Industry and Education (CANARIE), the Information Highway Advisory Council, and the National Broadband Taskforce. Even those government-initiated endeavours that included public participation found governments ultimately "non-responsive" in their outcomes (Barney 2004, 104). The effect of these and more recent public attempts to regain a place at the policy table represent what Barney (ibid., 97), referring to the CANARIE experience, has called privatizing and commercializing policy making. "Leave it to the market" is now the order of the day in Canadian media and telecommunication policy formulation.

Most recently, the Conservative federal government has sent a strong signal that it plans to continue giving market forces greater play in the allocation of media resources, announcing that it expects to relax Canadian ownership regulations in telecommunications and satellite markets at the same time as it intends to "strengthen laws governing intellectual property and copyright" (Canada 2010). In retrospect, the CRTC's 1999 decision not to regulate the Internet is in keeping with what can now be seen as a trend toward marketization, a process by which governments change policy to facilitate corporate ownership and control. Moreover, as overextended large media corporations such as CanWest and Quebecor began to flounder and restructure or divest, Canadian media and communication policy in the first decade of the twenty-first century must bear some responsibility for ignoring report recommendations and calls from experts, media activists, and the public for a different kind of policy and political environment, one that would encourage diversity and participation in the public interest and allow community and local media to flourish and truly be public.

A cause for considerable concern has been the impact of shifting and tightening public space on alternative media practice, which has been marginalized from debates that focus largely on the media as an industry. Yet, despite the daunting political and policy environments, new examples of alternative media practices continue to be forged, although they are joined by some that are ephemeral and remain invisible to history. As the chapters in this volume attest, many of these new practices negotiate with dominant media to produce more flexible and hybrid entities and structures, disdaining purity, whereas others deliberately create pods of resistance to all matters dominant and act collectively and consensually as micro-movements. If, in the current Canadian experience, we cannot make the claim that Bennett is right about increasing networks of resistance, we can clearly see the potential for such a claim within an environment that is actively involved in alternative media practice – the politics of possibility – as this volume suggests, and as the history of alternative media in Canada indicates. It is to that history that we now turn.

Toward a Canadian Alternative Media History

Although scholarship in this field has stepped up over the last several years, a relatively few books have led analysis of alternative media in the Anglo-American context. John Downing's *Radical Media: The Political Experience of Alternative Communication* (1984) stood virtually alone in the international field for over a decade and was therefore key to constructing initial understanding of what he called "radical media." Atton (2007, 19) considers *Radical Media* the "starting point for contemporary studies in the field" of alternative media. Extended and revised in 2001 with a number of co-authors, Downing's contribution was joined by Clemencia Rodriguez's *Fissures in the Mediascape: An International Study of Citizens' Media* (2001), which explored the grassroots community media making she termed "citizens' media." DeeDee Halleck's *Hand-Held Visions: The Impossible Possibilities of Community Media* (2002) focused on the history of community television mainly in the US context.

Chris Atton's *Alternative Media* (2002) took a more methodical approach to the field as a whole and became the primary text for teaching courses in alternative media. These books were joined in 2003 by Nick Couldry and James Curran's collection *Contesting Media Power: Alternative Media in a Networked World,* which acknowledged the impact of technology on alternative media and situated the subject within a broader networked world. Atton followed suit with his *An Alternative Internet: Radical Media, Politics and Creativity* (2004), an examination of alternative media on the Internet. In a vein similar to Rodriguez's *Fissures in the Mediascape,* Kevin Howley's *Community Media: People, Places, and Communication Technologies* (2005) and Ellen Rennie's *Community Media: A Global Introduction* (2006) have provided volumes that focus primarily on case studies of what they term "community media" in the US and international contexts. More recently, Megan Boler's edited collection *Digital Media and Democracy: Tactics in Hard Times* (2008) features a number of essays that discuss alternative media as a means to overcome the domination of public debate by the mainstream press. Kate Coyer, Tony Dowmunt, and Alan Fountain's *The Alternative Media Handbook* (2007) provides an overview of various forms of alternative media and a DIY guide, whereas Olga Guedes Bailey, Bart Cammaerts, and Nico Carpentier's *Understanding Alternative Media* (2008, xi) makes a case for "a reimagining of the alternative media canon" such that it includes a "wider spectrum of media generally working to democratize information/communication."

In more focused recent contributions, Chris Atton and James Hamilton's *Alternative Journalism* (2008) provides a critical historical overview and discussion of the practice of alternative journalism, and James Hamilton's *Democratic Communications: Formations, Projects, Possibilities* (2008) offers a deep historical and philosophical consideration of the dimensions of the field and the scholarship that documents and describes it. From a somewhat different perspective, Kevin Howley's collection *Understanding Community Media* (2010) provides a broad perspective on the contemporary purposes and politics of community media as a form of democratic communication. Finally, the two comprehensive volumes edited by Clemencia Rodriguez, Dorothy Kidd, and Laura Stein (2010a, 2010b) under the title *Making Our Media: Global Initiatives toward a Democratic Public Sphere* provide particularly strong theoretical and analytic insight into the emergent structure of grassroots and alternative media at the international level.

There is considerably less literature that reflects on anglophone Canadian-based experiences and interactions with alternative media. Yet the field continues to grow and is marked by the inseparability of media and activism, which underpins the very foundations of the field of scholarship in Canada, as first articulated by Raboy (1984) in *Movements and Messages: Media and Radical Politics in Quebec,* published the same year as Downing's *Radical Media.* Much of the early published works on alternative media sought to identify their history in terms of the social relations and the social movements they articulated. This included the newspapers of the labour movement and labour journalism, as identified in Verzuh's *Radical Rag* (1988), which features a brief foray into the dynamic editors and fractious politics of a developing movement and its media from the late nineteenth century. The focus on social class and labour was also the purview of a vibrant immigrant press in Canada and was central in initial movements for democratic social change (Hoerder 1984; Hoerder and Harzig 1985; Hoerder 1987a, 1987b; Mazepa 2003). Book-length case studies of what has come to be called ethnic media emerged in the 1980s (see Chapter 8 in this volume) and indicate the complexity of immigrants' experiences, not the least of which was a volatile politics that included a range of fascism, nationalism, conservatism, socialism, and communism (Pilli 1982; Levendel 1989; Principe 1999). Canadian historians have also examined relations of class and gender in terms of providing case studies of a radical women's press (Sangster and Hobbs 1999; Lindstrom-Best 1985), and feminist media in Canada grew in tandem with the women's movement, as Chapter 4 in this volume confirms. As for many facets of Canadian alternative media history (Woodsworth 1972; Verzuh 1989), much research remains to be done in general, given the number of feminist periodicals that were published during the 1970s and 1980s, as Wachtel's (1982, 1985) listings reveal.

Alternative media and histories that espouse non-mainstream ways of thinking in challenging power and dominance are generally considered "radical." This was noted almost half a century ago by Margaret Fairley (1945), who sought to reclaim a general history of Canada via a number of "radical" writers who provided evidence of a long tradition of social struggle in Canada, beginning in the seventeenth century. Identifying the continuation of this phenomenon into the twentieth century, Doyle (2002) emphasized that it was in the radical newspapers and, particularly, the many booklets and pamphlets published during the 1930s that agit-prop – the combination of agitation and propaganda – was honed to motivate activism (Mazepa 2011a). These were published by small alternative presses and disseminated hand-to-hand as an effective method of distribution and public education to which the culture of contemporary zines can be traced (see Chapter 13 in this volume). Regrettably, as Weinrich (1982) notes, many of these small publications have been lost or were destroyed by censoring provincial and federal governments. Nevertheless, the alternative venues for publishing, distribution, and exhibition remain crucial. Currently, what Betts (n.d.) identifies as a "small press movement in Canada" as an "alternative to the hierarchical, sales-driven model of commercial literary publishing" needs to be supplemented with the history, participation, and support of independent publishers such as Black Rose Books, Edmonton's Small Press Association, and the relatively few independent bookstores that remain in Canada (see Byron Anderson 2002).

As for alternatives in radio and television, save for an early discussion of community radio (Girard 1992) and of the initial developments in community television (K. Goldberg 1990), the primary written history focuses on the CBC, as its alternatives are historically identified as structural (public rather than private ownership and control), as well as practical (public service rather than for-profit goals) (Raboy 1990; Raboy and Taras 2005). Although mitigated by what Raboy (1990) calls a series of "missed opportunities," several examples indicate sustained attempts to democratize the CBC through experiments in developing radio and television beyond a commercial and technical transmission model (of one-to-the-many) to a model based on public interaction and participation. Radio programs such as the *National Farm Radio Forum* (1941-1953) and the *Citizens' Forum* (1943-1952) exemplify programming aimed at maximizing public discussion and participation in decision making (Raboy 1990; Romanow 2005; Mazepa 2007), and gained a worldwide reputation as models upon which to develop (Lewis 1993). These were complemented by diverse experiments in which religious groups, provincial governments, and independent organizations such as the Canadian Association of Adult Educators (Faris 1975) and the Workers' Educational Association (WEA) (Comor and Casella 1987) used radio to facilitate public education.

Many so-called radical elements at the CBC were quickly extinguished, however. The WEA programs had a brief life before they were officially cancelled due to "inferior technical quality" – and unofficially due to complaints by business leaders and a continuing red scare that identified such ideas or practices as communist (Klee 1995, 108). The persistent red scare has been an effective deterrent to experiential programming given government ownership of the CBC and marks one aspect of the political boundaries of how alternative the CBC can be and how far its programs can go in criticizing power, particularly as it is consistently under attack for both political economic and ideological reasons (see Chapter 12 in this volume).

After Canada's National Film Board (NFB) was established in 1939, it too was subject to a similar red scare with an attending scrutiny of staff, content, and policing of political boundaries (Kristmanson and McLaren 1998; Khouri 2007; Spencer 2003, 12). As Druick's (2007) book-length review of its history indicates, on the one hand, the NFB has been used as a tool for government propaganda or has censored controversial subjects; on the other, it is a significant example of progressive alternative media. This includes its recognition of working-class experiences and development of grassroots politics through its documentary subjects and discussion periods (Khouri 2007), an emphasis on public participation and explicit projects for social change (see also Waugh, Baker, and Winton 2010), and direct engagement with feminism (through Studio D), as well as specific support for Aboriginal media production.

The range of views on the NFB well indicate the pushing and pulling of government involvement, and support Williams' contention that the media can't be democratic when the state itself is not (Williams, cited in Sparks 1993, 84-85). The complexity of state involvement in communication is particularly acute in the development of Aboriginal media in Canada (which Chapter 9 in this volume addresses), as identified in Alia's *Un/Covering the North: News, Media and Aboriginal People* (1999) and Roth's *Something New in the Air* (2005), both of which document the character and history of Aboriginal media, largely in the Canadian North.

Although the proliferation and importance of web-based communication to the growth of alternative media is now a given, it should be remembered that just over twenty years ago computer networking was in its infancy, and significant attempts were made to secure it as a public space. Experiments in progressive computer networking in Canada began during the early 1980s when the Canadian Union of Public Employees developed the Solidarity Network. Known as SoliNet, it established the first national bilingual computer conferencing system in Canada and the first national labour network in the world (E. Lee 1997; Mazepa 1997). Its appearance was in tandem with the establishment of local computer networks in the 1980s and 1990s in cities across Canada and the US in Community FreeNets that provided public access to the web and e-mail facilities for little or no charge. These were primarily locally based operations in Ottawa (for example, the National Capital FreeNet) that depended on the work of volunteers and on the donations of those who could afford to pay for access for their sustenance and development (Weston 1997). As Murphy (2002, 36-37) states, by 1999, these "autonomous civil society computer networks" were unique to the US and Canada, with 114 operating in the

US and 67 in Canada, compared to only 10 in the rest of the world. They remain examples of an Internet prior – and in opposition – to its commodification and commercialization.

The emphasis on participation and social movement development using information and communication technologies has contributed to the burgeoning interest in alternative media, as the literature on the topic steadily increases in Canada. A number of theses and dissertations published in the 1990s and 2000s indicate additional bases for the further development of academic work in the field, as research combines with scholarship and scholarship combines with activism. This list, which is not exhaustive, includes dissertations and master's theses on computer networking and social movements (Balka 1992; Mazepa 1997; Kidd 1998; Milberry 2005; Powell 2009), Trepanier's (1991) application of Gramscian theory to alternative media strategies, Fairchild's (1993) dissertation on community radio in Toronto, and Mazepa's (2003) dissertation on alternative culture and media in interwar Canada. Additional work in Canada focuses on community media (Harris 1992; Dykstra 1999), community television (Lithgow 2008; D.E.B. Johnston 2005), and Aboriginal media (Buddle-Crowe 2002; Ferreira 2007; Hafsteinsson 2008), with some specific case studies (Gillett 1999; Falconer 2004; Winton 2007). Various articles and book chapters also provide general overviews of alternative media (see Skinner 2010) or more focused consideration of dimensions of the field (see Sullivan 1970; Demay 1993; Juniper 2002; Karim 2002; Avison and Meadows 2000; and a number of others in this book's extensive References section).

Additional volumes, such as Nancoo and Nancoo's *The Mass Media and Canadian Diversity* (1996) and Alia's *Media Ethics and Social Change* (2004), have touched upon English-language alternative media in Canada. The collection by Langlois and Dubois, *Autonomous Media: Activating Resistance and Dissent* (2005), draws upon many Canadian examples but was written by activists for a popular and largely activist audience rather than as a systematic study of the field. Thus, and with Mattelart's initial direction in mind, the consideration of the relationship between activism and scholarship led the editors of this volume to organize its chapters according to the three central characteristics of structure, participation, and activism. These characteristics are addressed in separate parts of the book but are treated as belonging to a central whole as one way of understanding the totality of relations of production and social relations manifest in alternative media. In this vein, although not directly addressing the subject matter of this book, Marc Raboy and Jeremy Shtern's recent volume *Media Divides: Communication Rights and the Right to Communicate in Canada* (2010) is particularly pertinent in that it provides a comprehensive overview of the larger political and legal ground that gives form to these relations.

Structure, Participation, and Activism

Led by Michael Albert's (1997, 1) central question "What makes alternative media alternative?" this book aims to develop both a history and a context of the field in Canada within the shifting trends and conditions that give it form. Like its historical predecessors, it intends to get at the heart of the term "alternative" by organizing its discussion around three central characteristics that distinguish these media: *structure, participation,* and *activism.* Although many alternative media forms have all three of these characteristics, together they provide an analytic frame for understanding how these media find form and function in the mediascape. Each contributor to the volume was asked to focus on one of these characteristics while considering the interplay of politics, policies, and practices as evident in the range of alternative media he or she reviewed and analyzed. Centring on structure, participation, and activism emphasizes the conditions that make these media, and the alternative public spheres they activate, temporal and vulnerable yet persistent and stubbornly enduring.

Structure accents how alternative media both develop out of and are structured into the larger media environment. This includes their intersections with specific national or international policies and institutions, and their administrative and economic organization. It highlights what Couldry and Curran (2003, 14) note are the "specific factors that enable or constrain challenges to [dominant] media power." For instance, many critical communications scholars have commented on global acceleration and consolidation of commercial media (Gibbs and Hamilton 2001), and in Canada specifically, on ongoing monopolization and corporatization within communications industries (Crow and Longford 2004, 356; Winseck 2002, 2010). However, as mentioned earlier, recent federal governments have not provided adequate support to public media, which keeps community and local media at risk and narrows the scope and diversity of information.

Participation focuses on the means through which these media extend democracy in communication and how this is facilitated (or not) in their internal organizational and discursive practices. Set in contrast to the top-down, or vertical, structure of corporate media that are seen as agenda setting and foreclosing on opportunities for expression, participation is often perceived as the key feature of alternative media. Atton (2002, 25) states, for example, that alternative media "typically go beyond simply providing a platform for radical or alternative points of view; they emphasize the organization of media to enable wider social participation in their creation, production and dissemination than is possible with mass media." Such participation attempts to establish a horizontal relationship between writers and readers – that is, a situation where there is as little filtering of news and information as possible.

Activism focuses on how alternative media are, as C. Rodriguez (2001, 20) puts it, "actively involved in intervening and transforming the established mediascape," and thereby working to transform established ways of seeing and operating in the world and to empower the communities of which they are a part (see also Frey and Carragee 2007a, 2007b; Rodriguez, Kidd, and Stein 2010a). The concept of activism highlights how social and political change is advocated and facilitated through the media as connected to external networking. Alternative media are thus seen as modes of prefigurative politics, providing examples of progressive political relations that are otherwise difficult to configure in the face of dominant social forms (Downing et al. 2001, 71), or as evidence of regressive social relations as a refusal to do so.

In attempting to trace and understand the dimension of these characteristics and challenges, the present volume foregrounds a number of critical questions that bring together the politics, policies, and practices of alternative media in Canada. These include the following: What are the conditions that inform and sustain alternative media? How does the Canadian policy environment enable and constrain their potential? How do the practices and structures of alternative media contribute to more representational and egalitarian forms of communication? How do alternative media actively challenge, subvert, circumvent, and/or undermine the power of dominant media? The chapters in this book address these questions by examining the specific conditions and environments that offer both possibilities and challenges for the work of alternative media.

In Part 1: Structure, Chapter 1 discusses the sustainability of alternative media in Canada. David Skinner argues that, with changes in media technologies, fragmenting audiences, and shifts in the ideological dimensions of media regulation, sustainability is a particularly important topic. With an eye to better understanding how to approach and deal with the issue of sustainability, he reviews and critiques some of the ways it has been taken up in the literature. He considers the conditions under which sustainability is viewed as a problem and how the key to sustainability might be seen as building and strengthening the social infrastructure that supports and gives form to these media. Set in the context of recent efforts toward media reform, the chapter goes on to examine attempts in both Canada and the United States to create different forms of organization and infrastructure to support alternative media. Of particular interest are what contributions, if any, these experiences offer to the further development of alternative media in Canada.

In Chapter 2, Kirsten Kozolanka examines the often overlooked field of public service educational broadcasters. Set between the broadcast policy responsibilities of the federal government and the educational policy responsibilities of provincial governments, the chapter illustrates how "educasting" was charged with a distinctive public service mandate and how its evolution has been structured by the shifting currents of politics and media policy. Kozolanka reveals how the forces of commercialization, unleashed by politics of the New Right, have severely affected the public interest mandate of these media and forced a range of organizational restructuring among them. Nevertheless, her analysis suggests that these evolving mandates may be a welcome antidote to the larger forces of commodification driving commercial media, and it identifies some encouraging signs of stabilization and growth.

Chapter 3 takes a more theoretical tack, as Scott Uzelman considers how studies and definitions of alternative media tend to concentrate attention on their organizational characteristics, thereby obscuring some important differences between them and their relationships to wider social and political movements. Uzelman is particularly concerned with the ways in which alternative media participate in radical democratic politics and challenge practices of oppression, and he illustrates how four common ways of conceptualizing alternative media tend to conceal their differences in this regard. He goes on to propose that the term "autonomous media" be used to provide a more concise way of differentiating this type of media from others.

In Chapter 4, Barbara Freeman offers a glimpse of the rich history of the feminist press in Canada. Developed with the express purpose of providing an alternative to the mainstream or "male bourgeois 'public sphere' of communication," hundreds of these publications came and went in various Canadian communities from the early 1970s into the twenty-first century. Focusing on *Kinesis* in Vancouver (1974-2001), *Broadside* in Toronto (1979-1989), and *Pandora* in Halifax (1985-1994), Freeman illustrates how their structure and operation, as well as the character of their stories and advertisements, worked to challenge dominant media in general and dominant women's media in particular.

In doing so, she provides an interesting counterpoint to both Chapter 1 – demonstrating that sustainability is the product of a complex range of political economic and social factors – and Chapter 3, giving a practical illustration of certain features of what Uzelman describes as autonomous media.

Rounding out the contributions to Part 1 is Chapter 5, Sonja Macdonald's case study of The Real News Network (TRNN), an independent, on-line, international video news organization launched in 2005. As Macdonald demonstrates, on the face of it, TRNN constitutes one of the more compelling recent challenges to commercial media as, without accepting advertising or government funding, it seeks to present news from a perspective not generally seen on commercial television networks. In doing so, TRNN draws on both mainstream and alternative media practices, and provides an interesting example of what can be called hybrid media. Macdonald traces four dimensions of hybridity in TRNN's operations and considers the impact of this blend of media structure and practice on the news it produces.

Indeed, as the chapters in Part 2: Participation indicate, and in community broadcasting in particular, there is consistent pressure by corporate media owners to extend their ownership to the ether itself and to obliterate both the concept and practice of public ownership entirely. As revealed in Chapter 6, Michael Lithgow's exploration of community television, government changes to regulations increasingly favour the private cable operators that have managed to reap the financial rewards of public funding with little or no accountability. The ability of these operators to aggressively manage both government policy making and the airwaves has meant that community television itself is almost invisible to Canadians, who are generally unaware of the possibilities of public ownership and its attendant participation in decision making and production. In emphasizing the importance of what he calls cultural citizenship, Lithgow discusses two local examples of what can politically constitute the "community" in community television and suggests that the traditional community centre be reconfigured to a community *media* centre, a central hub based on active communication and media production rather than sports and recreation.

Given the predominant structuring of the public as commodified subjects, public participation in media production is itself considered a political act. Chapter 7, in which Evan Light discusses community radio stations in Québec, underscores this recognition that public participation in media ownership and production is political (in terms of taking responsibility for it) but should not be assumed to be alternative or equated with political engagement in either formalized politics or social activism. In identifying such variations, Light submits that exactly *who* participates in radio, and *how* and *why* the community participates in the medium, largely depends on its constituents, access to resources (participant, financial, or technical), and the location of the station and its broadcast range (AMARC n.d.). Light highlights the differences between the organizations of the sole English-only campus radio station in Montréal and another station in the same area that manages no less than seven distinct language production units. In examining regional and rural examples, Light identifies significant differences between them and the urban stations in terms of what they perceive as their community mandate, particularly in the interpretation of "public service."

The diversity of the public and the degree of its participation is further expounded by Karim H. Karim in Chapter 8, on ethnic media in Canada, which he regards as ranging from the transient self-produced small press, to international broadcasting reception via satellite, to diaspora interaction on-line. Karim considers the question of what is alternative in media otherwise categorized by their language and cultural affiliation in a dynamic environment tempered by the global political economy of media (Chakravartty and Zhao 2008). Ethnic media in Canada have the added challenge of negotiating their relationship to federal government policies of multiculturalism while avoiding responses to commercial and international dominance that contribute to their further commodification and marginalization or result in exclusionary social practices to the extent that they digress into racism. As Karim concludes, dialogue among and between the diasporas and the communities with which they engage is based on public participation and shows ethnic media's independence and their progressive alternatives.

A growing independence from the structuring of state policies – or management through funding – as experienced in ethnic and community media, is indicated in Chapter 9, Marian Bredin's treatment of Aboriginal media. Contextualizing Aboriginal media in Canada, she reviews their historical development and focuses on three contemporary types, including independent film, regional broadcasting, and a national cable network. Bredin highlights active participation as essential to reposition an Aboriginal lead in policy making, to foster economic independence, and to facilitate cultural renewal and political activism. She identifies several factors that make Aboriginal media distinct, while emphasizing the necessity of activism on all accounts as fundamental to the democratization of public communication in Canada, demonstrating that participation is not restricted to the media themselves (their policy and practices) but necessitates political action and mobilization.

The four chapters in Part 3: Activism probe the meanings, degree, and challenges of prefigurative politics in alternative media practice. In Chapter 10, though valorizing the labour of alternative media as a commitment to an activist vision, Nicole Cohen also problematizes the actual conditions of that labour. Volunteer or poorly paid labour for alternative media directly challenges capitalism, but it can be (self-)exploitative and unsustainable. Moreover, alternative media are organized in such a way – informal and often run out of the home – that problems of gender, class, and workplace conditions and dynamics often remain unresolved. Cohen suggests that not addressing these issues contributes to alternative media's lack of sustainability and, in fact, challenges one of their underlying principles: "that anyone can make media" (this volume, 216). She argues that alternative media need to uncover the actualities of their labour practices in order to conduct the necessary conversation on how to create sustainable activist alternative media.

In Chapter 11, Kate Milberry covers on-line activism and addresses the key dynamic of our times: the social struggle between the public (the community model of the Internet) and private interests (the commercial model). Foregrounding net neutrality and fair copyright as two current and ongoing battles, she contends that the spectre of a two-tier Internet with different service and mobility for users in turn threatens to neuter the potential of cyberspace for alternative media. Within this fast-moving environment of on-line communication, "net freedom fighters" – many of them alternative media practitioners – have organized across a broad spectrum of action, both virtually and materially. In so doing, they are engaging in democratic media practice with the ultimate goal of democratic communication.

In Chapter 12, Patricia Mazepa tackles head-on another uncomfortable area of activist alternative media practice. She argues that the broad term "alternative media" covers both progressive and regressive communication forms, but rather than challenging conditions of domination and oppression, regressive communication reinforces them. Mazepa rejects the New Right's false presentation of its ideology as merely another perspective that is open to public debate and draws attention to the underlying power relations that must be uncovered to separate progressive activist media's quest for social justice from regressive media's exercise of power to legitimate and maintain the hierarchical order. Through examples drawn from the far right, religious right, and neo-conservatism, Mazepa examines the New Right's strategic framing and delineates its tactics of marginalization, scapegoating, demonization, and dehumanization.

In Chapter 13, on anarchist direct-action activism, Sandra Jeppesen provides a strong contrast and an excellent illustration of progressive prefigurative politics. Here, democratic media practice in the form of a zine collective's media activism and actions is situated within cultural spaces where collective principles and values challenge hierarchical economism. Jeppesen extracts her analysis of the media activism of an anarchist "horde" from Bourdieu's principles of legitimation, arguing that zines have a high social value within anarchist culture, largely because they disavow the economic and are seen as inherently anti-capitalist. Rather than being legitimated through Bourdieu's economic capital, the process of media production is consistent with the content it produces and the actions it describes. Such self-reflexive and collective self-production, Jeppesen argues, provides rhizomatic foundational efforts toward alternative media sustainability. Through her delineation of the horde and how it functioned, she addresses issues of labour and sustainability that are similar to those raised by Cohen in Chapter 10.

In the three interrelated spheres of structure, participation, and activism, our focus in this volume is on examining the conditions that democratize the media, both structurally and in representation, while recognizing that no democratic media are possible without democratic communication and a democratic government (Hamilton 2000). The chapters in this book attest to the challenges facing alternative media in Canada in reaching these goals, while also examining the practices that continue to define and redefine alternative media in Canada.

In the face of escalating commercialization and concentration of ownership worldwide, the breadth and diversity of media practices, and the roles and purposes played by various media in the development and circulation of public communication, need to be better understood and advanced. Given that communication is central to our species, our collective relationships, and our future, this book also aims to provide encouragement to its readers to (re)consider and further activate the democratic alternatives.

NOTES

1   The editors are painfully aware of the dearth of history on alternative media in Canada and recognize that the present discussion is but a brief sketch confined mainly to

publications in English. We welcome contributions to ongoing projects such as the Canadian Alternative Media Archive (www.alternativearchive.org/) and future research collaborations.

2 This includes direct lobbying as indicated in the list of the Registry of Lobbyists (Office of the Commissioner of Lobbying of Canada 2011a), to indirect lobbying through industry-sponsored conferences, such as the 2010 Canadian Telecom Summit.

3 Indeed, even the CRTC identifies the public as "consumers" as one of its four constituents, together with the broadcasting, telecommunication, and media sectors (see CRTC 2011).

PART 1: STRUCTURE

Sustaining Independent and Alternative Media

DAVID SKINNER

Sustainability is a particularly important issue today, not only for independent and alternative media, but for corporate media as well. Changes in media technologies, such as the expanding television universe and particularly the Internet, are fragmenting audiences and, in concert with shifting labour regimes and changes in the ideological dimensions of media regulation, have led to a profound restructuring of the media field. Corporate responses to these developments have focused largely on shifts in economies of scale and scope, and have been characterized by escalating concentration of ownership, convergence of varying types of media properties, the repurposing of media content from one medium to another, layoffs of professional media workers, a struggle to invent new types of content to attract and hold audience attention, and the solicitation of audience participation in media production. Of course, this new environment has not been solely imposed upon the media field. Rather, media owners, driven by threats to corporate profits and opportunities for new ones, are complicit in facilitating these alterations in terms of adopting (and adapting) new technologies, modifying labour requirements, and soliciting changes in the structure of regulation as they vie for position and profits in shifting markets (McChesney 2008a; Skinner, Compton, and Gasher 2005).

But for independent and alternative media – already in many ways marginal within the larger system – this fluid environment presents its own challenges and has made the issue of sustainability particularly acute, especially for on-line and other new forms of media. For the most part, these media have de-veloped out of a concern for the expression of a particular set of ideas and values, and consideration of a business model has generally taken a back seat to this goal. Because of their small size, they have few economies of scale and lack economic stability. Staff and contributors often work for little or no pay (Cohen 2007). And, unlike their corporate counterparts, alternative media are sometimes organized along collective or prefigurative lines, which, as Atton (2002, 25) points out, "emphasize the organization of media to enable wider social participation in their creation, production and dissemination than is pos-sible with mass media." At the same time, the size and demographics of their audiences are often unknown, making advertising and subscription sales dif-ficult. Even when this information is available and audience demographics amenable to commodification, the small size of their audiences and/or ideo-logical concerns over the impact of advertising revenue on content often miti-gate against this form of financing.

In the face of the challenges to the media system over the last ten to fifteen years, regulators in both Canada and the United States have been sympathetic to the demands of large private media companies and have relaxed a range of regulations, particularly those around ownership; they have also developed a number of production funds to help enhance their economic positions (see CRTC 2001b, 2007b, 2009f; McChesney 2008b; Skinner, Compton, and Gasher 2005). At the same time, however, there has been little by way of regulation to facilitate the development of independent and alternative media, and through the late 1980s and early 1990s, the neo-liberal turn in government policy yielded cutbacks across a wide range of what government supports there were for these kinds of organizations (see Vallantin 2008; Senate of Canada 2006, 40-42; Canada 2003, 337-41; Demay 1993). The result is a highly concen-trated corporate media sector occupying centre stage in the media system and little availability of independent, not-for-profit, or non-commercial media, particularly in the broadcast sector but also in print. And although the web offers seemingly infinite possibilities for independent media, finding ways to finance and sustain them in this venue generally remains elusive.

Here, "sustainability" is defined as facilitating media organizations' ongoing operation, improving their abilities to report on events and circumstances sali-ent to public life and engage in public discussion and debate. More specific-ally, sustainability is about having the resources to acquire staff, technologies of production, and avenues of distribution, and to develop audiences. In the face of a fluctuating media environment, the purpose of this chapter is to highlight new, innovative forms and modes for developing sustainable media organizations and to consider the role of the contemporary media reform movement in this regard.

Independent and alternative media are defined as a range of generally small outlets that work to develop and animate community and enable public discussion across a broad range of issues. Following Couldry and Curran (2003, 7), the main feature of these media is that they challenge, "at least implicitly, actual concentrations of media power, whatever form those concentrations may take in different locations." This definition includes media designed for specific communities, such as those left out of or marginalized by dominant media, but is not confined to them. Rather, the project of sustainability is to put a greater range of media voices – that is, a greater range of perspectives and ideas – at the centre of public life and increase their circulation both within and between the communities that comprise Canadian society.

From this perspective, independent and alternative media might be seen not as a separate field unto themselves but, loosely following Bourdieu's (2005) notion of a journalistic or media field, as a subset of a larger system within which a wide variety of media operate, each offering a somewhat distinct perspective on social events and circumstances depending on their position within that field and how they are structured into it.[1]

The field itself is highly diverse in its modes of financing, organizational structure, and public policy relations (see Curran 2005, 138-44). And, in turn, its organizational elements – that is, the media outlets themselves – are highly diverse in connection with public policy regimes, modes of financing, and audience relations.[2] These relationships are generally key to sustaining their ongoing operations.

With an eye to better understanding how to approach the issue of sustainability, this chapter begins by reviewing and critiquing some of the ways it has been taken up in the literature on alternative media. It considers the conditions under which sustainability is perceived as a problem and how the key to sustainability is often seen as building and strengthening the social infrastructure that supports and gives form to these media. Set in the context of contemporary media reform efforts, the chapter goes on to examine select examples of organizations and infrastructure designed to support alternative media in both the United States and Canada. Comparing and contrasting approaches to this problem in these two jurisdictions reveals what, if any, lessons the American experience might offer Canadians.

Sustainability in the Literature on Independent Media

The literature on independent and alternative media is somewhat ambivalent on the issue of sustainability, and at least three perspectives can be identified. The first views the various forms of such media as underdeveloped and generally doomed to remain marginal in the larger social context. This stance – often attributed to Comedia (1984, 95) in the mid-1980s – locates the source of this underdevelopment in "the absence of a clear conception of target audiences and ... marketing strategies ... and inflexible models of organization." Here, the focus is on the organizational practices of individual media outlets, and the call is for them to develop more efficient structures, larger audiences, and a market presence by modelling themselves more along the lines of their corporate mainstream cousins.

Although some notable successes have been realized in this direction, it is certainly not a universally viable strategy for achieving sustainability in this field (ibid., 101-2). What are sometimes seen as cumbersome collective and cooperative forms of organization go right to the heart of the representational practices of many independent media outlets, and rationalizing these to make them seemingly more efficient and effective, or shifting content to make them more popular, cannot help but dull or alter their original mandate or focus. One has only to consider the myriad of formerly radical publications of the 1960s and 1970s that morphed into entertainment weeklies to see the impact that these kinds of changes can have on content and organizational structure (see Verzuh 1986, 3). This is not to say that independent media should not and could not have a stronger grip on the economics of production, but how this is undertaken is crucial.

A second perspective does not foreground sustainability as a key problem or issue. Rather, it frames alternative media as ebbing and flowing along with the social and political issues that give them form. As C. Rodriguez (2001, 22) puts it, "democratic communication [is] a live creature that contracts and expands with its very own vital rhythms." From this viewpoint, independent media are by their nature somewhat ephemeral, called into being by the political will or context of the moment and fading as the urgency of the particular struggle or social formation of which they are part ebbs in strength. Here, organizational structure and relationships with the constituencies they serve are key to sustaining media projects, and when that particular configuration of circumstances passes, so does the organization (see Atton 2002, 7-52).

Certainly, independent media are sometimes so heavily engrained in particular issues, movements, or technologies that trying to extend their lives beyond the political and social circumstances that spark them may be a moot exercise. For instance, quite an extensive list of feminist publications of the 1970s and 1980s might fit this mould, as would a number of publications allied with specific political movements, such as the British *Marxism Today,* once much mourned in cultural studies circles (Jacques 1991). A number of Indymedia centres might be seen as a more contemporary example here (see Whitney 2005). Similarly, what are sometimes called "tactical media" – that is, media events and products that are designed to address particular events or situations – are dependent on "very specific circumstances in space and time," and thereby, are fleeting by nature (Garcia 2007). This is not to say that these media simply wither and disappear. Rather, the people and resources that comprise them are often re-formed as circumstances alter, much in the same way as many of the people and ideas driving Indymedia a few years ago have been taken up in new media operations.[3]

Although independent media products and outlets may often be inextricably tied to particular historical circumstances, this is not a reason to downplay or ignore the problem of sustainability. Whether linked to a very specific issue or mandated to a broader set of social purposes, most alternative media struggle to reach their audiences and communities. Here, the blind spot of this second perspective is how the social forces that characterize the mediascape undermine the operation of these media. In Canada, for instance, media policy increasingly favours market-oriented arrangements over direct regulation (CBC 2008b). Ownership restrictions are far from rigorous in protecting diversity and continue to be called into question (see Kierans 2008). Subsidies to print publications are increasingly based upon market criteria, and within established broadcast policy streams, public service broadcasting continues to suffer financially (Senate of Canada 2006, 42-43; Robertson 2008). Community television is under escalating attack, and in policy terms, community radio continues to be subordinated to its commercial cousins (CBC 2009; Vallantin 2008). Although the Internet does make distribution easier, finding means to support operations in this venue remains elusive. Hence, in this environment, independent media are operating in a social field characterized – to borrow from Williams (1989) – by increasingly asymmetrical relations of power.

Faced with this difficulty to establish and maintain independent media, a third perspective is developing that, like the first, also takes sustainability and marginality as key problems (Clark and van Slyke 2006; Hamilton 2008). Like the second, however, it also sees the organizational characteristics of these media as somewhat key to their appointed missions, as well as important in linking them to the social issues and movements that give them form (hence, simply adopting commercial media forms and/or strategies is not an option). At the same time, this stance varies from the second in that it takes a more critical view of the larger social field in which these media operate and emphasizes addressing the power relations found there.

Here, the key to sustainability is to build and strengthen the social infrastructure that frames these media. Drawing on Bourdieu, Hamilton (2008, 265) sketches the broad dimensions of this project: "Bourdieu places great importance on what are in practice two inseparable needs: generating creative responses to current situations, but also creatively remaking conditions that enable the generation of creative responses in the first place." From this standpoint, sustaining the creative responses of alternative media to everyday life involves developing the supports to maintain a wide variety of such media. Such responses might range from public education programs on the importance of these kinds of media, to instituting policy measures to support them, to creating new models for financing and sustaining them. Set in the context of a broad media reform movement, some of the dimensions of such a project appear to be visible in the United States. Because the American media system has recently confronted forces similar to those shaping its Canadian counterpart – ongoing deregulation, convergence, and concentration of ownership – the American experience in this regard may be instructive for similar efforts in Canada.

The US Experience

The US has a long history of alternative media and a complex range of support programs for community and public television and radio that span national, state, and local government (see Rennie 2006). However, forged in the broad sweep of New Right politics and galvanized by a concern that corporate media failed to question the premises of the Iraq war, as well as the proliferation of media commentators and outlets unabashedly allied with the ideological right, what Hackett and Carroll (2006, 93, 103-9) characterize as a new wave of media activism has been developing in the United States (see McChesney 2008b). A central element in the project of media reform in the US has been raising public awareness of media issues and helping people "understand that there is nothing natural about the media system and that they have a right and responsibility to participate in policy deliberations" (McChesney 2008a, 498). Here, the point is to create a larger climate for sustaining a wide variety of media, including independent and alternative media.

Toward this end, a broad range of groups have been working to develop progressive media policy and organizations. A key dimension of this effort is to raise the media reform issue on the agenda of other social movement and social justice bodies, to involve them in developing policy that supports alternative media, and to engage them as both producers and consumers of media. To an extent, these groups are all involved in developing forms of participative politics whereby media are viewed as a vehicle for either directly or indirectly engaging people in political processes.

Although these efforts are sometimes seen as heavily fragmented and "characterized by a diverse array of conceptual frames (ranging from 'media reform' to 'media justice' to 'communication rights' to 'media democracy')," taken together they represent the outlines of a social field aimed at both holding corporate media to some forms of public accountability and providing a broad infrastructure of supports for independent and alternative media (Napoli 2007, 2). In terms of independent and alternative media, this field contains a broad range of organizations. Some focus on creating policy and other kinds of supports at the national, regional, state, and local grassroots levels. Others work to generate supports for particular media outlets. Often these various organizations work in tandem, creating coalitions to address particular issues. Generally speaking, however, these capacity-building endeavours are taking place at three broad overlapping levels: public policy, organization, and public education. Public policy and public education often go hand in hand as these organizations work to educate constituencies, including politicians, on the implications of policy issues and to engage a wide range of groups and people in policy processes. McChesney (2008b, 498) draws the broad relationships between the elements of this movement and independent media: "Although the media reform movement concentrates on policy activism, it is closely linked to groups creating independent media ... and those who provide criticism of the mainstream media. Those doing independent media need success in the policy realm to assure they have a possibility to be effective while those doing criticism and educational work do so with the ultimate aim of changing the system. The three branches of media activism rise and fall together."

Although building supports for alternative media is not the central focus of most media reform associations, some have been working in this direction. These efforts range from lobbying various levels of government to achieve policy supports, to fostering strategic partnerships between media outlets, to forging connections with both media reform organizations and non-media civil society groups that can be utilized to build audiences and broad public support for independent media. Much of this work occurs in the context of developing research and education around public policy. This policy/education nexus is to some degree the product of the funding structure, as in order to qualify for foundation funding in the US, associations must draw a clear line between their educational and advocacy activities.

In this context, public education takes a different tack than either tradition-al media literacy or alternative media practice (see McChesney 1999, 301). Rather than focus on creating critical readers or consumers of media fare or the development of media production skills, it emphasizes community en-gagement and providing people with an understanding of the dimensions of social change necessary to produce a more diverse media system, as well as eliciting their active collaboration in generating those conditions. It recogniz-es that people may not have the time, skills, resources, or inclination to "be the media" but that for the most part they do have the capacity to intervene in the process of creating the conditions necessary for a healthy and diverse media to survive (see Action Coalition for Media Education, n.d.).

Perhaps the largest and most visible of these new media reform organiza-tions is Free Press. Its mandate describes its orientation as "challenging con-centrations of media power": "Through education, organizing and advocacy, we promote diverse and independent media ownership, strong public media, and universal access to communications" (Free Press, n.d.). Founded in 2002, Free Press had more than thirty employees by 2008 as well as offices in both Florence, Massachusetts, and Washington, DC. Financed largely by philan-thropic gifts and grants, Free Press and its companion organization, the Free Press Action Fund, had about $4 million in revenue in 2009 (Free Press 2010). Although Free Press is generally concerned with the policy dimensions of issues, its educational efforts are widely drawn and concentrate on research and other activities designed to raise awareness and understanding of media issues among legislators, other organizations, and the public at large (Josh Silver, pers. comm., 12 September 2007). Free Press is mainly focused on broad policy issues such as media ownership and Internet and wireless policy, within which independent and alternative media occupy niche positions. The importance of these topics, such as net neutrality, to alternative media cannot be understated, however, as without unfettered access as a means of distribution, these media would be heavily marginalized in the larger mediascape. Similarly, Free Press' work on media diversity includes concerns for "public media" – a term applied to community radio, public access TV, independent publications, and viewer-supported satellite channels. Most recently, Free Press has been involved in education and policy work around funding for public broadcasting, low-power FM radio, public access television, and postal rates. At eighteen-month intervals, it also hosts the National Conference on Media Reform, which regularly attracts two to three thousand people and carries a range of programming, including a particular stream directed toward alternative media (see Schechter 2005). As well, its website offers a range of information and tools related to organizing around issues of import to independent media.

Approaching the project of reform from a somewhat different direction, the Media and Democracy Coalition consists of twenty-five local and national activist media organizations, a number of which represent the interests of alternative media outlets and independent media workers and artists such as the Alliance for Community Media, CCTV Center for Media Democracy, Future of Music Coalition, the Media Alliance, and Prometheus Radio Project. Free Press is also a member. With two full-time staff, the coalition concentrates mainly on facilitating relationships between its members, other media, and media reform organizations at the national, state, and local levels, and helping develop the capacity to support media reform initiatives at various levels of government across the US. The coalition, a project of Common Cause, was established by funders to serve as a vehicle to help coordinate the efforts of its members and bridge the distance between national reform organizations and local grassroots activists and groups (see Napoli 2007, 53).

The coalition is largely focused on two policy ranges: media ownership and community media, and digital inclusion and an open Internet. However, as its campaign coordinator points out, "There's a lot of latitude in that framework. Specifically, we work on issues like net neutrality, building out an affordable and adequate broadband system ... and then under ownership to a certain degree that's where we get involved in low-power FM fights as well. Ownership isn't just about trying to make sure that a good number of companies own the media, but that communities own their own media infrastructure. So including radio, both low power and full power, and also community wi-fi and community broadband systems we have a strong interest in too" (Nathaniel James, pers. comm., 3 November 2007).

The coalition has been involved in a wide range of education projects on media issues and reform aimed at politicians, policy-makers, and social justice organizations at national, state, and local levels; promoting the development of low-power FM stations at the national, state, and local levels; organizing and support for reform interventions at Federal Communications Commission (FCC) hearings; organizing and information campaigns on issues surrounding concentration of media ownership; and developing an on-line facility for member groups to share information and resources.

Whereas Free Press and the Media and Democracy Coalition concentrate largely on public policy, a number of groups work to provide direct infrastructure and support for independent media. Of particular interest here are those that – borrowing from the convergence strategies of corporate media – focus on aggregating the resources of a number of separate organizations to harness economies of scale or scope.

Although forced to shut down operations in January 2007 due to cash flow problems in its distribution business, the Independent Press Association (IPA) provided a particularly innovative model of support for independent publications. Founded on the fringes of the 1996 Media and Democracy Congress, the IPA was a non-profit organization that helped small, generally progressive magazine and newspaper publishers develop their operations. At its height, it employed twenty-three full-time staff in offices in San Francisco and New York, and had over four hundred member publications based primarily in the US. About half of its $2 million operating budget came from grants. The IPA offered its members consulting services to help improve both content and production; business advice; a loan fund designed to promote circulation, increase advertising sales, improve newsstand distribution, or upgrade infrastructure; a service that promoted national distribution for over seventy of its members; an initiative designed to increase library subscriptions of members; active lobbying to keep postal rates down; and a branch office in New York.

Employing similar principles but situated at the local level, New York Community Media Alliance (NYCMA) was founded as the New York office of the Independent Press Association. It began operating on its own in early 2007 when the parent organization closed its doors (C. Anderson 2007). With about eighty members, the NYCMA is officially mandated "to promote social justice through media reform," and it exercises this mandate through encouraging civic engagement among ethnic and immigrant communities (NYCMA 2009). Toward this end, it has a number of programs designed to help sustain and develop immigrant, ethnic, and community newspapers and other media in New York City. With an annual budget of about $1 million, the NYCMA employs three full-time and three part-time staff, as well as three or four interns at any given time. Foundations provide 90 percent of its income. Key among its programs is an advertising service that collects circulation information from its members and, with one order, allows advertisers to purchase space in multiple papers and magazines, thereby affording these publications an economy of scale often available only to large chains. Through its Independent Press Institute, the NYCMA also holds press conferences and forums that provide members access to elected and public officials, in-depth background information on issues important to ethnic and immigrant communities, and technical assistance on things such as publication design and marketing.

The Media Consortium is another organization that works to supply supports for its members. It was founded in 2006 with two goals: "to increase independent journalism's voice in broader public debates about the crucial political and social issues of our day" and "to navigate the current wave of profound technological change that is reshaping the media business and redefining the practice of journalism" (Media Consortium, n.d.). The consortium is a project of the Foundation for National Progress, a not-for-profit that owns *Mother Jones* magazine. With a budget of approximately $500,000 in 2008, it receives in excess of 90 percent of its funding from foundations. It has roughly fifty members, among which are some of the largest and better-known independent and alternative media outlets in the US, such as *Mother Jones, The Nation, Progressive, In These Times,* AlterNet.org, Link TV, and Free Speech TV. It runs a number of programs to provide opportunities for members to establish relationships with each other, develop forums for their work, and build audiences. These include Building Connections, a program designed to foster relationships and collaborations between members; Media Wires, a news ladder that showcases stories from members and allows them to present each other's work on their websites; and Progressive Media Game Changers, a long-term creative and strategic planning exercise aimed at helping members meet with the shifting media environment. The consortium has also sponsored audience research for members and conducted a series of town hall meetings during the 2008 presidential election intended to place local issues in a national context and be covered by member media organizations. A key element of the consortium's strategy is to facilitate engaging a wide range of groups with their member publications and their audiences by pitching stories, advertising, and participating in on-line communities. The point is to make their members' media products more responsive to the constituencies they serve and become forums for the discussion and promotion of the issues that matter to those groups and communities.

Michigan's Grand Rapids Community Media Center (GRCMC) offers yet another model of organization. Located on the second floor of a public library in downtown Grand Rapids, the centre is a multi-faceted media organization that includes a community radio station, two public access television stations, a non-profit Internet service company, a community theatre, and an on-line citizen journalism site designed to promote community engagement. Working together, these elements of the centre yield an ever-evolving set of synergies focused on developing and delivering a wide range of not-for-profit media services, all designed to address social issues and effect positive social change in Grand Rapids. With an annual operating budget of approximately $1.2 million and the equivalent of about twenty full-time employees, the centre derives its revenue from an eclectic mix of individual contributions to the radio station, television franchise fees, fees for service, foundation grants, and other sources. Grant income is project-oriented and generally undertaken with community partners.

Although the very existence of these organizations would appear to signal a degree of success in sustaining independent and community media rising from the most recent wave of media reform, there is some question as to how one gauges that success. As some commentators point out, there is very little information regarding exactly how successful the reform movement has been in accomplishing its goals, including helping to sustain alternative media (see Napoli 2007, 56). The loss of the IPA was a heavy blow to the overall project of sustainability for print media, especially for magazines in the US, and changing funding patterns threaten cutbacks on other fronts. Moreover, except for the GRCMC, these groups are almost totally funded by philanthropic foundations. Such support can provide welcome seed money, but concerns have been raised about its sustainability, and as Hamilton (2008, 109) illustrates, it can also influence or shape the direction of projects. Stemming from their funding patterns, groups such as the Media Consortium and the NYCMA are largely focused on community engagement, which, though possibly producing a wide range of benefits for member media organizations, does not necessarily translate into increased income or economic security for them.

The Canadian Context

The United States provides interesting examples of support for independent and community media. The Canadian terrain, however, is very different, shaped as it is by the state's role in developing media and media policy, Canada's different legislative and regulatory structure, and the two solitudes of its anglophone and francophone communities. At the same time, with a population roughly ten times that of Canada and a much larger set of foundations and donors willing to supply seed money, the US has economies of scale and resources that differ drastically from those in Canada. Moreover, with the war in Iraq and the divisive politics engendered by the George W. Bush administration, the US political situation differs greatly from that of Canada. In this context, though there have been moments of public concern over issues such as convergence, concentration of ownership, and net neutrality, these have not coalesced into a broad movement for media reform or support for independent and alternative media (Hackett and Carroll 2006).

Historically, media regulation in Canada has been somewhat responsive to the development of alternative media. In the 1960s, the National Film Board's Challenge for Change program inspired people to use film and video to animate positive social change. In the 1970s, the Secretary of State's Native Communication Program helped fuel the development of Aboriginal newspapers, and through the 1970s community radio and television and Native broadcasting began to be mentioned in broadcasting policy. Although the 1991 Broadcasting Act recognizes community broadcasting as a key element of the Canadian system, in anglophone Canada, no comprehensive government programs or regulations have ever existed to support alternative media, and through the late 1980s and 1990s, most programs for other media suffered cutbacks or were discontinued.

Today, responsibility for media policy is divided between various agencies and departments at the federal level. Although the Department of Canadian Heritage has overall responsibility for most media policy, the Canadian Radio-television and Telecommunications Commission (CRTC) regulates broadcasting and telecommunications, and Industry Canada has some jurisdiction over telecommunications. Consequently, when it comes to developing and initiating public policy in areas such as ownership, community radio and television broadcasting, or the Internet, there are sometimes conflicting visions of the direction that policy should take.[4]

At the same time, policy fields themselves are characterized by asymmetric-al relations of power that both directly and indirectly favour corporate media. For instance, in the field of broadcasting, researching and formulating policy positions and appearing at regulatory hearings requires both resources and expertise that are often beyond the reach of small media organizations. Simi-larly, although the federal government offers a number of media support pro-grams through the Department of Canadian Heritage, navigating that field and lobbying to have particular interests represented in those programs is difficult for small groups, particularly those whose mandate and interests dif-fer from those of corporate media. Whereas in the US associations such as Free Press and the Media and Democracy Coalition help bridge these gaps, no groups are undertaking this role in Canada. Corporate media, on the other hand, are equipped with industry organizations and regulatory affairs departments that are focused on working to maintain and enhance their positions in media mar-kets. The strength of corporate media in this regard is evidenced in the wide range of economic supports they enjoy, such as access to production funds and the protection of advertising markets. To some degree, the CRTC recog-nizes this imbalance in the telecommunications policy process and has the power to award the costs of intervention to public interest groups, but no similar mechanism is at work in broadcasting policy or other policy fields.

In terms of media reform, although a number of voices are calling for change in the structure and operation of media in Canada, public pressure is fragmented at best. Historically, the only independent organization that has been actively engaged on issues of media regulation on a full-time basis is the Friends of Canadian Broadcasting, but its focus is solely on broadcasting policy as it relates to the CBC and corporate media. Media unions regularly intervene in CRTC proceedings and have made efforts toward developing comprehen-sive media policy, but these generally concentrate on reform of the corporate media system (including the CBC) and have little to say about alternative media. A number of other industry-related groups such as the Alliance of Canadian Cinema, Television and Radio Artists and the Canadian Media Pro-duction Association also work on behalf of their members but have done little if anything on the part of independent or alternative media.

In terms of Internet policy, the Canadian Internet Policy and Public Interest Clinic, a small legal clinic based at the University of Ottawa, provides a public interest voice, and the Public Interest Advocacy Centre often advocates on con-sumer issues in the field of telecommunications. With some issues, such as net neutrality, the work of these organizations may have an impact on alternative media. However, in terms of the direct representation of the interests of in-dependent and alternative media, very few groups are at play. One fledgling body, OpenMedia.ca (formerly the Campaign for Democratic Media), has been developing an organization that captures elements of both Free Press and the Media and Democracy Coalition, and has enjoyed some success in campaigns around media diversity and net neutrality, but it has only one full-time and two part-time employees, and it struggles with funding issues.

At the level of media production, in anglophone Canada the National Campus and Community Radio Association/Association nationale des radios étudiantes et communautaires (NCRA/ANREC) is one of the only organizations directly focused on supporting alternative media. Founded in 1981, the NCRA represents fifty-three community radio stations across the country. Its state-ment of principles points out "that mainstream media fails to recognize or in many instances reinforces social and economic inequities that oppress women and minority groups of our society" and commits members to "providing al-ternative radio to an audience that is recognized as being diverse in ethnicity, culture, gender, sexual orientation, age, and physical and mental ability" (National Campus and Community Radio Association 1987). The NCRA draws $12,000 to $15,000 per year from membership fees and from 2000 to 2007 was able to finance one employee and an office in Ottawa. Since then, a Trillium foundation grant from the Ontario government has paid for two employees, one at half time and one at two-thirds time. Over the years, the NCRA has run a number of programs to provide training and develop resources for its mem-ber stations, and it works with government and related industry groups on issues such as licensing, regulatory fairness, and copyright. It also hosts a well-attended annual conference with sessions on fundraising, programming, work-ing with the CRTC, and professional development. As a result of representations from the NCRA and similar francophone organizations, in early 2008 the CRTC announced the creation of the Community Radio Fund of Canada (CRFC). Seeded by a $1.4 million commitment by Astral Media as part of an ownership transfer community benefits package, funds from the CRFC will be available to community stations across the country to bolster programming and other ser-vices they deliver (National Campus and Community Radio Association 2008; see Chapter 7 in this volume).

More recently, the Canadian Association of Community Television Users and Stations (CACTUS) was formed to advocate on behalf of community tele-vision. Although community television stations have been operating in Can-ada for more than thirty years, faced with a lack of resources, there has been no national organization to represent their interests. Run by volunteers, CACTUS' main resource is a website constructed in drupal, an open-source content management system that allows the site's users to easily share content and information. The site provides a space to share programs, collaborate on projects, discuss and organize around policy issues, and pool information and ideas on "how [to] deal with volunteers, fundraising, technological changes, negotiating with cable companies, [and] creating programs" (CACTUS 2007). In 2009, CACTUS developed a comprehensive plan for increasing the presence and role of community broadcasting in the media system for upcoming CRTC hearings on community broadcasting (CRTC 2009a). Although that plan was not adopted by the CRTC, CACTUS has since been active in the public policy arena (see Edwards 2010).

A number of trade organizations are devoted to aiding periodicals at both the provincial and federal levels, but none focus specifically on independent and alternative media. Some small alternative publications such as *This Magazine, Canadian Dimension,* and *Briarpatch* belong to Magazines Canada, formerly the Canadian Magazine Publishers Association. But although Magazines Canada provides a number of supports to its members in the form of advocacy, distribution, professional development, and a variety of other services, by and large its services and programs are geared toward corporate and commercial members. Under the auspices of the Canadian Magazine Fund (CMF), the Department of Canadian Heritage also has a number of programs to help support periodicals. Programs here range from support for editorial production to business development and postal subsidies. However, the manner in which the CMF defines a magazine tends to preclude many alternative and independent media from being eligible for these funds, particularly as the CMF does not fund electronic, or on-line, media. Moreover, recent changes to the CMF that limit subsidies to only those magazines with more than five thousand paid subscribers could seriously affect those alternative publications that have been receiving funding as well as foreclose on the hopes of others to obtain it (Adams 2009).

Given the lack of larger infrastructural supports, independent and alternative media have been working to develop novel means of organizing and sustaining themselves. For instance, with no government support for on-line media, some small publishers have attempted to establish an organization like the Media Consortium in Canada. In 2006, the Canadian Independent On-Line Media Alliance began to develop shared software resources, shared technological infrastructure, ad swaps, and editorial collaborations; it also lobbied government on mutual policy concerns. This effort – what members call "co-opetition" (a blend of cooperation and competition) – has met with some success, but a lack of direct funding for the alliance itself appears to have limited its effectiveness.

At the structural level, some of the more successful outlets utilize a variety of resources and modes of organization to sustain their operations. For instance, rabble.ca, launched in 2001, is one of Canada's most popular on-line independent media sites, with an average of 140,000 unique visitors and 8 million page views per month through most of 2008. In that year, it had an operating budget of $154,000, 52 percent of which came from "sustaining partners" (mostly unions) and 16 percent from members (rabble.ca 2009). The rest was split among grants, advertising, donations, and income from special events. The staff is a mix of part-time paid employees, students, interns, and volunteers. Content, which consists of both original and reprinted material, takes the form of print, podcasts, and video. Although rabble.ca has been relatively successful in maintaining its operations and attracting visitors to its site, its relatively small budget mitigates against the production of original material, particularly news, and the dependence on sustaining partners leaves it in a somewhat precarious position.

The Tyee, founded in 2003, provides an independent on-line counterpoint to corporate media in British Columbia, one of the most heavily concentrated media markets in the country. *The Tyee's* content is not alternative in the radical sense of the word. Rather, with an emphasis on investigative journalism, it often goes head-to-head with corporate media. But given the generally conservative tone of much Lower Mainland media, it does challenge the dominant media powers in that region and boasts a number of prestigious journalism awards, such as the Edward R. Murrow Award and the Canadian Journalism Foundation's Excellence in Journalism Award, to prove the point. With six employees, *The Tyee* has an annual operating budget of about $600,000 and receives about 250,000 page hits a month (Morrow 2009). But even with its popularity and public acclaim, the publication is still struggling to break even, and despite the fact that about 20 percent of its income is derived from advertising and grants, donations keep it afloat (ibid.). *The Tyee's* management has been particularly innovative in finding ways to fund journalism and has managed to institute two charitable fellowship funds for financing investigative reporting. Although *The Tyee* provides the publicity to raise money for the funds, they themselves are managed by Tides Canada, a national foundation. Set at $5,000 each, the fellowships have a common goal, "to educate and engage citizens in thinking through our shared future" (*The Tyee,* n.d.). *The Tyee* is one of the most successful alternative independent news organizations in the country, but the fact that it still struggles financially underscores the difficulty of developing a sustainable business model for such media.

One of the most innovative alternative media organizations in Canada is the Dominion Newspaper Cooperative. Arising out of efforts to establish an alternative national newspaper, the *Dominion* newspaper has been published monthly in both print and on-line editions since May 2003 by a network of independent journalists across Canada. The Dominion Newspaper Cooperative is a federally incorporated body that has three types of members – readers, journalists, and editors – each with their own interest and role in the association. In an effort to promote a more horizontal relationship between readers and the cooperative, reader members are invited to participate in decision making in both developing story ideas and administrative issues. Journalist members are the main story contributors, and the editors do the administrative work. Membership consists of about four hundred readers, two hundred journalists, and five editors, although, with between thirty and fifty thousand page hits a month, members are not the only people reading the paper. The annual budget is about $50,000, with the vast majority of the money contributed by members. Although some of the published material is contributed by volunteers, the group does strive to pay contributors wherever possible and does so in both cash and exchange. The organizational goal is to set up local media cooperatives across the country that work to produce news at both the local and national levels. Local media cooperatives currently exist in Halifax, Toronto, and Vancouver, and more are being planned. Each of these has its own website for local news as well. Despite the ongoing struggle of raising money and developing resources, the cooperative has been steadily growing since 2003.

In media education, given the lack of foundation support of media reform in Canada and the generally fragmented nature of reform initiatives, there is no Canadian correlate to the kinds of educational activities being undertaken in the US by the reform bodies discussed above. In terms of working to develop support for independent and community media, however, one annual event does stand out. Organized by local Toronto and Vancouver chapters of the Canadian Campaign for Press and Broadcast Freedom, Media Democracy Day was first established in Toronto, Vancouver, and Kitchener-Waterloo in 2001 and has gone on to be celebrated in cities across Canada and around the world. Based on three themes – education, protest, and change – Media

Democracy Day events are generally intended to cast critical light on commercial media practices and the public policies that support them and to celebrate independent and alternative media. These events are locally organized and volunteer-driven, with some support often coming from universities, unions, and other not-for-profits.

Conclusion

Although not all the literature on alternative and independent media sees the sustainability of alternative media as a problem, in the context of the most recent wave of media reform, issues of sustainability are taking on increasing importance. In the US, a growing number of organizations are working to improve the sustainability of independent and alternative media through developing larger social infrastructure, most particularly in broad media policy and community engagement. To some degree, the focus of these efforts appears to reflect the fact that they are primarily funded through philanthropic associations. Although these measures may be effective in helping sustain independent media outlets in the long term, more research is needed to understand how successful they are in offering the outlets direct and immediate relief from economic exigencies.

In Canada, the context of media reform differs somewhat from that of the US, and without comparable access to foundation funding, fewer resources are devoted to promoting broad policy changes and community engagement. Although the Canadian state has sometimes provided some support for independent and alternative media, Canadian regulatory forums today are largely structured to accommodate the needs and interests of large privately owned commercial corporations. In this context, work needs to be done to provide independent media greater access to the policy process and to increase the flexibility of policy initiatives to allow for their application to a wider range of organizational forms.

At the same time, however, a handful of independent Canadian media outlets have been developing creative responses to financing their operations, particularly in the context of web-based media. Still, without government support, they struggle to survive. At the time of writing, no community media centres like Michigan's GRCMC are operating in Canada, though the W2 Community Media Arts centre, which recently opened in Vancouver, houses a diverse mix of media outlets, a performance space, a social enterprise café, and more (W2, n.d.). Also, CACTUS continues to press for a new set of multimedia community access centres financed through the monies allocated by cable companies to their community channels (Edwards 2010; Anderson and Lithgow 2009).

In public education, without foundation or some other kind of economic support, creating the kinds of initiatives found in the US would be all but impossible. However, a broad public education program could be developed in high school media literacy programs. Such programs are relatively common in Canada, but to be effective, they need to go beyond critical reading of media texts to provide a wider understanding of the ways in which structural factors, such as ownership and modes of financing, affect the manner in which media represent the world (Kozolanka 2007b). Such a perspective would complement young people's use and understanding of both traditional and Internet-based media.

At a more closely focused level, adding the study of independent media to the curriculum of journalism programs would offer journalism students a better understanding of the ways in which organizational imperatives impinge on media production and would also get them thinking about how to apply the skills they learn. Few journalism programs in Canada provide a critical perspective on the relationships between organizational structure and journalism practice (Gasher 2007).

In sum, unsustainable levels of debt, fragmenting audiences, and falling advertising revenues have precipitated a crisis in commercial media and resulted in severe cuts to media coverage, particularly at the local level in print, broadcast, and on-line media in both Canada and the United States. Although in the US, philanthropy may help seed independent and alternative media to fill this void, in Canada the issue of whether alternative media will surmount this challenge appears to be as much a question of government support as individual or community enterprise.

NOTES

The author would like to thank the Canadian Media Research Consortium for a grant that helped make this research possible.
1 Alternative media are sometimes seen as a field in their own right (Atton 2002) or are divided into various types of fields, each with their own peculiar characteristics and democratic potential (Hamilton 2008). However, if one considers that they are all implicated in the exercise of symbolic power, that their mandates and organizational practices are often constructed in reaction to dominant media, and that their regulatory

environments are generally similar, then to a large part they do in fact share the same field.

2 As Hamilton (2008, viii) puts it, "despite being grounded in often very different social formations, communications practices too-easily polarized as 'mainstream' and 'alternative' are often much more similar than different, not only in form and style, but also at the level of organization, technology, and social intention."

3 Research for this chapter turned up people who had worked for Indymedia centres in Canada and were now working for a variety of other media. Similarly, what is often referred to as "citizen's journalism" or "crowd reporting" can be seen to have its roots in Indymedia's open publishing (Skinner et al. 2009; see also http://www.nowpublic.com).

4 For instance, in terms of policy concerning media diversity, compare the recommendations of the Lincoln report (Canada 2003, 385-425) with the policies implemented by the CRTC (CRTC 2008b).

Public Service Educational Broadcasting
Between the Market and the Alternative Margins

KIRSTEN KOZOLANKA

Public service educational broadcasters are often overlooked in the Canadian mediascape, despite in recent years having made significant efforts to survive in ways that reflect the ongoing broader societal struggle between public service and the market. Against the odds, they provide cultural value while gaining economic value, yet they are still unable to become sufficiently commodified to survive without government support, which continues to diminish or be unreliable. This chapter examines public service educational broadcasting in Canada and its strategies to offer public service in a time of increasing privatization and marketization. It makes comparisons with similar policy and political environments experienced by the Public Broadcasting Service (PBS) in the United States and the Canadian Broadcasting Corporation (CBC). It also situates educational broadcasters as caught between marginalized alternative space and that of mainstream commercial broadcast media.

By definition and in theory, educasting – which is how public service educational broadcasters refer to their work – could be considered alternative media, as it is structured as non-profit-oriented media that exist outside the market and are independent from other media. In reality, however, educasters straddle the mainstream and the margins of space that continually shifts beneath them, as the policies of the New Right increasingly jeopardize the future of public service broadcasting.

The terrain on which the broadcasting-education hybrid of educasting operates in Canada and elsewhere is contradictory, difficult to categorize, and fraught with complex dilemmas. The underlying broadcasting-education duality is both a negative and a positive force in survival and continued viability. This duality inhibits potential as much as it provides a safety net, and educasting histories reveal both their vulnerability and their resilience. Within this environment, situating educasting organizationally and structurally must emphasize the importance of public service media within a broader media system as well as the societal role that they play in facilitating democratic communication. This does not mean that they are not or cannot be participatory or activist, the other overarching thematics of alternative media. Over the years, they have played an untrumpeted yet important role in fostering public debate, the construction of community, and awareness of social issues. This chapter will argue that these spheres of activity in fact are now key to the survival of Canadian educasting in hostile times. In addition, as the structural foundation of public educational broadcasting changes, educasters will need to adapt by enhancing their participatory potential. Key to this argument is Schiller's now classic view that when public space is contested, the culture in question must retain its centrality to social life and to democracy. In direct contrast to the New Right's prioritizing of the economic, Schiller (1989, 31) saw the economic as inseparable from the symbolic or cultural in a society. This chapter also suggests commonalities with alternative media that can be enhanced.

The ongoing uncertainty in the political and policy environment of recent years is at odds with the original purpose in setting up educasting institutions. They were created to serve and be responsible to the public in the public interest and are central to the project of democracy by fostering participatory democratic values by example. Garnham (2003, 194) has called this process democracy "as actual practice." An inherent complication for public service educational broadcasters is that their work goes beyond the general responsibility of service to the public. They are also guardians of a specific aspect of it: the production of knowledge through their mandate to educate. Fleisher (1995, 18) long ago pointed out that "educational broadcasting has been part of the dreams of greater equality and increased participation in society."

At the same time as diminished public funding has forced educasters to rethink and renegotiate their position, it should be acknowledged that the original remit of public broadcasting raised concerns for some in terms of its funding and relationship to the democratic state. Hamilton (2000, 361) reminds us of Raymond Williams' warning that a large public media institution such as the BBC with a state funding base could be "self-defeating" if it loses its partici- patory relationship with the community. More recently than Williams, Couldry and Curran (2003, 10) warn that "subsidies have only a limited effect in redress- ing the concentration of media power unless they are linked to community structures and practice," a position this chapter also takes up.

In contrast, the New Right has in recent years used privatization as its pri- mary counter-democratic tool. In the context of commercial media, it is useful as well to view privatization as an expression of the logic of commodification – the production of a good or service for a profit (Soron and Laxer 2006, 17). As Murdock and Golding's (1989, 184) trenchant definition suggests, it comprises the "economic initiatives that aim to increase the reach of market institutions and philosophies at the expense of the public sphere." Commercial media trad- itionally are assumed to have a public responsibility to circulate information and ideas, but the educasting duality of broadcasting along with a direct and specific mandate to educate is increasingly placed in contradiction with itself, as the ongoing trend to corporate media concentration narrows the space for public media, commodifies both content and audiences, marginalizes divers- ity and oppositional voices, and ultimately subordinates the media's public responsibility to private interests (McQuail 2005, 99).

Public services in general, such as public education, as well as education in the form of public service educational broadcasting, have felt the sting of commodification, which has shifted the public interest mandate of educasting away from the mainstream and closer to the alternative margins. New Right privatization was not only part of an overall offensive to contain the commons, but also to expand the market.[1] Public service and education are no longer merit goods in and of themselves, but have monetary value. They can be pri- vately owned and sold to viewer-citizens, who are repositioned as customers or consumers. Turk (2000, 4-6) distinguishes three forms of commercialization as applied to educational institutions: turning them into marketing sites for brand name products, altering how education is delivered so there will be greater usage of privately supplied goods and services, and driving education- al institutions to operate as if they were private. Such commercialization re- structures their organization, mandates, and decision making. Over time, the provincial educasters have also encountered these forms of commercialization in their embrace of marketing schemes through sponsorships, program under- writing, corporate fundraising, and joint ventures in attempts to generate non-public funding. Over a decade ago, Winter (1998, 124) provided an example of the broad response of educasters to the pressures from increasing commercialization. He suggests that a solution to financial deprivation in the public sector is establishing new partnerships with commercial enterprises, while also acknowledging that the ultimate price of this strategy might be the end of free educational television and even public service television itself.

Despite this quantum shift in the ethos of public service, very little research or critical reflection has focused on how Canadian educasting has fared under the New Right. One early paper laid out its rationale, mandates, and organization (Wilson, Bell, and Powell 1984), and a short on-line history exists (Keast 1986) as does an article that examines the values and state of educational broadcasting (Vaughn, Tobin, and Legault 1999). The struggle to keep TVOntario, the province of Ontario's educaster, in public hands has been documented and analyzed (Kozolanka 2001, 2007a). Most scholarly discussion on the subject, however, focuses on state-run public service broadcasters in Europe (Blumler 1992; Collins 1998; Jakubowicz 1999), with a long history of such analysis in Great Britain (Williams 1966; Garnham 1986, 2003; Keane 1991) and some scholarship in Canada (Gasher 1997; Raboy 1990).

Political, Policy, and Media Environment

From the beginning, educational broadcasters faced structural and institutional barriers to stability. They were situated dually within two overlapping policy jurisdictions: federal, which controlled broadcast regulation, and provincial, which controlled education (Wilson, Bell, and Powell 1984, 1). Federally, the objectives in the Broadcasting Act are both cultural and economic, and government has the power to decide on their relevance, as well as the appropriate balance between the needs of citizens and those of consumers (CRTC 2006b, 84). Individual provincial and territorial legislation is the foundation for universal public education. Both levels of government together defined educasting in 1969. This was important in setting out frames of reference, such as programming requirements for licensing. In 1972, the federal government agreed to "license certain independent corporations" in arm's-length relationships from the provincial ministries that would be funding them (ibid., 3). The result was a patchwork of agencies that developed independently of each other in five provinces: the Knowledge Network (British Columbia), ACCESS (Alberta), the Saskatchewan Communication Network (SCN), TVOntario, and

Télé-Québec.[2] All were based on the American PBS model of "a mix of program types and formats" that had already paved the way for successful educasting (Keast 1986, 24).

Among the unforeseen problems in this structure were the lack of national oversight (Wilson, Bell, and Powell 1984, 1), the 1996 release of the provinces to use federal transfer funds without restrictions, and, starting in 1997, the growth of specialty television channels that fragmented their audiences (Atherton 2001, E1).[3] First and foremost, however, was the shift away from public service itself.

Throughout the 1980s and 1990s in Canada, the federal government and some provincial governments, particularly in Alberta and Ontario, underwent extensive downsizing in response to New Right policies. Downsizing affected public services, whereas the corporate sector received tax credits and tax cuts (Ralph, Régimbald, and St-Amand 1997; Kozolanka 2007a). The federal response favoured outright privatization of public resources, whereas the provinces were inclined to opt for underfunding key areas of government, such as allocations to education ministries, where educasters tend to be housed. Underfunding education, as well as underfunding the educasters that were agencies of and received funding from ministries of education, created opportunities for the private sector to commercialize public education and broader educational services. Then as now, as Sumner (2006, 211) writes, "the void of deliberate underfunding is being filled by the infusion of corporate influence."

As a result, between 1994 and 1999, four of the provincial educasters were subjected to the threat of privatization, and the fifth (SCN) underwent a review. Most provinces pulled back on outright privatization and settled on lowering government allocations, which made it difficult for their educasters to operate fully in the public interest. Where initially provinces funded their educasters between 82 and 100 percent of total revenue, since 1990 they have reduced their support to between 59 and 73 percent. TVOntario was and is at the lowest end of the scale of this funding, dropping from 82.2 percent in 1990 to 58.4 percent in 2008. In 1990, the Saskatchewan Communication Network had the highest level of government funding, 99.8 percent, and currently Télé-Québec has the highest funding, at 72.5 percent in 2008. In addition, overall budgets are less, often considerably so, than they were in 1990. In 1991, the actual dollar investment by federal and provincial governments in the five educasters was $195.1 million.[4] In 2008, it was only $123.1 million, or 63.1 percent of the 1991 funding.

Most of the impact of lower budgets was felt directly in labour, job losses that brought with them a diminishment of institutional memory, expertise, and local knowledge. The second area of impact was in the loss of in-house production. Although outsourcing production does save money, drawbacks are the loss of local control, representation, and cultural specificity (Hoskins, McFadyen, and Finn 1993; Kozolanka 2001). In recent years, only SCN produced its own local and regional programs (Richard Gustin, pers. comm., 10 December 2007), and all educasters outsource to independent producers.

Canadian educasters are not the only public service broadcasters to have felt the anti-public-service economic policies of New Right governments. Over a period of decades, as commercial media grow in size and power, public service broadcasting has declined worldwide to the point that it is battling for survival (Fleisher 1995, 19). The shift away from public broadcasting was also a move from the "elaborate system of public accountability" that underpinned public broadcasting and other welfare state systems (Blumler and Hoffmann-Riem 1992, 219).

In the US, PBS survived a major overhaul during the early 1990s. As Hoynes (2003, 123) writes, its newly devised commodified brand – which it publicizes as high-quality educational programming for a loyal audience – is its primary asset, yet it also "makes the idea of non-commercial broadcasting increasingly dubious." Changes to PBS included less local focus and more centralization, advertising before and after programs, licensed products, and co-productions with commercial media. In undergoing the branding process, it has targeted its existing educated and high-income audience, and introduced a new audience: business (ibid., 123, 126). According to Hoynes (ibid., 128), in creating its economically successful short-term strategy, PBS is losing its "distinctive public service identity ... becoming just another brand competing for consumer attention in an increasingly cluttered commercial marketplace." Just as Canadian educasters in the beginning looked to PBS for a model of educational broadcasting, they echoed its shift of redefining themselves to become more commercial and to find new revenue streams.

Like European and other public service broadcasters, the Canadian Broadcasting Corporation (CBC) has also faced New Right underfunding policies and the threat of outright privatization. The unique situation of Canada, however, should also be recognized. The CBC was created as and continues to be a mixed public-private system, thus always playing to both public service and the market. Cutbacks to the CBC began as long ago as 1984, when Conservative

Party leader Brian Mulroney became prime minister. With cutbacks from its $1.5 billion budget well under way, it was the subject of a mandate review in 1995. The review was supportive of the role of the CBC as public broadcaster, however, and it quickly dropped from view without the implementation of its recommendations for strengthening the CBC. From 1990 to 2008, the CBC's annual operations allocation for radio and television from Parliament decreased from 73.1 percent of all revenue to 56.2 percent. The funding slack was taken up by becoming more commercialized through advertising and merchandise and program sales. Although the CBC made gains in increased children's programming and its website services, it did so by "cutting jobs, streamlining production, converging [its] newsrooms, downsizing the corporation, and showing reruns" (Padovani and Tracey 2003, 138). In so doing, according to Richard Gustin, executive director of programming at SCN, the CBC "abdicated its regional role and responsibility" (Gustin, pers. comm., 10 December 2007). Educasters have taken over the regional space vacated by the CBC, becoming more like a public broadcaster overall and leading to criticism that they have become CBC 2 – a public broadcaster rather than a public service educational broadcaster (Atherton 1995, A1).

At $930 million in 2008 (CBC 2008a), federal government financing of the CBC is still less than it was in 1990. Although public service broadcasting was contracting in many countries, a 1999 study for the Organisation for Economic Co-operation and Development (OECD) conducted by Laval University's Centre d'études sur les médias found that federal money for public television in Canada dropped 28.8 percent in just three years. This was the largest drop in funding among all the twenty-nine OECD countries (*Toronto Globe and Mail* 1999, A8). Despite this, public television in Europe and elsewhere still holds 30 percent of the viewing audience (Kiefl 2003, 3), whereas in Canada and the US, its audiences have always been small by comparison.

Educasting in New Right Times

In order to survive, educasters turned to market-driven strategies to diversify revenue streams, thereby entering into direct competition with private commercial broadcasters. This included fostering growth of products and merchandise sectors. It also entailed finding creative ways to gain advertising dollars, such as through program underwriting and sponsorships, without actually using ads in accordance with Canadian Radio-television and Telecommunication Commission (CRTC) regulations. This intrusion into semi-private broadcasting also served to habituate the educasters to a commercial environment and make it easier for Ottawa to reorient policy to include them.

Survival strategies were based on strategically targeting and emphasizing their strengths. In the federal broadcasting policy environment, Association for Tele-Education in Canada (ATEC), the umbrella group for the educasters (ATEC, n.d., 6-7), said that its response to the challenge of media consolidation was "to focus more clearly on what makes us unique in the market and to cleave more closely to our educational mandate ... to define ... more and more clearly how we bring a unique contribution to the market in which we work."

In the diverse provincial education policy environments, the educasters had differentiated strategies of survival. As noted by Light in Chapter 7 of this volume, Québec broadcasting in general is unique. Télé-Québec has always broadcast commercials within a programming schedule that stresses the cultural, situated as it is, "surrounded by television stations based in North American anglophone culture" (Vaughn, Tobin, and Legault 1999, 18). The small francophone market it serves gives it little broad potential for sales and sponsorships, so the Québec government continues to be a key source of funding (ibid., 27). In British Columbia, the Knowledge Network made early and successful programming moves toward general-interest public television broadcasting (Shandel 1994), and its public satisfaction rating and loyalty remain strong (Ian Morrison, pers. comm., 18 June 2008). SCN generated revenue by being a distributor of high-speed Internet via satellite (Gustin, pers. comm., 10 December 2007). It also placed considerable focus on in-house independent production in a region that is not otherwise well served. In contrast, TVOntario had closed down much of its in-house production by 1993 but maintains a solid and large membership base (Kozolanka 2001), relative to those other educasters that have a member base.

Survival does not come without cost. A key element in the shift away from public service in general was the reformulation by provincial governments of public education into training and, additionally, the glorification of technology-driven education (Mosco and Mazepa 2003; Kozolanka 2009). Both were intended to feed the labour and knowledge needs of the private sector. To meet the imperative of provincial governments intent on cutting costs to public services and filling private-sector training needs, the educasters themselves have refocused their role away from public service. An examination of changes to their mandates clarifies how public education and public education broadcasting have become more market-driven. TVOntario's original 1970 mandate stressed that its purpose was to "provide educational opportunities for all

people in Ontario where the use of such media will complement the educational opportunities being offered by other agencies, or alternatively, will provide educational opportunities not otherwise available ... , and further, to
cooperate with other organizations in attaining social and educational goals"
(Wilson, Bell, and Powell 1984, 1). In 2006, TVOntario laid out its "mission" in a
"strategy map" and said it "uses the power of television, the Internet and other
communications technologies to enhance education ... inspiring learning for
life." Its major goals were "establishing TVOntario as essential to building a
knowledge-based society ... , providing a safe, non-violent, commercial-free
educational service for children ... , building a strong and secure financial future, and managing the organization to the highest standards of business
practices, demonstrating effective use of funds" (TVOntario 2006, 4). In 2008,
the mission changed again to become shorter, more vague, and less business-
oriented, but It sounds more like an advertising slogan: TVOntario now "informs, inspires, and stimulates curiosity and thought" (TVOntario 2008a, 1).

Another example of a substantive shift in mandate comes from BC's
Knowledge Network. In an interview with the *Vancouver Sun* between the
broadcaster's 1996 review and its 1999 review, its CEO said, "It's about being
true to our mandate and building a brand identity" (quoted in Strachan 1998,
C8). The CEO went on to say that the Knowledge Network is "ideally positioned
to exploit its content creation business and extend its operations beyond TV
into the business of Webcasting" and that "it's more important than ever to
demonstrate [that the Knowledge Network] can deliver good value for the
money invested" (Morgan 2001, C2). In 2008, the Knowledge Network underwent a branding process yet again (Knowledge Network 2008).

Part of TVOntario's success in remaining a public agency lay in its strategy
in the early 1990s of recognizing the dangers of the status quo. It underwent
its own internal review voluntarily and created a long-term strategic plan to
take it through the 1990s (Kozolanka 2001). The "TVO model" was imitated by
the other educasters. It involved broadening its traditional audience, increasing memberships, finding non-government revenue, and supplying and selling curriculum programming to other broadcasters here and abroad (Atherton
1995, A1). Ominously, the TVOntario plan borrowed from the American PBS
model, which included "heavy reliance on corporate sponsorship," and also
from the private sector, for international program sales and "aggressive merchandising." In 1995, an added incentive for TVOntario to restructure and
downsize was to repel the interest from private investors in purchasing the
station (ibid.).

Whereas four of the educasters continued to struggle within diminishing or unstable funding, Alberta had the distinction of being the only province that privatized its educational broadcaster outright. The Alberta government of Conservative Ralph Klein sold off ACCESS, an institution built and operated with public money from 1978 to 1994, for the grand sum of one dollar to a private-sector group of which the media corporation CHUM was the majority shareholder.[5] Not only was the public investment given over to private hands, but, to add insult to injury, the Alberta government ministries continue to fund ACCESS by purchasing its curriculum programming – at one time enough to fill 60 percent of its schedule (Vaughn, Tobin, and Legault 1999, 15). ACCESS' focus was and is narrowly on training and education (Harris and Dafoe 1995, C2). Despite this public investment, ACCESS is not accountable to the public. Very little financial information on its operations is available publicly, and it was virtually ignored in CHUM annual reports, confirming that it held an insignificant position within the corporate structure. In fact, early post-privatization records were lost in the 2006 corporate merger of CHUM into CTVglobemedia. Despite being privatized, ACCESS remains a member of ATEC. At the time of the ACCESS privatization, the Knowledge Network's Glen Farrell described it as "smoke and mirrors" – a political decision, not an economic one (quoted in ibid.) – and presumably ATEC still considered ACCESS as one of its own.

Currently, a key factor in educaster survival lies in the potential blowback from the fate of the Canadian Television Fund (CTF). The CTF was a policy mechanism that encouraged high-quality Canadian programming in our small domestic market. It was co-funded by cable and satellite distributors from their cable profits and by the Canadian government. ATEC had a seat on the CTF board of directors, as did CBC, and educasters received a stable and proportional amount of CTF funding, which in 2008 totalled $265 million (CBC 2007, 1). Revenue from the fund was so important to the public broadcasters that Friends of Canadian Broadcasting's Ian Morrison has referred to the fund as "the oil in the engine" (Morrison, pers. comm., 18 June 2008). In 2007, two key media corporations – Shaw and Quebecor – threatened to withdraw unless rules were changed to allow them to collect and keep cable subscriber fees intended for the fund's coffers. Although the federal Conservative government said it would not change the CTF, the CRTC held hearings in 2008 and recommended that the fund be divided into separate public and private streams. The public stream would receive its funding through the Department of Canadian Heritage, leaving the CTF funding for the private-sector broadcasters. Funding to the public broadcasters would decline by $150 million over five years, and only the private sector would benefit from the growth from industry contributions to the fund (CBC 2008a, 1). ATEC stated that the change in the fund's structure would "jeopardize high-quality, independently produced Canadian educational programs ... [that reflect] diverse regional voices and viewpoints" (Association for Tele-Education in Canada 2008, 1).

The development of large corporate broadcasting channels has also changed the market for educational programming. At one time, prior to the flood of specialty channels in 1998, educasters could share the costs for developing programming and the licensing with other small channels and have an exclusive window in which they could show the program. The new corporate broadcasters, those with many channels, such as Alliance Atlantis' large group of specialty channels, and who thus have more clout, are more territorial. They set the terms for programming sharing and can demand exclusive rights for extended periods. This excludes the educasters from both participating in educational program development and broadcasting such programming while it is still current. SCN's Richard Gustin has said that development of some kinds of programs, such as history and science, subsequently dried up, and the educasters had to find alternative – and more expensive – programming directions (Gustin, pers. comm., 10 December 2007). The provincial educasters also work less with the Aboriginal Peoples Television Network and A&E Network. Moreover, the corporate broadcasters receive payments from the specialty channel distributors, giving them extra profits, whereas educasters provide their own programs for free. As former ATEC president Ken Alecxe has said succinctly, "our main interest is to get good Canadian programming out the door, theirs is ratings" (Alecxe, pers. comm., 7 November 2007).

This raises the broader issue of the impact of media concentration and audience fragmentation on public television. It is worth noting that changes to media structures affect all broadcasters, both public and private, large or small. The profusion of television channels has made the medium more competitive for audiences, and content has shifted away from information and education toward soft news and entertainment, as well as to narrowcasting to specific segments of audiences. The educasters are not exempt from this. Their traditional program mix of entertainment, information, and education has also moved toward entertainment. Although they tend to have niche audiences, they have not traditionally narrowcasted, believing that it "enables audiences to watch only what they are familiar with and, consequently, our dreams of reaching new audiences and inspiring them to want and seek more education – enlightenment – are evaporating" (Fleisher 1995, 18).

This issue of familiarity versus enlightenment has slipped into the background as all television broadcasters try to hang on to disappearing audiences. Canada, already with the lowest viewing of home-produced programming of any country (Kiefl 2004), is experiencing a decrease in conventional television viewing, as well as a decline in Canadian TV viewing in particular (CRTC 2006b). The few viewing numbers that are available on educational broadcasting are vague, and historical data are scanty or unavailable, but viewing trends affect all broadcasters. The CRTC reports its viewing figures only for educational broadcasters folded into the same category as CPAC (the Canadian Public Affairs Channel), TV Guide, and the Shopping Channel, among other niche broadcasters (ibid., 35). However, the educasters' own data indicate that together they have 11 million viewers per week (Association for Tele-Education in Canada, n.d.). TVOntario alone reaches 3.5 million viewers and has a 2 percent Ontario audience share, "equivalent to most Canadian specialty and digital channels" (TVOntario 2008c). The Knowledge Network reports 1.5 million viewers per week (Knowledge Network 2006, 1). Overall, as of the mid-1990s, according to the Association for Tele-Education in Canada's promotional video, the five educasters broadcast three hundred hours of non-commercial children's programming per week, have "tens of thousands" of viewers learning in telecourses, and "tens of millions" invested annually in programming that triggers $100 million in Canadian independent production (Association for Tele-Education in Canada, n.d.).

Commodification of the Educasting Commons

Educasters have managed to attract new revenue by putting the ethos, objectives, and marketing tools of the private sector into action. Their very survival is a testament to their ability to adapt to market capitalism. In so doing, they are operating, as PBS does in the US, by promoting a brand they may not have. Their original niche was for high-quality educational television programming with a sharp program focus that was clearly differentiated and had a distinctive identity (Vaughn, Tobin, and Legault 1999, 5). It was also explicitly non-commercial. Today, they are differentiated less as a niche in which citizens participate as a public right and more as just another specialty channel with competing interests and equal claims to their individualized viewer-consumers.

In the long term, the foundations for continued survival remain shaky. Financial data show that new revenue streams that were developed to replace government funding have stalled. Although TVOntario's membership base has reached its strongest point since 1998, revenue from sales and licensing bottomed out in 2003. Since 2004, the Knowledge Network lost its last federal government funding of $5.1 million, sales have dropped considerably, and donations and sponsorships have increased only slightly. SCN – considered stable in terms of government funding over its lifetime – posted high increases in memberships but garnered most of its non-government revenue from channel rentals and did not have an active merchandising sector. Overall, advertising is not as easy to find as it would be for private broadcasters, as audiences are too small.

The move to "commercial public" broadcasting has meant a shift away from the original ideal of enlightenment through education to a broad audience, which has been replaced with increasingly niche-oriented and limited targeted audiences. For instance, SCN's demographic was split between the older generation – "a CBC-type audience" – and young families (Alecxe, pers. comm., 7 November 2007). Generating non-government revenue requires marketing, both to current audiences through membership drives and other fundraising and to projected audiences, such as potential partners and for corporate giving. In this, the audience demographic of public broadcasting is exploited as a commodity. Hoynes (2003, 124) suggests that the same process is happening at a restructured and branded PBS, at which "the very idea of public service itself is being commodified ... Public service is increasingly something to be packaged and sold to consumers who are brand loyal to PBS. This branding strategy targets an audience of consumers – educated, interested, high income – and it sells 'content,' various program-related products, and an image to these consumers. And, increasingly, PBS trades this image to major commercial media for new revenue streams, in the form of corporate sponsorships and strategic partnerships."

The fly in the ointment for Canadian educational broadcasters seeking new revenue streams and doing so by marketing their audiences is that viewing research shows a drop across all television broadcasting, particularly in the youth demographic (CRTC 2006b). In other words, educasters are both commodifying their increasingly smaller audience and losing their sense of public service while taking public money. Over time, this may have a ripple effect and cause them and the CBC to lose the distinctive character that the management consulting firm McKinsey and Company, in a report on the BBC, believes sets off a "virtuous cycle" in which "there is a strong linkage between the health and funding model of the [public service broadcaster] and the overall quality of each national broadcasting market" (quoted in Padovani and Tracey 2003,

139). One of the contradictions and ironies in educasting is that at the same time as it becomes more commercialized, public opinion research conducted by the Friends of Canadian Broadcasting indicates strong overall satisfaction and support from all demographics and regions for educational broadcasting across Canada (Ipsos-Reid 2002). Educasting has, as Ian Morrison (pers. comm., 18 June 2008) puts it, "a reservoir of audience esteem ... that the public, although it doesn't use it very often, understands is distinctive."

The audience capital and cultural value that educasters have built are based on the old brand, whereas the new commercialism has redefined public space. As Polster (2000, 19, 30) has written about public knowledge in the similar and relevant context of post-secondary institutions, commercialism "prevents fulfilling the public service mission" and "reduces the use and limits production of public knowledge." By themselves redefining public service, educasters have been complicit in producing private knowledge for sale to their viewers and enclosing the commons. As in the case of PBS, formal privatization is not necessary, as they are slowly and incrementally privatizing themselves in what Habermas (1989, 175) has called "pseudo-privatization." Like the CBC, they have been deliberately underfunded or defunded to the point that they cannot fulfill their original mandates of public service. That failure opens them up to policies that further destabilize them and jeopardize the audience capital they have enjoyed to date.

The Road Ahead: To the Margins or to the Market?

The political and policy-making ground has shifted considerably in a relatively short time, and decommodifying educasting may not be possible since some no longer consider pure public service to be a viable option. In their discussion of public service broadcasting in 2001, Collins et al. (2001, 12) assert about the choices to be made by educasters that "the prospects are good if change is embraced rather than resisted." Less than a decade later, the bar is much lower, as educasters have indeed embraced the market model, and both the discourses and actions of the New Right have become further embedded into public service models. To many, like Collins et al., it remains a matter only of degree of acceptance.

Yet educasters are well placed to resist such market relationships. Over time, they have recast themselves as regional voices and have shown respect for and understanding of local and participatory society building. Their members are loyal viewers who consciously choose to support public service educational broadcasting and funding for public service broadcasting in general. If one measures viewer satisfaction instead of only the share that programs get, as does Kiefl (2004), Canadian television has higher ratings than we have given it credit for. Loyal viewers played a key role in helping TVOntario avoid privatization in 1997 and could be brought to bear again (Kozolanka 2007a).

In addition, the policy-making environment is not altogether negative. In 2003, the Lincoln report (Canada 2003, 244) devoted a self-standing, although short, chapter to them and other not-for-profit broadcasters and recommended "that the *Broadcasting Act* be amended to recognize not-for-profit public broadcasters as integral to the Canadian broadcasting system." The report also recommended that CBC funding be increased to match OECD levels. In 2006, a Senate committee report recommended that the CBC drop advertising completely and that the federal government "commit to long-term and stable funding" (CTV.ca 2006). In addition, in 2007, ATEC – the usually low-key umbrella body for educasting – appeared before the CRTC hearings on diversity, and it has made other such submissions. This was doubtless in a much-needed effort to raise the profile of its members and keep their perspective in the policy-making arena (CRTC 2007d).

Moreover, not all educasters are alike in how and to what degree they have commercialized. Télé-Québec, which currently has the highest proportional public funding, accentuates cultural value in a culturally isolated francophone province, yet commercials abound. SCN emphasized cultural value to isolated and First Nations communities, and enjoyed relatively stable funding from the province with little market activity. The ability to adapt and represent communities of interest and regions will be a strong factor in the survival of public educational broadcasting. Altogether, educasters have managed to satisfy audience appetite while maintaining audience conceptions of getting a unique product. Further, the CBC's budget-led abandonment of much regional programming has given the educasters room to establish and emphasize a unique role through local and regional programming.

How the CBC handles change will also be a factor in educaster survival. As Richard Gustin at SCN has said, "Anything that makes CBC [in Saskatchewan] a better broadcaster is good for SCN and is good for the people of Saskatchewan" (quoted in O'Connor 2000, A2). Years ago, at the beginning of the crisis in public service broadcasting, Fleisher (1995, 19) saw the same connection between the common future of educational and public broadcasting, noting that "more and more public broadcasters have declared that providing educational programming is one of their major tasks."

Nonetheless, the 2008 CRTC recommendation to divide the Canadian Television Fund into two separate public and private streams was considered a severe blow. Immediately prior to the restructuring, which took place in 2009, the CTF's budget for funding production decreased for the first time in five years (Canadian Television Fund 2008, 30). However, indications are that some educasters – TVOntario (including TFO), SCN, and Télé-Québec – initially benefited from a higher percentage of post-restructuring production funding (ibid., 48). In early 2010, the government completed the transition and formally amalgamated CTF with the Canada New Media Fund, creating the Canada Media Fund.

In addition, although the then new Saskatchewan Party government in that province did not mention SCN in election literature or its policy platform, SCN was concerned that it might be among the government's many reviews of public agencies and boards (Gustin, pers. comm., 14 July 2008). SCN's provincial funding remained stable for the first two years under the new administration, but in early 2010, the Saskatchewan government unexpectedly sold SCN to a private company. Bluepoint Investment plans to emulate the ACCESS model by selling curriculum and possibly other educational services to the government (A. Hall 2010). Also, in late 2006, Ontario announced it was once again creating a "strategic agenda" for TVOntario that is more in alignment with Ministry of Education priorities. In the face of ten straight years of provincial funding stagnation, the ministry asked TVOntario "to build a sustainable business model," which would include advertising (*Ottawa Citizen* 2006, C4). Coupled with the Knowledge Network's rebranding process, which follows a failed attempt by the BC government in 2005 to sell it (Palmer 2005, A3), this may signal yet another round of provincial reviews and continued uncertainty in the educasting environment.

The remaining educasters now find themselves in an untenable and contradictory position: marginalized but also mainstreamed through incremental market orientation. They are marginalized in the sense that they have lost their broadcasting niche and are slowly losing their public service purpose. They are mainstreamed in that they have become one of many commercial television choices.

As the original identity of educasting, as producing knowledge in the service of the public with cultural value, is overtaken by market imperatives, educasters generate less of what Polster (2000, 38) has called "alternative knowledge" – knowledge that is not oriented toward the production of economically valuable goods. Structurally, however, they are still nominally non-commercial and not-for-profit agencies at arm's length from government. They remain in tension with themselves, partly within the embrace of the market, partly enclosed with a shrinking commons as the political, policy, and media ground continues to shift. Thus, they also face the classic dilemma of alternative media: to commercialize further to survive or to stay true to their values and risk becoming irrelevant (Comedia 1984).

Politically, they continue to encounter challenges from both the conservative market advocates and their political alternatives. The New Right currently has discursive strength, growing political and economic power, and the upper hand in policy; it sees publicly funded broadcasting as part of big and therefore unneeded government. Yet progressive media organizations at the other end of the political spectrum do not see the educasters automatically as partners in struggle. One danger in the ambiguous public identity of the educasters is that they are so pervaded by the market that they do not see themselves situated within increasingly marginalized space or linked to alternative media. Thus, they do not make connections to alternative media movements but operate in isolation either on the corporate level of broadcasting, at the policy level with education ministries, or in one-to-one encounters with local and regional content providers and independent producers. Although these spheres of activity are legitimate, awareness of their common ground with the aims and audiences of alternative media and linkages to them would enhance knowledge and support for the public service purpose of educasting. It would also provide avenues for lobbying and resistance for the inevitable challenges that lie ahead.

Educational broadcasters are well placed to contribute with more precise and concrete dedication to democratic communication, but they will need to insert themselves more vigorously into public policy debates. Early in the struggle to retain vulnerable public service values, Blumler (1992, 220) suggested that public broadcasters take up "accountability activism" against regulatory authorities to ensure there was no slippage in obligations. Similarly, as Chapter 1 in this volume argues, broadcasters and others with better access to the policy process can advocate for policy flexibility in order to widen the range of voices and perspectives being heard. As well as intervening in policy matters, they can forge alliances with groups such as OpenMedia.ca, which is supported by many industry members, academics, and citizens with whom they can partner on research and lobbying.

Although educasters are not on the radar of media activists, they already excel at various aspects of grassroots activity, with the force of comparably large budgets and the ability to broadcast to audiences behind them. They are adept at public debate and the construction of community, and they could strengthen their existing close producer-creator relationships as well as build on the public desire for local programming. Also advantageous is the plethora of devices they already use in their work, from audience participation devices to viewer panels, not to mention the reciprocity of tele-education itself, which involves not just teacher-student, but also citizen-citizen interaction. Add to this their intersections with diverse voices and audiences, especially in those educasters that have memberships and thus a captive group of committed fans, and they could easily become sites for direct and indirect political action.

Educational broadcasting can also benefit from a fluid media environment that blurs the lines between media producers and media consumers. Web 2.0 will make this commonplace on-line, and alternative media have always had a close creator-audience relationship, but educasters are also developing this capacity. As an example, TVOntario has been using its website to engage consciously in what it calls a form of citizen journalism by "blending citizen-generated content with our own resources ... and acting as a ... 'smart aggregator': a trusted source of content, analysis and background in an age of participatory user-generated digital media" (TVOntario 2008b, 10). Here, TVOntario is essentially using its brand for citizen engagement, instead of commodification. Further, it lays out an unmistakable public service mission that is also participatory and activist: "Democracy can't work without public education, public broadcasting and the principles of journalism" (ibid., 16). TVOntario's 2008 strategic agenda echoes this in its focus on citizenship and public engagement, along with a digital media priority of reaching out to "users" (TVOntario 2010). Together, this evokes overlaps and synergies with community television that need to be explored (see Chapter 6 in this volume). TVOntario and the other educational broadcasters have also kept pace with social media and have upgraded to digital platforms.

Conclusion

Is there still space available in a crowded and concentrated media universe for educational broadcasters caught in these contradictions, fighting for survival by commodifying at the risk of losing their ethos and niche, and unaware of the common democratic and advocacy ground they share with alternative media? As Garnham (2003, 194) sees it, democracy is "an unfinished historical development," and public service broadcasting is still "a model to be improved rather than discarded." The very complexity and contradictions that could see them weaken and fall prey to further privatization and commodification may also compel them to find space to not only survive, but to develop and improve. To do so, they must be prepared to engage in democratic media building beyond their already phenomenal ability to construct community, deemed crucial by Couldry and Curran (2003), and thereby foster the centrality of culture in social life that Schiller (1989) theorizes. To be able to do so requires recommitment to public service ideals and values, as alternative media will not support a corporate media culture. At heart, it requires recognition that although their public support and financial stability come from the educated demographic (Fleisher 1995), to whom they target their market strategies, a more powerful invocation of public service and the most growth potential for advancing democratic media and communication lie in stimulating broader participation and enlightenment – and even action.

NOTES

1 As defined by Soron and Laxer (2006, 16), the commons is "those areas of social and natural life that are under communal stewardship, comprising collective resources and rights for all, by virtue of citizenship, irrespective of ability to pay."
2 TFO is hereby acknowledged as the stand-alone French-language companion to TVOntario. Community television and Aboriginal media, considered to be part of not-for-profit media, are examined in Chapters 6 and 9 of this volume.
3 The Canadian Health and Social Transfer, which transferred funding to the provinces with stipulations as to its use for health and education, was reconfigured in 1996, after which the provinces were allowed to use the transfer money as they chose.
4 The 1997 funding amount was used for Télé-Québec, as it was the earliest available.
5 The same company that purchased ACCESS also owned Canadian Learning Television (CLT), billed as "Canada's only national educational television broadcaster specialty service" (Canadian Learning Television 2008). CLT was not an agency of a provincial government. In 2008, it was sold by new owner CTVglobemedia to Corus Entertainment and renamed VIVA for a different audience.

Autonomous Media
Re-conceptualizing Alternative Media Practices

SCOTT UZELMAN

In writing on the subject of alternative or community media, the complaint is often expressed that they remain under-examined in the social sciences and humanities. Yet considerable activist and scholarly work, including the present volume, is currently being carried out that describes and theorizes such media. Much of this work has revealed important case studies detailing the efforts of individuals and grassroots organizations to create and sustain, for example, small circulation newspapers, community broadcast outlets, or websites. But efforts to theorize these have been equally important.

Alternative media theory has tended to focus attention on the characteristics of media organizations. Specifically, concepts such as "alternative media" and "community media" help to differentiate these forms from mainstream media institutions via the objectives they seek, the content they produce, the subjects involved, and the production and regulatory practices in which they engage. But because these concepts tend to focus attention on organizational characteristics, they often obscure important similarities and differences both between varied media projects and with practices seen in wider social life and political movements.

This chapter begins by providing a very brief survey of some of the major concepts developed to understand alternative media and then discusses some of their limitations.[1] Of particular interest are the effects of well-established

terms on concentrating attention on organizational characteristics of alternative media outlets. To resolve some of these problems, the concept "autonomous media" is offered to draw attention to communication practices that not
only attempt to remain independent in the traditional sense – independent
from dominant institutions – but also strive to ward off more subtle relations
of oppression. The concept is more precise and narrower than others in the
field of alternative media because it focuses on practices articulated to radical
democratic politics.[2] However, at the same time, because it emphasizes strategies and practices of communication in struggle, the concept allows for wider
vision extending beyond formal organizations. "Autonomous media," then, is
an analytic tool, but like most concepts it also advances prescriptive elements,
in this case, for radical democratic politics.

Conceptualizing the Alternatives

Several concepts have become widely used and cited by academics and activists in making sense of grassroots media organizations and practices. Concepts such as alternative media, radical media, community media, and citizens'
media are used to distinguish grassroots media groups from mainstream
media – that is, from corporate, state-controlled, and public service media. A
number of characteristics are commonly chosen to make these differences evident: objectives and content, subjects involved as producers and managers,
production and regulatory practices, and, to a lesser extent, organizational
size and scope (the audiences/participants reached). Although other concepts
could also be explored, the four noted above will be briefly outlined because
they are most widely cited in academic literature.

Of these four concepts, alternative media is the best established and most
widely used. Although it is often applied to a wide range of organizations and
practices, many authors use the term to refer specifically to overtly politicized
media projects and set them in opposition to dominant media institutions,
often situating them as part of a wider movement to democratize media and
society (Atton 2002; Couldry and Curran 2003; Downing et al. 2001). To these
ends, such media organizations seek to produce and disseminate content
(such as perspectives, issues, and formats) that is routinely marginalized or excluded from their mainstream counterparts. Moreover, alternative media are
often defined as specifically oriented to democratic, progressive, or left-wing
politics (see Albert 1997; Kidd 1999). Some authors leave the question of political orientation more open by suggesting that these media are distinguished

by efforts to enact social change (see Atton 2002). Most, however, do not restrict the definition to content; instead, organizational form figures prominently. In particular, these projects are differentiated from the mainstream by their participatory nature – that is, their openness to non-professionals in content production as well as management and development of the organization (Hamilton 2000). Additionally, this participatory dimension extends to the nature of flows of communication (horizontal as opposed to primarily vertical; dialogic as opposed to point to mass). Further, being alternative to mainstream media is suggestive of relative independence from the principles that guide dominant media forms; broadly speaking, these entail accumulation of profit via commercial corporately owned media, control via state-run media, and even the priorities of public service media, which often do not meet the needs of specific communities.

Numerous authors have attempted to lighten the burden that alternative media carries by developing parallel concepts that make distinctions often obscured by the more encompassing term or to make even more inclusive concepts. For instance, Downing and his collaborators (2001, xi) employ the term "radical media" to specifically distinguish overtly political forms of small-scale media from the mainstream. These media have as their goals expression of dissent "vertically" – that is, toward dominant "power structures," as well as "laterally" in order to build solidarity and support for movements of opposition. In addition, Downing et al. stress that these media often challenge dominant media practices and forms. For authors such as Rennie (2006), Howley (2005a), and Jankowski (2003), community media are distinguished from the mainstream primarily by their orientation and accessibility to local communities. However, where corporate media seek to maximize profit, and public service media tend to be oriented to generally broad public concerns, the concept of community media refers to those small outlets that look to serve local community interests that are not met by larger-scale media. Rennie (2006, 9) suggests that community media are not necessarily oppositional or even progressive. Instead, they have as their primary objective the provision of access to a diverse range of perspectives and voices not regularly seen in mainstream content. The last concept considered here is C. Rodriguez's (2001) citizens' media. Like that of community media, the concept refers to "ordinary people" gaining control over media to engage in self-representation. However, Rodriguez's concept draws more attention to the micro-political effects of such practices. That is, she contends that the impact of citizens' media should be evaluated not so much in terms of their ability to foster the development of mass unified movements of resistance to macro-structures of power (including mainstream media), but rather in their ability to transform and empower communities and individuals – their identities and understandings of themselves, and their relations to others.

Limitations of the Concepts

There are, of course, other perspectives on these concepts – and indeed, other concepts altogether – that capture similar practices and organizational forms (such as democratic media or activist media). Despite the differences between them, they share a common orientation to organizations and the communication practices they employ. To be sure, some authors do include other tactics and forms of expression such as street theatre, murals, dance, and song within the range of communication practices encompassed by their term (see Downing et al. 2001, 8). But, for the most part, the concepts addressed above tend to focus our attention on collective and enduring media outlets. In this, they offer important lenses through which to see and understand communication practices of social movements and local communities, as well as individual voices often excluded from mainstream media. However, by concentrating our attention on organizations, they also carry with them four important limitations, particularly for understanding possibilities for democratic social change in and through communication practices.

First, these concepts tend to obscure resonances between practices constitutive of alternative media projects and those increasingly part of the highly mediated lives of affluent societies. As communication technologies become more integrated into everyday life, especially for those of us living in the over-developed countries of the global North, it becomes necessary to think about communication practices in a more diffuse and decentred way. In particular, those practices once associated primarily with alternative or community media – such as dissemination of marginalized representations, participatory content production by non-professionals, horizontal and dialogic flows of communication – have become considerably generalized by growing accessibility of digital communication technologies. Indeed, these developments have been widely and perhaps overly celebrated as presenting new possibilities for democratic communication and social change. Regardless of the hyperbole that often surrounds these technologies, it is necessary to better account for this diffusion of mediated communication and the manner in which similar communicational practices and strategies of resistance are exhibited both within formal organizations and in everyday practices constitutive of what some refer to as Web 2.0 (O'Reilly 2005). This includes, for example, e-mail, text messaging, blogging, social networking such as Facebook, Twitter, MySpace, YouTube, and so on. At the same time, caution should be exercised in assigning democratic valences to these practices. As Huesca and Dervin (1994, 59) advise, the widespread assumption that "egalitarian communication processes ... lead to liberating outcomes" needs to be problematized. Consideration should also be given to the ways in which capital has harnessed these energies as new forms of largely unpaid "immaterial labour" (Terranova 2004; Coté and Pybus 2007).

Second, by focusing our attention on organizational structures and practices, concepts such as alternative, radical, or community media can obscure common logics of struggle that exist within the wider media democracy movement. These wider resonances have been addressed to some extent by concepts such as "democratic media activism" (Carroll and Hackett 2006) and "democratic communication" (Hamilton 2008), which highlight similarities between the practices informing alternative media projects and broader struggles to democratize mainstream media. Stated differently, alternative media projects are linked to broader efforts to democratize media by two common logics of struggle. The first is the motivation to distribute marginalized or excluded content – a strategy of alternatives. Emphasis here is placed on using media primarily as means for distributing marginalized or critical discourses, representations, and styles. Thus, strategies are directed at both opening up mainstream media to a wider range of content or bypassing them altogether (as alternative media do). Efforts to diversify mainstream media content include, for example, media manipulation strategies (such as press conferences and demonstrations), media monitoring, media education campaigns, and promotion of reforms to government media regulations. A second logic linking alternative media projects with broader media democratization efforts is less instrumental in its view of media, seeing them instead as institutions and practices that themselves need to be democratized. In these instances, strategies are directed toward transforming the relations and practices constitutive of dominant media forms. Moreover, the manner in which people relate to and practise media is very much bound up with their practices of self (subjectivity). Thus, as C. Rodriguez (2001) and others have emphasized, transformation of media, from this perspective, is also a matter of transformation of subjectivity – our beliefs, attitudes, habits, dispositions, and affects. We might refer to this logic of struggle as a "strategy of autonomy," to draw attention to the wider transformations aimed at through such practices, a point developed below. Of course, the concepts "strategy of alternatives" and "strategy of autonomy" are analytic in nature. They do not reveal pure tendencies or exclusive binaries but instead are useful in drawing attention to the assumptions informing communication practices or the way particular strategies and tactics are emphasized.

A third limitation of these concepts is the tendency to collect politically divergent projects within a single category. For the most part, the concept alternative media has been articulated to outlets espousing progressive or left-wing politics, ranging, for instance, from more liberal-democratic outlets such as rabble.ca to radical projects such as *Upping the Anti* (a biannual journal). Because it has also been applied to groups that differ widely in their organizational structure, objectives, and modes of governance and production, the concept often conflates bodies that emphasize a strategy of alternatives (such as The Real News Network) with others that stress a strategy of autonomy (such as Indymedia). But the tendency to blur serious political differences is particularly pronounced with the rather wide-angle term "community media," which, because it refers to locally oriented, locally produced media, captures an eclectic menagerie of organizations and practices on the basis of their differences from established norms. Examples of this are media created by radical democrats, religious fundamentalists, and far-right extremists, as well as a host of more mundane and ordinary community groups. Although this might make for a useful sociological tool to create distinctions between mainstream and community practices, its utility for political analysis and struggle is dubious.

This critique connects to the fourth and final limitation – namely, the propensity to assume that more equitable access to the means of communication, and therefore more widespread opportunities to engage in self- and collective-representation, necessarily produces democratic outcomes. In an essay written in the early 1990s, Huesca and Dervin suggested that this tendency was widespread in Latin American alternative media literature. Almost twenty years later, it persists in alternative media literature written in the global North and is especially pronounced in work on community media. Authors employing the concept demonstrate that seizing the means of communication need not be a radical act; indeed, media can be put to use for far more mundane and even conservative or repressive purposes (for example, to reinforce and intensify relations of domination such as racism or homophobia). But at the same time, authors such as Rennie (2006), and to a lesser extent Howley (2005a), tend to suggest a fairly stable linkage between locally oriented media outlets produced by and for local communities, and democratic outcomes. The assumption here is that pluralism and freedom of expression are fundamental to democracy. What is problematic, however, is the idea that any increase in the number of voices and range of expression works to strengthen democracy. Because community media contribute substantially to communicative pluralism by offering avenues for community and self-expression, they are seen as inherently democratic media forms. But how democratic outcomes are achieved when white supremacists use locally oriented media to create and grow communities promoting racial hatred is entirely unclear. The same goes for other attempts to sediment relations of domination such as religious fundamentalists using small-scale media to promote patriarchy or homophobia. These are extreme instances to be sure, but they serve to make the point that more attention needs to be paid first to what is meant by "democracy," and second, to the strategies employed in democratization. This in turn means paying careful attention to the manner in which these strategies articulate with specific relations of domination and relations of freedom (such as conditions for self- and collective determination).

Most authors theorizing grassroots media do not restrict democracy to procedures for the ratification of elite representatives (such as electoral or representative democracy) but instead emphasize the term's roots: rule by the people. Democracy refers, then, to more participatory forms of popular governance in wider social life. If participatory processes are truly integral to democratic life, this means accounting for and confronting deeply rooted structural inequality and sweeping relations of domination such as sexism, racism, homophobia, and even capitalism (the subordination of social and ecological life to profit). In short, too often, democratization is said to occur simply via opening media to more voices, as if quantity of communication or proliferation of differences were guarantees of emancipatory power effects.

Autonomous Media

To account for some of these limitations, in particular the two political limitations outlined above, the remainder of this chapter develops a concept that is at once narrower and more focused, yet also perhaps more far-reaching: "autonomous media strategies," or just "autonomous media." Previous activist

and academic work has used this concept to capture attempts to create genu-
inely democratic and participatory forms of media, as well as more dispersed
communication practices within wider movements for radical democracy
(Langlois and Dubois 2005; Uzelman 2005; see also Dyer-Witheford 1999; for a
critique of the concept, see Hadl and Dongwon 2008). The concept resonates
sharply with Williams' notion of "direct autonomous composition." As Hamilton
(2008, 234-37) explains, Williams uses the term to refer to forms of association
that privilege autonomous self-regulation over outside management or control, direct participation over representation, and continuous formulation and
construction over solely presenting interpretation and critique of the existing
order of things. Thus, as in more traditional definitions of alternative media, a
strategy of bypass is a key aspect of autonomous media in which the aim is to
create and preserve media institutions that allow for expression of critical opinions, under-represented issues, and novel formats. But autonomous media
strategies also crucially involve challenging ossified forms and practices of
communication that are implicated in domination.

The concept of autonomous media focuses attention on practices of autonomy within both media organizations and wider communication practices.
With a few exceptions (for two in particular on the Indymedia movement, see
Pickard 2006; Pickerill 2007), autonomy is an under-examined dimension of
alternative media practice. Yet as Fuchs (2009, 98) has noted, "the meaning of
the concept of autonomy is not self-explanatory." He points out that the concept has figured prominently in a wide range of philosophic, economic, and political writings. To be clear, autonomy here indicates the common sense notion of
independence from the influence of hegemonic institutions such as governments, corporations, religious bodies, and unions. That is, as Williams suggests,
autonomous media practices stress self-management and self-creation rather
than control or influence from outside actors or institutions. This is also not
the autonomy of liberal economic theory that treats individual freedom as
paramount and, indeed, views individuals as self-determining monads seeking to maximize pleasure and wealth. Rather, emphasis is placed on autonomy as a collective and social practice that seeks to install and reproduce
relations of power that allow for more widespread forms of self- and collective
determination.

This notion of autonomy also rejects the binary understanding of power
that sees it only as a resource possessed by the powerful or concentrated within powerful institutions, which is then exerted on less powerful entities.

Instead, autonomy here draws upon a relational notion of power that proposes that we think instead of the manifold relations, practices, and techniques that constrain our capacities to act, think, and relate to one another – and even to ourselves – in new ways. But at the same time, as Foucault (1988, 2002) cautions, power should not be thought of only as a repressive and constraining force. Relations of power are also generative; they enable and encourage particular outcomes even as they restrain others. Thus, radical democratic struggles must pay attention to and resist various forms of domination – which is, in effect, the persistence of asymmetrical relations of power – such as racism, sexism, ableism, homophobia, and class. At the same time, these struggles must also work to foster more fluid, equitable, and open relations that allow for more democratic outcomes. Such situations would then make possible, and indeed be constituted by, less oppressive practices, ways of relating to others, and more democratic subjectivities (that is, modes of practising and relating to self). More concretely stated, as more democratic relations of power come to life, individuals and groups are better able to engage in practices of self- and collective determination (such as enacting new relations that are less constraining and oppressive in the limits they present).

The concept autonomous media highlights the ways that radically democratic movements have reoriented and expanded struggles away from efforts focused solely on opposing, undermining, or seizing particular institutions where power has traditionally been understood to reside. Instead, such movements have also dedicated themselves to opposing particular forms or techniques of power that have come to be seen as oppressive (Foucault 2002). This is not to say that democratizing struggles should not be waged against and within specific institutions, but rather that they need to resist the particular relations of power that generate oppressive institutions, relations that these institutions then amplify.

From this relational perspective on power, many of the characteristics assigned to alternative media can be thought of as practices of liberty. That is, the strategies and tactics that constitute many alternative media projects can be seen as a means of warding off oppressive relations of power and creating and preserving more emancipatory relations. These tactics include democratic management of media outlets, participatory content creation, establishing possibilities for horizontal and dialogic flows of communication, making room for opportunities to challenge established conventions and representations, and building and maintaining working environments that are relatively free of oppressive forms of power. Indeed, these tactics are deployed in the recognition that processes as much as products can work to unsettle relations of domination.[3]

However, in keeping with Foucault's understanding of power, it is important to emphasize that these tactics are never necessarily or completely successful. Not only is it impossible to be rid of power relations once and for all, since they are inherent to human relations, but we must also be aware that oppressive power relations always threaten to emerge; that is to say, there is always a danger that power might cease to flow, transforming enabling limits into limitations that unduly constrain. Foucault thus counsels continuous vigilance and permanent resistance (Simons 1995).

So What's New about Autonomous Media?

"What difference does it make?" should be the first question asked of any concept employed to make sense of the world around us. Specifically, autonomous media emphasizes experimentations with new forms of democratic communication that explicitly encourage participatory and/or dialogic practices of governance and content production. Mainstream media in general, and indeed many alternative media forms, are characterized by hierarchical relationships, professionalized production norms, and unidirectional point-to-mass flows of communication. As a result, representation tends to be privileged over participation and monologue over dialogue, in both governance and content creation. Autonomous media strategies seek to disrupt these relations and the power effects of oppression they tend to produce by experimenting with new relations and modes of organization.

Although it incorporates many characteristics often assigned to other conceptual tools used to understand alternative media, autonomous media break from other formulations in several key ways. First, because they are explicitly articulated with radical democratic politics, they are much narrower in scope than a concept such as community media, which tends to lump diverse organizations into a single category based primarily on their differences from dominant forms. Moreover, although some formulations of alternative media do explicitly link these organizations to radical democratic politics (see Albert 1997), often insufficient attention is paid to the precise manner in which relations of domination are confronted. For instance, media groups such as Democracy Now! provide crucial avenues for the distribution of counter-information;

in this they are clearly alternative to the mainstream. Also, in many respects they are considerably different from dominant institutions in their organizational forms (they are non-profit, non-commercial), a fact that clearly enables them to disseminate under-reported issues and perspectives. However, associations of this type are primarily engaged in a strategy of alternatives, rather than strategies of autonomy. Autonomous media then draw specific attention to attempts to undermine relations of domination through content, but also via challenging hegemonic practices and social relations.

At the same time, the concept does not presuppose that emancipatory power effects follow from specific practices, a tendency sometimes evident in, for example, C. Rodriguez's (2001) formulation of citizens' media and Atton's (2002) presentation of alternative media.[4] Instead, autonomous media try to draw attention to practices based on explicit ethico-political commitments whose outcomes are never determined in advance. As Williams hints in his notion of "direct autonomous composition," because autonomy is never an achieved state, but instead a strategy to ward off multiple relations of domination that always intersect in unpredictable ways, it is necessary to engage in continuous formulation and construction rather than follow blueprints for emancipation.

Even though autonomous media is a narrower concept that focuses on radical democratic politics, it allows for a wider vision in that it is not confined to formal media organizations. The rapid growth of Internet access has fostered an explosion of participatory and dialogic Internet-based projects. This diffusion of communication technologies makes it increasingly important to think in terms of communication practices and strategies, rather than only about the characteristics of organizations. Although digital technologies offer increased opportunities to blur the line between media consumers and producers, participatory and dialogic communication is not, of course, merely the product of the tools we use. Instead, they are products of relations that are established between communities and technology, between each other, and to ourselves. That is, the new wave of "unmediated" media activism is also the product of a new ethic in which direct access to the means of communication by non-experts or ordinary people has become much more widespread and even normalized (Strangelove 2005). Thinking in terms of practices, relations, logics, or strategies allows us to see beyond formal organizations to include more distributed communication practices in the digital era and how more new democratic relations might emerge from them.

For the most part, theorists of alternative media have looked beyond what Gilbert (2008, 206) has called "a politics of disclosure." He uses the term to refer to the assumption that hidden truths of exploitation and oppression need only be revealed to largely ignorant populations for democratic effects to emerge. That is, it is primarily a lack of information that keeps people apathetic and passive in the face of injustice. Although this assumption remains widespread, most concepts used to understand alternative media also include a participatory dimension in their definition. Concepts such as radical media and community media, for example, incorporate political practices beyond merely distributing marginalized content. However, more attention should be given to precisely how such participatory processes might produce democratic political effects.

On the content creation side of things, participatory media practices have the potential to disrupt traditional hierarchies of knowledge (that is, who has the authority to speak), hierarchies of expertise and capacities to make valid meanings (who is authorized to create media content), and hierarchies of form and genre (the ways of speaking and representing traditionally privileged as authoritative). In other words, implicit in these practices is a suspicion of sedimented hierarchies, mediation, and representation by others in processes of governance, production, and in the content itself. Of course, hierarchy, mediation, and representation are not in themselves necessarily modes of domination. But whether in politics or media making, the potentials for effects of domination certainly seem to be enhanced when, for example, decisions regarding policies to be enacted or what constitutes valid media content are centralized or left solely to representatives or "experts."

Perhaps more profoundly, participatory media processes also have the potential to provoke subjective transformations that might not be possible through engagement with alternative content alone. For example, the new relations enabled by these processes can disrupt established habits or rechannel desires that are constitutive of dominant relations of power. More concretely stated, direct participation in media governance and media making has the potential to disrupt the ways ordinary people normally relate to media. Participatory media processes encourage people to see themselves as producers and even as managers rather than solely as observers and consumers of media content (and advertised goods and services). Additionally, these media forms can foster the development of new capacities and knowledges as people learn the skills of collective and democratic management or the techniques necessary to speak for themselves via media content.

Such participatory processes also have the potential to reveal the workings of relations of oppression in very intimate ways. Collective projects that are sensitive and in opposition to multiple forms of oppression can, for example, bring to light the small acts of sexism that pepper daily life as men dominate group discussion or otherwise act to silence or discredit the voices of women. Participatory processes can also be sources of joyfulness as we develop our capacities for creation and self-expression. This in turn can lead to a more profound sense of our ability to exert control over our lives, to engage in acts of self- and collective determination. In short, by fostering a less mediated relationship to media, participatory process can provoke new relations of freedom.

Seeing through the Lens of Autonomous Media

The concept autonomous media can be applied to a wide range of organizations and practices. Groups such as the Toronto Video Activist Collective, which encourages participatory video production for social justice purposes, or the Resist! Collective, a Vancouver-based "autonomous body" working according to anarchist principles to provide "communications and technical services, information and education to the greater activist community" (Resist.ca, n.d.), could be seen as instances of autonomous media. Both not only seek to foster the distribution of marginalized information and representations, but also to transform dominant relationships to media and communication as part of wider struggles to challenge various relations of oppression. Similarly, to the extent that they encourage new, more participatory relationships to media and communication, and promote social justice in the ends they seek, more dispersed and decentralized practices such as culture jamming ("billboard liberation," adbusting, stickering, and postering), street theatre (such as the Surveillance Camera Players [2006]), or other forms of creative expression such as murals or graffiti might also be categorized as autonomous media strategies. Likewise, activist use of social media such as Facebook or YouTube might also be seen as a strategy of autonomy, despite the commercial nature of these tools. Again, the concept's utility is not in revealing singular tendencies or pure expressions of autonomy, but rather in highlighting political assumptions often implicit in various communication practices. In order to better demonstrate the usefulness of this analytic concept, two specific organizations, the Independent Media Centre movement and the *Dominion,* will be briefly examined through the autonomous media lens.

The Independent Media Centre movement (IMC or Indymedia) has been the subject of considerable scholarly attention.[5] The focus here will be on its characteristics as a form of autonomous media. Briefly stated, at its height, the movement was composed of a network of individuals and activist collectives in over thirty countries, which maintained websites in more than a hundred locations that allowed for users to post content (text, photos, audio, and video) directly to an "open-publishing" newswire and also to comment on the postings of others. Thus, the websites were open to multiple voices, genres, and forms of expression. In some instances, these collectives also maintained physical spaces that served as work and meeting sites for the collective and the wider community. These virtual and physical spaces were utilized to pursue Indymedia's primary purpose of facilitating opportunities for activists and ordinary people to create media content directly. As evident in the slogan often taken up by Indymedia activists – "Don't hate the media, become the media" – the movement is informed by a strategy of bypass, where the goal is to create new, more democratic methods of communication instead of focusing on confronting the mainstream media directly or making symbolic demands of the state (Day 2005).[6] This creative dimension of the movement – the attempt to directly establish democratic and participatory forms of media – provoked considerable excitement in activist and academic circles. However, the movement has declined considerably since its peak in the early 2000s.

Indymedia is distinguished from hegemonic media institutions in several key ways. First, like many other forms of alternative media, the various website nodes in the network serve as conduits through which marginalized content (primarily critical or left-wing perspectives) can flow. In this, the movement is informed by a strategy of alternatives. But it also exhibits characteristics of a strategy of autonomy. It is highly participatory in the manner in which content is produced, in the management of the individual collectives, and to a great extent at its peak, in the network itself. Collectives worked via a process of democratic consensus-based decision making, and most were explicitly committed to anti-oppression and social justice principles. These principles were operative, or at least stated, in decision-making processes at the network level, within individual IMC collectives, and in many instances in the editorial policies of individual newswires. Structurally, the movement is non-profit and non-commercial, and driven primarily by non-professional volunteers, thus allowing it a degree of relative autonomy from the forces and compulsions of capitalist markets. Paradoxically, however, this same commitment to autonomy was also one of the principal factors in the movement's decline.

Given that the Independent Media Centre movement relied almost exclusively on volunteer labour and donated resources, the continued existence of many nodes in the network ten years after the first IMC appeared in Seattle is remarkable. However, the waning of Indymedia also speaks to the difficulty of sustaining strategies of autonomy, not just with regards to the enclosing forces of capitalism, which places strict limits on human endeavours not oriented toward the creation of profit, but also with respect to the stubborn persistence of other relations of domination. Lack of space prevents a thorough analysis of the factors that contributed to the movement's decline, but a few salient points can be addressed here.

The retreat of the global justice movement in the post-9/11 era is an obvious factor in the diminishment of the IMC. Not only did Indymedia spread with the wider movement against corporate globalization, it also drew much of its energies from the concerns surrounding the growth of unaccountable private power, the undemocratic implementation of free trade agreements, the increasing unresponsiveness of elected governments to public interests, and even the corrosive effects of intensified capitalist relations. In a sense, as the wider movement went, so went Indymedia. Other factors, however, both internal and external to Indymedia, especially those related to relations of domination, were also responsible for its decline. For instance, complaints were frequently voiced regarding the failure or inability of collectives to adequately regulate and edit their open publishing newswires (Chuck0 2002). The open-publishing feature was seized upon by "trolls" (individuals attempting to disrupt websites or listservs via offensive or inflammatory postings) and right-wing ideologues, with the result often being a stream of racist, sexist, homophobic, and generally reactionary postings. In some cases, this laissez-faire approach derived from an uncritical commitment to "free speech," whereas in others it sprang from an inability of volunteer editorial collectives to keep up with non-stop assaults on the newswire. The results, hardly in keeping with Indymedia's general commitment to social justice, discouraged many users and participants from continued involvement with the movement (Whitney 2005). The inability to adequately confront relations of domination was also evident within many Indymedia collectives (Langlois 2005). For organizations bound together by relationships of affinity and mutual trust, the persistence of sexism, racism, classism, and other forms of domination is particularly disruptive (Uzelman 2002; Jones and Martin 2010).

In a more mundane way, Indymedia may have diminished simply because in some senses it has become redundant in an age where the dialogic, participatory, and do-it-yourself logics that made the websites unique have now become generalized. In a relatively short period of time, the practices constitutive of IMC and other activist websites integral to the global justice movement have become generalized throughout a wide variety of Internet forms, such as social networking sites, blogs, wikis, and even corporate news outlets. Despite their contradictory status as profit-making entities, there is plenty of evidence to suggest that websites such as YouTube and Facebook are being used for activist purposes. Although their distributed nature makes them difficult to research, more work needs to be done in this area.

With all the factors noted above kept in mind, strategies of autonomous media such as Indymedia face perhaps an even more daunting challenge: the forces of enclosure generated by capitalism. The network-wide commitment to remaining autonomous from the commercial logics fuelling most mainstream media outlets, as well as from corporate, state, and even non-profit foundation funding (Pickard 2006), means that the movement is driven almost exclusively by volunteer labour power. The price of autonomy has often been physical, mental, and emotional burnout of activists who committed themselves to the movement as well as engaging in paid work, schooling, domestic duties, familial relations, and so on. In much of the work on alternative media, capitalist relations tend to recede into the background as the natural foundation upon which human endeavours are conducted in the modern era. However, in a time of mounting crises, we must not lose sight of the fact that capitalism is a colonizing ensemble of social relations that works to continually subordinate greater aspects of social and environmental life to itself. As it expands, it acts as a disciplining force that restricts alternative possibilities and futures, and encourages the emergence of certain outcomes that increasingly threaten social and ecological existence. Moreover, because capitalism is so powerfully colonizing, it is difficult to speak of "outsides" – relations existing beyond its compulsions. And yet, clearly alternative possibilities and futures are crucially necessary, despite the formidable barriers presented by the structure of capitalist culture.

To overcome the problem of sustainability of autonomous media strategies in market society, media activists have experimented with creative organizational solutions while at the same time fostering new relationships to media. The Dominion Newspaper Cooperative (or the Media Co-op, as it is also known) offers an interesting example of autonomous media attempting to establish a viable long-term organization producing independent news and to offer new, more participatory ways of relating to media.

The Media Co-op developed out of the *Dominion,* a monthly newspaper available on-line and in hard copy. Founded in 2003, it operates much like other forms of alternative media – that is, according to a strategy of alternatives. Its mission statement explicitly sets its operations in opposition to mainstream corporate media. Accordingly, it seeks to provide coverage of stories omitted or marginalized by mainstream media.

Although in many respects the project resembles other forms of alternative media, it also exhibits characteristics that resonate with autonomous media strategies. For example, it is explicitly committed to journalism guided by principles of participatory democracy and social justice. It has carried exposés on, for instance, the negative social and environmental impacts of Canadian mining corporations in Latin America, the involvement of the Canadian state in the 2004 Haitian *coup d'état,* and the condition of migrant farm workers in the US and Canada. However, the organization is perhaps more easily understood as a form of autonomous media with respect to its participatory dimensions. Although not based on an open publishing model like Indymedia, the *Dominion* allows for other modes of participation in content creation and governance. With respect to the former, though the paper has a number of regular professional contributors who are often paid for their work, it also solicits contributions from non-professionals not currently affiliated with the project. Like other forms of web-based alternative and corporate media, the newspaper also allows for moderated comments to be posted to articles.

Where the project becomes particularly distinctive as a form of autonomous media is in its cooperative organizational structure. A "solidarity cooperative," the Media Co-op has various types of members with differing interests engaging in a collective project. Membership types include managing editor, writer and editor, and reader. The managing editors are involved in the day-to-day workings of the *Dominion,* contributing at least twenty hours of work to it. Many of them perform double duty as writer and editor members who produce stories for the newspaper or edit its sections. Reader members support the project through their annual dues and to a lesser extent through their participation in co-op governance. In keeping with the federal legislation governing cooperatives in Canada, the Media Co-op also has a board of directors elected at a yearly annual general meeting (Dominion Newspaper Cooperative, n.d.).

Thus, as noted above, in many ways the *Dominion* resembles other point-to-mass forms of media. However, more avenues are available to reader members for direct participation in the newspaper and in the Media Co-op than in traditional alternative and mainstream media organizations. First, the newspaper encourages members to suggest story ideas to editors and writers on issues under-reported in mainstream media. This way, the co-op is attempting "through continuously-expanding grassroots organizing" to involve "communities which are negatively affected by the misinformation and omissions of the corporate media" (Media Co-op, n.d.). Second, members have limited opportunities to participate in the management of the cooperative and the newspaper via voting rights at annual general meetings and member meetings. Third, the co-op website resembles the Indymedia newswire function, allowing registered members to upload content and create blog postings available to other members and users of the website.

In many respects, the *Dominion* is a much more restricted form of autonomous media than Indymedia, especially as regards its participatory dimensions. However, it does offer an interesting example of the ways in which activists are experimenting to create new, more democratic ways of relating to media. Whether the Media Co-op will survive is uncertain at this early stage in its development. However, at the time of writing, Media Co-ops have been established in Halifax, Montréal, Toronto, and Vancouver.

Before closing this short discussion of autonomous media examples, we should emphasize that, though the rapid spread and increased accessibility of new digital media technologies during the past ten to fifteen years have greatly enhanced possibilities for decentralized, autonomous, horizontal, and participatory forms of communication, they are not entirely new. Activists and artists have long experimented with media forms to open them up to a wider range of users and for novel purposes. Chandler and Neumark (2005), for instance, have compiled a very interesting collection of essays that detail a long history of artistic experimentation with established and new media forms such as the postal service, telephone, and photography to encourage dialogic and participatory communication. Similarly, many authors have noted experiments with participatory forms of radio (Kidd 1998; Riismandel 2002) and television (Stein 2001). More recently, participatory and dialogic radio practices played a crucial role in mobilizing and sustaining the 2006 uprising in Oaxaca, Mexico, in which dozens of radio stations were established or taken over by ordinary people (Stephen 2007). Clearly, the concepts of autonomous media or strategies of autonomy do not necessarily draw attention to what is new in strategies of media democratization or even possibilities made available by new communication technologies. Rather, they help us to recognize long-standing tendencies and practices.

Conclusion

The utility of the term "autonomous media" lies not only in the way in which it highlights independence in the traditional sense (from dubious alliances with governments or corporate entities). More importantly, the concept also emphasizes autonomy from hegemonic communication practices, organizational forms, modes of governance, processes of production, relationships to audiences and users, and professional norms. In other words, we can use the term to emphasize the practices that attempt to break with these hegemonic processes on the assumption that they tend to be bound up with a multiplicity of forms of subordination that function to unduly constrain our capacities to act, to realize potentials, to self-determine. That is, the communication practices illuminated by the autonomous media lens seek to challenge specific forms of oppression (including patriarchy, racism, environmental destruction, and economic exploitation) not only via the content they provide, but also through the social relations and subjectivities they foster by experimentations with new and more democratic relations with media and communication.

The conceptual lenses developed in this chapter are not proposed as a means of constructing rigid separations between various types of communication practices; instead, they help us to see relative emphases within and between various communication practices and to draw attention to the assumptions implicit within the strategies about how political change occurs. In this way, the concept autonomous media in particular can draw increased attention to under-examined dimensions of grassroots media practices in struggles for social justice.

NOTES

1 To simplify matters, the terms "alternative media" and "alternative media theory" will be used as shorthand to capture this varied set of practices and the wider range of concepts developed to understand them. "Alternative media" is used to indicate the specific concept.

2 Radical democracy indicates political struggles for democratic social change in the broadest sense. These endeavours emphasize more participatory forms of governance in all realms of social life, as well as efforts to challenge relations of oppression and domination in everyday life, and generalize conditions for self- and collective determination (see Laclau and Mouffe 2001).

3 Moreover, in recognizing the possibilities for new relations to self to emerge ("empowerment" in more everyday language), there is perhaps an implicit perception that

subjectivity is not only constituted by specific relations of power but also that, at the same time, subjectivities are constitutive of these relations (see Read 2003). We breathe life into enduring relations and structures even as they shape who and what we are.

4 More attention also needs to be given to the politically problematic concept "citizen," given its articulation to nation-states. This is especially the case in colonial contexts such as Canada, where many indigenous peoples' struggles explicitly reject citizenship within the settler state in favour of building and strengthening indigenous nationhood.

5 For examples of more comprehensive examinations of the Indymedia movement, readers should consult Downing (2003), Kidd (2003), Coyer (2005), and Skinner et al. (2009).

6 Downing et al. (2001, 71) and Downing (2003) have taken up the anarchist term "prefigurative politics" – "the attempt to practice socialist principles in the present" – to describe this strategy.

"One Part Creativity and Nine Parts Hard Work"
The Legacy of Feminist Periodicals

BARBARA M. FREEMAN

In 1983, Philinda Masters, Toronto-based editor of *Broadside,* devoted a two-page feature to the vicissitudes of publishing a feminist periodical, which she likened to the reproductive life of a hen: "We take the germ of an idea, get it out, fertilize it, incubate it and at the end of the process we start all over again. It is a process of one part creativity and nine parts hard work in a never ending cycle. And, unlike real hens, we feminist egg-layers have to market the fruits of our own labour. After all that gestating, we have to get up off our bed of straw and *sell*" (Masters 1983, 8).

For Masters and other feminist media activists of her era, it was not enough to plan, write, edit, lay out, and print these periodicals. It was also important to develop schemes to ensure their survival, dedicated as they were to readers who shared a desire for full citizenship rights for women (*Kinesis* 1979). As is the case with most alternative media (see Chapter 1 in this volume), the structure of their newspapers both mirrored and subverted the editorial, advertising, subscription, and circulation tactics that were accepted practice in mainstream women's publications with broader distributions. The feminist publishers used a variety of financial strategies to meet the challenge of sustainability, including varying degrees of government funding, and threw themselves wholeheartedly into the intense production tasks that are always involved in establishing and maintaining any form of alternative media (Cohen elaborates on labour in alternative media in Chapter 10).

Between the early 1970s and the turn of the twenty-first century, some of the longest-running feminist periodicals in Canada managed to establish themselves as alternatives to mainstream newspapers and magazines, despite circulations that rarely exceeded two thousand to twenty-five hundred readers (Masters 1983; author interviews with Philinda Masters and Esther Shannon 2008).[1] They included *Kinesis* in Vancouver (1974-2001), *Broadside* in Toronto (1979-1989), and *Pandora* in Halifax (1985-1994). Despite their regional differences, these publications had much in common ideologically and structurally as they all had to juggle feminist politics, editorial subjectivity, financing strategies, and strenuous production demands. They were representative of hundreds of Canadian feminist publications that came and went (Coffey 1991; Wachtel 1982, 1985), but they stood out for being among the ones that endured the longest.[2] Each of the three was available for close to ten uninterrupted years between the 1980s and 1990s, co-existing with the other two for some of this period. *Kinesis, Broadside,* and *Pandora* broadly and respectively represented the urban West, Central, and Eastern parts of the country during a crucial period in the Canadian women's movement. Using feminist critical and cultural media theory, oral history interviews, and archival evidence, this chapter focuses on their structure and survival tactics, arguing that their eventual demise was not solely due to diminishing government grants. The other important factors included major shifts in feminist politics, individual career decisions, staff burnout, and – in the case of *Pandora* – a legal challenge to its woman-only publishing policy.

The key commonality among the three periodicals under discussion was the desire of their staffs to cover news and views of the women's movement because they wanted to foster communication among women who were committed or potential feminists. Although each publication team had its own ways of operating, all three were dedicated to countering the mainstream media's neglect or negative views of women and feminism (S. Fraser 1987; Davis 1986). They dismissed the concept of objective journalism, which demands that a female journalist take a neutral ideological position on the subject of women's rights, juggling conflicting views in a "fair and balanced" way (Freeman 2001). As one of *Kinesis'* earlier editors, Gayla Reid (1981, 21), once put it, "This paper believes in certain things and promotes them with all the objectivity of a mother bear."

Their editorial and advertising policies, design changes, and distribution methods were all aimed at shaping and reflecting the "counter-public sphere" of feminist expression. By terms such as "counter-public" (Marshall 1995), "sub-altern" (Valaskakis 1993), "sphericules" (Karim 2002), and "alternative" (Atton 2002; Squires 2002), scholars mean specific media representing and attracting women and/or racial, cultural, and political minorities, as opposed to citizen engagement with the mainstream or the male bourgeois "public sphere" of communication, as originally envisioned by Habermas as being crucial to participatory democracy. Marshall (1995), borrowing from Habermas (1989) and his feminist critics N. Fraser (1989, 1992) and Felski (1989a, 1989b), underlined the importance of the contributions that feminist publications made to a "feminist counter-public sphere" that challenged mainstream media's narrow view of both women's roles and their aspirations. These women-run publications not only promoted feminist "ownership, inclusion and accountability" in communication (Riaño 1994, 7), they allowed writers and readers of different feminist stripes to challenge one another, thus creating the type of forum in which "diversity is actively promoted, identities are constructed and political claims are formed and pressed" (Marshall 1995, 463).

Taking charge of their own periodicals in these ways gave Canadian feminists outlets through which to demand the political changes they regarded as urgent. Their demands included decriminalization of abortion, protection against discrimination for lesbians, Aboriginal women, and women of colour, laws against unequal treatment of women at work and in the home, limits on pornography, an end to female poverty, and universal access to national child care (Adamson, Briskin, and McPhail 1988). Rather than seek changes for women within the established political system, as did most liberal feminist voices in the mainstream media (Freeman 2006, 2001), most of them saw themselves as radicals. Whether they faulted capitalism, patriarchy, or both for women's oppression, they wanted to bring about fundamental change to gender relations in Canada and internationally (Descarriers-Belanger and Roy 1991; Adamson, Briskin, and McPhail 1988).

All three newspapers were organized as editorial collectives, in which members aimed to share their political viewpoints and individual abilities in an equitable manner with each other and with their readers, a model of communal responsibility already common among a number of left-wing feminist organizations (Adamson, Briskin, and McPhail 1988). They brought their differing skills in journalism, photography, print production, academic research, community service, and political activism to the task at hand (*Pandora* 1985a). Although one woman might have taken on the busy role of coordinating editor, giving her "power commensurate with responsibility," as Nancy Pollak of *Kinesis* put it (author interview 2008), the ideal was for all members to operate as equal partners and decide by consensus on the content, production, advertising policy, and distribution of the papers. There were variations in this pattern depending on the periodical, but each editor relied on the advice and skills of the rest of the collective and the labour of dozens of volunteers. As another marker of their difference from mainstream media, the editorial collectives tried to make their newspapers as accessible as possible to women of varying incomes by promoting donations from better-off subscribers to cover cheaper subscription prices or, in the case of *Pandora,* issuing it free of charge and billing subscribers only for mailing costs (author interviews with Emma Kivisild 2009; Shannon, Pollak, Fatima Jaffer, Masters, Bethan Lloyd, and Debbie Mathers 2008). This structure instilled a sense of community and responsibility among those who were most involved as writers, editors, and production workers. They offered training for women who were interested in publishing, journalism, and advertising, gathered at national feminist publishing conferences in 1985 and 1986, exchanged articles, and advertised in each other's newspapers (Kivisild 1985a, 1985b; MacDonald 1986; Sand 1985), all of which provided both mutual support and social networking. As Pollak explained (author interview 2008), not only was it exciting to work closely with other feminists in this way, it was rewarding to hold the results of their labour in their hands: "So much political work is intangible ... very process-oriented, but publishing is gratifying because you get something visible at the end to show for your efforts."

In principle, Canadian feminists generally believed that women should be paid for their work, but most of their publications could not afford to do so and relied greatly on volunteers (Masters 1983). Godard (2002, 209), borrowing from Bourdieu (1993), has described their efforts as a "gift" or "labour of love." This is true of *Pandora* but not entirely of *Kinesis* and *Broadside,* whose editors received regular salaries throughout their tenures. Even so, most of the women involved in all three periodicals sacrificed personal monetary gain to the feminist publishing cause by working for modest wages or none at all. Because the other collective members and volunteers often had to support themselves with regular paid jobs elsewhere, they usually showed up at the newspaper offices only for editorial meetings or production and distribution days, all of which typically involved bursts of intense activity (author interviews with Masters, Shannon, Pollak, and Lloyd 2008).

The History and Structure of Feminist Periodicals

Kinesis (1974-2001), Vancouver

Kinesis, published ten times a year, was the oldest and certainly one of the longest running of the feminist periodicals in Canada. Its motto was *"Kinesis –* News about women that is not in the dailies." Vancouver Status of Women (VSW), a broad-based feminist advisory group that relied on federal and provincial government grants to survive, began publishing *Kinesis* as a newspaper in 1974, with the editor also acting as a vice-president of the organization (Lazenby 1975-1976; Reid 1976-1977). These grants permitted VSW to pay its staff, including the *Kinesis* editor, the same full-time wages, which in the early to late 1980s ranged from a very modest $18,000 a year (author interview with Kivisild 2008) to a more generous $31,000 after the employees made their case to the VSW board for more money (author interview with Shannon 2008). Short-term government work grants provided hourly part-time wages to advertising and production coordinators and trainers (author interviews with Kivisild, Shannon, and Pollak 2008). Both VSW and *Kinesis* tackled the same women's issues, but the paper's masthead consistently declared that the opinions expressed in its pages, "unless specifically stated" (*Kinesis* 1975, 19), did not reflect VSW policy (author interviews with Kivisild, Shannon, and Pollak 2008).

Kinesis was edited by a succession of women, each with her own set of skills and unique feminist perspective. They included Emma Kivisild (1984-1986), who was interested in the punk arts scene as well as peace issues; Esther Shannon (1986-1988), a working-class single mother who liked to cover government and union politics; Nancy Pollak (1988-1992), who was instrumental in introducing an affirmative action policy at the newspaper; and Fatima Jaffer (1992-1994), the first woman of colour to take over the helm (author interviews with Kivisild, Shannon, Pollak, and Jaffer 2008). *Kinesis* was the only one of the three periodicals discussed in this chapter to conduct readership surveys for marketing purposes. These response rates shifted with the political times, reflecting a myriad of concerns such as lesbian rights, the decriminalization of abortion, and the perspectives of women of colour (Canadian Women's Movement Archives 1984; *Kinesis* 1984c, 1988, 1994b).

Although it had its own editorial perspective, *Kinesis* used accepted journalistic practice when it came to interviewing politicians or other spokespeople, even those who opposed feminism (author interview with Shannon 2008). Its regular news and editorial features developed as time went on. The paper ran a regular column called "Movement Matters" (*Kinesis* 1987), which consisted of news briefs about the feminist movement locally, in Canada, and around the world. "Inside *Kinesis*" (Shanahan 1989b) discussed funding issues, editorial decisions, and the turnover in the collective's membership. Because some of the community announcements were outdated by the time the newspaper appeared, it introduced "As *Kinesis* Goes to Press" (*Kinesis* 1992a), a compendium of last-minute items (author interview with Pollak 2008).

Broadside: A Feminist Newspaper (1979-1989), Toronto

Broadside was established by a Toronto feminist grassroots collective, but unlike *Kinesis,* it was not tied to a pre-existing feminist organization. In order to finance the paper, the editorial collective formed a non-profit publishing company with the members' own start-up money. Philinda Masters, who was the coordinating editor for most of *Broadside*'s existence, explained that the decision to structure the paper in such a way was essentially a defensive move. The left-wing political scene in Toronto was so divided that the collective feared radicals on the far left would try to infiltrate or otherwise influence the paper. The *Broadside* women wanted to maintain control, even if doing so meant following certain capitalist practices, such as filing corporate tax returns and selling investment shares in the company: "Essentially, because we were not really corporate-minded, we tended to run it as a collective anyway. So the corporate structure was basically there, but not very useful to us after all" (author interview with Masters 2008). They spent at least a year carefully planning the publication and establishing their editorial philosophy for a paper initially targeted at feminists and non-feminists alike (*Broadside* Papers, box 6, file marked "Minutes and related material, 1976-1979," various documents). The newspaper's title raised some eyebrows because of the apparent pun on the disparaging term "broad" for women (author interview with Masters 2008). The intent, however, was to aim critical feminist broadsides at the patriarchal establishment. The first editorial described the goal of creating a dialogue among all women, not just politically active feminists, and providing a voice for progressive perspectives that were not often found in the mainstream news media, as "the battered term feminist must be rescued from media-conceived notions and given a new lease on life." The collective expected the publication to be provocative in its responses to world events that affected women: "Often what we see and hear may provoke anger, anger which we want to express freely, creatively and with wit. *Broadside* will be a tough, vivid exuberant paper which, however it strikes you, will never be dull" (*Broadside*

1979, 1). The newspaper used similar words and expressions in its own subscription ads, intended to appeal to readers: "Feminist!" "Canadian!" "Independent!" and "Provocative!" It also promised that it would cover everything "from erotica to microchips ... Parliament to pornography" and "uncover women's culture and the women's movement" (*Broadside* Papers, box 6, file marked "Editorials, drafts, notes, clippings, publicity and other material, 1979-1989," subscription ad). The "Movement Comment" column (Gottlieb 1980) regularly provided news about feminist events and organizations, and the newspaper as a whole tackled a number of contentious issues in depth, such as the pros and cons of pornography (Cole 1985; author interview with Masters 2008). Broadside Publishing issued *Broadside* ten times a year and operated on an annual budget of about $30,000, Masters recalled (author interview 2008). It was sustained through a combination of grants from government agencies and arts councils (*Broadside* 1986, 2), as well as its "bedrock" subscriptions, some advertising, and occasional fundraisers. That was enough for Broadside Publishing to pay Masters a part-time salary of up to $14,000 – although she was working there full time – as well as part-time wages to two or three other women who helped out with production. All other labour was volunteer, but Broadside Publishing had to pay the costs of printing off-site as well.

Broadside kept in touch with its supporters through editorials, occasional public meetings, and letters to the editor, and some of its readers' suggestions did make their way into its pages (*Broadside* Papers, box 6, file marked "Editorials, drafts, notes, clippings, publicity and other material, 1979-1989," meeting flyers 1979, 1981, 1987; *Broadside* 1980, 2; 1982a, 2; author interview with Masters 2008).

Pandora (1985-1994), Halifax

Pandora was started by a small group of Halifax women who, like the *Broadside* collective, set up a non-profit publishing association (*Pandora* 1985b) to fund their paper as a vehicle to encourage and teach all interested women to write about their concerns, using personal pronouns that spoke to their own experiences (Lloyd 1985a, 1987). The collective chose the title to reclaim the patriarchal myth of Pandora, the foolish woman who unleashed evil on the world, as the "first woman who was sent down to earth with all-gifts ... She gave the good, knowing that the bad was also, therefore, possible" (Lloyd 1985a, 4). Co-founder Bethan (then known as Betty-Ann) Lloyd explained to a *Broadside* writer that *Pandora* put its emphasis on group process and outreach: "I'm not so much a journalist as I am a radical feminist. *Pandora* is providing a safe place for women who are so often silenced to find a hearing ear" (quoted in MacDonald 1986, 7). Even so, the collective deliberately referred to it as a "women's paper," rather than a "feminist" one because it wanted to involve all interested women. As feminists themselves, the *Pandora* collective members were among a political minority in the city. Maritime cultural values and influences were usually centred more on family and friends than on potentially divisive politics, Lloyd recalled (author interview 2008).

Initially, the collective had no set editorial policy, but Sharon Fraser, a local journalist, quickly persuaded it to adopt one. There was no point in publishing articles about spousal abuse, she stated, without providing a feminist analysis of the problem as well as information on where to go for help (S. Fraser 1985, 8). Consequently, *Pandora*'s collective members asked various women with medical, legal, or other expertise to write for the paper regularly and wrote articles themselves if they ran short of willing and knowledgeable contributors (author interview with Lloyd 2008). The collective kept in touch with readers through occasional editorials and public meetings (*Pandora* Coordinating Committee 1987; Lloyd 1985b).

Because it wanted to remain independent of political pressure, *Pandora* did not normally seek out government grants. It neither paid its staff nor charged for subscriptions, except to cover mailing costs, operating on a shoestring budget and publishing a maximum of four times a year. Most of its revenue came from advertisers, fundraisers, and some donations. At first, it was edited in Lloyd's living room and laid out using the equipment in the School of Journalism at the University of King's College, Dalhousie University, where she taught newspaper design. Though a busy co-parenting mother with a young son to support, she initially devoted much time and energy to *Pandora*, with the help of Brenda Bryan, Debbie Mathers, who later took over her job at King's, and other members of the collective. But after a couple of years, Lloyd left *Pandora* to attend graduate school in Toronto (author interview with Lloyd 2008). Getting the paper out was left to Mathers, her co-coordinators' committee, and the volunteers (Lloyd 1986). Two years later, Lloyd rejoined them and volunteered with distribution (author interviews with Lloyd and Mathers 2008).

Among Halifax feminists, the division between straight and openly lesbian feminists was a major local issue in the mid-1980s, as was abortion (author interview with Lloyd 2008; *Pandora* 1986a, 1986b), but *Pandora* remained resolutely supportive of lesbianism (Mathers and Ardyche 1987) and reproductive choice (*Pandora* 1990). Its editorial policy affected its distribution to some degree. The newspaper was sent to its subscribers in an unmarked brown paper bag to protect their privacy, Lloyd recalled, and it was received but not openly displayed at a Halifax battered women's shelter (author interview with Lloyd 2008). Persuading women who lacked writing experience to participate in the somewhat controversial *Pandora* was always a challenge. By the fall of 1987, the number of volunteers was dropping off, and the collective members wondered whether they were "speaking into a vacuum." To cut costs, they reduced the size of the paper from twenty-eight pages to twenty-four, a change that was evident in the one issue marked September-December 1987 (Ardyche 1987, 4). They were tired but they just did not want to give it up. As Mathers (author interview 2008) explained, "The importance of what we were doing was a big part of it ... You get involved and there's no one else to take over, so you keep doing it, you know."

Getting the Feminist News Out

Once they were established, *Kinesis, Broadside,* and *Pandora* quickly earned their feminist credentials in their own women's communities, cities, and beyond. Generally, it seems, readers expected the editor and the other collective members to decide on what to publish. In practice, however, such decisions depended on contributions of various kinds. Stories and opinion pieces were written only if and when there were enough volunteers to do the work and if the various women's groups gave advance notice about events to be covered. Consequently, the collectives had to be flexible in decision making and agenda setting, while still trying to adhere to their editorial policies (Zaremba 1986). As well as sounding boards, they were sometimes targets of criticism, but it is difficult to document their ability to appeal to readers and respond to various demands, except when the complaint itself was covered in the newspaper (Reid 1981; *Broadside* 1982b; Mathers and Ardyche 1987). People might write letters to the editor (author interview with Masters 2008), but they also might telephone her, drop into the office, or engage her or a collective member in a conversation during a chance meeting (author interviews with Pollak and Jaffer 2008). The editorial collectives quickly discovered that good writing, editing, and an attractive layout and design were key to wooing and keeping subscribers (Masters 1983, 8-9). They sought out well-written news and analyses of women's issues that reflected different feminist points of view, as well as book, music, and film reviews. They also published a calendar of regular women's group activities and advertised special events in their respective communities (*Broadside* 1985, 15; *Pandora* 1990, 12; *Kinesis* 1990b).

To keep their publications attractive to look at and handle, and easier to produce, the collectives undertook various design changes. Faith Jones, a writer and designer, described *Broadside* as among the better alternative publications in that it made good use of white space and photographs, although the reproduction quality was muddy: "Ink on newsprint invariably spreads, making *Broadside*'s crisp design difficult to pull off completely" (F. Jones 1987, 20). Later on, *Kinesis* and *Pandora* switched to degrees of desktop publishing, whereas *Broadside* did not last long enough to make the transition beyond using computer disks for typesetting (author interview with Masters 2008). As the technology improved, newspaper editing and production became faster and less communal than the earlier more intensive production routine of typing, editing, laying out, waxing, and pasting-up the contents manually before taking them to the printers (*Pandora* 1994c; author interviews with Masters and Mathers 2008). The editors were aware that the technological switch would not only change their structure but also their sense of solidarity on production days (author interviews with Pollak, Lloyd, and Mathers 2008). The feared loss of collective feeling was one reason *Kinesis* delayed the technical transition for a while, except to manage its subscription base (author interviews with Shannon and Jaffer 2008). Inevitably, there was the occasional costly technical glitch, such as the time the subscribers' names and addresses disappeared from *Pandora*'s hard drive (*Pandora* 1988).

Commercial Strategies

None of the three periodicals were successful in attracting more than modest advertising, despite their attempts to offer appealing rates. In 1983, *Broadside*, for example, was charging thirty-four dollars for a small ad, or twenty-five cents a word (*Broadside* 1983). Mainstream businesses were not interested in feminist periodicals, because of their low circulation and because these publications rejected copy, ads, or letters deemed sexist, racist, or otherwise discriminatory (De Rosa 1988). Courting ads from political parties could be both difficult and contentious as well. In Halifax, after a public meeting with its supporters to discuss the inaugural issue, the *Pandora* collective decided to accept ads up to the value of $100 from all political parties, but only the New Democrats accepted the offer (Lloyd 1985b). *Pandora* refused to accept ads from any politician who was anti-choice on the abortion issue (*Pandora* 1989).

Such policies limited the newspapers' advertising pools to business cards from women working in the professions, the trades, and the arts, as well as to display ads from unions, women's and alternative bookstores, women's centres, gay bars, organic food shops, and similar enterprises – the same venues that carried their publications (*Kinesis* 1994a). Every closing of such a venue created a distribution gap for the feminist publication concerned.

The editorial collectives tried to raise more money and their periodicals' profiles through various community activities – an energy-draining process. Much of *Broadside*'s fundraising in Toronto, for example, came from cultural events such as "a crazy talent night," a strawberry brunch for Friends of *Broadside*, bingo, entertainment nights with writers and musicians, and lectures from prominent American feminists (*Broadside* Papers, box 6, file marked "Editorials, drafts, notes, clippings, publicity and other material, 1979-1989," various flyers).

Despite all their efforts, government cutbacks and rising production costs led to crises over funding of various kinds, which also affected the way in which the periodicals operated. In 1986, for instance, *Kinesis* explained to its readers that it was losing $1,000 per issue and had to take action on a number of fronts. It bought new computer equipment to do in-house typesetting, raised its advertising rates, reduced its special theme supplements from ten to five annually, limited the number of pages per issue to thirty-two, and increased its subscription rate from $15.00 to $17.50 and the newsstand price by 50 cents to $1.75 a copy (*Kinesis* 1986).

Government Grants versus Editorial Freedom

The question of how much to rely on government funding was always difficult, especially as it increasingly came with some political strings attached. The decisions made by the editorial collectives of *Kinesis, Broadside,* and *Pandora* about government grants affected their structure and some of their activities. The federal and provincial governments had initially helped fund a number of services for women, such as Vancouver Status of Women, in order to give them a representative voice in the body politic, or run services such as battered women's shelters. In 1984, the right-wing Social Credit government of British Columbia stripped VSW of its core funding (*Kinesis* 1984a), but the federal Liberals restored it the same year (*Kinesis* 1984b), just before the Conservative Party defeated them in an election. But, by the late 1980s, Conservative members of Parliament, right-wing provincial politicians, and reactionary church

and civic groups, such as REAL Women, were arguing that feminist organizations and publications should not receive public funding at all because they
supported abortion and lesbianism. *Kinesis, Broadside,* and *Pandora* ran some
lesbian subject matter, but this content did not dominate the rest as the
editors wanted to appeal to as many women as possible (Freeman 2011, chapter 6). Nevertheless, any open support of lesbianism or abortion gave conservative politicians and lobbyists an excuse to stop supporting feminist services
and publications (author interviews with Shannon, Pollak, Masters, Lloyd, and
Mathers 2008). From 1988 through to 1993, the federal Conservatives repeatedly cut the budget of the Secretary of State (SecState), the government department responsible for funding women's programs, which in turn decreased
funding to numerous services, including VSW (Godard 2002; Pollak 1989c,
1990, 1993; *Kinesis* 1990a). Because of the right-wing backlash from REAL
Women and others, SecState told VSW and *Kinesis* to be "more market-driven"
(Pollak 1989b, 2) and not to overtly support abortion and lesbianism if they
wanted enough money to fund the editor's position the following year (Pollak
1989b, 1989a; Pollak Private Collection, her memo to the *Kinesis* editorial
board, 28 June 1989). Later, VSW assigned Jaffer to another position within the
agency, but she continued to edit *Kinesis,* she recalled. She also noted that the
budget cuts persisted through the 1990s under the Liberals, who were more
interested in short-term project spending than funding staff positions (author
interview with Jaffer 2008); for example, the regional SecState office did help
fund and distribute a twenty-fifth anniversary issue of *Kinesis* (*Kinesis* 1999-
2000, 9). In the meantime, the federal Conservatives had introduced the GST on
reading material, and the Liberals did away with postal subsidies altogether,
putting additional financial strain on the paper (Valiquette 1989; Vipond 2002,
59; *Kinesis* 1998a).

   In Toronto, *Broadside* had also found it more difficult to attract government
grants. By 1989, the collective was undergoing an internal crisis and was unable to issue the March edition, which would have celebrated International
Women's Day (*Broadside* Papers, box 6, file marked "Editorials, drafts, notes,
clippings, publicity and other material, 1979-1989," 16 March 1989, circular). A
letter to subscribers explained that the collective had suspended publication
but planned a special edition to mark *Broadside's* tenth anniversary later on.
The federal government would not help fund the special edition, because of
the collective's pro-choice and lesbianism stances (Shanahan 1989a). Luckily,
Ontario Women's Directorate, a provincial government agency, did step in
with partial funding (*Broadside* Papers, box 6, file marked "Editorials, drafts,

notes, clippings, publicity and other material, 1979-1989," 18 April 1989, letter to subscribers). Collective members, such as Susan G. Cole, also asked former contributors to donate $100, if possible (ibid., Cole letter, c. spring 1989).

Although *Pandora* did not normally apply for government grants, it raised the alarm about the right-wing lobbyists (Riggs 1987; Smyth 1987; Jefferson 1987) and felt the brunt of Ottawa's policies as well. The future of feminist periodicals would probably have been a topic of conversation at its next publishing conference, scheduled for Halifax in 1987 with *Pandora* as host. But when SecState insisted, as a condition of funding the proceedings, that issues pertaining to lesbianism and abortion remain off the agenda, *Pandora* refused to comply as a matter of ethical principle and the conference was never held (author interview with Lloyd 2008; De Rosa 1988).

Feminist Publishing in Crisis

Kinesis and Cultural Identity

By that time, much of the passion and sense of discovery over women's issues that had first inspired feminist publishing had dissipated. Pollak of *Kinesis* believed many of the concerns that had galvanized the earlier generation of white feminists appeared to have gone mainstream; these feminists were no longer perceived as the rebels they once were (author interview with Pollak 2008). Women of colour were fighting for recognition in the Canadian women's movement as a whole (Marshall 1995), a sea change that fundamentally shifted the content of *Kinesis* and the structure of the editorial collective itself, and to lesser degrees, broadened the outlooks of the other two publications as well. By the early 1990s, over half of the *Kinesis* collective members and a number of the volunteers identified as women of colour. This was a new configuration made possible by the newspaper's affirmative action hiring policy, adopted in 1991, while Pollak, who is white, was editor (author interview with Pollak 2008). It followed a deliberate attempt to get women of colour involved in *Kinesis* through their own caucus (Pollak Private Collection, minutes of the *Kinesis* editorial board meeting with the Women of Colour caucus, 3 January 1989; minutes of general board meetings, 31 July 1990 and 11 September 1991). They eventually became the majority on the collective, with Fatima Jaffer as editor. Jaffer, an East African–born Muslim of South Asian descent, actively solicited articles that reflected diverse racial perspectives on feminism in Canada and around the world (author interview with Jaffer 2008). With the switch to affirmative action hiring, cultural clashes sometimes made

the atmosphere tense at editorial and production meetings, where differences between individuals had to be understood and negotiated, according to
Jaffer. As a woman of colour, and an immigrant to Canada, she thought that
even the most "well-meaning" white feminists did not truly understand how
important it was for articles about women of colour to be written only from
their own perspectives, which she and her editorial collective insisted on.
They adopted journalistic practices that they thought were more inclusive of
minority women unused to being in the media spotlight, such as taping interviews and publishing the names of both the subject and the writer, in an "as
told to" byline. Women of colour were also featured on almost every *Kinesis*
cover because they'd "had white women on the cover 95 percent of the time
for seventeen years," and Jaffer wanted to "change the perception of who else
[were the] movers and shakers in the women's movement." She recalled that
despite what she termed a "huge backlash" to *Kinesis'* new publishing direction and structure, with many white readers and a number of advertisers
dropping the publication, it did gain in its supporters among women of colour and others who appreciated the shift. She believed that the paper still
covered issues of interest to all women. Unlike the other editors, she recalled
feeling some pressure from the politically vulnerable VSW to tone down or
delay coverage of contentious issues, but she believed that doing so would
be wrong. Generally, VSW supported *Kinesis'* new direction, she felt, even if
many white feminists did not (ibid.).

Pollak regretfully witnessed what she termed the "white flight" from the collective, the production volunteer group, and the subscription list by women
who felt left out and did not understand, she said, that the new *Kinesis* could
broaden their political outlooks. At the same time, she had her own reservations about its structure and policies. For one thing, she was afraid that the
pool of women of colour who wanted to work for the paper was too small to
sustain it (author interview with Pollak 2008). Jaffer acknowledges that it was
very difficult, especially in the beginning, to persuade enough women of colour to get involved and to train them (author interview with Jaffer 2008). At
the time, former *Kinesis* editor Esther Shannon warned the feminist community about a lack of vigorous analysis and debate in the paper, especially given
the neo-conservative backlash to feminism (Shannon 1994). By 1996, Agnes
Huang, who had no previous experience in journalism before she started writing for *Kinesis,* was editing the paper with the help of Jaffer, who stayed on to
support her (author interview with Jaffer 2008). In 1998, Huang explained in a
letter to subscribers that VSW was going through "difficult financial times" and

was unable to publish the April issue of *Kinesis* (Canadian Women's Movement Archives 1998). The *Kinesis* collective discussed new strategies for survival (*Kinesis* 1998b) and then, after Huang left, had a series of short-term or guest editors heading up special editions – for example, on Aboriginal women and Jewish women. But even after ten months of planning, the remaining workers could no longer produce regular monthly editions, publishing sporadically instead (*Kinesis* March, May, June 1998; February, October-November 1999; December-January 2000-2001). Part of the problem was the continuous turn-over at the paper. Pollak believed that the quality of its editing had diminished (author interview 2008), whereas Shannon was concerned that not enough attention was being paid to its economic health: "No matter how much fund-ing you get, and we never got very much, if you don't pay strict attention to the financial issues of an alternative publication you are not going to last" (au-thor interview 2008).

Finally, the paper stopped publishing altogether (*Kinesis* 2001). All the mar-keting ingenuity in the world could not compete against unremitting change in editorial direction and structure, and the withdrawal of white feminist read-ers and supporters. These circumstances were exacerbated by cuts to govern-ment funding for women's programs, including VSW; increases in publishing costs; and difficulties in attracting and retaining enough editorial, advertising, and production staff, and engaged readers.

Broadside and the Burnout Factor

During the late 1980s in Toronto, *Broadside* also wrestled with racial politics, but more in relation to its content than to the structure of the collective. Compared with that of *Kinesis,* the leadership of *Broadside* was fairly consistent and stable. It was split roughly between some of the founding members and several newcomers. A crisis of sorts occurred when one contributor was ac-cused by complainants of writing insensitive comments about the struggles of women of colour in the feminist community. *Broadside* initially published the piece because, as a matter of principle, "we almost never censored stuff," Masters explained. The collective listened to the objections and held sensitivity workshops to help white feminists understand the issues better. In Masters' view, this situation turned out to be "a good kind of trouble" since the collect-ive members learned from it (author interview 2008).

In 1988, Masters, then in her thirties, decided to leave *Broadside* for a more stable full-time publishing job (*Broadside* 1988). Most of the remaining collective members, who also had full-time jobs, found the work of getting the newspaper published almost every month very stressful (author interview with Masters 2008; Shanahan 1989a, 7), especially with the threatened loss of any government grant support. Their decision to fold after publishing the tenth anniversary issue in 1989 was part of a larger trend, Masters (1989) noted. The late 1980s saw the death of a number of other feminist publications, including *Herizons* in Winnipeg and even the francophone glossy magazine *La vie en rose* (LVR) in Montréal. Whereas *Herizons* fell victim to right-wing politics in the loss of its government operating grant (Godard 2002; Masters 1989), LVR tended to be more liberal feminist in its outlook, had a dedicated readership of forty thousand, more government support, and a broader advertising and circulation base. Nevertheless, it could not overcome internal political dissension, economic stress, and staff burnout (Lejtenyi, 2005; *La vie en rose* 1986; Guenette 1986; Guenette and Pelletier 1986a, 1986b).

The *Broadside* collective had hoped that a new group of volunteers would step forward to keep the newspaper going, preferably a far more racially diverse group than their own had been. As Masters (1989, 3) acknowledged, the established collective had been almost entirely white and inevitably "lopsided" in its perspective. Now that efforts were being made to incorporate much more diversity into the feminist movement, she wrote, "I think perhaps it's time for us to let go of our hold, and to pass on the responsibility for reflecting and shaping our political struggle to others." To compensate its subscribers, the *Broadside* collective negotiated with the Toronto Black Women's Collective to send them its newspaper, *Our Lives* (1986-1989), instead. Unfortunately, *Our Lives* did not survive very long; nor did a number of other periodicals published by women of colour. According to Godard (2002, 216), they had a much smaller readership and "even less symbolic capital to start with and so faced great economic difficulties."

Pandora and White Male Anger

Pandora fell victim to creeping collective burnout after it was forced to defend its woman-only publishing policy, which was stated on its masthead page, before the Nova Scotia Human Rights Commission in 1991-1992. The newspaper had published an opinion piece about child custody and then refused to run a letter in response from Gene Keyes, a white, well-educated fathers' rights activist (Huang 1991, 1991-1992; *Kinesis* 1991-1992). Its former coordinating editor, Lloyd, who disliked the offending article, still believed that the commission, which paid Keyes' legal costs but not *Pandora's*, was wrong to take up his case. She and other women testified on *Pandora's* behalf, emphasizing the need for woman-only publications, free of male intervention and appropriation of women's energy of any kind (author interview with Lloyd 2008; *Kinesis* 1992b; Cassin 1992).

The newspaper could have tried to defend itself on the grounds of freedom of the press or could have applied, as the commission recommended, for an exemption as an equality-promoting vehicle for women. The collective decided not to do either on political grounds. Instead, during the hearings its witnesses pointed out that it was as reasonable for women to have their own publications as it was for any other group, such as a charity, to focus on its own concerns (author interview with Lloyd 2008). Collective member Amani Wassef explained its reluctance to seek an affirmative action exemption in an interview with *Kinesis,* which was closely watching the case: "It would set a precedent requiring a similar exemption every time a women-only event, publication, meeting ... anything was scheduled" (quoted in Huang 1991, 3). Threatening phone calls to *Pandora* and its supporters from male harassers only added to the tensions involved in the case and made it difficult to find volunteers and fundraising participants (Huang 1991-1992; F. Jones 1994; *Pandora* Collective Member 1992; Nova Scotia Advisory Council on the Status of Women 1992). The newspaper won its case but had to pay its own legal costs. The collective managed to cover half the $38,000 debt through fundraising, and the all-female law firm forgave the rest (*Pandora* 1994b, 2).

For some of the women involved, the case was too draining, Lloyd believed (author interview 2008), but it galvanized others, such as Mathers, into keeping *Pandora* alive. "Stubborn! What can I say? We were stubborn," Mathers recalled (author interview 2008). But when she later left her job at University of King's College, the women no longer had a central location where they could put the paper together, making the desktop production process more difficult. They published only two issues each in 1992 and 1993, and a final, farewell newsletter in March 1994. The problem, the latest collective explained in an insert, was burnout (*Pandora* Collective 1994; *Pandora* 1994a), even though a few new volunteers had stepped forward. The collective wrote: "We finally, and reluctantly, had to accept that the thread of *Pandora* would be broken. It was an ending and needed to be honoured as such." The collective asked subscribers to donate their mailing cost rebates to a seed fund for a potential replacement periodical, to a women's group, or to *Pandora*'s law firm (Pandora Collective 1994). Although the human rights case was not mentioned as an underlying factor, former *Kinesis* editor Esther Shannon pointed out, "It was a very difficult atmosphere to publish in and a very diverse community that they were trying to serve, and the state played a major role in destroying that initiative" (quoted in F. Jones 1994, 3).

If *Pandora* had endured, it might have been able to develop a more racially diverse collective as well. The survivors were aware of the need to involve women of colour and other minorities in its structure, but it was slow going (see *Pandora's* published response to a survey query from Masters in Masters 1991, 28). The collective was able to hire one black woman for a summer job with the only grant it ever received. At that point, most African Canadian women in Nova Scotia either preferred to be identified as black "womanists" rather than "feminists" or were involved in their own long-time community-based groups, according to Lloyd (author interview 2008). It is also possible that local womanists might also have preferred to subscribe to *Our Lives,* which was publicized in *Pandora* (Black Women's Collective 1986). Amani Wassef, the daughter of an Egyptian father and a European mother, became involved in the collective in 1989, but newer members came and went, and it did not become more racially diverse until shortly before the paper folded in 1994 (Wassef pers. comm., 31 January and 4 February 2010). Despite its hopes to include more marginalized women's voices (*Pandora* 1994a; 1994c, 1, 4), the newspaper shut down before it could realize its dream (Pandora Collective 1994).

Conclusion

Kinesis, Broadside, and *Pandora* all strove to reach out to feminists and other women by informing them about their citizenship rights in ways that challenged conventional thinking and the reactionary spin against female equality in the public sphere of government and mainstream media. To do that, they acted in an essentially subversive way by courting government funding and/ or adopting mass media techniques in their counter-public feminist journalism, advertising, subscription appeals, fundraising, targeted distribution methods, and other strategies. The similarities and differences in their structures, which were mainly predicated on local conditions, helped them survive for a time. *Kinesis* and *Broadside,* both produced in large metropolitan areas, were able to publish ten times a year, paying and training skilled feminist editors and other part-time staff. Most of their writers were practised activist journalists and other professionals. *Pandora,* located in a smaller, more conservative city, published less often and on a shoestring budget, and, excepting the one-time summer job funding, without any grants. It relied on equally skilled staff who tried to train newcomers to write for themselves or their organizations. All three publications were blessed with strong editorial leadership in tandem with determined, politically aware feminist collectives. Fundamental to their survival was their ability to maintain these editorial structures, which, despite all their efforts, eventually crumbled under the weight of the difficulties they faced. Those difficulties included the conservative political backlash that feminists of all persuasions experienced, challenging cultural shifts in feminist thinking, and the intensive work required for producing alternative media, all of which affected their periodicals and their markets.

   Although it is beyond the scope of this chapter to recommend media strategies for today's feminists, it is important to remember the legacy of the past and build on those successes, rather than repeat the mistakes. *Herizons,* after all, was reborn in 1991 (Masters 1991; Marshall 1995) and survives by focusing on feminists of all ages and identities. It relies on sustaining subscribers and other loyal readers as well as advertisers (Gordon 2004), rather than government grants. *Shameless,* with its emphasis on teenagers and transgender youth, has been going strong since 2004 (see Chapter 10 in this volume, written by a co-founder of *Shameless*). These periodicals and others exist because all women still need feminist media that are structured not just to survive, but to thrive as "counter-public" (Marshall 1995) manifestations of women's determination to become equal citizens.

NOTES

This research was conducted with the aid of a grant from the Social Sciences and Humanities Research Council, and with the assistance of graduate research assistants Stephanie Dunn, Andrea Hunter, Susan Krashinsky, Ameera Javeria, Claire Brownell, and Chloé Fedio.

1 The interviews for this chapter were conducted and recorded as part of an oral history project on feminists in the alternative media, with a view to having the recordings archived after publication. Oral histories are used not just as primary research in their own right, but to supplement documents and other methods of evidence gathering. Accordingly, the academic term "personal communication" usually employed to describe this research method is inadequate to the point of inaccuracy, given that the same term also covers e-mails and brief telephone conversations.

2 There were over three hundred, including newsletters, from the late 1960s, but the total seemed to level out at between forty and fifty between the late 1980s and the mid-1990s (Godard 2002; Marshall 1995; Masters 1991).

The Real News Network as Hybrid Media
The Future of International Video News?

SONJA MACDONALD

The way that viewers experience video news has changed over the last two decades. Although video news was once the sole purview of television networks, that monopoly is now challenged by twenty-four-hour cable, satellite news services, and on-line options. The increased competition in video news has led networks to make significant changes, not all for the better. These include increased reliance on infotainment, or soft news, over hard news and a reduction in local and international reporting (Bennett 2008; Pew Project for Excellence in Journalism 2009). These developments reflect a more general shift in news production, particularly in commercial venues, where news is seen as one among several types of content for sale to advertisers to attract audiences. Alternatives to commercial news have materialized, although they have not attained the same scope or reach as commercial media. One of the more recent and compelling challenges to commercial media in this regard is The Real News Network (TRNN), an independent, on-line, international video news enterprise launched in 2005. TRNN aims to present news that is not seen on commercial television networks, without accepting advertising or government funding. TRNN's importance in the ongoing transformation of news is evident in the ways in which its production, funding, distribution, marketing, and audience development practices are structured. In these areas, it draws from both dominant and alternative media practices, and provides an interesting example of "hybrid media." In this regard, TRNN presents exciting opportunities for the future of news, but it also demonstrates the complex and often contra-dictory challenges in providing video news outside of the traditional commer-cial model.

Recent scholarly work on alternative and participatory media has begun to develop the concept of hybridity to understand the relationship between al-ternative and dominant forms (C. Rodriguez 2001; Atton 2004; Deuze, Bruns, and Neuberger 2007; Hamilton 2008; Atton and Hamilton 2008). Hamilton (2008, 3) argues, for example, that we need to move beyond positioning main-stream and alternative media as two opposing and fully formed forces work-ing against one another. Instead, he views mainstream and alternative media as "variations within a single, more general, yet highly contradictory social for-mation," mutually constituted and both part of a larger social complex (ibid., 4, 16). Rather than seeing the structure and practices of these organizational forms as distinctly dissimilar, he perceives the differences between them as constructed across a continuum. Atton (2004, 9) argues that this is the case when assessing Internet media projects, where one effect of the Internet has been to erode the agenda-setting and decision-making functions of journal-ism through the increased blurring of the line between producer and audi-ence in Internet media projects. Similarly, Deuze, Bruns, and Neuberger (2007, 323) see the Internet as contributing to the development of a participatory journalism that blurs the lines between professionals and amateurs in news production and, more generally, between its users and producers.

The Real News Network demonstrates at least four dimensions of hybridity. The first is how it straddles and negotiates national regulatory structures and how decisions around its organization both challenge and are constrained by these structures. The second dimension is reflected in how TRNN challenges both dominant and alternative production practices. The third is found in how TRNN is trying to create a funding model that differs from that employed by commercial media. The final dimension is demonstrated in how TRNN distributes content and engages audiences in a manner that merges old and new media forms. Each of these dimensions will be examined separately in this chapter.

The Real News Network

The Real News Network is a not-for-profit international video news service cur-rently available on-line but with plans to expand across many media plat-forms, from conventional and specialty TV to radio, the Internet, and hand-held devices. It was founded by Paul Jay, a Canadian documentary filmmaker and former producer of CBC TV's *Face Off* and *Counterspin* programs. The idea for an independent international video news service was inspired by the limited media coverage of the global protests against the war in Iraq (Peters 2006) and what Jay saw as a lack of verifiable fact-based reporting presented on domin-ant television news networks around these events (Jay, pers. comm., 6 February 2011). The first iteration of what would become The Real News Network was Independent World Television (IWT), which Jay launched on-line in June 2005, with funding from the Canadian Auto Workers, the Ford Foundation, the MacArthur Foundation, and the Phoebe Haas Foundation.

Jay's vision is to provide fact-based professional video news stories about world events with ordinary people's interests in mind. His goal is to break the monopoly in television video news held by dominant commercial media in the US and Canada; thus, TRNN is trying to become a mainstream news source reaching a mass audience of ordinary citizens. TRNN was founded in Canada and, for Jay, brings a much-needed Canadian intervention to US news media. It follows a legitimate and genuine Canadian tradition of questioning official narratives. As the producer of the independently produced flagship debate show *Counterspin* on CBC Newsworld, Jay worked to forward this critique from within Canada, but he concluded it wasn't effective enough as the US remains a centre of power and influence in global issues. TRNN's critical intervention is possible because of its commitment to independence from advertising and corporate and government funding, which Jay argues impose filters on what news and opinions are covered in dominant media (Jay, pers. comm., 6 Febru-ary 2011). His critique is in line with critical media scholarship that has noted a fundamental incongruity of democratic communications, especially news in the public interest within a market-structured media system (McChesney 1999; Herman and Chomsky 2002; Bennett 2008). Thus, one of the key challen-ges for TRNN is sustaining production without these sources of revenue.

As the project developed into The Real News Network in 2007, it raised $5 million from various Canadian and American foundations and individuals (TRNN 2008). This funding allowed TRNN to establish a high-definition studio facility in Toronto and offices in New York and Washington, DC. Additionally, TRNN forged links with independent journalists around the world (Cohen and Glassman 2007, 4). In the spring of 2009, TRNN moved its main news operation from Toronto to Washington, yet the web operations and administration re-main in Toronto, and a Canadian production unit is planned in the future (TRNN 2009, 8).

At this point, it is important to note Paul Jay's opposition to the categorical term "alternative media." He thinks it is too general, involving many diverse projects that are not necessarily committed to non-commercial funding models or professional journalistic practices. This concern about the generality of the term mirrors similar issues raised by critical scholars in the field (Hamilton 2008; Rennie 2006). Eschewing the term "alternative media," Jay classifies TRNN as "independent media," due to its funding model and its journalistic practices. One way that TRNN can be viewed as alternative is in the overarching class perspective that informs its content, which provides an alternative to official elite narratives of current events and issues. The dominant elite media, Jay argues, ignore the fact that differing class interests are at play in any story (Jay, pers. comm., 6 February 2011). Despite his concern about the term "alternative," useful concepts about funding and production can be drawn from the academic literature on alternative media that address the issues of independence central to The Real News Network model (Atton and Hamilton 2008; Atton 2002; Atton and Wickenden 2005).

Hybridity in Regulatory Relations

The Real News Network's first dimension of hybridity lies in its relation to national regulatory regimes. Although, as Joseph Straubhaar (2007, 80, 82) argues, cable and satellite television stations such as CNN, BBC World Service, or Al Jazeera are often framed as global news services, defining them in this way simply because they are global in reach hides the fact that they are part of a "complex system operating in different layers" and that these layers include regulatory structures that, in many instances, are "stubbornly national." For example, in Canada, mainstream television services such as CNN, BBC, or Al Jazeera must make application to the Canadian Radio-television and Telecommunications Commission (CRTC) for a specialty television licence that carries with it varying degrees of regulatory control (Salter and Odartey-Wellington 2008, 48-49). The licensing process can be costly, time consuming, bureaucratically laden, and politically complicated. Success is not a foregone conclusion, as exemplified by the complicated application process experienced by Al Jazeera in Canada. The Arabic station was approved for a licence in 2004, but it has not been able to secure a cable or satellite partnership because of onerous conditions of licence (Bourrie 2004). Following a year-long process, Al Jazeera English received approval in November 2009 (CRTC 2009b).

As an on-line news service, The Real News Network does not face the same constraints as a licensed television news channel. In Canada, the CRTC has stated that it will not regulate broadcasting in new media (CRTC 2009c). This allows TRNN to remain exempt from regulatory requirements such as content rules and licensing, thus, in some respects, transcending Straubhaar's (2007) claim of the stubborn national character of global television.

But, though the CRTC's silence on broadcasting in new media may allow TRNN more operational latitude, corporate regulatory practices such as Internet traffic shaping may pose a far greater challenge to its operations and result in the reterritorializing of The Real News Network. Traffic shaping is the practice in which Internet service providers (ISPs) control the speed and priority at which packets of data travel over their networks (see Chapter 11 in this volume; Barratt and Shade 2007; Faulhaber 2007). The CRTC decided in October 2009 that it would allow some degree of traffic shaping by ISPs (CRTC 2009g), which may affect TRNN's operations in two ways. The first is in the cost of doing business at the production level. Large Canadian ISPs recently instituted usage-based billing forcing customers using large amounts of bandwidth to pay more. TRNN has taken steps to circumvent this, primarily by embedding its videos on YouTube rather than hosting and streaming them directly from The Real News website, and secondly, through the shortness of its video segments, which are, on average, eight to ten minutes long. If TRNN progresses to providing half-hour news programs on-line, it may run into cost restrictions related to traffic shaping.

The second way that traffic management practices could harm TRNN is in its delivery of content to its viewers. If the network providers systematically slow delivery of high bandwidth data, the download time for video from TRNN's website may be significantly increased, making it less appealing for viewers. To date, TRNN has received no complaints from them. Consequently, although TRNN may avoid certain statutory regulatory restraints that face traditional television services, it is subject to different restraints in corporate regulation of the Internet.

Hybridity in News Production

The second dimension of The Real News Network as a hybrid form of media relates to how the news is gathered, presented, reported, and edited. In these areas, the organization both draws on and departs from dominant and alternative practices. Borrowing from dominant media, TRNN replicates the hierarchy and professionalism of traditional journalism, and it obtains a portion of its news stories from news services such as Associated Press Television Network (APTN), Al Jazeera, and BBC News. From alternative media, TRNN incorporates some localized and participatory reporting practices. It departs from dominant practices in how it employs a method of verifiable fact-based reporting and its commitment to questioning the official narrative often found in dominant media. Additionally, this commitment to traditional professional-journalistic practices is not found in many modes of alternative media.

In terms of presentation, the on-line format of TRNN's video news differs from what viewers are familiar with on television. Currently, it offers no structured news program, and no anchor people introduce or give context to the stories, which are ordered chronologically, thematically, and by region. Viewers search and select video segments on the TRNN website from two general types of news content. The first is produced by TRNN staff, and the second is Best of the Web and Breaking News, which contains video segments from other on-line media sources that are reposted on the TRNN website. The latter type of content demonstrates how TRNN participates in non-linear modes of delivery of news, which Webster (2009, 226) argues make "discrete items of content available to individuals as they request them." Webster (ibid., 224) states that this process of recommendation breaks with traditional boundaries on media consumption, creating "systems [that] alert you to things you weren't necessarily looking for" but all the while keeping the visitor within a community of related sites – in this instance, a community constructed by TRNN staff.

TRNN has a small staff of ten full-time employees, composed of journalists, media producers, and professionals with experience in conventional and new media. It is also working on building collaborations with independent journalists around the world to bolster its content, as well as those who work for other news services and agencies. A selection of these collaborative stories appears on the website, but it currently represents only a small portion of content. To supplement its own video coverage, TRNN augments its own reporting with footage and segments from other news services such as the Associated Press Television Network (APTN), BBC News, and Al Jazeera.

For Jay, TRNN's independence in news production is its main challenge to commercial television news. He argues that dominant television news media have strayed considerably from independent practices and are more reliant on repeating official reports from elite sources than on pursuing the context of stories that are reported (Jay, pers. comm., 6 February 2011). These practices narrow opinion and perspectives due to the external influence of advertisers and corporate and government funders on editorial management. TRNN's commitment to independence from these influences facilitates its ability to stick with the fundamental goals of professional journalism. Therefore, its legitimacy rests on following the rules of professional journalism and questioning the official narrative. In this vein, Atton and Hamilton (2008, 17) argue that it is not incongruous for an alternative news project to uphold professional standards of journalism; rather, they state that professional journalism is "the coin of the realm for legitimate public discourse and debate, regardless of the purpose or cause." They also suggest that when an alternative media project competes with commercial counterparts, professionalism aids in building the project's reputation (ibid., 50).

Another way that TRNN follows the rules of professional journalism is demonstrated in its use of footage from APTN and international news services. Until 2010, TRNN subscribed to APTN's video service and downloaded footage to complement stories it was covering, but due to the expense, it cancelled this contract and now relies on footage taken from other news services such as Al Jazeera and the BBC. TRNN does not pay for this material but does credit the organizations in its coverage. The footage is a valuable resource for TRNN, as it provides access to images from a far greater number of locales than could otherwise have been the case. In terms of APTN, Jay made a clear delineation between the range and quality of images and the editing and commentary provided by the networks that carry its content. As he states, "[there is] really good reporting from APTN that never makes it to TV networks ... It is surprising the range of stories and quality of what is being reported – networks just throw [it] in the garbage" (pers. comm., 7 March 2009). Using the footage from other international news services forces TRNN to rely on how those organizations have framed the stories in question. Yet, TRNN is also remodelling the content of other networks when it reuses the material in its own stories (see Hackett and Zhao 1998, 2005; Niblock and Machin 2007, 194).

TRNN also draws from alternative journalistic practices. Local reporting and participatory journalism are used not as primary modes of production, but to supplement and diversify existing content. Both assist in reducing the cost of content. "Local reporting" refers to TRNN's habit of seeking out local journalists in regions around the world to comment and report on current issues. The TRNN use of local reporting demonstrates the duality of its hybrid model. Local reporting differs from the commercial model, since rather than "following the network model of hiring Canadians and Americans and sending them everywhere" (Jay, pers. comm., 7 March 2009), TRNN uses indigenous reporters as its sources. However, this model is more about seeking local professional reporters to provide timely comment directly from specific regions on issues there, rather than inverting the power relations and democratically engaging the local community as the alternative practice of native reporting does (Atton and Hamilton 2008; Atton 2002; Atton and Wickenden 2005). The value of this practice for a poorly funded hybrid media outlet such as TRNN is to provide additional perspectives on international issues while also defraying the cost of sending TRNN reporters to various regions.

TRNN has a commitment to "diversify production formats to include viewer participation" (TRNN 2009, 15). A recent example of this is the inclusion of viewer comments at the bottom of the homepage, encouraging an ongoing dialogue between viewers about issues and events addressed in TRNN stories. There is a clear division between content that is produced by professional journalists and contributions from viewers, as Jay outlines: "Professional standards come first, if there is citizen user-generated materials then it is segregated into its own area clearly identified as that" (pers. comm., 7 March 2009).

TRNN also engages in participatory journalism, which is understood as a practice that has expanded in the on-line environment, where it is far easier to "share resources and outputs among widely distributed, loosely connected individuals who cooperate with each other without relying on either market signals or managerial commands" (Deuze, Bruns, and Neuberger 2007, 323). But there are varying degrees of amateur participation. TRNN's use of participatory journalism is limited to incorporating citizen involvement into the research and formation of story ideas. Its approach here is similar to that of commercial media, where editorial staff have control over the content, including how it is framed and presented. This reflects Atton's (2004, 37) observation that agenda-setting and decision-making functions become blurred in hybrid Internet media projects.

TRNN demonstrates hybridity in production by incorporating practices from both dominant and alternative media models. Yet, clearly it is structured more by traditional journalistic values and practices than alternative ones. Thus, its challenge to dominant news is more of a critique of commercial editorial practices such as framing, gatekeeping, and agenda setting, as the use of content from other news services exemplifies. Additionally, TRNN has yet to build the network of local reporters or content producers to provide much in the way of local footage.

Hybridity in Funding

One of the fundamental tenets instilled by the founders of The Real News Network is that editorial independence can be achieved only without the influence of advertisers or corporate and government funding. Yet, because of its focus on producing video news, TRNN is a costly endeavour. Unlike text-based news sites, TRNN requires a large-scale capital investment in technology, facilities, and staff to generate its video component. These financial challenges are not unique to TRNN, as most news producers, both in dominant and alternative media, face similar problems. To address this, TRNN is pursuing a diverse funding model comprising three sources: charitable grants, individual member donations, and merchandising. Each of these comes with its own set of benefits and limitations as it relates to the alternative-dominant hybridity continuum.

TRNN's initial and largest single source of funding comes from charitable grants. In its early stages, the management team secured $5 million in grants from both American and Canadian sources, including the Canadian Auto Workers, the MacArthur Foundation, the Ford Foundation, and the Phoebe Haas Foundation. This was used to get the project up and running, including investing in capital expenditures, purchase of technology, and investment in a professional staff to produce video news and seek out additional avenues for funding. TRNN has established two charitable foundations, in both the US and Canada, through which the funds flow. In 2007, it received an additional loan of $4 million from the Theanon Foundation, a Canadian charity. In 2008, TRNN's annual operating budget was $2.2 million, but due to the economic slowdown, the 2011 annual operating budget was reduced to approximately $750,000 (TRNN 2008; Jay, pers. comm., 6 February 2011). Although the majority of early funding came from larger charitable sources, this is no longer the case. The network anticipated total charitable funding of US$750,000 for 2010, but the actual amount was closer to $200,000 (TRNN 2009, 15; Jay, pers. comm., 6 February 2011).

There are unique benefits and problems associated with funding from charitable organizations. In terms of benefits, philanthropic funding is an effective way to move away from a market model of financing. As Hamilton (2008, 95) notes, "To the extent that democratic communications presupposes a struggle against the market, organizing as a nonprofit or volunteer group seems to be an ideal way to operate outside of market relationships. In contrast to producing capital by producing commodities, grants from philanthropic foundations provide capital from donors (occasionally from benefactors who are immensely wealthy). Such financial support is further removed from capitalist relationships because, in contrast to the imperatives of amassing and concentrating capital, the purpose of a philanthropic foundation is to dispense it according to criteria other than whether doing so helps the philanthropy become profitable."

Although the decisions and rules that govern news production supported by charitable grants are freed from the market imperative, the charitable route also has two significant pitfalls. The first, as noted by Atton and Hamilton (2008, 270), is that "although avoiding the pressures of the market, such a means of support ensures that the publication will work in concert with the interests of the patron, whether it is a philanthropist or wealthy benefactor, a foundation, or, in the extreme case, the state." In other words, the same influences on editorial independence that exist with advertising and government funding can also occur with philanthropic funding. This has certainly been the experience for TRNN. Although it had early support from a number of foundations, some declined to extend this funding because they found TRNN's content too "radical and provocative." Also, TRNN has turned down grants when the donor organization was too closely linked with government (Jay, pers. comm., 6 February 2011).

The second pitfall in funding relates to the recent transformation of charitable organizations themselves, which have become more professionalized and corporatized (Hamilton 2008, 101). In turn, this requires entities receiving grant money to also demonstrate a level of professional organization. Hamilton (ibid., 109) posits that in this process "not only are organizations themselves changed ... [but] the grant-funding system as a whole perpetuates itself by channeling philanthropic support to social-reform communications projects that already have the appropriate professional, reformist credentials, or that begin to take on such a form as a result of the need to gain support."

In selecting their board of directors, the founders of TRNN chose people who would defend the network's editorial independence and approach; expertise in fundraising was not considered important. Additionally, they avoided including financial donors on the board to ensure independence (Jay, pers. comm., 6 February 2011). Despite its challenges with philanthropic funding, though, TRNN is hiring a staff person dedicated to grant writing and fundraising for special projects, reflecting the time commitment and professional skills required to succeed in acquiring foundation money.

Due in part to the constraints of charitable funding, TRNN is shifting the funding model away from heavy reliance on foundation grants toward individual donor contributions. Its 2009 business plan outlines how "within three years The Real News Network will be sustainable based on small donors and e-commerce and will only pursue occasional special project-funding from foundations and major donors" (TRNN 2009, 18). TRNN highlights the success of the individual donor/membership models of PBS and National Public Radio as examples of organizations that have developed sustainable programming following this model. In the spring of 2009, TRNN received four hundred new paid donors per month, and according to Jay (pers. comm., 6 February 2011), the majority of funding for 2010 came from individual donors, estimated at approximately $600,000. This included a single generous contribution of $250,000 from one member.

The individual donor-funding model allows for a more varied stream of financial support from a more diverse pool of donors than does the foundation model. If successful, it would make the venture far less susceptible to the constraints of patronage funding and the influence of economic conditions on those charitable organizations. Another benefit of the individual donor model is that it creates more direct accountability between TRNN and its viewers/users, as they are paying for the service.

However, two potential problems emerge from this model. The first concern is a lack of certainty in terms of sustainable long-term funding. Although TRNN was fortunate to receive a significant individual donation of $250,000 in 2010, this is not assured for future years, leaving TRNN financially vulnerable. The second potential problem relates to the creation of a tiered service model for viewers, something that TRNN has contemplated. This is similar to subscription models used by traditional media companies for their on-line content. Although seen as unpopular in the early 2000s (Chyi 2005), this model is being reconsidered as a number of commercial newspaper organizations, such as the *New York Times* and News Corporation, envision "paywalls" for on-line content through agreements with Google and Microsoft's Bing search engines (Pfanner 2009). Thus, TRNN may be at the forefront of a new revenue model that is being adopted by conventional media.

A third source of revenue pursued by TRNN was e-commerce. For a few years, TRNN developed e-commerce relationships with Amazon.com, Expedia.com, Indigo/Chapters, and priceline.com, whereby TRNN received a commission for goods purchased through its website or for referrals to these other vendors from its website. On the surface, the practice does not seem out of place for TRNN, as the first products that appeared on the e-commerce pages were network-branded items and books on themes sympathetic to TRNN content. Yet closer inspection revealed that the commission relationship extended to a range of unrelated commercial products. This raises questions about whether or not the sale of these items is tacitly endorsed by TRNN because they are sold on its e-commerce site. The e-commerce experiment was short-lived. Jay states that, because it was not really promoted, it did not generate much revenue, only approximately 2 to 3 percent of total revenues (pers. comm., 6 February 2011). As a result of the limited returns and the resemblance of e-commerce to advertising, TRNN has abandoned this strategy.

Jay continues to pursue different options to diversify TRNN's funding model and is currently investigating two other sources. The first is somewhat similar to the e-commerce model but would provide TRNN with much more control over revenue generation. TRNN is looking to establish a separate company called Real Earth Catalogue, a merchandising business selling green, fair-trade, and union-made products – in Jay's words, "an Amazon for the social good" (pers. comm., 6 February 2011). A portion of the revenues (20 to 25 percent) from Real Earth would be invested in the operation of TRNN. This approach is still in the early stages of development, but essentially the catalogue would be an on-line store where consumers could purchase items that Real Earth staff have sourced as upholding green, fair-trade, and union-made standards. To ensure some rigour, space will be made for product peer review, where consumers can remove products if they do not comply with their claims (Jay, pers. comm., 6 February 2011). In addition, TRNN may provide some news resources to investigate the veracity of the claims of products sold via the catalogue. Real Earth would act as middleman between the vendor and purchaser, and would provide credibility to the items for sale based on the reputation of the catalogue and, by extension, TRNN itself. Although Real Earth Catalogue would be a separate company, it would be majority owned by TRNN.

Real Earth is a potential answer for how TRNN can monetize its entry into traditional television. Even though TRNN does not accept advertising, it will require supplementary funds if it is to move into television to garner a larger audience. Once on television, it can use ad space to promote the Real Earth Catalogue business as a means to generate income to support the high cost of production for TV programming. Jay argues that unlike advertising, where TRNN would be the seller and vulnerable to editorial intervention and the current challenges in advertising sales, the catalogue model inverts the power and places TRNN, through its ownership of the catalogue, in the position of buyer (ibid.). If a product owner dislikes TRNN's content, it doesn't matter, as the catalogue can source another similar product. As a separate organization, the catalogue will not draw on the current limited resources and staff time at TRNN.

The second potential source of funding that TRNN is pursuing is the sale of its content to other media producers. Specifically, it is proposing to sell original interviews, footage, and branded segments to APTN and McClatchy-Tribune. It is also preparing to establish a "dedicated business unit and to position itself as the leading broker of independent news footage" (TRNN 2009, 11). Although this is more closely related to its actual business model of news production than the merchandising option, it is unclear how the structure of the news service business could affect the type of content produced by TRNN. Will TRNN develop all possible stories on world issues, or will the focus shift to prioritizing reporting on those events and stories that will sell? This may demonstrate a step back into the arena of limitations found in the commercial media model that TRNN was established to challenge.

The diverse model of funding that TRNN is pursuing is designed to build a sustainable and stable revenue source for the project, yet the more it diversifies into other areas to raise funds, such as the individual donor model and e-commerce, the more it flirts with the boundaries of commercial media, potentially jeopardizing its claims to independence. In response to this, Jay acknowledges that "nothing is pure; there is no pure independence; it is all relative. You just have to kinda make a call that we can do this without compromising our core values, but we can't do that without compromising our core values, and we make those choices" (pers. comm., 6 February 2011).

Hybridity in Distribution, Marketing, and Audience

Distribution and Marketing

The Real News Network's modes of distribution also demonstrate hybridity in terms of bridging old and new media forms. In many ways, a connection to traditional media such as television is essential for TRNN in its efforts to reach a larger audience, as television continues to be "overwhelmingly popular with consumers" (Cartt.ca 2011b). As a web-based news service, TRNN is always looking for distribution and marketing options to expand its reach. Jay sees a blurring between the distribution of TRNN news content and the marketing of TRNN itself to small donors, especially through social networking platforms such as

Facebook. Thus, he refers to distribution and marketing interchangeably (pers. comm., 7 March 2009). It is in these two areas, within both mainstream media and other progressive and independent media enterprises, that TRNN has developed an extensive series of networks with traditional media forms.

Currently, TRNN is working on three distribution options, all through partnerships with other media entities. Its staff are constructing a one-hour news program and negotiating possible distribution arrangements with a patchwork of outlets. This includes deals with public access television stations and independent and privately owned stations, as well as ongoing discussions with Rogers Communication in Canada and ComCast and Time-Warner in the US (Karlin 2007). The arrangements all hinge on the development of the merchandising model, which provides TRNN with the ability to monetize television.

A second distribution arrangement through traditional media sources is the deal that TRNN has developed with the McClatchy Company. TRNN content is available on-line through McClatchy's regional websites, which reach an estimated 3.3 million viewers throughout the US. In addition, TRNN's planned sale of news content would be orchestrated through a deal with McClatchy-Tribune (TRNN 2009, 19). As one of the largest regional newspaper companies in the US, McClatchy has had to reassess its own business model in light of shifting news patterns, including a marked reduction in newspaper readership and advertising revenue. In the US, a 10 percent drop in readership of daily newspapers was recorded from 1998 to 2007 (Newspaper Association of America 2007). A 17 percent decline in advertising expenditures in print newspapers was reported for 2008, while at the same time, on-line advertising expenditures have increased by an average of 21 percent since 2004 (Newspaper Association of America 2008). The partnership with TRNN has offered McClatchy a means of moving on-line with quality video content without having to make an in-house investment in labour and technology. As a predominantly regionally based print news business, McClatchy can offer its audiences unique content via its association with TRNN, both in terms of international content and video format. For McClatchy, the arrangement with TRNN means expanding the content provided to its audience beyond what its competitors offer. In return, TRNN gets a small office in McClatchy's Washington space, access to more regional audiences outside the central urban areas, and the ability to link with an already respected and established name in US news as it tries to expand its viewer reach.

Finally, TRNN has developed significant avenues for both distribution and marketing on-line, beginning with its own website, www.therealnews.com.

TRNN estimates that it received close to 3.5 million visitors in 2008, almost 1.5 million of whom were new (TRNN 2009, 18). Paul Jay estimates that visits to TRNN through all on-line platforms have grown considerably since 2008, with almost 6 million views per month in 2010 (pers. comm., 6 February 2011). The blurring of distribution and marketing functions for TRNN occurs most directly in the use of Web 2.0 functions. TRNN employs social networking sites such as Facebook, MySpace, Twitter, and Digg to both distribute its content by re-directing viewers to its web page and as a central means of building its individual donor base by accessing audiences and donors through the group networks that are the core of these sites. TRNN (2009, 18) estimates that approximately 14,500 visitors per month are directed to its site from these social networking sites. It also has video syndication partnerships with Yahoo Video, Blip TV, and YouTube, the latter through its own YouTube channel, established in June 2006, which has led TRNN to claim that it is in the top five of YouTube non-profit channels (Jay, pers. comm., 6 February 2011). In addition, TRNN is a member of the Media Consortium, a cooperative of progressive and independent US media enterprises that includes *The Nation, Mother Jones,* and *Progressive* magazines, and that links TRNN to a larger range of potential viewers by building on the stated preferences of Facebook and Twitter users, employing the word-of-mouth marketing that these applications perfected, and by joining the community of progressive media enterprises in the Media Consortium.

TRNN's distribution and marketing model clearly demonstrates a range of hybridity of old and new media forms. Through distribution arrangements with "old" cable television, TRNN would gain access to a potentially larger audience than it reaches on-line while not having to incur the cost of licensing and regulation, yet in these arrangements it enters into the market structures of commercial television governed by the logic of the audience commodity.

Audience

With respect to hybridity in audiences, Jay's goal is to reach a mass "global" audience with TRNN video news. He has achieved some important success in this, as a result of the various distribution and marketing efforts under way. In addition, TRNN receives a significant number of hits on its website, and it reports that its visitors tended to stay longer on the site than the average for other news and media sites.[1] Despite this reach, the audience is not necessarily global in scope: 60 percent of overall visitors are from the US, followed by 17 percent from Canada, 6 percent from the UK, and 2.8 percent from Australia.

Of those who visit TRNN on YouTube, three-quarters are male, and approximately 20 percent are under the age of thirty-four (TRNN 2009, 19-20). The age and gender of the majority of visitors to TRNN parallel general demographic data about Internet users (Canadian Internet Project 2008, 39).

Despite this success, a picture of the TRNN viewer emerges as English speaking, male, and probably American. A number of factors contribute to this, language as the most significant. Since TRNN is an English-language website, it is not surprising that the top four countries that provide its viewers are all English-speaking nations. A related factor is that all these countries have well-developed Internet infrastructure and broadband penetration, both of which are necessary to view TRNN content.[2] Thus, we see that TRNN cannot be considered a fully global news service, due in part to language and technology, but also due to content, and is less hybrid and more mainstream in nature.

The Road Ahead for The Real News Network and Hybrid Media

The Real News Network is an ambitious venture that is presenting novel ways of producing independent international video news. It was founded mainly as a challenge to the media power of corporate television networks and in opposition to the perceived narrowing of opinion and reporting found on those networks. As an example of Hamilton's variations of social formations in alternative and dominant media, TRNN demonstrates hybridity in a number of ways: how it produces its news, how it is funded, how it distributes its content, and how it reaches its audiences. To some extent, the fact that it is an on-line news service has allowed it to permeate national boundaries and avoid the national regulatory structures that confine television networks. At the same time, however, it is also constrained by the technology it is built upon, as its viewers must have access to broadband networks, high-speed Internet, and a variety of software that can support video. In addition, as a non-profit media enterprise that does not accept government funding or advertising revenue, it is constrained financially and is reliant on diverse and often conflicting forms of revenue generation.

The hybridity of TRNN plays out in the continuum between dominant and alternative practices of news production and financing that it has adopted. Within these two aspects of its operation, it must delineate a fine line in preserving its independence. TRNN makes the case that professional journalistic practices are not in themselves limitations on providing viewers with a variety of perspectives on issues, but rather the narrowing of opinion in network news is a result of the relationship with the market model of corporate media, particularly in television and editorial decision making.

What needs to be acknowledged, however, is that maintaining the independence of news production is directly linked to financial health, a key structural determinant. TRNN has developed a diverse funding model, but one that comes with challenges in terms of operational balance between fundraising and news production, and that also provides a number of paths down which the network could slide into the arena of a market model, threatening the independence and breadth of perspective of its content.

TRNN is also bridging between old and new media in its methods of distribution and marketing. It has built potential opportunities to compete head-on with network television through a patchwork of partnerships with cable access television and independent and mainstream television stations. Yet, here again TRNN is bumping up against the market structures, where its success is contingent on monetizing its content for television.

The Real News Network model can offer important lessons for other independent media projects. The first is in the need to create and sustain a diverse funding model. Despite challenges facing TRNN in its funding structures, if fully developed, its multi-faceted plan will provide more freedom than would be available with just one source of funding. This model may prove useful not only for independent media producers, but also for dominant media faced with similar restructuring challenges. Another important lesson from the TRNN model is its success at building networks through social networking applications, which allows TRNN to construct a community of viewers using existing networks, and with other progressive and independent media enterprises, which enhances the possibilities for sharing knowledge, training, and distribution networks.

In addition, TRNN demonstrates some key lessons for the future of hybrid media. It is taking the lead in this type of media formation, particularly in video news, and presents an interesting model for how to cross over between media. It has built important partnerships with traditional media such as television and newspaper companies, while also developing distribution channels through on-line and Web 2.0 applications. It also blends the professional reporting and organization of dominant media with the inclusive, democratic, and community-building practices of alternative media, but here some cautions need to be acknowledged. The hybrid model is not fixed in place and is always in flux, as a constant struggle occurs with external structures and in internal decision making. Here, TRNN faces ongoing negotiation and struggle in retaining its journalistic independence while expanding revenue streams and partnerships with dominant media enterprises.

Perhaps because of its hybridity, The Real News Network offers a tangible challenge to dominant commercial video news, doing so across various media platforms. Yet a central question about the balance required for hybrid media persists: Can a project like TRNN blend commercial and alternative media practices, such as professional and participatory forms of journalism, and still retain its editorial independence? If the answer is yes, the lessons TRNN offers could transform not only how independent media are structured, but also how the overall social complex of video news production develops in the future. We need to stay tuned to see what emerges.

NOTES

1 TRNN (2009, 18) reports its bounce rate at around 30 percent, which is significantly lower than the industry average at 56 percent. The "bounce rate is a metric used to determine what percent of site visitors leave (bounce) immediately after arriving at the site's homepage."
2 In 2008, the US, the UK, and Canada were in the top ten ranking of OECD countries with the highest rates of broadband subscribers. Australia was ranked thirteenth (Organisation for Economic Co-operation and Development 2008).

PART 2: PARTICIPATION

Transformations of Practice, Policy, and Cultural Citizenships in Community Television

MICHAEL LITHGOW

Community television is like an invisible giant. It is a sector of the Canadian broadcasting system worth more than $100 million annually and yet this cultural behemoth remains largely unknown to most Canadians. Even public outcry in 2008 over the demise of local television and the subsequent creation of a $60 million Local Program Improvement Fund failed to bring community television issues into greater public focus. As is the case for the other kinds of non-traditional media discussed in this volume, the policies, issues, and especially potentials of community television remain misunderstood and understudied.

The creation of community channels was envisioned as a way for Canadians to make and see television about their own communities. It has been shaped from the beginning by the competing forces of broadcasting policy, commercial interests, and a desire for creative expression on the part of communities across the country. From its inception within the National Film Board's Challenge for Change project as a radical experiment in the democratization of mass media in the late 1960s, to its de facto commercialization and deregulation in 1997, to its subsequent re-regulation and emergence as a heterogeneous terrain of cultural production in the early twenty-first century, community television in Canada is the product of competing and often opposing cultural forces. As a result, broadly speaking, there are two kinds of community television in Canada: (1) cable-company-produced programming and (2) independent community production. It is in the latter that we find the only recognized contribution to televisual culture in the broadcasting system, independent of corporate and market constraints. It is the only legislatively recognized element within the Canadian television broadcasting system whose structure is founded on public action and participation.

An important question facing the community television sector in the early twenty-first century is its continued relevance in a digital age. What is often underappreciated are the unique opportunities offered in comparison to online experiences. Professional skills-learning in collaborative productions, access to costly professional facilities and equipment, and subsidized training and live broadcasting are experiences not typically available in online contexts. Community television remains – even with an active Internet culture – a vital opportunity for expanding cultural citizenships well beyond the democratically feeble offerings of consumerism and into the kinds of capacities that encourage and engender public action.

This chapter sketches some of the salient contours of these new geographies of community television in Canada by focusing on two cases of independent community production, one in rural Cape Breton and the other in one of Canada's poorest urban communities, Vancouver's Downtown East Side. By situating today's practices in a historical policy context and by examining how some of these practices help communities determine their own social, cultural, and political existence in both rural and urban settings, I argue that Canadian community television as it is emerging among independent producers is an overlooked and vital site for the expansion of democratic accountability through cultural citizenships. I conclude by briefly considering Canadian policy in an international context of trends that raise difficult questions about community television's future. Despite localized successes, the existing regime in Canada, I suggest, is a public policy failure. Most importantly, community television's complexity and potential social contributions have yet to be addressed in any meaningful way by regulators, elected officials, and the public alike.

Community Television as Cultural Participation

Community media has historically been theorized as a site for oppositional discourses – that is, for news and views that oppose or challenge dominant ideologies in any given culture (Waltz 2005). More recent scholarship recognizes community media's more politically heterogeneous practices and roles as a *constructive* as well as destabilizing element within civil society. Downing and Fenton (2003, 190), for example, describe the cultural territories of community media as "mediating space" between private and public interests, and Rennie (2006, 36) argues for recognition of community media as a "legitimate participant in social governance," along with market forces and the state. These views complicate the traditional counter-hegemonic expectation usually associated with the "alternative" in alternative media: "Within such a vision, community does not have to be marginal or defined by opposition, but is capable of offering new avenues for participation that work with an acceptance of the difference, diversity and power structures of the contemporary world" (ibid.). It is a vision of community media that can either challenge existing power structures or exist within them as a vehicle for addressing democratic deficiencies by facilitating greater participation in governance. In either case, shaping and defining the relationship between citizens and social institutions is central to its purpose and effect.

Community media, or "citizen's media," as C. Rodriguez (2001, 151) prefers, also play an important role by "reshaping identities, reformulating established social definitions and legitimizing local cultures and lifestyles." They emerge in civil society, a conceptual and cultural space where dominant powers of state and private markets can be scrutinized and challenged, and where tendencies toward monopoly – whether over the production of knowledge, allocation of resources, or public meaning – can be directly opposed (Habermas 1987; Howley 2005a; Carpentier, Lie, and Servaes 2003). Such tendencies don't preclude influence by market forces and state interests, but suggest a category of cultural production not dominated by either. For example, commercial sponsorships allow local businesses to support particular programs and changing government regulations continue to structure community television's operating environment. But production can and does occur with varying degrees of independence from either in community settings, and it is in this latter form that we encounter the greatest potential for participation by Canadians, not only as production volunteers, but as contributors with significant levels of creative control over programming.

The different kinds of participation offered by citizen's media point to a key issue in public communication – exactly *who* gets a say. Dahlgren (1995) describes a vast cultural landscape of overlapping and ever-widening concentric circles of knowledge and experience, the smaller circles associated with subgroups, with ever-larger circles widening out to include a more generalized public who share more and more generalized knowledge. Participation in the widest of the concentric circles, Dahlgren (ibid., 134, emphasis added) argues, "begins to pull us in the direction of *citizenship* as a form of identity." Community

television is one forum for ordinary Canadians (including the poor, marginalized racial and ethnic communities, and non-corporate producers) to express,
participate in, shape, negotiate, reconfigure, and determine relationships between individuals and the wider social and political realities encountered on a
day-to-day basis.

The concept of "cultural citizenship" helps to explain some of these broader
connections between social participation and culture through access television, for example. King and Mele (1999, 605) have observed that "by shifting
our analysis and critique from cable access programming (i.e., the 'product') to
its production (i.e., participation) we redefine the traditional notion of the
public sphere to include meaningful action on the part of local citizens from
various backgrounds in a medium otherwise dominated by commercial and
corporate interests." King and Mele (referencing Rodriguez) further suggest
that even if the motivations of public access producers are not political, production itself is fundamentally meaningful: "The experiences of media author-
ship and participation reveal the power of information production otherwise
mystified by advanced technologies and 'behind-the-scenes' decisions of television editors and producers (C. Rodriguez 1996)" (ibid., 608). Cultural citizenship also locates cultural production's excesses (that is, in excess of program
content alone) within a framework that recognizes independent public participation as essential to the development of civil society. Community television brings groups of strangers together to accomplish difficult technical
feats that can be achieved only through collaboration and with access to professional studios and equipment requiring specialized training; it thus invigorates a range of capacities that, at the very least, enhance abilities to participate
in public action.

It should also be remembered that people enjoin in culturally creative processes for many reasons, not only to exchange information. These include, for
example, to establish or strengthen a sense of identification, for sociability and
security, for expression, pleasure, and entertainment, and for personal and
community empowerment (J.P. Jones 2006; Stanley 2006). Community television provides important analytical and epistemological resources, but it also
operates on many other experiential and communicative levels, such as the
acquisition of technology skills, learning to get a message across, expanding
openness to diversity, creating social bonds, and addressing collective issues
(King and Mele 1999). There is also a range of individual and community capacities that can be developed and enhanced through participation in production processes: building self-confidence, collaboration skills, and conflict

resolution, developing community and social cohesion, constructing rhizomatic networks, assisting civic awareness and participation, preserving languages and local histories, and (re)creating institutional relationships (K. Goldberg 1990; Stanley 2006, 13-14; Lithgow 2008).[1] These all suggest the many ways of tracing the often ephemeral implications of cultural participation and by doing so help us gain a better understanding of how these practices work to shape Canadian society.

A History of Policy Uncertainty

When community television was first invented (c. 1967), it was an unexplored medium for cable companies, activists, and artists alike. By 1972, more than a hundred cable systems across Canada voluntarily offered a community channel, with most programming being created by independent community producers on their own equipment (K. Goldberg 1990, 15). The Canadian Radio-television and Telecommunications Commission (CRTC) introduced regulations in 1975 that required cable companies above a certain size to provide a community channel with financial support (at the time, 10 percent of gross revenues) (CRTC 1975). These early regulations were an attempt to standardize the quality of a service mandated as the "primary social commitment" on the part of cable companies in return for single provider regional licences (K. Goldberg 1990). Access channels were also an effective way to convince cautious Canadian households to purchase cable services. At the time, Canadians were reluctant to pay for television which they received for free through broadcast, but were intrigued at the prospect of seeing themselves and their communities on cable (ibid.).

Standardization of services brought pressure from cable companies for the standardization of programming. In 1972, more than 75 percent of programming was produced by independent community members; by 1978, it was less than half (ibid.). A report commissioned in 1982 by Rogers Cablevision in Toronto found that, even then, independent programming was virtually nonexistent and that programming had become increasingly conventional (ibid.). In the 1980s, artists abandoned the community channel after repeated conflicts over content with cable company managers (Abbott 2000). Cable companies were exercising a judicially untested authority over community expression by censoring programming they deemed unacceptable.

In 1986, the CRTC allowed sponsorship advertising – text over still images – for the first time on the community channel (CRTC 1986). This encouraged cable companies to explore the commercial potential of access programming, with some charging community producers for airtime and requiring minimum levels of paid sponsorship for programs. The commercialization of the community sector then accelerated, prompting a public outcry. In 1990, responding to these complaints, the CRTC initiated a review of community channel policy. The end result, Public Notice CRTC 1991-59, both encouraged and discouraged the commercialization of community programming. On the one hand, it ensured that commercialization would continue by allowing sponsorship advertising and reducing by a full half the expected level of financial support from cable companies. But it also protected community television's unique role in the Canadian broadcasting system by prohibiting cable companies from charging fees for access or tying access to advertising, and by setting out new roles and objectives for the community channel which importantly acknowledged community television's public service value.[2]

In the years following, cable companies continued to organize most community channel programming with the active participation of thousands of volunteers across Canada (Community Media Education Society 2008; Sid Tan, pers. comm., 21 September 2008). Some programs were entirely controlled by cable company employees, whereas others fostered higher levels of creative and editorial input from community members. In many jurisdictions, community programming was centralized through single regional offices. In others (Vancouver, for example), cable companies operated multiple neighbourhood production offices throughout a licence area. Typically, these offices were equipped with cameras, edit suites, and production vehicles, with a small number of cable company staff who provided training and volunteer opportunities for hundreds of community members.

In 1996, the CRTC proposed changes to the funding formula. Cable companies (including direct-to-home satellite distributors) were required to contribute not less than 5 percent of gross revenues toward "the creation and presentation of Canadian programming" (CRTC 1996), but only 1.5% (and only the largest cable companies were required to do this) needed to be allocated to the provision of a community channel. The remainder could be paid into a production fund that financed Canadian-produced commercial programming. When the changes were implemented in the following year, the CRTC included the surprise provision that the 1.5% contribution was a voluntary commitment. It (CRTC 1997) declared that the "community channel has achieved a level of maturity and success that it no longer needs to be mandated" and that "apart

from the benefits to the public through local reflection, the community channel provides cable operators with a highly effective medium to establish a local presence and to promote a positive image for themselves." In effect, the
CRTC had deregulated community television.

Fallout was swift. In Vancouver, for example, six out of nine neighbourhood
production offices were closed. Across Canada, cable companies began to aggressively manage their community channels like commercial properties. A
period of political conflict ensued, pitting cable companies – encouraged by
the CRTC to use community channels for corporate promotion – against community organizations and independent producers.

One of the central issues then, as it is now, was access to production resources and schedule time. Cable companies wanted more control over programming, which meant less community participation. In one particularly egregious
example, Vancouver's Shaw Cablesystems eliminated three hours of weekly
community-generated programming (produced through a non-profit group
with whom I was actively involved at the time called Independent Community
Television Co-op, or ICTV), offering instead a mere two minutes per week. At
the time, Shaw's community channel manager told a CBC news reporter that
at Shaw, "access is an evil word" (CBC 2002). By the end of 2002, in most jurisdictions, independent community programming had all but disappeared, and
in its place was a distinctly more conventional (and commercial) approach to
programming (Community Media Education Society 2008; Cathy Edwards,
pers. comm., 14 September 2008; Tan, pers. comm., 21 September 2008).

Another element of the ongoing conflict over community television was
corporate use of the channel to generate revenues. Cable company programs
resembled commercial programming to such an extent that even commercial
broadcasters complained to the CRTC that the new regulation had, in effect,
granted cable companies their own commercial channels which were being
used to compete with private broadcasters for advertising (Canadian Association of Broadcasters 2001). The cable companies themselves were not shy
about their designs. In a 2001 submission to the CRTC requesting a relaxation
of rules governing sponsorship advertising, Rogers Cable argued that existing
earnings from community channel sponsorships – at that time already well
over $1 million – could be increased an additional $1.7 million if moving images were allowed (Rogers 2001). In the same year, the CRTC launched a major
review of all community-based media policy, including that governing community television. Over the course of eighteen months, two draft policies were

proposed and over a thousand submissions were received from members of the public, community groups, cable companies, and broadcasters.

A new policy framework was introduced in 2002. The regulations expressly situated community television within the legislative framework of the 1991 Broadcasting Act, which identifies community programming as one of three *equal* elements that make up the Canadian broadcasting system along with "public" and "private" (CRTC 2002). Several comments made by the commission in the new policy are instructive. For example, the commission states that "access by citizens to the community channel has always been a cornerstone of the Commission's policy" and that "the factor that most distinguishes the content of community programming from conventional television services is the ability of community programming to turn the passive viewer of television into an active participant. From this participation flows programming of a nature that is as varied as the imagination and skills of the participants" (ibid.). The commission also reiterated its expectation that licensees should "give the community the widest opportunity for self-expression by actively encouraging groups and individuals to present program ideas, produce their own programs with or without the help of the licensee's staff, and submit videotapes and films produced by them for broadcast by the licensee" (ibid.). The new policy unequivocally restated that "the Commission considers that providing and encouraging citizen access remains one of the most important roles of the community channel" (ibid., appendix). The commission also incorporated the public service roles and objectives from CRTC 1991-59 essentially unchanged.

What was not addressed in the 2002 policy was control of the substantial financial contributions required of cable distributors to support their community channel activities.[3] In 1995, cable companies on average contributed 4.6 percent of gross revenues toward community programming, or a total of $85.5 million across Canada (Statistics Canada 1999). By 2003, contributions had declined substantially to 1.8 percent (Statistics Canada 2004). Despite significant increases in gross revenues for the cable industry overall (from $1.8 billion in 1995 to $6.1 billion in 2006, a whopping increase of 239 percent), community channel spending increased a more modest 43 percent in the same period, from $85.5 million in 1995 to $121.9 million in 2006 (Statistics Canada 1999, 2007). More problematic is that despite the size of these expenditures, there has been little precise accounting for how these monies are actually spent. Even the parliamentary committee responsible for its review, the

Standing Committee on Canadian Heritage, was unable to obtain detailed accounting information from cable companies for its 2003 report on the Canadian broadcast system (Canada 2003, 30).

Lack of financial accountability aside, the new policy created a tiered system of community television (cable company managed and independently produced), but ignored how these changes affected participation and the kinds of experiences fostered. Because independent production falls outside of the employee and management structures of cable companies, it allows for greater creative control by participants and thus fulfills the original policy mandate by presenting the widest opportunities for public expression in terms of aesthetic decisions (the look and feel of programming), notions of appropriateness or community standards, political orientations, and sexual, racial, and class preferences. These kinds of differences were more apparent in some jurisdictions than in others. In Vancouver, for example, where independent producers were the first to negotiate airtime and equipment-sharing agreements under the 2002 policy, programs were subsequently censored by the cable company because of concerns about professionalism, nudity, community appropriateness, and political sensitivities (for example, a commentary that accused the United States of being a "rogue" nation was deemed unsuitable to air) (Community Media Education Society 2008; Tan, pers. comm., 21 September 2008).

Under the 2002 regulations, 50 percent of the community channel (for the largest classes of cable company licence) was to be made available for programs produced by community members independent of cable company oversight (see CRTC 2002, paragraphs 55-70). Significantly, the commission acknowledged the centrality of these independently produced programs by noting that, "while access programs [i.e., independently produced] are a central element of community programming, licensee-produced [i.e., cable company produced] programs *may* be equally valuable" (ibid., para. 70, emphasis added). Independently produced programs were given primary importance. The new policy also created new classes of licence for different types of community television programming services: these included a stand-alone community programming licence that would allow non-profit community groups to operate the community channel should a cable licensee choose not to, a licence for community-based digital services, and a licence for community-based low-power television (50 watts or less on the VHF band, 500 watts or less on the UHF band) (ibid.).[4]

Under the 2002 policy changes, community television participation emerged in three distinct classes: first, cable company managed and produced programming (with varying levels of community participation from none to some but with production and creative management governed by company employees); second, independent community production, in which creative control and production remained in the hands of independent community members (with varying levels of cable company technical support); and third, broadcast organizations that are independent both financially and operationally from cable companies. Evidence indicates that the first category has significantly diminished production opportunities and tends to create programs that resemble commercial television (CACTUS 2009; Community Media Education Society 2008; Tan, pers. comm., 21 September 2008). According to public advocates, in many if not most jurisdictions, volunteer opportunities have all but disappeared, and community channel managers are emphasizing commercial measurements such as audience share as a means for gauging the success of programming. Given such constraints, expanding opportunities for cultural citizenships tend to be found in the latter two forms of community television production.

Case Studies: Fearless TV and Telile Community TV

Although in many municipal jurisdictions there are no independently produced programs on the community channel, important exceptions do exist. One of these is Vancouver's Fearless TV (FTV), established in 2007. FTV is an example of independent community-based production (category two from the list above), where creative control over programs is independent of cable company management.

FTV was created through a series of workshops on community television in the Downtown East Side (DTES) of Vancouver.[5] FTV describes itself as a "cluster" of the DTES Community Arts Network, an umbrella group for various arts-related initiatives in the community, and for much of its programming, FTV collaborates with local arts organizations (such as Gallery Gachet, a local artist-run space, which serves as a production studio). The group has twenty members; half are considered core members and the other half are more peripheral in their involvement. A majority of members work, live, or have lived in the DTES. Members include community organizers, activists, students, journalists, and artists. They are all volunteers. On average, FTV produces four hours of original programming monthly.

The social context in which FTV operates is unique. Despite being part of the "world class" city that recently hosted the 2010 Winter Olympics, the DTES is one of Canada's poorest communities: 67 percent of the population in private households is low income (City of Vancouver 2005a); 98 percent of households are rental units (City of Vancouver 2008); unemployment hovers at around 22 percent (the city average is 8 percent) (City of Vancouver 2005a); and the average household income is 70 percent less than the city average (ibid.). In this one-square-kilometre community, there are ten emergency shelters, twenty-eight free/low cost meal facilities, and nine community kitchens (ibid.). The DTES also has a severe drug and health crisis. Within a local population of sixteen thousand, an estimated one-third are intravenous drug users, and the area has some of the highest HIV infection rates in the Western world (Adilman and Kliewer 2000). In 2005, nearly a third of the province's drug overdose deaths occurred in this community (City of Vancouver 2005a). The DTES is home to North America's first safe injection site, where intravenous drug addicts can legally take heroin intravenously under the care of health professionals. And, in contradistinction to these alarming statistics and testament to its complexity, the DTES also has a number of positive community initiatives, including over ten thousand subsidized and cooperative housing units, seventeen artist-run centres and galleries, Canada's longest-running community radio station (Vancouver Co-op Radio, CFRO), and two community gardens (ibid.).

The DTES is also subject to ongoing upheaval from urban renewal and transformation. Development pressures are reducing the number of affordable housing units (mostly single-room occupancy hotel rooms) while increasing upscale market housing; neighbourhood gentrification is accelerating as the city looks for ways to expand housing markets near the downtown core (Lin et al. 1999; City of Vancouver 2005b). According to FTV founder Sid Tan (pers. comm., 21 September 2008), FTV was established to allow the people who already live and work in the DTES to have their voices heard and to represent their own community in response to these changes.

To fulfill this goal, FTV provides ongoing training for members in all aspects of television production: editing, camera, sound, directing, pre-production, and producing. According to Tan, the local cable company (Shaw Cablesystems) has, however, demonstrated reluctance and even outright refusal to offer training for FTV members. FTV's experience with Shaw has been unpleasant and antagonistic, to say the least. "It seems to us," Tan (ibid.) explained, "that the cable company would just as soon not have us; they are openly hostile."

Despite such poor relations, Shaw does provide limited access to equipment as required by the CRTC. Roughly once a month, FTV uses a three-camera mobile studio from the Shaw community channel studios to produce four one-hour television shows. FTV also uses cable company editing facilities but is allocated time in less convenient off-hour time slots. The programs appear on the community channel, on-line, at public screenings in the neighbour-hood, and at private meetings held by local community organizations (ibid.).

FTV programs focus on local community members, organizers, artists, and activists. FTV also shows locally produced documentaries (one dealt with the impact that the 2010 Olympics was expected to have on the neighbourhood, and another focused on a local housing group). According to Tan, local arts, housing, poverty, and homelessness dominate FTV programming. Much of it concentrates on finding solutions to local problems. "We're trying to figure out how luxury housing and subsidized housing can exist side-by-side," explains Tan (ibid.). Programming has addressed lobby efforts by local groups to in-crease the provincial minimum wage and welfare rates; health outreach, emer-gency shelters, and accommodating the needs of mental health patients; local initiatives such as arts festivals, projects such as Insite (the safe injection site constantly threatened with closure), and the Wills Project (a cost-saving initia-tive by the provincial government to get neighbourhood residents to create wills); and fundraising efforts by local community non-profits.

FTV programming satisfies the 2002 CRTC policy objectives in a number of ways. The CRTC has repeatedly stated that access is the cornerstone of com-munity channel policy and one of its most important goals. The CRTC has also acknowledged that participation is what drives diversity in programming. FTV is offering ways for highly marginalized groups to have their voices heard though creative control over production, their choice of guests, and their pre-ferred topics of coverage. In addition to engendering a high level of citizen participation, FTV provides alternative points of view, ethnic diversity, and coverage of local events, all expressly stated goals and objectives for the com-munity channel under the 2002 policy (CRTC 1991, 2002).

But the goals and objectives themselves recognize only some aspects of FTV's role in the local community. FTV programming (production and recep-tion) increases awareness in the wider region about the people who live in the DTES and about the DTES as a community. It provides a context for people to come together to work collaboratively to produce television that interrogates political, moral, and policy positions. In speaking about its constituents, Tan (pers. comm., 21 September 2008) states that "they're poor, yes; but it doesn't mean that they're not creative, politically active or socially responsible. They need an outlet, and we've got to show that real people live in the DTES who care about their neighbourhood. Fearless TV says: they're poor but they count. They're of value, because look at what they're doing."

FTV is actively involved in re-creating social identities, both of the neighbourhood as a whole and of the individuals and groups who live there. "Above all," says Tan (ibid.), "we are training community champions, giving voice to community champions, encouraging people to champion their community." FTV production and distribution demonstrates all aspects of cultural citizenship: enhanced capacities for community action, helping to build social networks, playing a role in negotiating collective values in the neighbourhood, and fostering civic participation.

The second case study is in an altogether different setting. Telile Community Television is an independent community broadcaster located on Isle Madame, a small island off the southeast coast of Cape Breton Island in Nova Scotia.[6] Isle Madame has a population of less than four thousand. Telile broadcasts over a radius of twenty-seven kilometres using a relatively small 450-watt transmitter. The station controls its own programming schedule, and because of Public Notice CRTC 2002-61, the local cable company is required to carry its signal, which is distributed on the west side of Cape Breton Island. The signal is also carried voluntarily by another cable company throughout the eastern part of Cape Breton. Telile does not receive financial help from either company.

Telile is located in one of the regional centres for Canada's Acadian community, a minority French-speaking culture whose ancestral roots date back over four hundred years in the area, and whose cultural identity remains an important aspect of public culture in the area. About half of Isle Madame residents self-identify as bilingual (CDÉNÉ 2006).

Like many Cape Breton communities, Isle Madame has depended on the fishery for its economic livelihood for centuries. But in the early 1990s, the federal government closed the east coast cod fishery, and overnight, one-third of the island's residents lost their jobs. Facing catastrophic economic and social collapse, residents mobilized to save their community. Telile Community Television was created in 1993 as part of that effort. Fearing a mass exodus of the population, and looking for solutions to the economic crisis, community leaders wanted to engage residents in a conversation about local economic development strategies. To get the word out, they began making programs in a little-used studio in the basement of the high school, and the programs were scheduled on the local community channel. Telile was born in 1993.

In 2002, unsure of its tenure on the local cable system, Telile applied for and received an independent community broadcast licence under the new regulations (CRTC 2002). The station operates independently. Most revenues come from the sale of bingo cards in connection with a weekly one-hour televised bingo program. Some (but significantly less) revenue is derived from advertising on what is called the "community scroll" (a text-based community message board that fills up more than three-quarters of all air time) and through the sale of copies of popular programs. Annual revenues available for production and operations range between $150,000 and $200,000.

Telile has three employees: a station manager, a producer (who also manages the scroll and sells advertising), and a bookkeeper. The vast majority of programs are produced by the employees. The board of directors, which is responsible for administering the station, consists of nine elected volunteers. Based on the personal involvement and affiliations of the individual directors, the board indirectly represents more than forty local community organizations.

Programming cycles are planned six to eight weeks in advance. In addition to the community scroll, a significant portion of programming consists of live-to-tape recordings of local performances, including music, dance, and theatre in community centres and local schools. Each week, at least one new show is presented and repeated throughout the week. Programs focus on such various subjects as coverage of council meetings and local elections, public service announcements and the rebroadcast of the provincial legislature's question period, and programs about local history and heritage. Telile also creates and airs profiles of local businesses and community leaders, provides coverage of community events and local economic development initiatives, and raises public awareness about local policy and planning. The station's cultural programming (involving musicians, festivals, religious events, and local artists) and its programs about local history and heritage all serve in the construction and maintenance of a unique Acadian and Cape Breton identity. Cultural programming underscores and valorizes local history, which helps shape collective values and preferences, and increases social cohesion through a shared sense of belonging. The community scroll also helps to build social inclusion by announcing community gatherings, job openings, and training opportunities. Programming also addresses community development issues by exploring strategies for local economic self-reliance and initiatives, such as the creation of a wind-farm.

The people of Cape Breton, like those in many rural areas worldwide, also experience significant levels of social exclusion and social fragmentation: 18 percent of the population lives in poverty (K. Lee 2000), and the unemployment rate hovers around 27 percent (CDÉNÉ 2006). The region has the tragic distinction of having the highest cancer rates in Nova Scotia, a cancer death rate 25 percent higher than the national average, and mortalities due to bronchitis, emphysema, and asthma that are a full 50 percent higher in Cape Breton than the national average (GPI 2003). A 2007 report suggests that current rates of out-migration will result in upward of fifty thousand young people leaving Cape Breton between 2007 and 2021, looking for better opportunities (CBCEDA 2007, 16).

The people in the communities served by Telile, like most Canadians, live in a cultural milieu dominated by non-local media flows that have little if anything to do with local life. Cable and satellite television services provide hundreds of mostly foreign-owned channels. Very little of what happens on Isle Madame and very few of the people or places that make up its communities ever appear within locally available media streams – except, that is, for the programming on Telile. The station was created in response to an economic and social crisis, and continues to play an important role in how residents define their identity and negotiate their rights, obligations, and relationships with each other, with the state, and with wider Canadian society.

Community Television in a Digital Age: What Next?

Despite their differences, Telile Community Television and Fearless TV both engage in building social identity and inclusion by expanding control over symbolic resources. These are practices of cultural citizenship that have emerged through independent control over programming and production. Telile, in its rural setting, valorizes Acadian identity, heritage, music, and place, and through its scroll and community events coverage, provides a kind of cultural "soft tissue" for inhabitants of a sparsely populated and impoverished region. These messages encourage residents to remain in the community by legitimizing and celebrating local experience and increasing access to social opportunities, or what Sreberny (2005, 246) identifies as "recognition," which is an important step in democratic communication building. Telile programming validates local identities that are ignored in commercial media and works to bolster a sense of pride in place, culture, and history. Similarly, FTV valorizes the humanity of people who must otherwise contend with prejudices in the dominant culture that stigmatize the poor, drug users, and many of the racial groups that make up the Downtown East Side's population. Community television in these instances shares an interest in building community from the inside out and from the bottom up. It is a politics of participation through cultural production.

Both communities have been subject to and in a sense failed by dominant economic and political systems. And in both, citizens have responded to this failure by taking advantage of an opportunity created through federal regulation to participate in Canadian culture via community television. These are remarkable success stories. And yet, current policies fail to acknowledge the important ways in which these approaches to community television – independent and community-driven – expand public action. In both cases, community television is helping local residents to define their relationships not only with each other, but also within networks of state agencies that at the very least are having difficulties adequately addressing issues of local poverty and social exclusion. For the residents of Cape Breton who see their community and local cultures reflected in Telile programming, the channel emerges as a site where local identity is defined through ongoing problem solving. FTV similarly presents a site where residents have the opportunity to identify problems, discuss possible solutions, and make decisions about collective action. In both cases, programming is produced largely independent of the traditional market pressures found in commercial media contexts and largely free of direct federal influence.

Regrettably, there are no statistics documenting how many hours of community television in Canada are produced independently and how many are generated by cable company employees (although this may change under recently introduced regulation). Advocates who work in the community television sector suggest that most programming outside of Québec is made by cable company employees and that this explains in large part why community channels increasingly resemble commercial channels and why there are fewer and fewer opportunities for volunteers (Edwards, pers. comm., 14 September 2008; Community Media Education Society 2008; Tan, pers. comm., 21 September 2008). Utilized in this manner, community television fulfills only a fraction of its public service potential.

Furthermore, control over the $100 million annual cable levy remains at the centre of community channel controversy. These funds have been spent with virtually no government oversight, and until very recently all attempts to obtain detailed accounting information from the cable industry – even attempts by Parliamentary committees – proved unsuccessful.[7] Given the important cultural and citizenship work undertaken at all sites of independent production, and more importantly, those that could be better accomplished with greater access to resources for independent community producers, the current arrangement suggests an expensive (and expansive) policy failure. If community channel monies are being spent primarily on what amounts to additional commercial programming, the policy objectives for community television have been eviscerated.

The most recent round of changes to community television policy is both encouraging and discouraging (CRTC 2010b). Most discouraging is that despite widespread support for an independent fund to be created for the management of community television assets, individual cable companies have retained control of the resources. But new regulations are requiring greater public accountability from the cable industry for spending, programming, and production decisions. The continued importance of the independent sector has also been reinforced with clearer rules about spending: no less than 50 percent of community channel revenues must now be spent on independent community production. More problematically, the CRTC accepted submissions from cable companies that suggested they are currently meeting and in some cases exceeding these targets despite contrary submissions from individuals and groups across Canada. In other words, where the new policy promises potential improvements, it reinforces the status quo by leaving control over community resources in the hands of corporate entities with private agendas.

It is worth noting that despite the dubious quality of some of these policy gains, public interest advocates did influence the policy review process in important ways. The Canadian Association of Community Television Users and Stations (CACTUS) presented to the CRTC a comprehensive proposal for reallocating community television funds to support a network of independent community media centres. In keeping with a general shift toward "networked information economies" (Benkler 2006) and "redactional cultures" (Hartley 2000) and expanding public participation in cultural processes, these media centres would have thus emphasized skills training and production/distribution opportunities for more than 90 percent of the Canadian public (CACTUS 2009). Although the proposal was rejected, it significantly reoriented the conversation during the policy review process. At least one commissioner filed a strongly worded dissenting opinion supporting the independent management of community television resources based in part on the CACTUS submission (CRTC 2010b).

Canada is not alone in raising questions about the relevance and continuing role of community television, although in most jurisdictions (with the notable exception of the United States), the importance of community participation is driving policy considerations. In the US, where there are over four thousand public access channels, there are growing concerns over the long-term survival of the PEG system (called PEG for dedicated channels for public educational and government-sponsored programming) in response to recent attempts by the larger cable companies to limit local municipal involvement (and thereby centralize programming in the hands of state governments), and by offering PEG channels only in low-resolution, poor-quality visual formats. Advocates also charge that access offices are closing at an unprecedented rate because, under existing regulation, PEG funds cannot be used to pay staff. Community access advocates are mobilizing public support for legislation that has been introduced in the Senate, called the Community Access Preservation Act (H.R. 3745), in an attempt to address these concerns (Alliance for Community Media 2010).

The European Union has called on all member states "to give legal recognition to community media as a distinct group alongside commercial and public media where such recognition is still lacking" and "to make television and radio frequency spectrum available, both analogue and digital" for community access programming (European Union Parliament 2008). Many European Union member states do have "open channel" policies of some kind as part of their terrestrial broadcast systems, but the type of support received and extent of public uptake varies widely (Edwards 2009).

In Japan, though there is no regulatory recognition for access television, most cable companies offer a community channel, and thirty-six of approximately five hundred over-the-air broadcasters also provide public access services (ibid.). In South Korea, the national broadcaster (Korean Broadcasting Service) is required to air a minimum of 100 minutes of citizen access programming per month; programs that air on KBS are compensated between $5,000 and $8,000 (ibid.).

We also find recognition of and support for community television in many South American countries, although their approaches also vary widely. Venezuela passed the "Organic Telecommunications Law" in 2000, allowing licences for non-profit television (there are now more than fifty stations);

Uruguay has set aside one-third of analogue and digital bandwidth for community television; Bolivia recently recognized community television as a distinct category; Brazil has some seventy community stations; and Colombia has more than five hundred licensed community stations in operation (ibid.). Funding, access, and expressive freedom range in each jurisdiction.

In Canada, the emergence of on-line culture continues to transform how we think about participation in public communication. There was a time, for example, when advocates sought to have a community programming "lane" set aside in the "information highway," an "electronic commons" for citizens' media, in much the same way as a community channel is reserved within the cable signal (Surman 1994). This is a laudable idea (at least in principle), but today it is the major telecommunications companies that want the Internet transformed from one network equally accessible to all into artificially managed parallel networks, with speed and access determined by ability to pay. As discussed by Kate Milberry in Chapter 11 of this volume, "net neutrality" has replaced the "electronic commons" as the vanguard call to protect the democratic potential of the Internet (Barratt and Shade 2007).

One of the most forward-thinking ideas to date remains the CACTUS proposal for the creation of a network of community-media resource centres that would provide studios and training for community radio and television production, broadcast, website development, photography, writing and literacy, and sound and audio recording and editing. This is a vision of subsidized cultural access, much like a public library system, but taking account of the many ways that digital and on-line technologies have expanded opportunities for cultural participation and how these new practices are in turn reshaping the kinds of cultural experiences that citizens want and expect.

Our communications systems are changing, but the central relevance of cultural participation to democratic accountability remains. And even though independent community television in Canada does offer significant opportunities for public action, as demonstrated by the cases examined in this chapter, most access channel resources in Canada are at risk of being squandered, if only because the surrounding policy discussions continue to lack a basic understanding of community television's role in expanding cultural citizenships. In a time of profound instability in the media industries, Canadians would be better served by community sector policies that took into account these democratic potentials when addressing the sleeping giant's role in the future of Canadian broadcasting.

NOTES

1 Similarly, a lack of participation has been observed to undermine community television's wider potentials. See Howley (2005b).
2 Briefly, the new roles and objectives included engendering a high level of citizen participation and community involvement, actively promoting citizen involvement and training opportunities, seeking out innovation and alternative points of view, affording balanced opportunities for differing views, reflecting bilingual and ethnic diversity, and providing coverage of local events (CRTC 1991, 9).
3 Broadcast distribution units (or BDUs, the regulatory term for cable companies) are the only content distributors to which community channel provisions apply; direct-to-home satellite distributors and mobile telephone services are not obliged under the regulations to provide community channel services.
4 The community programming licence policy comes into effect only if a cable company or other distributor elects not to operate a community channel. This has happened twice under the new policy. In the first instance, the licence applicant reapplied to carry a community channel; the CRTC issued new regulations exempting cable licensees under a certain size from having to provide a community channel. There has also been one application for a community-based digital television service (CRTC 2007a). The application was denied because of an insufficient business plan. No community programming licences or community-based digital service licences have been awarded to date.
5 The following discussion is based on interviews and private correspondence with Sid Tan, founder and current executive director of Fearless TV.
6 The following discussion is based on interviews and private correspondence with Telile staff and directors, key members from its past, and local residents, as well as a review of twelve months of programming (see Lithgow 2008).
7 In the report from the Standing Committee on Canadian Heritage, *Our Cultural Sovereignty*, the committee expressed "dismay" that it was unable to obtain financial information from the cable companies about how community television resources were being spent (Canada 2003, 30). This, too, may be changing with the introduction of financial accountability and transparency provisions (see CRTC 2010b).

Public Participation and Community Radio in Québec

EVAN LIGHT

Approaches to understanding alternative media often focus on their role as counterweight to the large corporate media that dominate the mediascape. For instance, Haas (2004, 115) notes that characterizations of alternative media often frame them as "counterinformation institutions" and "agents of developmental power," and adds that they are also identified by "the alternative values and frameworks that underlie their news coverage." In this context, alternative media enable communities that are under- or unrepresented in mainstream media to represent themselves. Participation in media production serves to overcome traditional barriers between media producers and media subjects/consumers. The work of alternative media can be seen as inherently political in that involvement in the making of media reconfigures modes of labour and production, as well as popular understandings of what media are, their roles in society, and who can take part in their production. By facilitating community participation in production, alternative media democratize access to resources as well as access to and creation and dissemination of knowledge. In their very composition and production, alternative media are projects of social development capable of empowering communities according to their specific traditions, values, needs, and desires. This concept of alternative media – one that privileges direct participation in media production – dominates related North American discourse and action. It is a concept that is radical, idyllic, and very much at a crossroads.

Although community radio in Canada is often mentioned in texts on the subject of alternative media, it has not been widely studied. Some early works focused on the role of First Nations people in advancing this form of media (Salter 1981), competing approaches to community radio in Québec (Ogilvie 1983), and the distinctions between community radio and local commercial radio (Savage 1985). More recent work has placed Canadian community radio in an international context generally (Girard 1992), as an instrument of social movements (Kidd 1998), and as a specific object of comparison (Light 2007).

The social project of alternative media in Québec has gradually changed over time, due in part to fluctuating social, political, and economic realities. It has also been transformed by the adaptation of urban-centred alternative media approaches to non-urban realities. In urban areas, alternative media are widely seen as something that goes against the grain of the mainstream. In Canada, community broadcasters are mandated to provide a complementary alternative to public and commercial broadcasting. Participation factors substantially in the organizational behaviour of these media institutions. Community radio stations, especially those in urban centres, are often understood to be composed of diverse communities with ties to social, artistic, musical, and political movements within the larger community. However, notions of alternative media as fundamentally participatory (in terms of production) and oppositional (in their distinction from the mainstream) begin to change when we look more broadly at the field of community radio and its history. What if a community media institution were to serve hundreds of people across a large rural area rather than thousands or millions within a dense urban centre? What if there were no local commercial media for community media to serve as an alternative to? How do differing experiences in physical proximity, population density and diversity, and financial resources affect the nature of alternative media? In this chapter, I consider the development of participation within these diverse localities by looking at five community radio stations in Québec. In doing so, I challenge some of the underlying notions related to alternative media and provide new perspectives on the concepts of community media and participation.

A Brief History of Community Radio in Québec

Historically, alternative media in Québec have been closely related to the social movements of the province, either working in concert with or independently of the state. The origins of these social movements lie in a period of drastic social, political, and economic change that started during the 1960s. Until this time, Québec's socio-economic infrastructure lagged far behind that of English Canada. Indeed, entering the late 1950s, the province "had reached a stage of marked underdevelopment relative to the rest of the continent" (Raboy 1984, 8). A change of government in the early 1960s led to what is now known as the Quiet Revolution, "an accelerated attempt to catch up in education, industry, social services" (ibid.). Following the early 1960s, a multitude of social movements sprang up in order to ensure their members' voices would be heard and understood, both socially and politically. These diverse movements included unions, feminists, sovereignists, immigrants, marginalized youth, and others (Boyer, Desjardins, and Widgington 2007).

Early community radio also had close connections to the community video movement. Coinciding with the National Film Board's Challenge for Change/ Société Nouvelle program, community video groups in Québec worked to demystify media use and production, and to give citizens access to communication resources. Each of these media received federal and provincial support of some sort, framed in the problematic of defending "national culture" from invasive and dominant forms of cultural hegemony. Speaking of the situation in the 1970s, Armand Mattelart notes, "It all goes to say that, in the current phase of capital accumulation, even in countries where the model of development is completely copied from multinationals, the internationalization of business processes stays on par with waves of 'cultural nationalism'" (quoted in Barbier-Bouvet, Beaud, and Flichy 1979, 25). In Québec, local media were all the more important as the province suffered from a doubled cultural domination. Canada was dominated by American media and industry. Québec, in turn, was dominated by anglophone culture, both from within and outside Canada. Thus, early in the development of community media in Canada, the federal and Québec governments adopted a strategy that promoted the use of community media within a larger framework of social intervention, serving to develop and reinforce Canadian and Québécois identity and cultural production (Ogilvie 1983, 72).

Québec's first community radio station, CKRL in Québec City, was founded in 1973. A student station, it was given an experimental broadcasting licence, as the Canadian Radio-television and Telecommunications Commission (CRTC) had not yet developed a policy framework for community-based broadcast media. The founding of CKRL was quickly followed by Montréal's CINQ (Radio

Centre-Ville) in 1974. Most early stations were urban-based and founded by a mix of community groups and students in order to create neighbourhood-focused and neighbourhood-managed social and media spaces. The development of Québec broadcasters was aided by a provincial government effort to build up community media under the guidance of local community production committees (Raboy 1990, 223-37). It grew in earnest through the latter half of the 1970s when the Parti Québécois government expanded its Programme d'aide aux médias communautaires (Community Media Support Program, or PAMEC).

The majority of community broadcasters in Québec are situated in non-urban environments. The Association des radiodiffuseurs communautaires du Québec (ARCQ) divides its non-urban membership, accounting for the majority of stations in the province, into two categories. Regional *(en région)* stations serve populations of twenty to seventy thousand. Rural stations *(en région eloignée)* serve communities of five thousand people in areas that tend to be geographically remote (author interview with Martin Bougie, 18 March 2008). These stations, known as *radios de premier service,* are often the only local ones in their communities. Many were founded in the early 1980s, though a few are of more recent date. In the first half of the decade, the minister of communications, through PAMEC, invested heavily in the province's community radio network, providing start-up and operational funding to stations. During this period of growth, many stations employed community development specialists to engage in outreach and to integrate the greater community. In the late 1980s and early 1990s, funding to PAMEC was reduced, and the majority of community development posts were abolished, leading to a gradual decrease in active volunteer participation in programming (author interview with Pierre Jobin, 30 April 2008). With diminishing revenues and rising inflation, community broadcasters were forced to develop commercial advertising as a revenue stream. At the same time, ARCQ engaged in a broad program of professionalization, helping stations to create structures that could manage the flux of volunteer labour and building fundraising capacity. This situation greatly altered the trajectory of Québécois community radio. It led to a high level of professionalization and changed the project of community radio from one focused on a process of participation to one of community-owned, professionally managed local media institutions. This occurred during a broad wave of professionalization in community activism and development as funding objectives began to change at provincial and federal levels (Shragge 2003, 49-55). Due to a decrease in volunteers, stations needed staff to produce community programming and to continue the project of community radio in one form or another. In need of new funding sources, they began to concentrate on producing a quality product that would attract advertisers. Thus, the loss of funding greatly affected the manner in which participation is approached at rural community radio stations (author interview with Jacques Chartier, 2 May 2008; author interview with Jobin, 30 April 2008). That being said, the Québec government continues to provide consistent and vital core funding to broadcasters without attaching conditions to its use.[1] Funding for community radio reached an apex in 2003-2004, when $1.9 million was distributed among thirty-one stations. This was slashed by more than 50 percent the following year but has since been largely increased (Ministère de la Culture et des Communications 2004, 2005, 2006, 2007). Québec remains the only province in Canada that provides financial support to community broadcasters. It is, in part, thanks to this sustained support over several decades that Québec community radio has developed a formidable collaborative network, whereas coordination within other provinces is quite minimal. Perhaps symptomatically, no other Canadian province currently has a provincial ministry dedicated to culture and communication. Likewise, Québec is the only province with a provincial community radio association that helps stations directly, serving as a communication hub between stations and representing them provincially and federally.

Urban Community Radio

Montréal is a very diverse city in cultural, political, and economic terms; its broadcast mediascape reflects this. It is the third-largest city in Canada with a population of more than 1.8 million (Statistics Canada 2006a), of which over 560,000 people are immigrants. An equal number identify their mother tongue as one other than English or French (Statistics Canada 2006b). Thirty-eight radio stations serve this population. CBC and Radio-Canada each operate two FM stations. In terms of commercial broadcasters, there are four French AM stations, five English AM stations, three multilingual AM stations, twelve French FM stations, and thirteen English FM stations. Three major broadcasting companies – Astral Media, Corus, and RNC Media (Radio-Nord) – own over 50 percent of the radio stations in the province of Québec and a large number of those in Montréal (Centre d'études sur les médias, 2008). Situated among these are two FM campus-community stations, CKUT at McGill University and CISM at Université de Montréal, as well as three FM community stations: CIBL, CINQ, and CKVL. Concordia University's Internet-based campus radio station, CJLO, was granted a campus-community AM licence in 2006 and began broadcasting early in September 2008 (CRTC 2006a). The Université du Québec à Montréal has an Internet-based campus radio station, CHOQ FM; it was founded as the first student radio station in Québec in 1969 (CHOQ 2008).

Policies governing community broadcasting in Canada have been reviewed several times (CRTC 1991, 1999b, 2000a, 2000c, 2009e, 2010a). The most recent review occurred in 2010. The stations included in this study are licensed as either community or campus-community broadcasters. The latter are mandated to play a distinct role, both in their universities and the community at large, often providing a vital link between the two. Community stations have no advertising restrictions, whereas campus-community stations are limited to a maximum of 504 minutes per week without any guidelines pertaining to advertising sources or pricing. The only limitations on maximum broadcast range are technical and financial. Previous to 2000, restrictions on community radio advertising existed so as not to undermine commercial radio revenue. Broadcasters must not interfere with any other broadcast signals, and the frequency and wattage are both determined with Industry Canada before a station begins broadcasting. Community stations occasionally upgrade their broadcasting power, but this is a lengthy and expensive process. As a condition of their licences, all stations must provide training in all aspects of their operations to all community members who are interested.

CINQ: Radio Centre-Ville, 102.3 FM, Montréal

The roots of Radio Centre-Ville lie in Québec's movements for social change during the 1960s and 1970s. In 1970, members of five Montréal communities – anglophone, francophone, hispanophone, Portuguese, and Greek – considered founding a community radio station. Their motives were to help members of their distinct communities to better integrate themselves into the larger Montréal community and to provide a means of mass communication to those without such access. Although the concepts of multiculturalism and multilingualism are today addressed in various venues, Radio Centre-Ville was an innovator, bringing people from various communities together expressly to take control of media for themselves (author interview with Evan Kapetanakis, 24 April 2008). Members of the core group of organizers incorporated the station in 1972, began broadcasting from the studios of Radio McGill (then a radio club, not a licensed broadcaster), and prepared an application to the CRTC. They started broadcasting from their own studios in 1975.

Radio Centre-Ville is organized hierarchically, with a general manager responsible for the daily functioning of the organization and ten other employees. Four volunteer coordinators ensure a continual presence at the station; one is an information coordinator who facilitates volunteer activities. Volunteers carry out all programming. The station has an accountant, a technical director, and an individual who is mainly responsible for interviews. The annual operating budget fluctuates between $350,000 and $400,000, with roughly half provided by grants. The remaining revenue comes from the following streams: advertising, sponsorships and community announcements, an annual lottery, membership fees, fundraising and special programming, and production studio rental.

As mentioned above, the coordination of programming is entirely in the hands of volunteers. Thus, the concept of membership at the station is taken very seriously. Seven linguistic production teams coordinate programming and collaboration between teams. Before volunteers can be fully integrated into the station as members, they must first involve themselves in its work. Eventually, they stand before the membership committee, which determines the extent of their participation based on their knowledge and ultimately grants them membership or not. The teams have no standard operating procedures and arrive at decisions according to their own devices. An "inter-team" committee of one representative from each linguistic team and a member of the board of directors coordinates programming more broadly in order to organize a unified station body and to encourage intercultural exchange (author interview with Evan Kapetanakis, 2 February 2006).

The mandate of Radio Centre-Ville is clearly defined and has not changed since its founding. Rather than "give a voice to the voiceless," it provides an organizational centre for sectors of Montréal society that are marginalized, both socially and in the media. Within this organization, the so-called voiceless can represent themselves. Participation can be defined as "the desire of citizens to implicate themselves in their milieu, to take their lives into their own hands and be able to effect change. Being able to speak for themselves" (author interview with Kapetanakis, 24 April 2008). Since its inception, Radio Centre-Ville has placed an emphasis on intercultural exchange and cultural representation through participatory media use. It provides a counterbalance to non-representative corporate media and a point of convergence for social groups working for common causes such as "citizen participation, solidarity, social justice and the democratization of communications media" (Radio Centre-Ville 2005, 7). By maintaining a permanent media environment for the station's seven distinct communities, Radio Centre-Ville helps new immigrants integrate into their cultural communities and the broader communities of Québec and Canada (author interviews with Evan Kapetanakis, 2 February 2006, 24 April 2008).

Community outreach and participation occur in myriad ways: programmers cover events in their communities, invite community members on-air, and regularly connect by telephone with individuals or other community stations in their countries of origin. Tracing this activity and its results is a project that has not yet been pursued, but this station has made a few attempts. Since 2002, CINQ has been relying on listener surveys to calculate how many listeners it has in order to provide potential advertisers with concrete proof of its impact. The last survey, conducted in 2006, tallied 100,000 listeners (author interview with Kapetanakis, 2 February 2006). The station keeps track of the number of daily phone call inquiries it receives, working relationships with social groups, and letters and e-mails from listeners. Another way it measures success is through monitoring new program proposals and communications between programmers and their audiences. Like other stations, CINQ receives a large portion of its funding from the Montréal community, and the fact that it is surviving financially is a testament to community appreciation of its work. Given the station's resources and the decentralized and non-standardized operating practices of its linguistic teams, determining the social impact of the organization in a thorough manner is impossible (author interview with Kapetanakis, 24 April 2008).

Regularized audience participation is necessary for such work to be successful, and CINQ has developed a series of operational principles to assure this community participation. Although many community radio stations operate according to such precepts, Radio Centre-Ville is the only one examined here that has defined them as operational guidelines. The following is an excerpt from the station's *Welcome Manual:*

Radio Centre-Ville will encourage listener participation by various means:

by permitting access to the airwaves;
by continually offering training in the production of radio programs;
by demonstrating local musical and literary talent;
by organizing or promoting the organization of forums of public debate;
by encouraging new approaches to programming and public interest;
by encouraging new and innovative approaches to radio;

by producing programs developed more in the critical spirit than that of conformity.

Formal ties with communities are embodied in the seven linguistic radio production teams: French, English, Spanish, Creole, Chinese, Greek, and Portuguese. These teams maintain open relations with various social groups within their communities and to ensure that programming and community outreach work adheres to the above principles.

Radio Centre-Ville has developed two projects directed at children and adolescents. Radio Enfant is targeted at primary school students between the ages of six and twelve (Radio Enfant 2009). Funded in part by Centraide, outreach workers from the station teach children how to produce radio. Recently, they have developed a similar program for adolescents, teaching radio production skills to youth aged thirteen to eighteen.

Radio Centre-Ville is the only community broadcaster in Québec with a multilingual broadcasting licence. This puts it in direct competition for listenership with Montréal's multilingual commercial stations and also means that its programming is subject to an extensive set of conditions. The station currently broadcasts in seven languages and "must provide ethnic programming aimed at a minimum of five cultural groups in at least five languages" (CRTC 2005). In addition, 65 percent of vocal musical selections broadcast each week must be in French, no more than 40 percent of regulated broadcast time (6:00 a.m. to midnight) can be multilingual and directed at a distinct ethnic group, and 50 percent of ethnic programming must be spoken-word programming in a language other than English, French, or a First Nations language *or* in French or English but directed at ethnic communities. On top of all this, 7 percent of the music played during ethnic programs must be Canadian (ibid.). Ultimately, these conditions mean that it is virtually impossible for Radio Centre-Ville to integrate more linguistic communities, not because the station does not want to, but simply because the bureaucratic mathematics are impossible (author interview with Kapetanakis, 24 April 2008).

One of Canada's oldest community broadcasters, Radio Centre-Ville has relied on an organizational structure that ensures that participation remains the underlying foundation of its institutional project. An increase in human resources has helped facilitate greater volunteer access to the station and maintain professional production space for volunteers. With over three hundred active volunteers responsible for programming and all associated activities (such as networking, fundraising, and advertising), Centre-Ville is in constant flux. As we will see, this is a positive characteristic of participatory community media, permitting them to adapt to the needs of their communities with immediacy and flexibility.

Radio CKUT: 90.3 FM, Montréal

CKUT is a campus-community broadcaster attached to McGill University in Montréal. Campus-based radio has existed there since the 1950s, first operating as a closed-circuit radio club. In 1987, the CRTC made a call for applications for a campus-community radio station in Montréal, which was answered by radio clubs then active at McGill and Concordia Universities. The licence was awarded to McGill's club, making it Montréal's first English-language community broadcaster. Given its unique status, the station has attracted a large anglophone and allophone community contingent interested in having access to media (author interview with Louise Burns, 22 March 2006). Today, CKUT is among the largest campus-community broadcasters in Canada in terms of budget, human resources, and broadcast power. In Montréal, it is a hub for the anglophone independent music scene, arts communities, and political activism. This station began broadcasting on-line in 1997 and was probably the first in Canada to do so.

CKUT is one of two campus-community radio stations in Canada to be collectively managed.[2] Staff facilitate community participation and maintain the large volunteer-based organization. As with Radio Centre-Ville, participation in station life is a prerequisite for station membership. The loosely monitored volunteers work an average of four hours a month. The station counts seven full-time and two part-time staff. It manages the largest volunteer infrastructure of its kind in Québec, including the regular integration of a migratory student body. The annual budget fluctuates between $300,000 and $350,000, with roughly half coming from a student levy paid by undergraduate and graduate students at McGill. This amounts to $4 per student per session, a result of a student-initiated referendum. The remainder is generated through advertising sales, benefit events, and an annual fundraising campaign.

Programming is entirely carried out by volunteers and is organized in a number of ways. A News Collective of open membership coordinates daily afternoon news programs, and looser affiliations of programmers coordinate regular morning news and culture programming. Since 2005, the station has created a variety of collectively run music and spoken-word programs to better integrate its four hundred volunteers. It also has a weekly program with a rotating monthly residency, recruiting hosts from Montréal's diverse creative communities and thus further promoting the practice of participatory media by generating working examples within social networks that may not be otherwise exposed to it.

CKUT plays many social roles in Montréal. As a campus-community broadcaster, it is mandated to provide training and broadcasting opportunities to volunteers and must equally engage the community of McGill University and that of greater Montréal. Rather than operating simply as a radio station, it is more of a "community social resource centre in the way that people come here, build friendships, create networks with other people in their community or people in other communities." The mandate of the station is to provide spaces of representation for all communities within Montréal and to "expose news, music and culture that isn't even being superficially examined anywhere else on the dial" (author interview with Sara Saljoughi, 22 March 2006).

Formal ties to communities are maintained through programming, with a large number of Montréal communities represented on-air. Spoken-word, community news, and music programming coordinators perform outreach in communities not yet represented. A volunteer-based committee of elected members – each of whom contributes to a balance in programming decisions and represents a constituency – makes all programming decisions. Paid programming coordinators sit on this body but cannot vote.

In recent years, CKUT has engaged in very innovative public broadcasting activities. These include live broadcasts from a metro station focusing on racial profiling affecting the immediate community (CKUT 2006); a monthly news program broadcast from a local church and hosted by an Algerian refugee living in sanctuary and fighting deportation; a nationally broadcast Homelessness Marathon (CKUT, n.d.); and the installation of a studio at the Native Friendship Centre to facilitate the production of First Nations programming. CKUT regularly facilitates workshops on community radio at local schools and homeless drop-in centres, and partners with community events by co-presenting advertising and/or maintaining a physical presence at events. The station organizes live broadcasts at concerts, marches, lectures, and other happenings.

All community radio stations in Canada are mandated to "provide for the ongoing training and supervision of those within the community wishing to participate in programming" (CRTC 2000d). CKUT holds regular training sessions on subjects such as record library management, radio production, interviewing, remote broadcasting, and documentary making. It also offers a trimesterly Training Days series, where station volunteers and community members share skills in formal workshop environments. Since 2007, it has organized two conferences aimed at integrating the general public into the making of community media (CKUT 2007, 2010).

In a manner similar to that of Radio Centre-Ville, CKUT has developed a sustainable organizational structure for assuring the continual development of participatory media practices. By refining this structure, it passes on the practice of participatory media use through generations and among the members of various communities. Without resorting to regular overhauls of programming, this station works to integrate numerous communities and diverse perspectives. The volunteers of CKUT and the many communities in which they live are foundational to every facet of this station.

Regional and Rural Radio

All regional and rural community radio stations in Québec are unaffiliated with universities, and a diverse range of stations exists throughout the province. Some were founded at the beginning of the movement in the 1970s and early 1980s, some serve remote and sparsely populated rural areas, and others have formed in the past decade.

Radio-Acton: CFID 103.7, Acton Vale
Radio-Acton was the product of both natural disaster – the ice storm of 1998 – and lack of local media. In early 1998, parts of Ontario and Québec were hit by three successive storm fronts, resulting in what has been called the greatest natural disaster in Canadian history. The town of Acton Vale and its surrounding area were among the hardest hit in Québec; some residents lived without electricity for over six weeks. Although there are a number of community stations in nearby municipalities, none serve Acton Vale. This lack of publicly available local media became a matter of public safety when rescue workers had no way to contact those affected by the storm. The idea to start a community radio station serving the region was put forward in 1999, and the project started in 2002. CFID began broadcasting in 2004 (author interview with Patrick Fortin, 2 May 2008).

CFID serves Acton Vale, a town of 7,978 people (Ville d'Acton Vale 2008), as well as outlying areas for a total potential listenership of fourteen to fifteen thousand. Thus, unlike urban stations, Radio-Acton has a very small pool from which to draw its volunteers. Of the fifteen thousand people in the extended community, thirteen hundred are members paying annual fees. Some actively participate in station activities. Seven community members sit on the station's board of directors, five have been integrated into regular on-air programming, and five others help with various tasks. Paid administrative staff make all programming decisions, and community members can apply to host a program. The station has six full-time and three part-time staff. The budget has doubled over the past four years to $400,000, half coming from advertising and the rest from radio bingo, fundraising, and government.

Because Acton Vale is situated among numerous other towns and within range of Montréal-based commercial broadcasters, the general manager of CFID believes the station is in direct competition with other broadcasters (author interview with Patrick Fortin, 2 May 2008). Although it aims to be a local broadcaster focused on the needs and realities of its community, CFID also tries to develop its "accessible" or "commercial" appeal. The majority of the population is employed in farm or factory industries and not necessarily highly educated. For this reason, Radio-Acton attempts to "speak to people in their own language" unlike "elitist stations such as Radio-Canada or alternative radio stations." Financial realities appear to be at the base of this station's organizing principles, as it acquires half of its $400,000 budget through local advertising and has doubled its overall budget during the course of three years. The station does not proactively engage in outreach to incorporate distinct sectors of the community: instead, it offers a certain number of offbeat musical programs to satisfy local needs (ibid.).

As a relatively young community station, Radio-Acton appears to have little desire to embody or relate to the history of social projects that precedes it. However, the manner in which it conceptualizes community participation begins to challenge the way in which this subject is traditionally approached. Rather than consciously create a form of alternative media, Radio-Acton aims to be a regional community broadcaster, accessible to the widest listenership possible. It measures its success in its membership, radio bingo participation, and local advertising, and sees these activities as important forms of community participation.[3] Alternative media are often positioned within radical politics and projects of social change. For the general manager of Radio-Acton, such practices would serve to alienate the market and listenership his station needs to survive. However, by creating a form of media that is explicitly local and speaks to citizens about their own experience "in their own language" against a wave of non-local media, Radio-Acton unconsciously engages in these very practices. Although the station may not self-identify as an alternative media institution, it does play the role of one, providing media made by and for its immediate community. Community participation, as invoked in the community management and ownership and underlying financial support of the station, ensures that this remains the case.

CFBS Radio: 89.9 and 93.1 FM, Blanc Sablon

CFBS was founded in 1983 as the province's first bilingual community radio station. It serves six immediate communities in the municipalities of Bonne-Espérance and Blanc Sablon, as well as many small communities in Labrador. The total population served by CFBS is five thousand, with the largest town counting fifteen hundred residents.

In the early 1980s, social development projects and popular education were concepts spread widely throughout Québec. At this time, Blanc Sablon considered starting a community radio station as the region, like many other geographically isolated areas, was grossly under-served by media institutions. In 1982, CKNA in nearby Natashquan renovated its studios and donated its old equipment to the founders of CFBS. The station also received support from the health centre, which donated a trailer where the station was housed until 1990. Today, CFBS owns its own small building in Blanc Sablon. It has an annual operating budget of $120,000 to $130,000. Half of this comes from the province, and the remainder is generated through advertising and weekly radio bingo (author interview with Melva Flynn, 27 April 2008).

CFBS is a small station that takes advantage of its lightweight administrative structure. Broadcasting eight hours per day, it maintains a semi-structured programming schedule that easily adapts to its community's needs. Its two full-time and two part-time staff produce half of the programming, and six volunteers contribute on weekly or bi-weekly rotations. Staff regularly facilitate programming by community members with interest but limited technical knowledge. The station enjoys a close proximity to local communities. Instead of creating formal bureaucratic structures for community participation and outreach, CFBS relies on its reputation as an accessible and interactive media institution that belongs to the community. Formal ties to the communities lie in its board of directors, whose seven members come from various socio-economic sectors and communities.

Unique among the rural stations profiled here, CFBS promotes itself as an open door and a centre of community communication, identity, and expression rather than a professionalized media institution. It recruits residents to provide voiceovers for advertising and promotes use of the station according to immediate community needs. It is "free for all, all the time." One example is the use of the station for community healing following the death of local children in a car accident:

> Being a small community, every tragic accident impacts all of us ... There was a car accident on the Labrador side of the border, about a ten-minute drive from where I am right now [at the radio station]. Grandparents who live next door to me. Just three days ago, one of the kids who was involved in the accident, he finally passed away. [One passenger's seatbelt malfunctioned; the others had not worn theirs.] So seatbelts became a community issue ... All of this took up hours on our phone line on the air because of this accident. It's people wanting to vent and say their piece, and listen to what others have to say. And to express their sympathies for the parents. Our programming went out the window, and it has been out the window since this accident occurred last Wednesday. (ibid.)

CFBS has twenty-five years of history and presence in a community with access to very little broadcast media, let alone any local media. Rather than entertain its communities or "cover" them in a journalistic manner, it provides a centre for community expression, communication, and dialogue. It has also become a locus for organizing, recently networking with three other stations on Québec's North Shore to publicly address issues in the region's health network. CFBS engages in participatory communication and is a grassroots community-based and community-managed institution. However, by maintaining a historically central place in its larger community while adhering to a practice of community ownership and participation, it calls into question the oppositional foundation of alternative media. Rather than framing themselves as oppositional and exclusive, perhaps alternative media should work toward a greater project of inclusiveness and participation. Indeed, given that participatory democracy is a foundation of alternative media, should the latter not be as inclusive as possible if we hope to prompt a change in how we organize our society?

Radio Gaspésie: CJRG 94.5 FM, Gaspé

Radio Gaspésie is situated on the Gaspé Peninsula at the eastern tip of Québec's South Shore. Among the oldest community radio stations in the province, it was part of a larger project promoting, facilitating, and maintaining local culture and history that was founded in 1976-1977. The first portion of the project was to create a regional museum, Musée de la Gaspésie. The radio station was founded in 1978, followed by a community television station and then a community newspaper. These were the first local media created in the region, which until then had been dominated by print media from urban Québec and received only CBC/Radio-Canada radio, one regional AM radio station, and Télé-Québec, a cable television channel (author interview with Chartier, 2 May 2008).

Initially, Radio Gaspésie was almost entirely volunteer-run. With time, volunteer interest decreased and those who remained were unable to regularly generate quality radio. Eventually, the volunteers who produced the best radio became employees of the station. Today, CJRG has developed a structure whereby community members can regularly contribute without committing to the management of entire programs, which is done by paid staff. The station has forged strong links with local cultural and community non-profits to ensure that community events and interests receive mass media exposure. CJRG is an example of the gradual process of transition from volunteer-based participatory media to professionalized community media outlet. However, because the station is solidly rooted in its past, it has made an effort to maintain regularized community participation in media making, preserving a project of participatory community media while altering its structure to serve its community adequately. With thirty thousand potential listeners, Radio Gaspésie has twelve paid staff and twelve regular volunteers. Its annual budget is approximately $750,000; $425,000 comes from local and regional advertising (the station has four transmitters to cover a very large territory), $150,000 from radio bingo, and $25,000 from membership fees. Provincial advertising coordinated by the Association des radiodiffuseurs communautaires (ARCQ) produces an additional $150,000 of revenue (author interview with Jacques Chartier, 18 March 2009).

The history of this station is an exemplar of the general evolution of community radio in Québec. CJRG was originally founded and managed by members of the community who volunteered their time and energy. From the beginning, it was given the mandate of providing any and all programming not offered by CBC/Radio-Canada (locally focused programming for everyday audiences) to a community lacking media institutions. Somewhat paradoxically, though, the community members who were initially most attracted to it fit the listener profile of CBC/Radio-Canada, which led to conflict within the community and the station. The current success of CJRG probably indicates that this conflict has since been resolved, perhaps through its ability to adapt to the changing needs of its population while maintaining historical perspective on its mandate as a community broadcaster.

Changing Dynamics

The development of alternative media is at a critical juncture in Canada. Community radio has been largely approached within a macro framework of communicative democracy and individual and community participation. Today it faces the challenges of professionalization, a rapidly changing technological landscape, and precariousness of funding resources. These challenges originate in competing visions within the community radio movement and the strategies adopted to address changes taking place in society. The history and current state of Québec community radio clearly demonstrate some of the ways that these tensions manifest.

As with much alternative media in North America, community radio is often understood to exist in opposition to dominant media production and dissemination practices. In Québec, however, the development of the medium is largely controlled by the socio-economic realities these stations face and the ways in which their communities respond to such pressures. In its origins, community broadcasting was a crucial part of a broader social development project – the organized appropriation of a mass communication medium to build and maintain communities. Community media developed throughout Québec at a steady rate with investment from the provincial government and a broad-based dedication to participatory community organizing. The initial idealism that accompanied the large-scale project of community broadcasting declined during the 1980s, with losses in funding and resources and a decrease in active volunteers. This led to a revisioning of community radio in most of the province, which began to place the goal of sustainability and a living wage above the project of participatory media. With the wave of professionalization that has taken place throughout the Québec community broadcasting sector since the late 1980s, few institutions continue to operate according to a participatory and community-based tradition (author interview with Jobin, 30 April 2008). Although community volunteers maintain a strong presence at urban stations, their role has markedly diminished in non-urban settings, due in part to a lack of funds, human resources, and evolving local populations. For these stations, direct community participation in media production has been largely replaced by a professional template designed to create media environments that attract traditional advertisers. With the consolidation of commercial broadcasting, these broadcasters also increasingly play a role once filled by local commercial stations that have fallen victim to the economies of scale afforded by corporate mergers.

Retaining Alternative Media Spaces through Policy Reform

Although the CRTC gives community broadcasters a wide social mandate to serve their communities in a participatory manner, there is little or no oversight and historically little expert authority on community media within the regulator.[4] This media sector has been largely left to its own devices in determining funding and management structures, permitting for, in the case of Québec, a redefinition of the role of community broadcasting. Radio-Acton presents us with one extreme result of this situation whereby a community broadcaster has fine-tuned its programming to sell advertising. However, all the stations profiled here periodically face financial and institutional precariousness. As with any social project, institutional knowledge and tradition at community radio stations are refined and maintained over time. Although the oldest stations in Québec have weathered countless challenges, community participation in media production remains central to their mandate. The evolution of these stations may be natural, yet certain policy changes can help ensure that participation, in its various forms, remains at the core.

Canada is one of few countries in the G8 that does not fund community broadcasters (Stevenson 2007). In order to release the pressure valve of advertising and to enable community broadcasters to wholeheartedly fulfill their mandate, such funding is necessary. After more than two years of development and advocacy activity, Canada's three central community radio associations – the NCRA, ARCQ, and ARC du Canada – created the Community Radio Fund of Canada (CRFC) in 2007. In 2008, the CRFC obtained seed funding ($1.4 million over seven years) from Astral Media as part of the mandated benefits package associated with its 2007 purchase of Standard Broadcasting.[5] The CRTC ruled in 2010 that this fund would receive an additional $775,000 annually in mandated commercial radio contributions (CRTC 2010a). Attempts to obtain federal funding have been unsuccessful.

Communications policy making in Canada privileges commercial media over non-commercial alternatives. Policy making is predominantly expert-driven and relies on processes of consultation rather than dialogue. One example is the

September 2007 Diversity of Voices hearing. At its inception, this hearing – which was initiated in order to examine the effects of media consolidation on the diversity of editorial voices in Canadian media – focused narrowly on commercial media. Community media advocates inserted themselves into the process, yet commercial media were ultimately granted three days of time before the CRTC, whereas forty community media groups and independent producers were granted fifteen minutes apiece over the course of one day (CRTC 2007d). Such hearings are rarely reported in mainstream media, and the general public is not often invited to attend or intervene. Thus, policy making is developed and delimited as a forum for experts and professionals who represent their narrow interests and for decision-makers, whose rulings affect society on a massive scale.

Community radio has made significant advances throughout the world in recent years, and the Canadian model, as well as those of Australia and the UK, will be increasingly looked to as an example by emerging radio movements.[6] Such movements have appeared in Nigeria, which legalized community radio in October 2010 (AMARC 2010); Bangladesh, where licences were first granted in April 2010 (Bangladesh NGOs Network for Radio and Communication 2010); Uruguay, where community radio was legalized in 2008; India, which introduced community radio legislation in 2006 (Community Radio Forum 2010); Jordan, where community radio was legalized in 2000 (International Media Support 2010); and Japan, where it was fully legalized in 1995 (Kanayama 2007).

In the years ahead, Canada will be undergoing a transition in broadcast technology and infrastructure as the world moves from analogue radio and television broadcasting to digital. This transition will be the most radical redistribution of radio spectrum resources ever seen and has great potential. What this potential becomes, however, depends on how its related policy is developed and who is included in its development (Gómez 2007). Digital transition could provide an infrastructure to support thousands of more independent voices on the airwaves, or it could lead to their ultimate privatization. Rather than continue to monopolize the decision-making processes related to our communication networks, policy making must become participatory and deliberative. Including community broadcasters in the policy-making process (and ideally the revision of this process) is an initial and vital step toward assuring a future for alternative and community media. The direction to take should be determined collectively, allowing communities to truly maintain ownership of the radio spectrum, just as they do their radio stations.

NOTES

Research for this chapter is supported by the Fonds québécois de recherche sur la société et la culture.

1 Campus-community stations are not eligible for this funding. Stations must be licensed community broadcasters.
2 CKDU in Halifax is the other.
3 Radio bingo is a primary source of funding for many community broadcasters in Québec.
4 There has never been a commissioner at the CRTC with a background in community broadcasting.
5 The author of this chapter was a director of the NCRA from 2006 to 2008 and was involved with the development and founding of the CRFC.
6 Australia's first station started in 1972, whereas that of the UK dates from 1978.

Are Ethnic Media Alternative?

KARIM H. KARIM

If participation is considered to be a key criterion of alternative media, ethnic media can be viewed as intrinsically alternative. They enable minority ethnic groups to participate in the mediascape. However, not all ethnic media demonstrate an attachment to progressive causes, which is another important characteristic of alternative media. The former are produced by varying interests, whose only commonality in a media category is that they address readerships or audiences that are primarily characterized by ethnicity. The main causes for such media to come into existence relate to the fulfillment of groups' need for access to information in their own languages, reception of material in a culturally familiar manner, and remaining abreast with news about members of the group, the homeland, or diaspora.

Presentations of issues solely from the basis of ethnicity, however, risk its essentialization. Focusing primarily on a particular group may engender notions such as those of ethnic superiority and racial purity, which inevitably come into conflict with society's common good. Certain ethnic media that do not subscribe to broader social values tend occasionally to engage in the vilification of others. This underlines the tension between the militant particularism and universalism of respective social movements (Harvey 2000, 33). Producers of media content who place themselves in opposition to universal values cannot be considered progressive.

However, S. Hall (1997, 184) argues that "ethnicity is the necessary place or space" from which minorities who are marginalized by hegemonic ethnic groups communicate to counteract dominant discourses. The broad consensus of hegemonic interests on major issues at particular junctures is reflected by the dominant discourses that provide the definitions, theoretical paradigms, agendas, and frameworks within which meanings are constructed. These reference points form the bases for public communication about key topics such as culture, democracy, citizenship, and the economy. The mass media are vital channels for dominant discourses, which continually reproduce themselves intertextually through interaction between various means of communication. They engage in a constant competition with oppositional and alternative discourses, seeking to sideline, subvert, or co-opt them. Despite the widespread acceptance of the equality of citizens of all backgrounds in public life, minority ethnic interests are frequently assailed in mainstream media (Henry and Tator 2002) as well as in the alternative media of the extreme right (Downing and Husband 2005). A nexus exists between the populist discourses of the extreme right and dominant discourses (Karim 1993; van Dijk 1993). Minority groups find themselves having to develop countervailing discourses to support their integrity. And due to their lack of access to the mainstream media, ethnic media often become the channels through which such resistance is expressed.

One of the major reasons for the existence of ethnic media is that the mass media primarily address the interests of the largest demographic groups and tend to exclude the cultural expressions of the smaller ones. Ethnic media are viewed as serving two primary purposes – they contribute to cultural maintenance and ethnic cohesion, and they help members of minorities integrate into the larger society (Riggins 1992; Husband 1994; Browne 2005). Newspapers are the most common form of these media. There are several hundred ethnic newspapers in Canada. They have large variations in form, quality, and frequency. Some are well-staffed established dailies that compete with mainstream papers; these print media usually have full-scale production facilities and strong advertising revenues. At the other end are very small operations run by enthusiastic individuals out of their homes – such ventures tend to have fairly irregular production cycles and are usually transitory. They appear and disappear quickly, only to be replaced by other similarly short-lived publications.

Governments strictly control the use of electromagnetic space for radio and television broadcasting, and there is strong competition for licences to enter this field. A significant number of ethnic broadcasters run programs on rented time slots with commercial operations' schedules or on community stations. Such slots on the schedules of existing operations are frequently at the most inconvenient times for their potential audiences. A number of stations devoted entirely to ethnic programming have obtained licences in Canada over the last two decades. Technologies such as satellite, digital, and subsidiary communication multiplex operation (SCMO) broadcasting are facilitating the proliferation of ethnic stations.

Internet-based media seem especially suited to the needs of ethnic communities. Increasing numbers of linguistic fonts can be accommodated through developments in software, and the structures of electronic systems are able to support ongoing communication in the widely scattered groups. The decentralized nature of on-line networks stands in contrast to the highly regulated and controlled model of broadcasting. Internet-based technologies are also interactive, relatively inexpensive, and easy to operate. They facilitate non-hierarchical organization as well as one-person operations, and lateral communication as opposed to the generally rigid top-down structures of the mass media. Ethnic groups are extensively using on-line media such as e-mail, Usenet, listserv, and the World Wide Web (including social networking programs), and are also publishing content on off-line digital formats such as CDs and DVDs.

This chapter looks at the ways in which ethnic media may be considered alternative. Before scrutinizing their placement and operation within the Canadian and diasporic contexts, one must understand how they relate to public spheres, ethnicity, and diasporic migration. Ethnic networks of communication are not confined to the borders of nation-states, and therefore it is also important to view them within the larger transnational contexts with which they have connections. The operation of ethnic media in Canada has been affected by the policy of multiculturalism, which is also examined below.

Public Sphere and Public Sphericules

If we are to understand the participation of ethnic media in the public sphere, it is necessary to unpack the latter concept. Habermas' (1989) notion of the ideal public sphere implies the existence of a largely monolithic civic discourse. This model was based on his perceptions of eighteenth-century Europe, where enlightened upper- and middle-class white men conducted discussions about public affairs. According to Habermas, these members of the bourgeoisie, who met regularly to converse in coffee houses, gave sole expression to civic discourse along with the newspapers owned by their socio-economic classes. Some of the most vigorous early challenges to these ideas came from feminist writers such as N. Fraser (1992) and Benhabib (1992). Criticizing the exclusion from the idealized space of civic discourse, they proposed decentred and heterogeneous models of the public sphere.

Highlighting the need to recognize cultural diversity in contemporary societies, postmodernist and post-colonial theories suggest more inclusive alternatives. Kalantzis (1995, 2) proposes a model of "civic pluralism," which "means that all people have access to political power, economic resources, social services, and most importantly, cultural symbols regardless of their cultural affiliations and styles." Her vision includes a national ethos based on the creative virtues of internal diversity, an outward-looking global perspective, a new relationship between the state and the citizen, the recognition of differences as productive resources, the state as a broker of symbolic and cultural capital, the use of media – especially digital media – to provide voices for minorities, and the overlapping of multiple communities of work, interest, affiliation, gender, and ethnicity.

Bhabha (1994) suggests that marginalized immigrant minorities operate in a "third space," distinct from the hegemonic public spheres of both the country of settlement and that of origin. This space allows for a high order of creativity and cutting-edge modernity. (For example, the phenomenal success of writers such as Salman Rushdie, V.S. Naipaul, Anita Desai, M.G. Vassanji, Rohinton Mistry, and Jhumpa Lahiri – all first-generation migrants to Western countries – appears to be indicative of such ingenuity.) D.T. Goldberg (1994) proposes the establishment of official spaces where institutions may negotiate relations between dominant and subordinate groups, thus allowing all citizens to participate in civic culture in a way denied under the concept of a monolithic public sphere.

But Gitlin (1998) laments the fragmentation of the public sphere into what he terms "public sphericules" that isolate the sole interests of those who occupy them. However, Cunningham and Sinclair (2000, 28) disagree with this pessimistic scenario: "In contrast, we argue that the emergence of ethnospecific global mediatised communities suggests that elements we would expect to find in 'the' public sphere are to be found in microcosm in these public sphericules. Such activities may constitute valid, and indeed dynamic, counterexamples to a discourse of decline and fragmentation, while taking full account of contemporary vectors of communication in a globalising, commercialising and pluralising world." The alternative messages of ethnic media unfold in sphericules bound primarily by ethnic interests but tend to overlap and interact with many others in the broader public sphere. Downing and Husband (2005) make Habermas' original concept much more reflective of the way in which multiple discussions take place in society between and across the various groups shaped not only by ethnicity, but by a range of social characteristics.

Ethnicity

Weber (1978, 389) remarked that "the whole conception of ethnic groups is so complex and so vague that it might be good to abandon it altogether." It is often used as a synonym for a series of terms that include tribe, race, and nation, all of which are similarly vague social constructions. Nevertheless, ethnicity remains a key concept in the social scientific study of human beings. It refers to the belief in a common ancestry of a particular group. Even though, in many cases, this belief has little basis in reality, it is significant because it forms the basis upon which individuals in the group organize their lives and the ways in which others deal with them. Classifications of ethnicity are also frequently imposed externally, as was carried out by European colonialism in various parts of the world.

Members of an ethnic group may also be viewed as having a common language, culture, religion, and/or history. But in many cases, people who consider themselves or whom others consider to be of a similar ethnicity have substantial linguistic, cultural, religious, and historical differences. On the other hand, they may share these characteristics with other collectivities to which they are not seen as being related. The concept of ethnicity is so diffuse that people of mixed ancestry may come to see themselves as single ethnic groups – for example, the emergence of "Canadian" and "American" ethnicities. Also, Muslims of different national origins living in Western countries are coming in certain contexts to be treated as a single ethnic grouping.

Some peoples identify respective territories upon which they make historical claims and to which they attach their names. Such claims are often consonant with aspirations of nationhood. *Ethnos,* the ancient Greek word from which the term "ethnic" is derived, denotes "nation." In fact, the concept of the nation-state, which emerged in seventeenth-century Europe, was based on the general idea of a shared ethnicity of the population that lived within a particular territory (Renan 1990; Smith 1989). Such notions have implied that all or the vast majority of people in a nation-state have the same language, culture, and religion. In reality, virtually no country's population is monolithic.

Whereas in the past there was a general reluctance to recognize minority groups as belonging within a nation, ideas of multiculturalism have promoted an acceptance of ethnic diversity. But what tends to emerge in many cases is the privileging of larger ethnic groups' language, culture, and religion over those of the smaller ones. Also, the ethnicity or race of dominant groups actually becomes invisible and is presented as the national norm, with the smaller groups being referred to as "ethnic groups" and "visible minorities." In Canada and the United States, the term "ethnic" as opposed to "race" has been used to distinguish dominant European-origin groups from non-dominant ones. Hierarchies and "us versus them" polarities are maintained in these manners within nations among various peoples who are identified according to their perceived ethnicity or race.

Migration, Diaspora, and Globalization

Contemporary changes in the idea of the nation are occurring in a time when transnational communications are increasingly enabling individuals and communities to remain in touch across the seas. The telephone, Internet, satellite television, and other media help construct a web of connections among ethnic diasporas living in various parts of the world, making them more resistant to assimilation into national populations. These "transnations," as Appadurai (1996, 172) terms them, extend around the planet with the help of modern-day communications. Giving the example of the US, but citing what is almost universally true, he notes, "No existing conception of Americanness can contain this large variety of transnations." They reside in one country but also straddle many others. Ethnic groups and their media within national contexts cannot be fully understood without standing back to look at the larger picture of their diasporic connections.

The word diaspora is derived from the ancient Greek *diaspeirein*, which refers to the scattering of seeds. Diaspora has come to denote the existence of a particular ethnic group in a number of countries and continents. Diasporas are frequently described as "imagined communities" (De Santis 2003; Tsaliki 2003). Borrowing from Benedict Anderson's (1983) description of nation-states, this characterization emphasizes both the improbability of first-hand acquaintance of all members of the group with each other and their adherence to a common set of cultural references. Diasporic links are enhanced by the simultaneous consumption of the same media content by members of a global community. However, as with an ethnic group, membership within a particular diaspora is based on a belief about a common descent whose veracity is often obscured by the mists of time.

Unlike nations, which are traditionally placed within a defined location, transnations are deterritorialized communities. Migration removes the diasporic members from the homeland, but they transport with them its imaginary, which they frequently invoke in their lands of settlement. (Some view themselves as exiles, dreaming of returning to the ancestral home some time in the future.) This contributes to their desire for media content and other cultural products that celebrate their emotional links to the old country.

However, cultural goods and services do not originate solely from the homeland, but are exchanged in the worldwide networks of settlements that constitute the transnations (Cunningham and Nguyen 2003). For some groups, politics in the homeland or in other parts of the diaspora are of abiding interest, especially in times of crisis (Bunt 2003). Media are often used to mobilize support for the homeland causes (Hassanpour 2003; Santianni 2003). The utilization of media by transnations challenges the incorporation of immigrant groups into the countries of settlement. But, before we examine this issue further, it is useful to explore the relationship of diasporic cultures with global structures and globalization.

The large migrations of the eighteenth, nineteenth, and early twentieth centuries were a consequence of colonization and trading connections as well as of the steady improvements in transportation. More recent human flows from Africa, Asia, and Latin America to Europe, North America, and Australasia seem to have been prompted in part by the economic involvement of the latter in the former. The off-shoring of production, foreign investment in export-oriented agriculture, and the power of multinationals in the consumer markets of developing countries have often led to mass movements of people (Sassen 1996).

These movements have created diasporas, members of which are located around the world. However, the characteristics of all such transnations are not the same; indeed, major differences exist even within respective diasporas. Complex historical, social, and cultural dynamics in specific groups have shaped varied identities. Mandaville (2003, 135) views these communities as being continually "constructed, debated and reimagined." In order to appreciate better how individual diasporians situate their own selves, researchers need to understand how worldwide communities are internally layered according to periods of migration, the historical receptivity of societies to various waves of migration, and the continuation of the diaspora's links with the home country and with other parts of the transnation. These sociological factors have produced a range of differences in the strength of such groups' internal and external attachments. The characteristics of diasporas are also shaped by factors such as the extent of the retention of ancestral customs, language and religion, marriage patterns, and the ability to communicate within the diaspora.

Multiculturalism policies tend erroneously to view members of immigrant communities as having engaged in a one-way move that broke all ties with their past. Migrants often follow non-linear routes, frequently backtracking and returning to particular locales in sequences that vary between persons and groups. As well as having multifarious connections with their land of origin, worldwide diasporas develop intricate networks linking their various settlements. The resulting identities are complex and dynamic – sharing different cultural characteristics with specific parts of their transnational community and simultaneously with the national populations of which they have become a part.

Canadian Multiculturalism and Ethnic Media

In 1971, Canada became the first country to initiate a multiculturalism policy and is presently the only country to have a full-fledged multiculturalism act of Parliament, passed in 1988 (Canada 1988). Although the policy remains contentious, its origins in Canada are reflective of the history of relationships between its various peoples. Multiculturalism has validated the public presence of cultural diversity in Canada, particularly in the country's institutions. Over two hundred ethnic origins were reported by the total population of Canada in the 2006 census; this included eleven that had passed the 1 million mark (Statistics Canada 2008, 5-6). Whereas the languages and cultures derived from its British and French ethnic groups remain dominant, room has been made for others in certain expressions of public life. Multiculturalism does not stand on its own but is integral to the Canadian state's overall social policy framework, which addresses broader issues of pluralism. A number of other actors have helped to give form to the policy. Civil society has been vital to the institutionalization of pluralism in Canada. This includes the work of ethnocultural groups, social organizations, social entrepreneurs, academia, artists, and media. The Canadian Ethnic Media Association, for example, represents the interests of members who are engaged professionally in print and electronic media as well as creative writing.

Ethnic media have had a long history of ensuring diversity of coverage in this country. This had engaged numerous entrepreneurs either working alone or in teams. Ethnic media have grown significantly in Canada over the last decade. They range from small newspapers run from home basements to well-established and professionally run broadcast stations. Most of them have substantial diasporic content. Third-language media are also the only source of information on matters such as public health, education, training, job seeking, and business opportunities for many newcomers who have not obtained proficiency in one of the two official languages. However, a significant number of ethnic media appear in English or French. Most ethnic newspapers across the country publish on a weekly or monthly cycle. Some larger dailies include the Chinese-language *Ming Pao, Sing Tao,* and *World Journal,* and the Italian *Corriere Canadese.* Ethnic print organs are becoming increasingly sophisticated in terms of operation and content, and in some cases compete directly with non-ethnic newspapers.

Whereas ethnic programming has been present in Canada for more than half a century, the primarily third-language CHIN Radio (established in 1966) and OMNI Television (which arose from CFMT – "Canada's First Multicultural Television," established in 1979) have been pioneers. A unique approach to ethnic broadcasting has developed in this country under official multiculturalism. The Multiculturalism Act proclaims the federal government's policy to recognize the diverse cultures of Canadian society. In the same vein, the Broadcasting Act asserts that the Canadian broadcasting system should reflect the diversity of the country's cultures. The Canadian Radio-television and Telecommunications Commission (CRTC), which introduced an Ethnic Broadcasting Policy in 1985 (revised in 1999), specifies the conditions under which the dissemination of ethnic and multilingual programming can be carried out.

The policy is based on section 3(d)(iii) of the Broadcasting Act (Canada 1991), which states that the Canadian broadcasting system should reflect the circumstances and aspirations of Canadians, including the multicultural and multiracial nature of Canadian society: "As one way of furthering this objective, the Commission has licensed ethnic television and radio broadcasters that specialize in providing ethnic programming. Ethnic programming is programming directed to any culturally or racially distinct group other than one that is Aboriginal Canadian, or from France or the British Isles. Such programming may be in any language or combination of languages" (CRTC 1999a). According to the licences that the CRTC dispenses under this policy, radio and television stations are required to devote at least 60 percent of their schedule to ethnic programming.

The federal Cabinet has also indicated an interest in enhancing ethnic broadcasting in Canada. The minister for the Department of Canadian Heritage, within her limited authority to give directives to the CRTC, asked the commission in 1988 to reserve the next available radio frequency in the Greater Toronto Area (GTA) for use in promoting the "multicultural and multiracial nature of Canadian society" (Saunders 1988). Cabinet also issued two Orders-in-Council in 2000 asking the CRTC to report on the future establishment of a television service in Greater Vancouver and a radio service in the GTA that would meet the needs of minority audiences (CRTC 2000a, 2000b). In both cases the government referred to the growing linguistic and cultural diversity of the metropolitan areas.

Ethnic radio programming is present in most Canadian cities of significant size (for example, see Murray, Yu, and Ahadi 2007). This includes time slots acquired on mainstream stations, community radio, and campus radio, as well as twenty-four-hour multilingual broadcasters such as CHIN in Toronto and Ottawa. The CRTC has granted several ethnic AM and FM licences in metropolitan areas as well as a number of Aboriginal station licences. SCMO technology has allowed several third-language stations operating on sub-carrier frequencies to emerge in various cities. However, subscribers need to acquire specialized radio equipment to access this programming. Ethnic and multilingual television content is provided by the multicultural channels OMNI (Ontario, BC, and Alberta) and CJNT (Montréal), but it can also be found in various time slots on community cable, commercial stations, and a national network (Vision TV). The Aboriginal Peoples Television Network, which is national in scope, was established in 1999. Various specialty television services in languages including Arabic, Chinese, Farsi, Greek, Hindi, Italian, Korean, Polish, Portuguese, Punjabi, Russian, Spanish, Tagalog, Tamil, Ukrainian, Urdu, and Vietnamese are available on a national basis via satellite and digital cable services. These Canadian channels carry a blend of programming produced in this country and in other parts of their respective diasporas. A growing number of foreign-based services are available in some cable packages.

However, the CRTC has dealt with competing ethnic and religious interests in a number of licence applications. Telelatino, the national Italian and Spanish specialty TV channel, opposed the arrival of RAI, the Italian state-owned public service broadcaster, on national cable services in Canada (Canadian TV Forums

2003), arguing that its market share would be substantially diminished. However, RAI's bid was successful in 2005 following a petition by Italian Canadians and pressure from the Italian government. The Canadian Jewish Congress (2004) opposed the application of Al Jazeera, on the basis of the broadcaster's perceived anti-Semitism. The Qatar-based Arabic-language channel had strong support from Arab Canadians. Although the CRTC granted the licence, it imposed onerous monitoring conditions on the carrier, which effectively dissuaded any cable company from offering it. Al Jazeera's English-language service was approved by the regulator in 2009 without similar conditions. Falun Dafa (Canada 2006) and Tibetan organizations (Little and Chan 2008) protested the permission granted to China's CCTV also to be made available in this country.

Yu and Murray's (2007) study of Korean media in British Columbia found little Canada-related content. However, some ethnic media provide extensive coverage of Canadian current affairs and other information that would help members of minorities remain informed about the larger society (Karim, Eid, and de B'béri 2007). This type of coverage would presumably also promote integration into the Canadian public sphere and encourage active citizenship. However, not all ethnic media offer such information. The smaller the publication or broadcast production, the lesser the likelihood that civic discourse relating to Canada will be carried. A primary goal of most ethnic media seems to be to provide cultural and informational programming related to the respective community, which is generally unavailable in Canadian mass media. Once this goal is met, the medium can use additional available time or space for discussions about Canada-related public affairs.

Whereas relatively little research exists on Canadian ethnic media, there are some indications of the alternative discourses that they support. Mazepa's (2003) study of the Ukrainian press in the first half of the twentieth century indicates a great diversity in ideological positions. There were active sections of the pro-communist, nationalist, and religious press. Mazepa sees Ukrainian Canadian newspapers playing an important role in the development of collective activism. The pro-communist press viewed conditions in both Canada and Ukraine through the perspectives of the national and international exploitation of labour, and during wartime it emphasized commitments to pacifism and anti-fascism. Women's political participation was also encouraged by the pro-communist Ukrainian Canadian press.

Punjabi-language newspapers in British Columbia championed the cause of Indian independence in the early twentieth century (Tatla 1991). This was contrary to the interests of the British Empire, which was generally supported

in the mainstream Canadian media of the day. Later, in the 1980s, elements of
the Punjabi press supported the cause of the separatist state of Khalistan in
India. Given the acts of terrorism that Khalistan supporters are believed to have
perpetrated, this was viewed as extremely controversial (Bolan 2005), raising a
question about the categorization of alternative media: do they include radical media?

On the other hand, several South Asian media in BC have significant coverage of mainstream provincial and federal politics, mirroring the active participation of South Asian politicians in these parts of the public sphere (Karim
2002). Several ethnic media expressed strong opposition to the anti-terrorism
legislation proposed by the federal government in 2001. These included newspapers such as *India Abroad,* the *South Asian Voice,* and *Share* (an African Canadian publication), and the on-line vehicles of the Canadian Islamic Congress
and the Council on American-Islamic Relations–Canada (Karim 2003). This was
certainly an alternative discourse, especially in the aftermath of the terrorist
attacks of 11 September 2001, when the mainstream media tended to favour
strong security measures.

Ethnic media are not only sites for expressions of alterity vis-à-vis mainstream media. Competitions between discourses also occur within them, reflecting internal differences of opinion within communities. Bernard's (2008)
study of present-day Tamil-language radio programs in the GTA reveals the
tensions between various sections of their listeners. An attempt by young
Tamils to address issues of caste discrimination raised the hackles of some
members of the audience. The owners of the station subsequently put an end
to the program. This attempt to promote alternative discourses was thus
stopped by the social conservatism of the owners.

The lines between mainstream and ethnic media have become blurred in
some cases. Torstar, the proprietor of Canada's largest circulation daily, the
Toronto Star, publishes *Desi Life,* a South Asian magazine. It also owns part of
Sing Tao, whose other owner is a Hong Kong–based media corporation. *Ming
Pao* and *World Journal,* the other Chinese dailies in Canada, are also owned by
foreign corporate interests as is one of the largest South Asian newspapers,
India Abroad. "Canada's First Multicultural Television" (CFMT) was bought by
Rogers and expanded into markets outside Ontario as OMNI. However, it
should be noted that CFMT also relied on mainstream programming in prime
time to remain financially viable. Nevertheless, these and other ethnic media
continue to draw readers and audiences. They are also engaged in promoting
the participation of minorities in the larger public sphere. But with corporate

ownership come limits on the extent to which alternative discourses can be expressed in these media.

Diasporic Media

Until the early 1990s, the global flows of communication were almost completely controlled by media companies owned by states or large private corporations. Whereas their domination still continues, many more voices are being heard transnationally. New technologies and certain aspects of globalization have enabled diasporas to engage in lateral communication among their members and with others. Transnational ethnic-based commercial broadcasting infrastructures are becoming increasingly integral to the global economy. This touches on the question of whether diasporic media are alternative or part of dominant structures. The answer is that, due to their heterogeneity, they have a relationship with both.

Ethnic media have extended operations within countries and across borders. Niche marketers look upon advertising in ethnic radio and television as a way to reach growing minority populations in a time of fragmenting audiences. The two largest Spanish-language US networks, Univisión and Telemundo, are available across the US and are watched avidly by the fast-growing Spanish-speaking population (A. Rodriguez 2000; Dávila 2001). However, obtaining space for ethnic broadcasters in the electromagnetic spectrum has involved a continual struggle with national regulators. For example, in the early 1990s, France's centre-right government actively encouraged the exclusion of Arabic stations from cable networks. In response, many Maghrebi immigrant families subscribed to satellite television for programming from Arab countries (Hargreaves and Mahdjoub 1997).

The relatively small and scattered nature of the communities they serve has encouraged diasporic media to seek out the most efficient and cost-effective means of communication. Technologies that allow for narrowcasting to target audiences rather than those that provide for mass communication have generally been favoured. As a result, ethnic media have often been at the leading edge of technology adoption. As Gillespie (1995, 79) notes of the Indian community in Southhall, England, many families obtained VCRs as early as 1978 "well before most households in Britain." In Mexico, videotape became the means to increase television program exports to the Hispanic geo-cultural region. Later, satellite technology was used to interconnect the various Spanish-language TV stations throughout the US (see Dávila 2001).

Whereas governments in developing and developed countries have expressed fears that direct broadcast satellites (DBS) would erode their sovereignty by transmitting foreign programming to their populations in unregulated manners, this technology provides remarkable opportunities for diasporic communities. Ethnic broadcasters, previously having limited access to the electromagnetic spectrum, find far greater options opening up due to DBS. Diasporic programming using this technology has grown exponentially, well ahead of many mainstream broadcasters. Even as mainstream networks in Europe were making plans to introduce digital broadcasting, the Arab-owned and operated Orbit TV in Rome had begun by 1994 to provide extensive programming via DBS to Arab communities both in Europe and the Middle East.

One of the most fascinating uses of DBS technology in the Middle Eastern context is MED-TV, a Kurdish satellite television station (Hassanpour 2003). Several other Kurdish stations have been established in the wake of MED-TV's success. This is a case of a diaspora within and without the divided homeland attempting to counter forceful suppression and to sustain itself through the use of communications technology. MED-TV has faced resistance not only from governments of the various states straddling Kurdistan, but also from anti-terrorist police forces in the UK, Belgium, and Germany. It was determined to provide a view that differed from the dominant global discourses about Kurdish identity.

Quite apart from the DBS television offered by global conglomerates such as Rupert Murdoch's Star TV, which beams programming to several Asian countries, a number of diasporic DBS-based networks now serve Asian diasporas. The Chinese Television Network, headquartered in Hong Kong, has been broadcasting to East Asia, Australia, the Pacific Islands, and the United States since 1994. Hong Kong's Television Broadcasts International "reaches into several Asian markets and to Chinese communities just about everywhere" (Berfield 1997, 31; also see Sun 2002). The London-based Chinese Channel's programs are received in the UK and in continental Europe. Among various transnational satellite services from India, Zee TV has emerged as a very popular global Indian network (Thussu 2000, 197-99). Satellite TV service providers in the US have realized the viability of diasporic channels and are making them an integral part of their services. This, in fact, contributes to their mainstreaming.

With the availability of new communication technologies, diasporas are increasingly able to obtain cultural materials from elsewhere in the world. A number of ethnic television broadcasters export their programming to other parts of the diaspora; for example, Canada's weekly Vision TV program *Aspire*, produced by a group of South Asian diasporics in Toronto, is regularly re-broadcast in Guyana and the US. On a much larger scale, almost all cable systems in Latin America carry either Telemundo or Univisión. The picture that Latin Americans see of American society in these North-South news flows is different from that presented by US networks such as CNN or by global TV news agencies such as Reuters because the two US-based Spanish-language networks also seek out Hispanic perspectives on national news stories. However, A. Rodriguez (2000), who studied Univisión's content, argues that its news values are similar to those of the mainstream American broadcasters.

The ability to exchange messages with individuals on the other side of the planet and to have access to community information through the Internet almost instantaneously changes the dynamics of diasporas by allowing for qualitatively and quantitatively enhanced linkages. Diasporic websites already contain global directories of individuals, community institutions, and businesses owned by members of diasporas. Some sites have hypertext links to sites of alumni associations. The availability of on-line versions of newspapers from countries of origin further enhances intercontinental connections. As the number of language scripts and translation capabilities of on-line software grows, non-English speakers are increasingly drawn to the medium.

Many websites and blogs catering to transnational communities enable individuals to participate in global conversations. Discussions range over topics that include culture, literature, entertainment, politics, and current events in the countries of origin and settlement. Indeed, the electronic chat room becomes the "place" where some members of global communities come together to reconstitute the relationships that existed before migration. Social networks such as Facebook and MySpace are also allowing diasporic members to connect with each other. Although cyberspace does not allow for the same level of interaction as face-to-face meetings, it enables communication to a much greater extent than was previously possible for scattered groupings of people. Indeed, information about reunions, festivals, and worldwide locations of community institutions facilitates the physical gathering of diasporic individuals. Current events and new publications of materials relating to the transnational group are regularly discussed in on-line news groups and blog chat rooms. All these forms add to the growing knowledge base of the diaspora as it interacts within itself and with others.

Diasporic cybercommunities centred on very specific topics attempt to bring communal knowledge to bear on contemporary issues. Chat groups allow for people interested in these topics to communicate from any place where they have access to the Internet. Santianni (2003) discusses how Tibetan Buddhists have used universalist human rights discourses on the Internet to obtain Western support for their nationalist cause. Shams is a news group that enables discussion of issues relating to the rights of women in Muslim law; Bol is a listserv for issues of gender, reproductive health, and human rights in South Asia; and KoreanQ, also a listserv, caters to lesbian and bisexual women of Korean heritage. These examples point toward the dovetailing of particularist and universalist interests in ethnic media.

Cooperative arrangements between young professionals who have recently left China and who work in high technology sectors in Canada, the US, and the UK have led to the emergence of on-line magazines that express their particular concerns (Qiu 2003). These new arrivals feel that their information needs are not met by the content of the thriving print and broadcast Chinese ethnic media, which are produced largely by older groups of immigrants from China. Despite being separated by great distances and, in most cases, not having met each other, the virtual editorial teams are electronically publishing regular issues that cover events happening in the homeland and the Chinese diaspora. However, the content of these publications tends to be conservative and cannot be characterized as alternative.

A number of diasporic websites are designed to correct what are considered misperceptions by outsiders and to mobilize external political support. Several web pages of the transnational Roma ("gypsies"), who have been vilified for centuries in many countries, function in this manner. Guillermo Gómez-Peña, a Mexican commentator on issues of cultural hybridity, has extended his postmodernist literary and artistic criticism to cyberspace in a deliberate effort to confront the hegemonic structures of knowledge production and to respond to their globally dominant images of Chicano identity. The Council on American-Islamic Relations and the Canadian Islamic Congress run electronic mailing lists that provide updates on issues affecting Muslims, and they encourage subscribers to lobby relevant media, community, and government organizations to redress what they view as unjust treatment. Several groups also use on-line media to challenge hate propaganda and to carry out polemics against other websites. Some anti-government organizations have taken even stronger action with the use of electronic technology. From time to time, Tamil activists have electronically disabled the websites of several Sri Lankan embassies that they viewed as disseminating propaganda. The speed of simultaneous worldwide demonstrations in March 1999 by Kurdish protestors, who reacted immediately to the capture of a guerrilla leader by Turkish forces, was the result of the Internet links maintained by that global community. From the perspective of the state, such uses of media would probably be moving beyond the alternative to the subversive.

Although some diasporic websites do carry scholarly and archival material, their major strength lies in functioning as interactive repositories of cultural knowledge. In facilitating global accessibility to Asian, Latin American, and African views of the world, community on-line networks provide a small but important counterweight to the enormous production and export capacities of the cultural industries of developed countries. This becomes a way to mitigate the effects of cultural imperialism and to foster worldwide cultural diversity. A primary motivation for immigrant communities to go on-line seems to be survival in the face of the overwhelming output of the dominant culture and the limitations of immigrants' access to the cultural industries in their countries of settlement. In these ways, isolated members of diasporas who are using on-line media participate to some extent in cultural production rather than merely consuming media content. It is difficult to see how such media enterprises could be co-opted by mainstream media.

The opportunity that Internet-based media create for users to participate in producing materials appears to allow them to circumvent the hierarchical mass media as well as to counter material from dominant government and commercial sources. However, even though the use of on-line media and DBS is increasing around the world, there remain wide differences in how various ethnic groups employ them. As we move beyond North America, Europe, and Australia, the ownership of computer hardware and subscription to Internet services falls dramatically. Ethnic-based programming on DBS uses a market model and is targeted at fairly affluent members of various diasporas. Mainstream companies are increasingly interested in ethnic media, with corporations such as CBS acquiring Telemundo (renamed TeleNoticias) and Rupert Murdoch's expanding empire to reach South Asian audiences in the UK. As ethnic broadcasters become successful, they are increasingly identified as targets for takeovers by global media conglomerates.

Conclusion

Ethnic and diasporic media occupy a diverse universe that offers a very broad range of content. Their primary goal is to provide what they view as the information needs of their readers and audiences. Insofar as they enable marginalized minorities to participate in society, they do form an alternative to the mainstream media. Ethnicity also becomes the ground from which to resist hegemony, especially that which seeks to diminish ethnocultural pluralism. However, the inclinations of a few ethnic media to promote ethnocentrism and even racism compromise this effort. It is gratifying that the Canadian experience does not bring forth many examples of this kind.

Canadian multiculturalism has facilitated the autonomy of minority cultures and growth of their media. Its promotion of integration (rather than assimilation) also encourages participation in the larger society and adherence to universal values. Whereas the content of most ethnic media in Canada reflects communal and homeland concerns, a number of outlets engage with the larger society. They inform their readers and audiences about Canadian history and institutions, and also use media as tools to stimulate participation in the political sphere. They have fostered dialogue on issues such as labour and human rights, speaking from universalist positions that rise above their particularisms. Ethnic radio talk shows highlight important social issues that often remain unaired in communities. The concern, however, is that whereas some of the ethnic public sphericules intersect with that of the larger society, others do not due to differences in language and culture or due to tendencies toward isolationism. Multiculturalism has not been able to resolve this issue.

Nor has it sufficiently recognized the transnational connections of ethnic groups. Diasporas seek to overcome the restrictions of national borders and maintain networks that span continents. The far-flung dispersal of their communities often leads them to become early adopters of communications technologies that enhance their abilities to remain in touch with each other. Whereas they are part of globalizing processes, they are also pursuing alternative forms of transnationalism that attempt to assert their own particular interests. The cultural flows being facilitated by the Internet and satellite technologies work in favour of the circulation of materials that are usually neglected by Western state and corporate entities. In this, diasporic media have become major players in countering cultural imperialism. However, in some cases the larger transnational media networks, such as those of people with origins in India and China, may be overwhelming others and producing newer manifestations of cultural imperialism.

The picture that emerges of ethnic and diasporic media is fairly complex. They operate at multiple levels – spatial, cultural, and ideological. The answer to the question, are ethnic media alternative? is not simple. They challenge the conceptualization of the alternative. Clearly, they differ from mainstream media; however, some of them are becoming increasingly allied with them.

On the other hand, their multiple manifestations continue to provide newer and hybrid ways of engaging with society. They represent one of the fastest-growing segments of the media, nationally and internationally, and thus bear watching. Their future appears to hold an intriguing potential for creative engagements with the alternative.

The space in which ethnic media are alternative is where they engage with issues relating to social justice. Highlighting societal and institutional prejudice, discrimination, and marginalization contributes to the broader effort to ensure justice for all. The discourses of a significant number of ethnic media frequently address human rights at large, since they recognize that their own claim to equity and access draws on a universalist worldview. There is considerable room for alternative media that pursue other issues to make common cause with like-minded ethnic media. Commitment to social justice and the end to discrimination of all types, already a hallmark of non-ethnic alternative vehicles, could encourage contributions from writers who are engaged in ethnic media. Collaborative efforts in sharing resources to reduce production costs in several locations – especially small towns – would enable alternative media of various kinds, including print, broadcast, and Internet-based ethnic operations, to build sufficiently large user groups. This becomes especially important in economically difficult times. The consolidation of infrastructure as well as advertising among coalitions of this kind can be vital for survival. Such collaboration that brings together a diverse range of ideas and creativity leads to the development of broad communities of alternative media organizations and workers. They would have a greater potential of preventing vulnerable media from being swallowed up by media conglomerates that diminish their expressions of alternative views of the world.

Indigenous Media as Alternative Media
Participation and Cultural Production

MARIAN BREDIN

In Canada, the trajectories of alternative and indigenous media share several points of convergence and divergence. This chapter focuses on the historical emergence of Canadian indigenous media and considers the factors that made alternative and indigenous media possible. It reviews several points of comparison and contrast over time and discusses those common factors that continue to make them both vulnerable, while highlighting those that make indigenous media distinctive. This is followed by a brief overview of the political economy of indigenous media in Canada, which frames a more detailed examination of both the structures of participation and cultural production within three specific media organizations: Igloolik Isuma film and video production company, Wawatay Radio Network (WRN), and the Aboriginal Peoples Television Network (APTN).

Alternative and Indigenous Media Histories

In the early period of local, low-cost, low-tech, non-professional media use, Native, non-Native, urban, and remote community radio and television were treated alike. Seen as experimental and transitory, these alternative media drew on a variety of funding sources and were subject to minimal regulation. Indications that Aboriginal, or indigenous, media would develop separately came as early as 1974, with a satellite communications experiment in northern

Native communities called the Northern Pilot Project (NPP).[1] Specific federal policies and programs for Native broadcasting did not begin to crystallize until 1983. During this period, the term "Native communication" was gradually replaced by "Aboriginal broadcasting." In reference to the global experience of colonized peoples in settler societies, the term "indigenous media" is now more commonly used to refer to local and culturally specific use of media by Aboriginal peoples. The Canadian history of indigenous media can be compared to its global development, especially in Australia and Latin America. Indigenous people in Canada share the technological, social, and cultural factors that generated movements for indigenous rights and autonomous indigenous media in other countries. As Wilson and Stewart (2008) explain, the emergence of indigenous activism was organized around concepts of the Fourth World and internal colonialism within settler societies in the latter third of the twentieth century. As the contributors to Wilson and Stewart's anthology on global indigenous media clearly demonstrate, the multiple instances of local indigenous media activism share some common practices with other forms of alternative and community media.

Although Aboriginal communities in Canada have unique communication needs, their media practices are similar to those of community and alternative media on university campuses, in small towns, among urban communities of interest, and in minority ethnic and linguistic communities (see Chapters 6 and 7 in this volume). Current broadcasting policy identifies distinct categories of Native broadcasting: campus and community radio, ethnic or multilingual broadcasting, and cable community television. These categories are treated separately by regulators and funding agencies, they are situated differently within public and private sectors, and they engage public interests, market forces, and technological imperatives in varying combinations depending on locale. It is thus difficult to speak of a homogeneous alternative media or community sector, despite several commonalities.

Alternative and indigenous media both emerged out of post-war Canadian social formations. The 1960s and 1970s were characterized by extensions of the welfare state into Aboriginal communities that included liberal policies of assimilation embodied in documents such as the 1969 *White Paper on Indian Policy*, "culture of poverty" models, and modernization strategies that were imposed upon Native communities.[2] These liberal ideologies and policies of the settler state had the unintended consequences of contributing to the political organization of Native people and the rise of cultural activism, along with demands for media access.

Beyond Native communities, affordable volunteer-operated media were first established in the 1960s using new technologies such as portable video, low-power FM, and local cable networks. Early media projects took advantage of funds from federal programs such as Opportunities for Youth, the Local Initiatives Program, and the Company of Young Canadians, whose terms of reference were very broadly defined within the context of "participatory democracy" (Wilkinson and Associates 1988, 7). Local media experiments in Québec were more explicitly shaped by what Raboy (1981, 4) refers to as "alternative communication practices" – the strategic use of media by activists and labour groups, already organized around specific political and economic objectives.

Community Media: From Innovation to Regulation

The experimental movement in low-tech local media interventions reached a peak during the 1970s. By the end of that decade, the social configurations of new technologies such as portable audio and video, low-power FM, and cable television had become more stable. Local media experimentations were captured within the CRTC's regulatory framework and codified in policy statements. During the same period, Canadian communications policy shifted from a passing concern with small-scale recording and distribution techniques to a preoccupation with the implications of satellite technology, cultural industries, telecommunications infrastructures, and the profitability of private broadcasting. In 1980, the transfer of jurisdiction over cultural agencies from the Secretary of State to the newly created Department of Communication marked the merging of goals for broadcasting with those for industrial development. Mitchell (1988, 169) argues that this was partly a response to the unintended political consequences of the earlier emphasis on local cultural development models. This conjuncture was further reinforced by the findings of the 1982 Federal Cultural Policy Review Committee (the Applebaum-Hébert committee), which mounted a substantial critique of public sector cultural institutions. The Department of Communication followed this up with a series of policy papers in 1983 that advocated the market as a more effective means of achieving public policy goals for communication (Collins 1986, 93; Canada 1983). As a result of these shifts, community and indigenous media were somewhat arrested in their progress, as no clear mandate for their inclusion within the public sector and no decisive definition of their role at the community level emerged from this period.

Community radio developed many common characteristics across Canada, with variations according to the size of community served and the linguistic and cultural content of programs. In 1985, the CRTC issued a definition of a community radio station that remains relatively unchanged in the 2000 policy revision (CRTC 2000d). This definition identified community radio as "owned and controlled by a non-profit organization whose structure provides for membership, management, operation, and programming primarily by members of the community at large" (CRTC 1985, 5). The 1980s were characterized by a contradictory policy and funding environment for community media. Community radio was primarily dependent on government grants, generating inevitable conflicts between the bureaucratic criteria of the granting agency and the objectives of the media practitioners. In Québec, as Light reviews in Chapter 7 of this volume, community radio funds were tied to cultural development. In the North, funding for local and regional media was implicitly linked to job creation and economic development agendas. Northern Native community radio networks created during early satellite and telecommunications experiments, for example, were made possible only by the broader demand for satellite infrastructure for resource exploitation and administration in the region. The contradictions arising from the reliance on government funding follow from the fact that few programs are dedicated specifically to the development and support of community radio.

Today, community radio includes provincially funded stations in Québec, local member-funded stations in the rest of Canada, campus-community stations, minority francophone community stations in Ontario, and Native community stations. Each type of community radio draws on different combinations of public funds and commercial revenue. In size, transmission power, and operating budget, community radio stations range from ten-watt stations in tiny isolated Native villages, with no paid staff and minimal operating costs covered by band council grants and radio bingo, to several thousand-watt stations in Montréal and Toronto, with paid managers, producers, and technicians, and combined revenues from grants, advertising, and on-air funding drives. What these stations have in common is that some or all of the programming is done by volunteers, and administrative structures within the station – boards, committees, general meetings – allow volunteers and the community or group they represent some degree of participation its operation.

Native community radio and regional Aboriginal radio and television networks represent the most distinctive elements of the heterogeneous community

sector. Many Native community radios operate as the sole service in their remote communities, and though the lack of funding, training, and technical
resources is challenging, there is little pressure toward commercialization.
Native community radio was already established in many areas before the arrival of commercial broadcasting and satellite service. Native media broadcast
in a variety of indigenous languages and function as a truly local information
source. They are treated separately for most policy purposes, but motivations
and aspirations similar to those in non-Native community broadcasting are
sometimes overlooked. Fragmented policy agendas for community media in
their multiple forms have inhibited the creation of any clear priorities for this
sector and have prevented its entrenchment as a valuable component of the
national broadcasting system.

Community cable television channels also emerged from the experimental
attitude of policy-makers and regulators during the 1970s, but their development differed from that of community radio because of their distinct technological and economic situation. The case of community cable TV is a good
illustration of how the critical potential of local alternative media has been
constrained by commercial imperatives and the lack of accountability (see
Chapter 6 in this volume). The difference between community television and
community radio is that the channel itself is not owned and directed by the
volunteer producers, but by the cable company. The cable operator is responsible to the CRTC for the program content on the community channel and to
its shareholders for turning a profit. Although cable subscribers pay for the
channel, there is no direct relationship between the cable company's profits in
any given community and citizens' access to the local channel. Salter (1988,
246) refers to the cable community channel as an example of "privatized public
broadcasting" because though it carries mainly local programming and almost
no advertising, it is financially supported by the cable company. Thus, "the responsibility for determining what is in the public interest falls to a private corporation." Despite this inherent conflict between local needs and private profit,
urban indigenous groups have used cable channel programming very effectively, especially in Western Canadian cities.

The model of the cable access channel converges with the history of indigenous broadcasting in some important ways. Before the creation of Aboriginal television networks such as Television Northern Canada (TVNC) and
Aboriginal Peoples Television Network (APTN), indigenous television in the
North functioned as a kind of community access model.[3] Regional Native

communications societies made television programming that was then incorporated into the schedule of existing TV services such as CBC Northern Service, Cancom, and TVO. Although the Native production groups had direct control over the content and design of their programs, they were subject to the commercial imperatives of the distributor and often relegated to the late night and Sunday morning time slots. This model of limited access to existing channels, whose programming priorities and commercial strategies do not include local or indigenous content, reflects Salter's argument about the privatized public sphere.

It might be argued that APTN's mandatory carriage on basic cable represents a similar form of community access in a national multi-channel environment. In this context, the guarantee of direct income from cable subscriber fees gives APTN a degree of economic and political independence not possible for community cable channels, Native communications societies, or even TVNC. Yet notions of access need to be complemented with analyses of accountability and control: accountability must be defined not only in terms of consultation, participation, or audience response, but on the basis of transparency of decision making and program planning to all community members.

Like all alternative media, concepts such as "democratization" and "participation" are difficult to actualize, and ways of linking audiences and communities to procedures of accountability need to be fully worked out in local contexts. These concerns are as valid in indigenous communities as in any other, and they cut across differing technologies, whether film, broadcasting, or the Internet. The claims for alternative media's radical potential might thus be localized in an effort to express specific needs and to create structures that locate control of media firmly within particular groups. The remaining question is whether communities are most successfully mobilized by media, or whether other instruments of change (such as education, economic development, and political action) are ultimately more effective, but these are not mutually exclusive.

Creating the Conditions of Possibility for Indigenous Media in Canada

Ginsburg (2002) and other media anthropologists recognize that most indigenous groups, whatever their location, live under neo-colonial conditions of territorial dispossession, political suppression, and introduced diseases, and have histories of cultural genocide and economic dependence on the state.

Ginsburg locates the emergence of indigenous media as an integral part of political resistance and self-determination movements. She is explicit about the ways in which media are used by Fourth World groups – indigenous minorities in settler societies such as Australia, New Zealand, and South and North America – as a form of what she calls cultural activism. Media are employed to transmit and transform traditional cultural knowledge in these contexts. Ginsburg (ibid., 230) sees indigenous media as a form of cultural invention that, like the post-colonial concept of hybridity, "refracts and recombines elements from both the dominant and minority societies."

Canadian indigenous media reflect a condensation of complex histories, networks of power, and discursive constructions of Aboriginal identity, cultural contact, and technological change. Southern-originated radio and television programming was first introduced to many of the isolated communities in the northern parts of the provinces and the territories when they had access to few other forms of public communication. Northern indigenous people were already exposed to established institutions of the settler society and participated in religious missions, colonial economies, and the extraction of resources. The missions and compulsory education promoted the use of non-Native languages and created assimilationist pressures. When radio and television were extended to the North, they were accompanied by the underlying assumption that existing Native cultures, societies, and economies were part of the past, and that, except for a few folkloric residues, they would disappear in the face of Southern expansion and settlement.

This neo-colonial narrative was challenged by Aboriginal people on many fronts. In Canada during the 1970s, emerging expressions of cultural identity were grounded in a strong sense of respect for the land and communal values. Aboriginal cultural activism developed in concert with the strategies of the national Indian and Inuit political organizations but was shaped by the threats to identities and communities posed by major resource developments and the economic and social upheaval they generated.[4] For the Cree, the Inuit, and the Dene, for example, cultural activism involved the overt challenge to northern development through the land claims process. Decolonization was linked to increasing indigenous control of their own education, health and welfare, and local economic development, and to the appropriation of media technologies. The development of indigenous media well illustrates the productivity of power at its margins. Resistance to the one-way flow of information and to centralized media production transforms indigenous subjects, shapes cultural identity, and alters relations between cultures. The lived experience of cultural tradition brought to bear upon new communication technologies also has a transformative effect upon the social construction of the technology itself. The tools, practices, and formal conventions of dominant media are subtly, and sometimes radically, reconstructed through indigenous media practices.

Prior to 1980, Aboriginal broadcasting mainly consisted of local ventures into community radio, either community-owned stations or access programming on the CBC. Beginning in the early 1970s, a series of experimental and short-term video, radio, and satellite telecommunications projects were undertaken in Native communities. These projects involved local volunteers and outside animators, and made use of government funds available for "community development." The first Native communications societies emerged during this period, beginning with the Alberta Native Communications Society in 1970. The federal Native Communications Program was established in 1973 under the Secretary of State, providing limited funding for one Native communications society in each of thirteen northern regions. However, just as the construction of pipelines or hydro-electric projects in the North contributed to the underdevelopment of existing Native economies, the extension of expensive technologically sophisticated satellite networks from the south undermined the potential development of indigenous media. The emphasis on national communication networks diverted attention away from the need for local, low-cost, low-tech community radio networks, regional Aboriginal-language broadcasting, and basic telephone service. Where viable Native community broadcasting did emerge, there was an official attitude that these were merely interim measures until plans for universal coverage could be fully implemented (CRTC 1976, 2). Furthermore, satellite television was introduced without any consultation with indigenous groups and little attention to Native needs and priorities (Inuit Broadcasting Corporation 1982, i). Indigenous cultural activists were thus forced to challenge the technological and commercial imperatives driving federal communications policy.

Indigenous Media, Communication Policy, and Cultural Autonomy

Indigenous media must also be considered in relation to broader concepts of cultural autonomy and the "right to communicate." Newly organized Native broadcasters established a presence in national communication policy debates, articulating the need for Aboriginal-language programming. Neither the CBC nor commercial broadcasters offered significant amounts of Native-originated programming. Northern Native television audiences were confronted by a novel

and visually appealing medium in non-Native languages that made no reference to local experience or cultural contexts. Indigenous people wanted to see
their own language, knowledge, and modes of representation conveyed by
television, given its central location in their homes and communities.

The struggle for Native-controlled television production and distribution
was to prove long and difficult, from the first Inuit interventions in CRTC hearings, through participation in satellite experiments, the development of the
Northern Native Broadcast Access Program (NNBAP) in 1985, the creation of
Television Northern Canada (TVNC) in 1992, and the launch of Aboriginal
Peoples Television Network (APTN) in 1999 (see Roth 2005). Radio, by contrast,
was more easily and effectively appropriated, and the bulk of Native broadcasting activity was concentrated in community radio throughout the 1980s.
This sector of Aboriginal broadcasting came under regulatory definition with
the CRTC's 1990 Native Broadcasting Policy (CRTC 1990). In practice, community radio has followed a fairly uniform pattern of growth in indigenous communities. Community-owned stations are predominantly volunteer-run, have
minimal operating costs, are often located in less than optimal facilities, and
make use of very simple studio and transmitter technologies.

Currently in Canada, thirteen NNBAP-funded broadcasters create radio and
television programs in twenty or more Aboriginal languages, as well as English
and French. In 2003, eleven of these groups produced 1,146 hours of regional
radio programming per week, and nine groups produced twenty-seven hours
per week of television (Canada, Department of Canadian Heritage 2003, 25).
The amount of programming in Aboriginal languages varies considerably
from region to region, and between radio and television, but in all cases levels
of Aboriginal-language radio content have increased substantially since the
NNBAP was created (see Table 9.1). Apart from the regional Native communications societies, there are also forty-five Aboriginal "Type B" community radio
stations that hold a licence to operate in markets with competing commercial
radio service (CRTC 2010c). There are also as many or more community radio
stations operating as the primary local service in remote Aboriginal communities. These small far-flung stations have been exempt from licensing requirements and radio regulations since 1998 (CRTC 1998), but little consistent data
on their operation are available.

Aboriginal broadcasters funded by NNBAP and the community radio stations have created an invaluable space for indigenous media content within
the Canadian broadcasting system, yet in the twenty-five years since NNBAP

TABLE 9.1

Percentage of Aboriginal-language programming on NNBAP broadcasters and APTN

Organization	Radio (%)	TV (%)
Aboriginal Multi-Media Society of Alberta	3	N/A
Inuit Broadcasting Corporation	N/A	N/A
Inuvialuit Communications Society	N/A	60
James Bay Cree Communications Society	80	N/A
Missinipi Broadcasting Corporation	20	90
Native Communications Incorporated	30	??
Native Communications Society of the Northwest Territories	75	N/A
Northern Native Broadcasting, Terrace	0	N/A
Northern Native Broadcasting, Yukon	20	50
OKalaKatiget Society	50	50
Société de communications Atikamekw-Montagnais	95	N/A
Taqramiut Nipingat Incorporated	100	100
Wawatay Native Communications Society	90	10
APTN	N/A	20.5

Note: N/A means not applicable.
Source: Canada, Department of Canadian Heritage (2003), using information supplied by NNBAP organizations and APTN.

was created, these broadcasters have seen an exponential increase in competition for northern Aboriginal people as audiences. The past two decades have also witnessed a decline in indigenous-language use, as more and more Aboriginal youth are exposed to outside media (Canada, Department of Canadian Heritage 2003, 31). As increasing numbers of indigenous people live in urban settings in southern Canada, there is a pressing need for media to serve off-reserve Aboriginal communities. To address this need, Aboriginal Voices Radio, a national radio network with stations in Vancouver, Calgary, Edmonton, Toronto, and Ottawa, was established. Launched by well-known indigenous actor, director, and publisher Gary Farmer, the network is intended to broadcast "the music of Aboriginal and Indigenous artists to Canada's largest cities. This allows millions of Canadians to appreciate the talents of these artists and their cultures. We believe this encourages better relationships and more understanding between Aboriginal and non-Aboriginal communities" (Aboriginal Voices Radio 2007).

Although in seemingly disparate remote and urban contexts, indigenous community radio conforms to similar participatory media practices in that its goals are to engage listeners in the negotiation of social change at the local, regional, and even national level. Native community radio is characterized by several similarities, including strategies of horizontal communication, an inclusive non-professional style, and the open transparency of the station's daily operations within the community. In remote Aboriginal communities, residents come and go at the station, listen regularly, phone frequently, play radio bingo, and often take part in broadcasts. In many of these small reserves, community radio preceded the introduction of other mass media, so residents simply regard the community station as indigenous, as something locally initiated and controlled, and not compromised by its association with the foreign origin and content of other forms of public or commercial radio and television (Valentine 1994; Buddle 2005).

In comparison, because of the high costs and lack of access, by the 1990s, Aboriginal-language television represented just a fraction of the amount of Southern-originated TV available in indigenous communities. Aboriginal content on TVNC and APTN had to compete with commercial television and broadband Internet access, which became widely available in even the remotest areas. This competition with non-Native media, together with the increasing decline in Native-language use over the last two decades, means that in practice, Aboriginal broadcasters have had to take a flexible approach to language of production. They have argued that a wider interpretation of the "cultural" objectives of Aboriginal broadcasting allows them to determine their own linguistic priorities and concentrate on providing culturally relevant content to contemporary Native audiences in indigenous languages, English, or French, as appropriate.

As Aboriginal groups began to engage more extensively in regional radio and television production, however, the need for the transfer of basic broadcasting skills in a culturally appropriate manner became a related issue. Although advanced technical and administrative skills are not really necessary for the successful volunteer operation of community radio, the ability to fill a regular regional program production schedule and to produce several hours a week of high-quality television and radio requires training. Now, in the third decade of indigenous radio and television, a second generation of producers is being trained at the regional level, often in its own language, by other Aboriginal people who have been working in the field for several years. This avoids some of the tensions and mistranslations that occur when an outside "expert" provides skill training to Aboriginal broadcasters, but it also ensures that training is designed in a way that accounts for the unique cultural and social contexts within which Aboriginal media are used. However, there are few resources available for this kind of culturally situated media training, and young indigenous media producers must still travel long distances to larger centres to gain the skills they need.

Developing technological skill is complemented by political awareness as subject to the various levels of government and norms of professional journalism. Although regional Native communications societies are formally organized at arm's length from Aboriginal political groups, the objectives of Aboriginal media and a wider commitment to indigenous self-determination overlap. Indigenous reporters and journalists working in Aboriginal media may view the tactics of Aboriginal politicians with a certain degree of healthy skepticism, but most share their dedication to the principles of self-determination and Aboriginal rights. Professional ideologies of journalistic balance are consciously or unconsciously subsumed within strategies of cultural activism and are not seen as contradictory. Aboriginal voices, values, and interpretations of political events are clearly more likely to be reflected in indigenous media in compensation for their absence from non-Native sources.

Participation and Cultural Production

Native control of media has a significant impact upon internal organization and participatory structures. Internal "relations of production" must be understood as mutually determined by economic factors (the extent of indigenous ownership and control), technological biases (the degree to which media technology may be successfully appropriated for local use), and socio-cultural contexts (how media practices are shaped by indigenous cultural norms and communal sanctions). Visual anthropologists seeking to locate a culturally specific indigenous visual language or formal aesthetic tend to look for textual or discursive traces of cultural precepts. But to understand relations of production and participation in indigenous media, researchers must also consider the cultural determinants of who speaks, under what conditions, and within which constraints. Native community radio, for example, embodies the grassroots principles and cultural norms upon which other types of Aboriginal media are modelled.

The participatory practices of indigenous community radio are also often carried beyond the geographic confines of locality. In her study of Aboriginal off-reserve radio, Buddle (2005, 12) draws attention to this process, suggesting that Aboriginal media practitioners use "media to say recognizably 'Native' things about appropriate conduct, ways of relating to one's environment, and the responsibilities that inhere (or that they feel ought to inhere) in the new forms of sociality that are emerging in particular urban settings." Similarly, Santo (2004, 394) considers Inuit video making in the community of Igloolik, for example, as a form of cultural citizenship due to its collective and consensual production processes. Evidence from these studies and others suggests that indigenous media represent an effective working model of the participatory principles of alternative and community broadcasting. Participatory practices and articulation of Aboriginal perspectives and goals within the media organization are vitally linked to "media-internal" strategies such as organizational structure. In turn, these are linked to "media-external" strategies that connect indigenous media to existing or emerging social movements for political rights and cultural autonomy.

Political Economy of Indigenous Media

The political economy of indigenous media in Canada is increasingly diversified from the early period of state-supported satellite experiments and government-funded regional media production under NNBAP to the independent production and national distribution of television on APTN. Today, indigenous media draw upon various combinations of public funding, advertising revenue, cable subscriber fees, box office income, and broadcast agreements. Aboriginal media producers and policy-makers still emphasize the need for stable and sufficient government support for indigenous media. However, in some ways, the most participatory and culturally representative organizations are those that have reduced their reliance on direct state support and have a mixed revenue base. Most local Native community radio stations are primarily volunteer operated and dependent on mixed support from band council grants, radio bingo, and federal training or employment grants. These small unlicensed stations carry little or no advertising. Larger "Type B" Native community stations in urban areas have a similarly mixed funding model, but according to the CRTC, less than 20 percent of their revenue comes from advertising (CRTC 2007c, 34). The regional Native radio networks (Wawatay, Aboriginal Multi-Media Society of Alberta, Northern Native Broadcasting Yukon, Native Communications Incorporated in

Manitoba) have no restrictions on the amount of advertising sold, though most carry very little. As stated by the CRTC, the limits were discontinued in 2001 after the Native licensees argued that "the ability to access more revenues from advertising would allow for greater self-sufficiency and less reliance upon financial support from governments and band councils" (CRTC 2001a, 1). Native broadcasters recognize that government funding comes with constraints, expectations, and unpredictability. Relying on federal programs usually requires that cultural objectives be secondary to economic and employment strategies. Dependence on band council grants or programs from First Nations agencies can also create the perception of lack of political independence in indigenous media. Reliance on more generous government funding in the early period established a degree of dependency on the state that is now difficult to surmount, but increased dependence on commercial models comes with its own constraints and conflicts. For these reasons, indigenous media need to continue to develop a mixed revenue base and independence from state funding programs to help promote long-term stability. Indigenous film and video, on the other hand, have little opportunity for advertising revenue and rely instead on federal subsidies for film and television, occasional distribution deals, individual program sales to schools and libraries, and broadcast agreements with APTN, provincial broadcasters, or commercial networks. In both cases, a mixed funding model with as much local indigenous control as possible will ensure the survival of indigenous media.

Indigenous Media in Practice

Indigenous media can be distinguished from other alternative media primarily by the degree to which they mobilize Aboriginal cultural knowledge in all its forms, including use of indigenous languages, reference to the accounts of elders, exploration of traditional values, and documentation of the past and present experience of colonialism. The second criterion for distinguishing indigenous media is by how much they support media-external movements for social change and indigenous rights. This involves the challenge of measuring social linkages and the long-term impact of indigenous media practices but might include their role in Aboriginal community development, regional alliances, national politics, and their negotiation of social relations of gender, age, and class in indigenous communities. Third, and more broadly, indigenous media enact a participatory form of cultural production within and beyond the media organization. Media-internal strategies include participation within the organization through culturally appropriate production practices, sharing of technological skills through training, indigenous ownership, and participatory management. Cultural participation also occurs through representation and identification: creating media space for Aboriginal narratives, stories, perspectives, and critiques from individual media practitioners and their communities that also circulate within the larger society. Analysis of these three attributes can show how indigenous media support social participation and cultural citizenship, and generate reflection, action, and change for indigenous and non-indigenous peoples in Canadian society. A closer look at specific indigenous media organizations can illustrate how each embodies these three characteristics in different ways.[5]

Igloolik Isuma: Independent Indigenous Film and Video

Igloolik Isuma Productions was launched in 1990 as Canada's first independent Inuit production company under the direction of three Inuit and one non-Inuit partners: Zacharias Kunuk, Paul Apak Angilirq, Pauloosie Qulitalik, and Norman Cohn. The company has been creating community-based films and video, historical documentary ("re-lived" drama), and feature films that are widely distributed and have achieved international recognition. Isuma's stated mission is to "preserve and enhance Inuit culture and language; to create jobs and economic development in Igloolik and Nunavut; and to tell authentic Inuit stories to Inuit and non-Inuit audiences worldwide" (Isuma 2008, 1). Isuma has used the domestic and international success of its award-winning historical drama *Atanarjuat: The Fast Runner* (2000) to trigger new federal financing for its films and to reinvest those funds in Inuit film production.

Isuma mobilizes Aboriginal cultural knowledge in all its forms, and local participation in every aspect of film and video production is high. Isuma videos are produced entirely in Inuktitut and rely upon the imaginative representation and reinvention of local Inuit history and lived experience. Scripts are grounded in a synthesis of elders' narratives and work toward a regeneration of traditional values associated with living on the land and collective decision making. Isuma videos also document the Inuit experience of colonialism and contact with dominant society. *The Journals of Knud Rasmussen* (2006), set in the early 1920s, explores the initial period of Inuit conversion to Christianity through the dramatized experience of a local shaman and his family. Isuma also actively generates and supports movements for social change. The organization has a strong focus on mobilizing women and youth in Nunavut and has partnerships with a women's video production collective and a youth video performance group in Igloolik (ibid., 3). Through skills training and employment opportunities generated by its productions, Isuma actively pursues economic development for Inuit according to Inuit needs and priorities. In the strongest sense of the term, Isuma engages radical processes of decolonization and cultural autonomy through filmmaking. It has actively challenged the structures of government funding for Canadian cinema in an effort to get equal recognition and support for indigenous productions. Finally, Isuma enacts a participatory form of cultural production within and beyond the media organization through ongoing consultation with elders and community members in its documentation of Inuit history. Although the company is owned by specific individuals, the partnership is strongly linked to modes of communal participation. At Isuma, mainstream production roles (such as actor, producer, writer, director) are fluid and non-hierarchical, and individuals may shift between these roles from one production to the next. Isuma trains and employs local people, extends film and video technologies to other groups in the community, and actively creates new forms of visual culture in Nunavut. The presence of Isuma films and videos in the Canadian cultural landscape and upon international screens has generated a greater national and global awareness of indigenous peoples' history and culture.[6]

Wawatay Radio Network: Regional Radio Production in Northwestern Ontario

Wawatay Radio Network (WRN) was created in 1974 to produce regional content for a network of indigenous community radio stations and is now broadcast on Bell satellite television service to thirty-seven local stations in northwestern Ontario. Production offices are located in Sioux Lookout and Moose Factory, and programming languages are English, Ojibway, Cree, and OjiCree. The programming from Sioux Lookout addresses OjiCree communities in the northern interior of Ontario, whereas content from Moose Factory is produced for Cree communities along the James Bay coast, although all communities receive the programs from both studios. Revenue sources include federal NNBAP support, some advertising, contracted services such as translation at meetings and government events, and paid programming from local churches and gospel jamborees. Wawatay's program content includes indigenous music, religious programs, youth productions, sports, news, and political coverage. The majority of this content is produced in the local indigenous languages of Omushkego (Swampy Cree) and OjiCree (an Ojibway dialect). WRN mobilizes Aboriginal cultural knowledge through its high level of indigenous-language content, strong links to communities and elders, focus on storytelling and oral history, and exploration of local issues and concerns from an indigenous perspective. It indirectly supports indigenous movements for social change through its current affairs programs and involvement in some elements of distance education. WRN provides detailed coverage of regional politics and national Aboriginal affairs in local languages, but re-source constraints prevent it from taking strong leadership in community de-velopment. The religious content on WRN reflects the strength of mainstream and evangelical churches in this region, but those community members who are not churchgoers may feel alienated by this programming. WRN has also tried to reach a younger audience with more contemporary popular music genres and youth-oriented content. The urgency of engaging younger listen-ers in indigenous-language radio is demonstrated by a recent language survey commissioned by Wawatay. Results showed that 79 percent of youth respond-ents said their parents spoke an Aboriginal language at home, whereas only 52 percent indicated that they themselves did (Wawatay Native Communications Society 2008). Young Aboriginal people in this area have had greater exposure to English than their parents through earlier and longer schooling and the in-creasing availability of non-Native media. The challenge remains one of at-tracting indigenous youth to WRN programming in the face of many competing media choices.

WRN enacts a participatory form of cultural production within and beyond the media organization because internal radio production roles are shaped by a strong collective ethos. Most WRN employees are able to perform most pro-duction tasks, so that organizational hierarchies are fluid. But a small core of established employees has operated the network from year to year, and pos-itions on the Wawatay board have also been held by many of the same individ-uals in the communities represented. Although this is important for the stability of the network and its operation, it may inhibit a sense of wider involvement and participation beyond the paid staff. The local community stations supply some content for the regional network schedule, and some communities cre-ate their own programming in place of the WRN feed, but resource constraints and centralized locations of the two network studios prevent widespread com-munity participation beyond regular news reports and phone-in programs.

WRN does not have the same national and international profile as Isuma or APTN, but it represents an important example of a regional indigenous media network that has become relatively self-sustaining and open to local participa-tion in an environment of constantly constricting public funding for Aboriginal broadcasting. It has created a viable communications link between relatively isolated and impoverished indigenous communities that has ultimately contributed to their growing political autonomy and cultural revitalization.

Aboriginal Peoples Television Network: A National Indigenous Cable Channel

The possibility that a national cable television network represents a form of alternative media constitutes a substantive challenge to the conceptualization of alternative media structures and processes. But APTN, through its evolution, its organizational structure, and its content, stands as a significant alternative to the commercialized model of "specialty" cable channels predominant in Canada and to the centralized and elitist conceptions of national public broadcasting represented by the CBC. Indigenous television production grew out of the regional Native communications societies described earlier and was first distributed directly to indigenous communities in 1992 by TVNC, Canada's first indigenous-controlled network. Formed as a result of grassroots effort by Northern and Southern Native cultural activists, APTN was licensed and launched in 1999. The network has built a presence in the Canadian television landscape and generated the development of new indigenous programming from across the country. Moving into its second seven-year licence term, APTN continues to establish cultural and economic roots within Aboriginal communities and to cultivate a small but significant non-Aboriginal viewership. Before the creation of APTN, there was no national outlet for indigenous television in Canada and relatively little incentive for mainstream networks to acquire or develop information or entertainment programming that reflected the nation's indigenous peoples.

APTN clearly mobilizes Aboriginal cultural knowledge through the wide range of indigenous television content it carries. It has commissioned new programming in genres including documentary, children's, "lifestyle," drama, music, and variety. The network has its own in-house news production team based in Winnipeg, with content from regional offices across the country. APTN maintains the earlier commitment of TVNC to television in indigenous languages, and at present it broadcasts approximately 28 percent of its content in a variety of Aboriginal languages including Inuktitut, Cree, Inuinnaqtuun, Ojibway, Inuvialuktun, Mohawk, Dene, Gwich'in, Miqma'aq, Slavey, Dogrib, Chipweyan, Tlingit, and Mechif (Aboriginal Peoples Television Network 2005). It is important to note that APTN receives little or no direct government funding for this content, but purchases the completed programming from the regional Aboriginal producers. The regional producers, with their immediate links to diverse Aboriginal communities, remain in control of the content that is developed for television.

Unlike most other Canadian cable channels, APTN functions as a hybrid non-profit public network with a specialty television funding model. The network relies on revenues from cable subscription fees and so is less dependent on government funding, ad revenue, or the resale of imported US prime-time programs. Because the carriage of APTN on basic cable is mandated by the CRTC, the restrictions of the privatized public sphere that affect the community cable channels have no impact on APTN. APTN uses its economic independence, its social and cultural mandate, and its public service objectives as an indirect trigger for Aboriginal cultural production. Through its program content, it can also be seen to support movements for social change, especially those linked to Aboriginal rights and cultural autonomy. The network confronts the daily experience of Canadian Aboriginal people living through the legacies of colonialism and economic and political marginalization. As an example from APTN's current affairs genre, the weekly phone-in show *Contact* is distinguished by the high degree of representation from Aboriginal people and extensive participation by callers and on-line comments from across the country in Aboriginal and non-Aboriginal communities. The program takes on issues and conflicts that the mainstream networks rarely address in any sustained manner. Examples of issues covered in individual programs include the long-term effects of residential schools, the Ipperwash Inquiry in Ontario, the land reclamation at Caledonia, the development of Aboriginal education programs, drug and alcohol addictions in indigenous communities, and specific challenges faced by Aboriginal women and youth.

Much of the news and current affairs programming on APTN goes directly to indigenous activists and ordinary people in Aboriginal communities for its sources and so makes room for Aboriginal perspectives in the national media. The network plays an important role in ensuring that federal and provincial governments are more accountable to indigenous people, but also in making the workings of First Nations governments and indigenous organizations more transparent. Through its board structure, APTN also reproduces an alternative model of participatory engagement beyond the media organization. The original NNBAP Native communications societies are represented on the board, and though these board members have no direct involvement in the day-to-day management of the network, they bring the concerns and interests of their communities to its overall direction. Further, as APTN continues to acquire more programming from independents, a number of key new indigenous television production companies have been established. These independents enact a much broader form of cultural participation in Canadian society, as they are increasingly able to claim space within domestic cultural production for indigenous stories and images. Within APTN, however, internal divisions of labour and management processes seem to replicate those at mainstream commercial or public television networks. From this point of view, the network is more accurately seen as a conventional broadcaster in the business of producing indigenous content. The kind of internal participatory structures more common in small community-based local or regional media organizations such as Isuma and Wawatay are less apparent at APTN.

The Cultural Future of Indigenous Media as Alternative Media

Canada's diverse and highly developed indigenous media sector represents the culmination of the early aspirations of alternative media practitioners and indigenous cultural activists. As the examples explored above clearly demonstrate, indigenous media organizations are established at the community, regional, and national level as an integral part of contemporary indigenous cultures. Although they are not invulnerable to economic pressures or political upheaval, their social relevance and cultural importance are indisputable. As models of participation through media alternatives, the indigenous media examples documented here have much to teach us. Their engagement with indigenous cultural knowledge, strong links to local communities, and commitment to fostering cultural participation for Aboriginal people make them unique in the rapidly transforming national and global mediascapes. As the principles and practices of alternative and indigenous media undergo the transition to digital forms and computer networks, they continue to share the potential for cultural engagement and social action in constantly shifting public spheres.

NOTES

1 In this chapter I have used the terms "Native," "Aboriginal," and "indigenous" throughout. They are not entirely interchangeable and signal the historical shifts in names that are most frequently used by indigenous individuals or groups and by policy-makers and broadcasters in different time periods being discussed. The terms "Native people" and "Native broadcasting" were most commonly used in the 1970s and early 1980s.

CRTC policy for broadcasting by indigenous groups is still officially titled "Native Broadcasting Policy." The term "Aboriginal people" was defined by the federal government in the 1982 Constitution to include Indian, Inuit, and Metis groups. Not long after this, the phrase "Aboriginal broadcasting" became more frequently used. "First Nations" is now the more common term used by Indian groups in Canada, but Inuit and Metis people do not usually apply this name to themselves. Although "indigenous people" or "First People" are probably the most inclusive of all these designations, in this chapter I have chosen to use the historically appropriate terms when discussing policy development and to employ more specific cultural and linguistic designations used by indigenous groups themselves, such as Cree, Inuit, or Dene, when referring to particular groups.

2 Culture of poverty models current in the 1960s and 1970s suggested that poverty and marginalization generate a "culture," which inhibits development. Constructed in this way, culture could also be seen as a remedial force through which the cure for the problems could be introduced. According to this model, the demonstrable benefits of adopting aspects of the dominant culture would induce indigenous people to give up the elements of their traditional culture allegedly contributing to their poverty. However, the uncritical use of this model located the causes of poverty in Aboriginal culture itself and sought to eliminate poverty by manipulating elements of that culture. This was simply the latest variant in a series of assimilationist policies and did little to challenge the hierarchical and paternalistic nature of the relationship between First Nations and the Canadian state, or racist elements of Canadian society. It also sidestepped substantial historical evidence that poverty and dependency among First Nations had been created and sustained by earlier actions of the state itself.

3 Roth's (2005) detailed history of First People's television describes the creation of TVNC and APTN in much greater detail than is possible here.

4 Examples of cultural activism among Canadian Aboriginal peoples in the 1970s and early 1980s are well documented in works such as Harold Cardinal's *The Rebirth of Canada's Indians* (1977), Mel Watkins' *Dene Nation: The Colony Within* (1977), and Leroy Littlebear, Menno Boldt, and J. Anthony Long's *Pathways to Self-determination* (1984).

5 The case studies of indigenous media presented here are based on personal observations and interviews conducted with staff and volunteers at these three organizations in the summer of 2003. Many thanks to all the indigenous media practitioners who took part in my research.

6 The risks faced by independent indigenous media are highlighted by recent developments at Igloolik Isuma. While this chapter was in the final stages of publication in the summer of 2011, the Inuit-owned company was forced to file for receivership by a Nunavut investment firm to whom Isuma owed several hundred thousand dollars in unpaid loans from 2009. The future of the company and its extensive archive of Inuit-produced film and video remains uncertain.

PART 3: ACTIVISM

From Alienation to Autonomy
The Labour of Alternative Media

NICOLE S. COHEN

Thousands of people spend thousands of hours working for alternative media in Canada. They produce magazines, journals, websites, zines, broadcasts, podcasts, and newspapers. Some earn small salaries or honoraria, but most volunteer. All of them take their work as editors, publishers, reporters, artists, writers, designers, board members, and circulation managers seriously. Some move between corporate and alternative media; others contribute to alternative media while working in non-media jobs. They are the workforce that constitutes the production of alternative media, which, although no official count exists, comprises a large chunk of Canada's media landscape.[1] Yet, little research exists on the labour of alternative media. This is surprising, as theories of alternative media as a form of radical or democratic communication have long foregrounded processes of production in their understandings of what makes alternative media alternative (Enzensberger 1974; Williams 2005; Downing 1984; Downing et al. 2001; Atton 2002, 2004).

Enzensberger (1974, 96, 107) considers developing forms of electronic media to be politically strategic, able to transform consumers into producers through collective media production. "It is wrong to regard media equipment as mere means of consumption," he writes. "It is always, in principle, also a means of production" (ibid., 106). Similarly, Williams (2005, 50, 51, 53) argues that the "means of communication are themselves means of production," not devices through which to pass messages between abstract individuals, but socially and materially produced and reproduced. Atton (2002, 3) characterizes alternative media by the social relations flowing from their organizational structures. As he states, alternative media can "radicaliz[e] the methods of production" and enable different thinking about what it means to be a media producer (ibid., 4). Indeed, challenging the notion of who can produce media has fuelled alternative media, encapsulated in slogans such as "Don't hate the media, become the media." Despite this emphasis on processes of production, however, little attention has been given to what constitutes that production: the actual work of creating alternative media. That is, the hours of writing, editing, fundraising, promoting, meeting, designing, distributing, and problem solving that media production requires. If we follow Atton in understanding alternative media through organizational processes and resulting social relations, we need to consider labour. Indeed, the idea of labour directly intersects with the three elements that this book proposes characterize alternative media: structure, participation, and activism.

In some ways, it is not surprising that few have tackled this question. Problematizing labour in alternative media is difficult, primarily because most alternative media workers are not paid and are therefore not usually considered to be workers. Most people contribute to alternative media because they are committed to the politics or vision of a project, not because they require paid employment. For this reason, involvement is defined in terms of resistance against the dominance of corporate media and efforts toward democratizing media production (Atton 2002; Downing et al. 2001; Langlois and Dubois 2005). Rarely is this resistance or production considered in terms of labour, a notion that raises challenging, even uncomfortable, questions. For example, how do we reconcile ideas of media activism with concepts that underpin the notion of labour, such as commodification and exploitation? Activist-participants generally accept that there is a difference between being exploited by profitable media conglomerates and working unpaid for non-profit media that contribute to a community or to a movement.

It is critical to value the important contributions volunteers and activists make to alternative media, but it is just as important to consider the labour of alternative media in order to inform strategic thinking and to raise new conceptual questions. This is not an attempt to solve what might be understood as the problem of labour in alternative media, but rather an effort to build on established approaches to enrich debate and challenge the limiting notions that alternative media are democratic solely by virtue of existing. By foregrounding the idea of alternative media production as labour, we can conceptualize alternative media in Canada as a particular type of activism that seeks to resist not only dominant messages of mainstream or corporate media, but also the commodification of labour power by corporate media firms. This is especially the case under current conditions of intensifying concentration, conglomeration, and lean media production. Viewed this way, alternative media become a space for the expression of non-commodified, non-alienating labour, and new ways of understanding the relationship between alternative and corporate media emerge.

This chapter examines the labour of alternative media in order to expose the space of tension these media occupy: resistance to a market-based logic of production makes alternative media significant, yet the model itself challenges the sustainability of many media projects. Following Hamilton (2008, vii), this chapter approaches alternative media as a "problem to engage instead of an answer to be found" by uncovering some tensions involved in their production. By exploring the conditions of labour in corporate commercial and alternative media, I propose that the latter provide space to seek non-commodified and non-alienating labour. This allows me, again following Hamilton, to locate corporate and alternative media on a continuum of media forms, as two instances of media production constituting one another in complex and contradictory ways. Instead of conceiving of alternative and mainstream or corporate media as being in opposition to one another, this chapter attempts to understand the spaces of continuity and exchange between media forms as those occupied by labour.

Celebrating alternative media projects is important, but romanticizing the real and often difficult work of producing them risks masking problems that can limit efforts to build sustainable alternative media. To begin, we must trouble the notion of alternative media work as a labour of love.

Theorizing the Labour of Alternative Media

Alternative media work is usually described as a labour of love (Duncombe 1997, 95; Cohen 2007; J. Johnston 2008). Labours of love are performed for little or no pay, requiring participants to depend on other, paid, employment or sources of income. Labouring for love means undertaking productive work voluntarily without financial compensation or other benefits that may be associated with paid work. The term evokes ideas of passion and selflessness, notions historically separated from ideas of production by a capitalist division of labour that situated men's work in the market and women's in the home, unwaged (Dalla Costa and James 1972).

It is this gendered labour – unpaid domestic work historically performed by women – that "labour of love" usually refers to. Traditionally understood as work to which women are biologically predisposed, this labour has not been assigned a market value and is therefore not counted as work (ibid.; Waring 1999, 21). Feminist political economists argue that the discipline of economics has given particular meanings to terms such as "labour," "production," "value," and "work" that limit our ability to conceive of labour that takes place outside of direct market exchange as work (Waring 1999, 17). By challenging a narrow conception of labour as waged labour and exposing the value of unwaged or non-market work, feminist political economists have expanded the notion of work, broadening understandings of what constitutes productive labour, including work performed for no wages and outside of direct capitalist production (Dalla Costa and James 1972, 26).

This understanding can position participation in alternative media as productive labour – as work. The value it generates is not surplus value (although bookstores and printers, for example, do profit from alternative media), but rather building social movements and communities, engaging with social and political issues, and constituting ourselves as citizens, activists, and thinkers. This value has to do with the creative rewards of engaging in work that contributes to something in which a person believes. Understanding participation in this way, we can turn to Marx's conception of work as the manner in which humans exercise creative capacities and come to understand the world and their place in it (Sayers 2005, 613). This is a view of work as inherently rewarding, as an end unto itself, as something that can unite people over shared interests (ibid., 610). Of course, work under capitalism looks drastically different, for the human capacity to labour is commodified.

In his understanding of the dynamics of capitalism, Marx (1990, 270) distinguished between labour, the activity of work, and labour power, a person's capacity to work. Labour power is a peculiar commodity because it is not produced expressly for sale on the market, but rather is embodied in a person's living being. Labour power becomes a commodity only when that person sells it for a wage (ibid., 272). This process results in estranged, or alienated, labour (Marx 1978, 72), which is commonly understood as "a feeling of meaninglessness, or a general malaise, discontent or unhappiness, particularly in relation to work" (Sayers 2005, 609).

Alienation means that a worker's labour is objectified, appearing as something detached from her. Once a worker sells her labour power, her labour becomes external, no longer part of her essential being. Work ceases to affirm her and is experienced as a loss of reality (Marx 1978, 71, 74). Alienation manifests in several ways. Workers are alienated from the products of their labour and from the process of production (ibid., 74, 75, 77). They are separated from one another and alienated from their species being or human essence, the characteristic that, for Marx (ibid., 75), is what makes humans human, the "vital activity" that enables us to be creative, productive beings.

Alienation results from a particular historical mode of production that causes work to be regarded as something forced upon us, determined not by workers' autonomous needs, but by the needs of capital (Sayers 2005, 610; Wennerlind 2002, 5). This suggests that if work were shaped by workers' needs and desires, if it were liberated from the market system, we could regain control over our productivity and creativity. Work could become a "free expression of life," a way to connect with people, to the products of labour, and to the processes of realizing one's creative capacities (McLellan 1969). Indeed, argues Sayers (2005, 610), the very experience of alienation suggests that work has the potential to be non-alienating.

The notion of self-determined work is reflected in the autonomist Marxist concept of self-valorization, or "an alternative social structure of value that is founded not on the production of surplus value but on the collective needs and desires of the producing community" (Virno and Hardt 1996, 264). The term describes self-managed, local forms of social organization that are relatively separate from capitalist relations. This is a useful way to conceptualize alternative media that seek to create autonomous forms of media production within, yet against, capitalism. It situates alternative media as an attempt to realize fulfilling, creative work. This becomes particularly clear when the work involved in alternative media is contrasted with that available to those labouring for corporate media, who may seek in alternative media non-alienating, non-commodified labour.

Commodified Media Labour and Alienation

Evidence of discontent among media workers is mounting, exposing alienation in industries that are often imbued with notions of inherent rewards and creative fulfillment (McRobbie 2002, 517). In recent years, Canadian media workers have experienced waves of layoffs, hiring freezes, strikes, station closures, and a lockout at the Canadian Broadcasting Corporation over issues of contract labour and outsourcing (Sandborn 2007). Canadian freelance writers are in the process of collectively organizing to address declining wages and control over copyright to their works.

As Cottle (2003, 3) notes, media workers are "often at the forefront of processes of organizational change," which has recently meant the imposition of flexible work regimes and technologies that require reskilling and multi-tasking. The forces driving change in media industries include deregulation, concentration, technological development and convergence, international competition, and outsourcing (Winseck 2002; Deuze 2007, 57, 59; Mosco and McKercher 2008). Underlying these forces are processes of marketization, or shifts in policy that have "enlarged the scope of market relations," allowing corporations increasing freedom while using market measures to assess levels of success in both private and public media (Murdock 2003, 19). Under these conditions, media companies' mandates are aggressively focused on the bottom line, and unsurprisingly, labour costs are first to be cut. This means fewer jobs, lower pay, and deteriorating working conditions (Deuze 2007).

Although some workers benefit from these changing conditions, many have experienced the negative dynamics shaping media and cultural production. Media workers face growing insecurity as work is outsourced and their industries casualized, creating low-paid and insecure temporary, contract, and freelance positions. Competition is fuelled by an increasing number of media production programs, whose graduates are prepared to work for free, keeping wages down (Hesmondhalgh 2007, 206; Gollmitzer and Murray 2008, 22). Much like their counterparts in other industries, media workers experience declining autonomy and a resulting lack of control over their work, which is increasingly regulated through workflow standardization and surveillance (Deuze 2007, 70). This is what welcomes those who can get through the newsroom door. Landing a job means having the right contacts and the time and resources to complete unpaid internships. It is not surprising, then, that many who labour for corporate media have sought work – paid or not – in alternative or community media, either instead of corporate work, or concurrently (Hamilton 2008, 3). Alternative media can provide the type of work envisioned by Williams and Enzensberger. Williams (2005, 61) saw radical potential in self-managed autonomous communication to go beyond "representative" communication and enable people to speak directly to each other. By resocializing the process of production, alternative media can be a place to seek productive, creative, fulfilling, self-organized work (Enzensberger 1974, 113; Sayers 2005, 612).

Workers resist processes of commodification in various ways, and for many, participating in alternative media provides relief from degraded working conditions, a way to express desire for non-alienating, non-commodified labour. In one of the only texts to link alternative media producers and their relationships to paid employment, Duncombe (1997, 74) roots the emergence of American zine culture in the neo-liberal restructuring of the 1970s and 1980s and resulting precarious employment. Zine creators were clear in defining their creative efforts as labour, "as protest against the drudgery of working for another's profit" (ibid., 2). In zines they found fulfilling work that gave them control over production processes. Zines were a form of non-alienating work for which people employed their creative capacities. Producing zines enabled people to identify a connection between the processes of their labour and the results, over which they felt ownership (ibid., 96). As Duncombe (ibid., 15) writes, the concerns of zine creators include "how to count as an individual, how to build a supportive community, how to have a meaningful life, how to create something that is yours."

Although zines occupy a marginal slice of cultural production, they indicate the desire to express the ways in which work could potentially be organized (ibid., 94). This echoes Downing's (1984, 23) argument that alternative media represent a form of prefigurative politics, "an attempt to practice [a particular politics] in the present, not merely to imagine [it] for the future." For many, work in alternative media can be a prefigurative form of a particular organization of labour, a way to resist intensifying processes of commodification and to express a desire for non-alienating labour. They demonstrate what it would mean to transform capitalist forms of media production, how to reunite people with the processes and products of their labour. As a founder of now defunct US activist magazine *Clamor* writes, creating media is "one example ... where activists have the opportunity to model a different world, one that we want to live in ... By building viable alternative institutions and providing concrete examples of how society could be run, we help challenge the dominant structure" (Angel 2007, 2).

Alternative media offer alternative ways of working. They are not produced expressly for sale on the market, which enables people to maintain control over the production process and products of their labour. Work conditions enable the overlap of skills and roles, and often involvement in the entire production process, from conceiving ideas, to working with writers, to distribution and promotion. People join projects to connect with other people and to express their creative capacities. These are small self-managed workplaces where

creative or challenging ideas are welcome. For Atton (2002, 16), fostering fulfillment "as a total human being" is a critical goal of alternative media, expressed through the organization of production in non-profit, participatory, or
collective modes, by non-hierarchical decision making and by ownership over
the means of production.

Kidd (2002, 65) offers the Seattle Independent Media Centre (IMC) – a virtual
activist news centre where anyone can upload stories, photographs, and video
– as an example of a space to directly challenge the practices and norms of
corporate news production, a "communication commons." She frames the IMC
in terms of its production, describing participants as a "new class of cultural
workers" reacting to corporate control of information and the logic of privately
owned media. Kidd (ibid., 67) notes the drive for self-valorization and the way
in which this productive self-activity is an attempt to overcome feelings of
alienation: "[IMC producers] use the concept of the commons to proffer an alternative conception of development and of communications that begins
with attention to the self-activity of common people, demonstrating how sub-
altern groups actively and concretely have organized their space, time, and
rebellion in the midst of and against the development of global capital."

Although alternative organizations of media production can be understood
as expressions of a liberatory form of labour, these spaces are not inherently
free from dynamics and asymmetrical power relations at work in traditional
media, and labour manifests as a problem in many aspects of alternative media.
For one, alternative media operate on very little funding and what has come to
be known somewhat admiringly as "self-exploited labour" (Atton 2003, 43).
And although this operating model is often recognized as being detrimental
to the financial stability of alternative media, at its core is the question of
labour, of not being able to materially support the people whose productive
work is fundamental to the project. Exposing the problems of labour in alternative media is a step toward conceptualizing the possibilities of alternative
media as a viable space for the creative expression of labour.

Labour as a Problem of Alternative Media

Most argue that financial challenges lead to the failure of alternative media
(Atton 2002, 44), and labour is part of these challenges (Comedia 1984).
Alternative media have subsisted for decades on volunteer or low-paid labour,
people who contribute due to a political or creative commitment to media
that, without their involvement, would not otherwise exist. However, people

who work long hours for little or no pay, usually while working elsewhere for income, quickly burn out. People regularly move on, leaving alternative media in a pattern of short life spans, high staff turnover, and limited morale for projects that usually begin with fervour (Hackett and Carroll 2006, 131). Publications often die when key members depart. When the co-founders of *Clamor* became too overwhelmed by the financial difficulties of publishing independently, they closed the magazine (Angel 2007).[2] *Undercurrents,* a British video magazine, blamed its closure on overwork. Its members could no longer produce the magazine unless they "[found] a way to clone [themselves] and survive without sleep or financial support" (quoted in Atton 2002, 50).

The people who remain must often spend their most productive and creative time on paid employment, which means their unpaid media work suffers (Angel 2007, 12). New publications regularly repeat mistakes others have made, as there is little continuity between staff and publications, and the alternative media movement as a whole often lacks institutional memory.[3] Media producers are usually too busy making media to find time to develop strategies for becoming sustainable. As Atton (2002, 36) notes, the financial problems of alternative media are self-perpetuating: "Given that capital investment is minimal, and that producers of these titles are already working for no wages, there is not only little margin for expansion, there is hardly space in which to survive."

Although they would if they could, most alternative media cannot afford to pay contributors or staff (those that can afford it, do pay). Projects have tiny budgets, with most resources allocated to printing and distribution costs. These projects are born from big ideas rather than a desire for big profits, and people prefer to spend their time creating content rather than figuring out how to budget for wages. Most decide to start a project first and worry about how to pay for it later. This limits the ability to save for future financial crises or to enable "capacity (of time, of energy, and money) for innovation and strategic thinking" (Angel 2007, 8). Many people involved in alternative media projects do not understand finances or are determined to try work outside of capitalist modes of production (Comedia 1984, 96; Atton 2002, 32). Discussions of money usually focus on how to get enough to pay the printer, rarely as something needed to pay staff. This has implications for alternative media beyond sustainability.

When people are overworked, or if they have no time to attend meetings because they are juggling alternative media work with jobs and other responsibilities, practices such as collaboration or democratic decision making are sidelined in favour of getting things done. As well, attempts to forge a new way of "doing business" (Atton 2002, 32) – or operating outside of capitalist organizations of production – may have the unintended effect of limiting who can afford to work for alternative media. As Hackett and Carroll (2006, 131) write, "the difficulty of making a living doing progressive media work explains why so many activists are young people without families to support." Indeed, many people's paid employment leaves little time to volunteer for alternative media, and those whose waged work allows for stealing time or resources usually contribute the most. Working for alternative media often requires personal funds for travelling for reporting and purchasing equipment, thus limiting involvement from people who lack the necessary disposable income (Zeleke 2004, 13).

These factors challenge one of the underlying principles of alternative media: that anyone can make media. It is often those who already work in media – corporate or independent, established or aspiring media workers – who are able to contribute. Incorporating volunteers into projects is an important way to involve a range of people in media production; yet relying solely, or even mostly, on unpaid or low-paid labour narrows the range of those who can steadily contribute. This raises important questions about class and alternative media, an area under-explored in both activist and academic literature. In one instance, Kidd (2002, 80), an advocate of the Independent Media Centre model, notes its limitations, particularly inadequate resources that demand a reliance on volunteer labour: "Already, those people who are able to volunteer tended to represent a small minority of young, white, North Americans and Europeans who could afford to share their time ... There will have to be very creative solutions to overcome the huge inequality of access to media production and Internet technologies that exists for working-class communities of colour."

Clamor was founded thanks to loans and access to credit cards, without which it could not have published beyond its fourth issue (Angel 2007, 14). It is admirable that activists are willing to take personal financial risk for media they believe in, but it is a risk many cannot afford. *The Walrus* and *Maisonneuve*, two Canadian independent magazines that aim to provide critical and intellectual engagement with politics, social issues, and culture, were launched with and are sustained by family foundation money. Their success is disheartening to struggling media projects that cannot access such funds. It is critical to examine the class composition of alternative media projects in order to evaluate the degree to which alternative media provide a true alternative to their corporate or mainstream counterparts, which, argues Weaver (1998), are predominantly composed of white, highly educated, male workers who share upper-middle-class values. The stories told in media depend on who is doing the telling or on who decides which stories are worth being told. In this way, alternative media can also be limiting.

As McRobbie (2002, 522) notes, the lack of a workplace, or running a media organization as an unconventional workplace – out of homes, virtually, or with inadequate office space – results in a lack of workplace policies to mitigate potential problems. The power dynamics that shape alternative media are not well documented, but a report funded by the National Campus and Community Radio Association reveals that alternative media are not inherently immune to sexism, ageism, or class-based exclusion, which can undermine mandates of democratic practices (Zeleke 2004). For example, independent campus-community radio has long been an important outlet for feminist media producers. Stations across the country are committed to training volunteers, making it theoretically possible for anyone to participate. Campus-community radio has provided space to discuss gender and feminist politics, as well as a place for women to develop skills and learn to be media producers (Cohen 2006). Yet the report reveals a range of issues that may lurk behind other alternative media projects.

Many women find campus-community stations intimidating to join, as they can be perceived as boys' clubs or the domain of hipsters – those who are in the know about indie rock and hip hop music, genres that have not been overtly friendly to women (Zeleke 2004, 13; Cohen 2006, 26). Women expressed concern for their safety, as many stations are in out-of-the-way spots, and volunteers often work alone late at night. Many volunteers experienced harassment from male listeners and even other staff, both verbal abuse and unwanted sexual advances (Zeleke 2004, 9). Even more troubling is that many stations and their board members do not take these issues seriously. As Zeleke (ibid., 9) writes, "harassment charges were seen as divisive and were therefore swept under the carpet." Few stations have a policy on sexual harassment, and if they do, it is "not well publicized and ... not ... incorporated into the culture of the station." Stations can be inaccessible to older or low-income women and those with children (ibid., 8, 10). At some stations, a gendered division of labour persists: men do technical work and women answer phones and keep the office clean (ibid., 7). Although this division may not be intentional, writes Zeleke (ibid.), "the overall 'good vibe' of the station [made it] difficult to create a space where the ... situation could be discussed." This report demonstrates the problems that can arise from having staffs composed of volunteers: because workers are unpaid, it is unclear what rights they are entitled to and to whom they can address problems.

The report also demonstrates the need for empirical research into the social relations shaping the production of alternative media, including workplace policies and practices. For example, little research exists on gendered and racialized dynamics in alternative media, which could be related to several factors.[4] Conversations about oppression often occur in private. People who are passionate about the politics of a project may not want to disrupt already stressful operations or be seen as not committed enough to the cause, and it may be difficult to raise issues of harassment and marginalization in informal settings. Leaving an organization can be easier than confronting colleagues and friends, which results in problems remaining unresolved. Research demonstrates that women experience inequality and forms of oppression in many areas of media production (Pitt 2003; Byerly and Ross 2006), and there is no reason to assume that these issues do not persist in alternative media. In fact, alternative media settings may exacerbate problems, particularly through informal organizational structures, casual job descriptions, implicit assumptions about democratic practices, and lack of time and resources to develop strategies to address problems (Brooten and Hadl 2009).

There is a great need for empirical research into people's day-to-day experiences of producing alternative media. Conceiving of alternative media producers as workers, regardless of their status as volunteers or paid staff, can open the conceptual space needed to explore these questions. A recent example demonstrates possible areas of inquiry. In January 2007, a Toronto paper *(Eye Weekly)* published a story on the challenges facing independent magazines, with a cover photo of the people who ran them. As co-editor of *Shameless* – a feminist magazine for teenagers – I was part of this group. Waiting to be photographed, we could not help noticing that all six of us were white women and that none of us earned living wages (or any wages) from these projects. This demonstrates the need to probe connections between women's low-paid affective labour and women producing independent or alternative media. Have women been historically conditioned to work for free?[5] Is our participation a reflection of the gender dynamics in mainstream media? How can some women afford to devote so many unpaid hours to alternative media projects? How do issues of race and class shape this participation? If the aim of alternative media is to offer an alternative to mainstream and corporate media, to create space for the expression of non-alienating, non-commodified labour, questions about the social relations of labour must be examined.

Sustaining Labour in Alternative Media

Although emphasis on sustaining alternative media may always come down to money, conceiving the problem as that of labour may enable broader thinking about making alternative media sustainable, financially and otherwise. David Skinner discusses some of these issues in Chapter 1 of this book. Here I offer a few examples of broad thinking about questions of labour.

Unlike corporate media workers, most alternative media workers in Canada cannot access organizational forms such as unions or even a loose network for financial or social support. This is due not only to the character of alternative media projects, but also to the way in which "worker" has traditionally been understood by trade unions: as someone who works full-time for a single employer in a single workplace. Many contributors to alternative media do not fit this model. Some cobble together a living from contributing to various media, whereas others work in both commercial and alternative media. Many are students, activists, teachers, or academics, or are employed in completely unrelated occupations. This makes joining already existing media unions difficult.

Several unions represent media workers, but none have extended their organizing efforts to alternative media. The largest are the Communications, Energy and Paperworkers Union of Canada (CEP), which has twenty-five thousand members in a range of media industries, and the Communications Workers of America, whose subsidiaries the Canadian Media Guild and the Newspaper Guild represent journalists and technical workers across the country. These unions represent workers at for-profit media outlets (and the CBC) who are on staff or contract and who tend to have an adversarial relationship with freelance workers due to their differing, at times competing, material interests (the Canadian Media Guild does represent freelance workers at the CBC). Staff want steady employment and have struggled to limit the contracting out of labour (Mosco and McKercher 2008, 121), whereas those who freelance depend on outsourced work. This tension does not make unionized workers and freelancers obvious allies. For the most part, trade unions organize workers on a workplace-based model to achieve collective bargaining. This is difficult to apply to alternative media workplaces.

It is possible that the nascent Canadian Freelance Union (CFU), a local of the CEP launched to address the labour struggles of freelance writers, could include alternative media writers. The CFU president suggested that *This Magazine* – a small progressive politics publication – should become the first union "shop" to sign with the CFU. Then editor Jessica Johnston was surprised

by the suggestion. It makes sense politically (*This* began as a socialist magazine in 1966), but the practicalities of publishing *This* would inhibit a push for
increasing writers' pay. *This* is a charitable non-profit with a writer-friendly contract that claims only first printing rights – unlike corporate contracts, which
can demand "all rights, in perpetuity, throughout the universe" (Professional
Writers Association of Canada 2006, 35) – yet the magazine has such a small
budget that pay "is more symbolic than anything" (Jessica Johnston, pers.
comm., 1 February 2009). A small organization such as *This* would have problems with a collective agreement provision to pay writers on time. The magazine is often obliged to wait until grant money arrives to pay its writers. "The
reasons that a union could be unworkable are the same [reasons] that would
make one desirable," says Johnston (ibid.):

> The protections we would want a union to offer would be next-to-
> impossible in practice, given the overall lack of resources. For example, I
> worked an average of twenty hours of overtime each week, typically every
> day of the week. Those were the demands of the job, and no union would be
> able to protect me from that. The 'exploitation,' though, was voluntary. I
> knew what I was signing up for when I took the job ... If there was a will
> there, we probably could have figured something out. But that would have
> involved prioritizing ourselves over the project, and we weren't willing to do
> that. Who wants to reallocate scarce resources in a charity to staff salaries? ...
> There's not much time to try to affect the status quo when the day-to-day is
> already way too much to do.

No agreement emerged from the CFU's brief discussion with *This,* but Johnston
sees value in the broader political project of affiliating with unions.

A unique example of unionized alternative media staff is *Briarpatch,* a news
magazine based in Regina, whose few staff members belong to Local 568 of
the Retail, Wholesale and Department Store Union. They pay dues, receive
benefits, are protected from arbitrary firing, and can access grievance processes. Most importantly, staff negotiate their contract with the magazine's
volunteer board every two years. "The challenge for us is more often to make
sure the work environment and expectations actually reflect the contract
(which is quite good), rather than fighting to improve the contract," says former editor Dave Oswald Mitchell (pers. comm., 3 March 2009). Contract negotiations can seem humorous – staff, familiar with the magazine's finances, will

argue against more holidays or a raise – but he emphasizes the importance of these negotiations:

> [Negotiations have] played a role in keeping me from burning out these last few years. Both sides [staff and the volunteer board, many of whom are union activists] share a desire to see the organization grow and thrive (or at least sustain itself), which is only possible if the staff feels valued and fairly compensated. In the non-profit sector, it's easy to sweep frustrations about feeling underpaid or overworked under the table for the sake of loyalty to the organization, but when there's an honest examination of finances, the compensation being paid, and an exploration of both monetary and non-monetary perks that can keep staff happy and energized, innovative and important solutions can emerge.

If joining a union is not possible, opportunities may lie in other organizational forms. San Francisco–based Media Alliance provides an example of a group that advocates for community access to media as well as for media workers (both alternative and progressive journalists in corporate media), provides services, and links ideas of media justice to media labour. The group was founded in 1976 to support social justice journalism but now focuses mainly on media access. Until 2006, it provided medical insurance to media workers. It will intervene in situations where it feels media workers are being economically hurt or censored, such as layoffs after a merger or when journalists are threatened for not revealing sources to the state. Managing director Tracy Rosenberg finds that though Media Alliance's membership is active around certain issues, media workers are difficult to engage, as they are often overworked and cannot afford to do free work. "I hope in time there will be a long-term goal [for Media Alliance]: making media workers' careers more sustainable," she says (pers. comm., 29 December 2008).

Although Media Alliance does not provide a model for funding alternative media labour, its work is instructive. It demonstrates what a broad-scope media justice centre could look like and presents an opportunity to envision ways that alternative media workers in Canada could organize to not only address issues around producing media, but also to create space to talk about labour. Canadian conditions differ from those in the United States, where there are more alternative media publications, many of which are able to pay contributors, and where media producers can access foundation money and a

222 *Nicole S. Cohen*

comparatively vast readership. However, Media Alliance demonstrates that bringing together a community of workers with shared interests is a good place to start.

Although there is an overlap of contributors to various projects, Canadian alternative media organizations usually operate in isolation. Instead, media projects could create collaborative structures through which to exchange ideas, strategize, and share labour costs. Groups could share business plans, pool resources to hire someone to sell advertising or work for multiple publications, hold joint fundraisers, and share office space. Generating research on organizational formations is important, which suggests that education and research institutes need to be brought into the alternative media fold. Journalism schools, often sites of privilege that train the next generation of corporate media workers, have potential to become partners in developing this research and alternative media in general. Few journalism schools offer space to discuss or produce alternative media, despite the fact that many students, facing limited or unfulfilling options in media labour markets, will spend some time in alternative media. Trained journalists can bring professional production skills to these projects, yet they have little to offer in the way of business or structural development. Not only could more journalism programs teach alternative media and media economics, but schools can help found student-community partnerships and research centres to develop and support alternative media.

Taking labour seriously means rethinking fundraising in terms of generating money to pay for labour. The Media Co-op, which publishes an alternative newspaper called the *Dominion,* is currently developing a financial model with the explicit goal of paying for articles. *Briarpatch* recently began paying for articles, and long-running *Canadian Dimension* has made it a priority to pay those who write for a living and low-income contributors (Cohen 2010). Several organizations, including *This* and on-line magazine *The Tyee,* have established funds to directly support the labour of investigative journalism, acknowledging the need for critical reporting and the importance of paying for good work. Unions could play a role here, funding the work of alternative media by paying salaries or funding investigative reporting on labour and political issues.

These suggestions demonstrate the need to be honest about the fact of labour. When alternative media appeal to readers and supporters for donations, rarely is the work involved in production discussed. By adopting more transparent business processes so that the community (readers/listeners, contributors, and supporters) can understand the true cost of production, alternative media may generate support in areas where it is needed most. Angel

(2007, 8) suggests that readers become more economically involved in alternative media production, beyond taking out yearly subscriptions, a model that the Media Co-op hopes will fund its work: so far, 130 sustaining reader members have signed up to donate five dollars or more a month, which has enabled the Media Co-op to pay for three articles per month.[6] Practices such as transparent budgets and collaborative business plans can incorporate readers into developing solutions.

Angel (ibid.) urges alternative media producers to invest time and money in training someone to handle financial planning and accounting. Placing greater importance on this aspect of alternative media while bringing the broader community into the planning process may enable projects to develop innovative business models that can foster stable, sustainable organizations. This does not necessitate adopting exploitative capitalist modes of production. For example, Arbeiter Ring, a Winnipeg-based not-for-profit book publisher, is a worker-owned collective organized around principles of participatory economics, which privileges collective ownership, self-management, and equity. These suggestions for supporting alternative media are based on acknowledging labour and understanding that, to be effective, these media need to be inclusive and fulfilling for workers. Projects will always include volunteers, but ways must be found to maintain the momentum of media projects, to curb burnout, to stop publications from folding, and to prevent working for alternative media from becoming a privilege that few can afford.

Labour and Alternative Media: Conceptual Possibilities

Problematizing alternative media labour enables an assessment of the limitations and possibilities for creating meaningful work that connects people to communities and to other workers, enables participation in entire processes of production, and encourages creative and political expression that may be stifled in corporate media. Furthermore, thinking about alternative media in terms of their labour allows a new consideration of the relationship between alternative and corporate media. Hamilton (2008, viii) argues that it has become difficult to make a clear distinction between alternative and mainstream media in terms of content, form, "organization, technology, and social intention." Examining labour can expand Hamilton's nuanced view of the flows between alternative and mainstream media.

The fact that contributing to alternative media requires time and resources to support non-waged work can account for the reasons why many who participate in alternative media are, or have been, paid workers in mainstream media, either seeking relief from a contracting corporate system (Deuze 2007, 62) or because of creative desires. *Undercurrents,* for example, was an activist project that drew on the skills, expertise, and equipment of professionals to produce and distribute the video magazine (Atton 2002, 50). As Atton (2004, 44) writes, "the value of acquiring conventional training in journalism has been recognized by many alternative media projects and journalists (indeed, some of those who work for the alternative media are 'moonlighting' from day jobs in the mainstream)." This speaks to the desires of media workers to pursue creative, gratifying work outside of a directly commodified relationship.

Labour also flows in reverse. Because access to paid employment in corporate media has become so difficult, many aspiring writers and producers work for free for alternative media to gain experience that can lead to paid positions. Many writers moved from *Clamor* to larger magazine work (Angel 2007, 4). Indeed, a scan of the terrain of Canadian media reveals back-and-forth flows between corporate and alternative media. During my time at *Shameless,* I encountered dozens of writers who had paid media jobs but found in *Shameless* space to pursue feminist ideas and satisfying work relationships. I also encountered aspiring writers for whom *Shameless* was an opportunity to gain exposure and experience that led to work for the largest publications in the country. Alternative media workers may be considered activists whose focus is on changing the ways in which producers work and resisting being reduced to mere content providers by media firms. Yet they can also be viewed as non-professionals seeking entry into media production.

This suggests that, following Hamilton's observation, we should understand mainstream and alternative media to be on a continuum of media forms, with flows of people, ideas, and practices between them. They constitute one another in complex, often contradictory ways. Media concentration, convergence, and shifting labour practices are revealing these contradictions at a rapid pace, enabling us to expand our understanding of alternative media solely as spaces of social justice. In some ways, alternative media can be understood as subsidizing the corporate press by training aspiring workers and enabling them to develop diverse perspectives and work practices. In other cases, we see "labour of love" discourses used by corporate media outlets to justify cutting writers' wages, as *Publishers' Weekly* (owned by publishing giant Reed Elsevier) did when it asked contributors to view their pay as an honorarium rather than a salary and to write for the magazine because writers "love books and believe in *Publishers' Weekly* as much as [it] believes in them" (Book Critics Circle 2008).

These conceptual suggestions demonstrate the opportunities for research into the labour of alternative media, which is necessary to uncover the dynamics of both the alternative and corporate press, and to understand the relationship between the two. Problematizing the labour of alternative media raises challenging questions, but it can also shed new light on dynamics of the Canadian media landscape and spark ideas to help create a viable, sustainable alternative media movement. This begins by recognizing the thousands of hours of labour thousands of people put into alternative media, work that cannot be understood simply as a labour of love.

NOTES

This chapter is based on ideas developed for an article written for *Briarpatch*. Thank you to Dave Mitchell for valuable feedback on that article and to Patricia Mazepa for sparking some of these ideas and pushing me to grapple with them.

1 An out-of-date but somewhat comprehensive list exists on the IndependentMedia website (IndependentMedia.ca, n.d.).

2 Unfortunately, there is little documentation of recent alternative media projects in Canada, particularly accounts of their operating practices and processes, reasons for staff leaving, and for publications folding.

3 In 2009, the Canadian Alternative Media Archive was launched to begin to remedy this situation. This digital archive, located at www.alternativearchive.org, is administered through Carleton University in Ottawa.

4 One notable exception is Brooten and Hadl's (2009) work on issues of gender in Independent Media Centres, which argues that some of the approaches to running non-hierarchical activist media spaces can reinforce gender oppression.

5 A member of an activist media project that pays a few contributors a month notes that "the people who come from more privileged backgrounds" are usually most assertive about being paid and being published (Cohen 2010, 144).

6 The advantages of a co-op model are further demonstrated by Vancouver Co-op Radio (CFRO). The station is owned cooperatively by thirty thousand members and employs four part-time staff who manage it collectively, working closely with the board and decision-making committees.

Freeing the Net
On-line Mobilizations in Defence of Democracy

KATE MILBERRY

Calls to regard the Internet as a basic public necessity are growing more insistent, particularly as on-line access becomes increasingly required for participation in social life. In this context, net neutrality and fair copyright are two of the most critical issues facing Internet users today. Net neutrality refers to Internet service providers (ISPs) treating all content and applications equally, without degrading or prioritizing service based on their source, ownership, or destination. Fair copyright seeks to counter proposed radical changes to "modernize" copyright laws that restrict or criminalize legal uses of digital content. These issues striate the new media landscape. But despite their unique complexities and challenges, they meet along a common fault line that demarcates the Internet into community and commercial models. They portend a two-tier Internet, with different services and mobilities for different users, and they cast uncertainty on the potential of the Internet as a democratic media system. This threatens fundamental values such as freedom of speech and expression, access to information, fair dealing, and the right to communicate online – issues that are all key to the development and operation of alternative media. Concerned citizens and activists have responded to these threats by rallying to defend an open Internet, mobilizing at the grassroots as well as the policy table. This chapter examines this civic mobilization by situating the issues of net neutrality and fair copyright in their historical context and considering their implications for democratic communication, which is the core of on-line alternative media.

Canadian Telecommunications Policy: From Common Carriage to Convergence

The outcome of current debates over policy formation and legislative reform will shape how the Internet and its content are deployed and accessed in the future. The evolution of telecommunications policy in Canada reprises a now familiar theme of competing interests, a conflict that increasingly sees public-interest-oriented regulation cede to regulatory liberalization that privileges the mobility of private capital. As Winseck (1997) argues, over the last several decades the focus has shifted "from protecting natural monopolies, industry boundaries, and balancing competing interests toward expanding markets, ensuring that competition works, and reconciling the contradictory interests between historically dominant telecommunications operators, new competitors, and large users."

Early regulation of the telephone system emerged out of railway legislation. The Railway Act of 1879 treated telecommunications as point-to-point communication systems carrying a variety of content and ensured that rates were "not unjustly discriminatory or unduly preferential" in order to facilitate the flow of information. However, vertical integration between publishing and telegraph interests threatened the flow of information as telegraph companies charged rival press agencies exorbitant rates for transmitting news by wire (Babe 1990, 57-59). A ruling by the Board of Railway Commissioners in 1908 ended this practice, in effect forcing a division between content providers and content carriers in Canada's nascent telecommunications system. This ruling established common carriage, both in principle and practice, and meant that telegraph, and later telephone, companies had to allow messages to be sent over their networks without alteration or interference as long as the appropriate rates were paid. By the end of the Depression, a capitalist political economy had taken deep root in telecommunication regulation. Nonetheless, a certain equilibrium was achieved between public and private interests, with the government often granting telephone companies monopolies in particular geographic areas in exchange for the delivery of universal affordable service. Inherent in this accord was the principle of common carriage, which is recognized today as an essential component of a democratic media system for its role in severing "mediated communication from the distorting influence of power that stems from ownership and control of the means of communication" (Winseck 1997).

Conflict around Canada's telecommunications policy agenda began to emerge as part of an uncertainty about the demands of a growing information economy. In the 1970s, a Department of Communication report titled *Instant World* suggested the key to future economic prosperity lay in the development of a seamless web of telecommunications, broadcasting, publishing, and computing, all woven together through common ownership and relaxed regulation. Here, for the first time in sixty years, the principle of common carriage appeared under threat as the convergence of what were, at the time, separate industries and technologies was touted as industrial strategy. Both consumers (wary of information control and worried about media diversity) and established telecommunications companies (fearful of losing their monopolies) shunned the idea (Winseck 2002). But the die was cast, and in the 1980s, the Canadian telecommunication environment began to shift from a tightly regulated monopoly to a competitive market. This new policy direction would have profound implications for the fledgling Internet in Canada. When a national telecommunications policy was enshrined in the 1993 Telecommunications Act, it bore the stamp of a view that promoted an increasing reliance on market forces over regulation (Anderson et al. 1998; Rideout 2003). Importantly, however, the act did preserve the historic practice of common carriage, reaffirming the tradition of non-discriminatory service (Barratt and Shade 2007).

Through the 1980s and the early growth of electronic publishing, telecommunications companies began to commingle carriage and content through developing and controlling databases, owning publishing houses, and generally moving to become information service providers (Babe 1990, 231-33). In 1996, in the wake of numerous government studies and reports, the Canadian Radio-television and Telecommunications Commission (CRTC) approved full-scale convergence, allowed telecommunications firms to acquire broadcasting licences, and permitted cable companies to provide local telephone service (Rideout 2003; Gutstein 1999). By the end of the 1990s, the long tradition of monopoly in the telecommunication sector had ended, and the vision of telecommunication as a public resource – an essential component of citizenship, democracy, and national identity – that had evolved over most of the twentieth century was fading as communication, information, and culture became increasingly commodified and treated much like other sectors of the economy.

This switch from telecommunications regulation in the public interest to regulation as industrial strategy brought increased media ownership concentration and a "new hierarchy of values that privileged expansion of information and media markets over concerns about freedom of expression and the role of communication in democratic society" (Winseck 2002, 796). According to Ruggles (2005, 708), this regulatory approach threatens to subvert "fundamental and long-standing Canadian cultural policy goals and ... the diversity of voices publicly audible in Canadian political and cultural spaces." It was within this context that the Internet arose as the new technology on the telecommunications scene. Fearful of discouraging investment and guided by free market rhetoric, the CRTC decided in 1999 against regulating content on the Internet, although the regulation of certain aspects would continue (Rideout 2003). This meant that Internet technology was left to the vagaries of the market to shape its growth and guide its development according to the narrow objectives of commerce: in a telecommunications environment that consistently favoured corporate interests, the Internet was thus exposed to manipulation and control by telecommunication corporations.

Net Neutrality: Protecting an Open Internet

Wu (2003) calls network neutrality a normative principle applied to broadband networks founded on non-discrimination. A neutrality regime preserves the Internet as a common medium, which treats all content equally, regardless of its origin or destination. In other words, a neutral network does not privilege one application (such as e-mail) over another (such as peer-to-peer). Structurally, net neutrality is enabled by the Internet Protocol suite (TCP/IP), a set of rules that allows computers to communicate over a network. The network layer (IP) is indifferent to the link layer (the physical infrastructure) over which it runs, as well as the application layer (content) running above it.

TCP/IP exemplifies the end-to-end principle, a design feature intended to push intelligence to the edges of the network – the end-users – creating a decentralized network that is dumb but efficient. As Wu and Lessig (2003, 6) explain, "By vesting intelligence at the edge or 'end' of the network, the Internet shifted the capacity to discriminate from the network to the user." According to Wu (2003), the fundamental argument for net neutrality rests on an evolutionary theory of innovation, wherein the innovation process is a Darwinian competition among user-developers of new technologies. Although initially considered a pragmatic engineering philosophy for network system design, the end-to-end principle is inherently political. This is because placing control with the user ensures that the network itself remains neutral in terms of the information and applications that pass through it. In this way, neutrality encourages freedom of speech and participatory democracy while discouraging centralized corporate and/or state control (Isenberg 2003). As Moll and Shade (2008, viii) point out, "net neutrality ensures that the Internet contains no centralized control mechanisms and that those who own the networks do not also control the content that runs over them."

The spectre of a non-neutral network raises fears that ISPs that own the system might have an increased financial interest in discriminating against competitors or differing classes of users. Indeed, this is what early telecoms policy, beginning with the Railway Act, sought to prevent. As they stand, existing laws do not stop wholesale ISPs from offering new services that prioritize some content (either that of their subscribers or of particular applications) over other content. This would authorize a two-tier Internet with a "fast lane" for those willing or able to pay higher fees – namely, corporate clientele – and a "slow lane" for the public, which would include small content providers (such as alternative media outlets), content creators (bloggers, artists), and regular users. Although this creates a more profitable system for incumbent ISPs, it also has the effect of gating the Internet, creating a closed non-neutral network requiring additional fees for priority access.

A related issue is that of throttling, or traffic shaping. Here, ISPs control the speed with which particular types of traffic travel the Internet. Some have already begun to slow traffic originating from peer-to-peer (P2P) applications, creating a de facto two-tiered Internet. ISPs use deep packet inspection to identify P2P downloads and slow their travel through the network ostensibly to make space for other traffic on a congested network, whereas those transmitting approved content remain in the fast lane. P2P traffic uses similar amounts of bandwidth as the proprietary services such as iTunes or Bell Video Store. However, no punitive measures against "bandwidth hogging" have been undertaken against these services (Mezei 2009).

Concern has also been voiced about unfair practices at a deeper structural level – the physical components that make up the Internet's "backbone." Where secondary ISPs sometimes connect users to the Internet, primary ISPs control the backbone – the main trunk connections that form its foundation. These are the high-capacity data routes and core routers that carry data around the world. In North America, they are owned by major telecommunication companies and to a lesser extent, governments and academic institutions. In

Canada, secondary ISPs pay large telephone and cable companies to connect to the Internet, and discriminatory and anti-competitive behaviour is a real threat.

According to a 2002 study conducted for Industry Canada, the most common complaint of secondary ISPs was "unfair competition and pricing on the part of large ISPs" (Industry Canada – Telecommunications Policy Branch 2002, 4). As the on-ramp to the Internet, primary ISPs occupy a powerful position and can act as gatekeepers, deciding who will enter and at what price. They have the incentive and the means to discriminate, extracting higher rents from those wishing to connect to the Internet via their pipes. Similarly, a non-neutral Internet enables primary ISPs such as Bell and Rogers to privilege their own search engines, Internet telephony, and video streaming services while slowing down or entirely blocking content from their competitors. This would force users – small ISPs and the public – to pay higher premiums to prevent bandwidth-heavy content such as videos and music from being shunted to the slow lane. Moreover, the use of deep packet inspection enables primary ISPs to collect detailed data on all individual users, including those of their competitors. One critic has labelled this as "akin to industrial espionage," noting that "such data must be considered to be ... highly confidential between a service provider and its customers" (Mezei 2008, 2).

Under the Telecommunications Act (Canada 1993), such actions might be considered "unjust discrimination" as derived from the principle of common carriage. However, due to the CRTC's 1999 decision not to regulate the Internet, provisions from the act have not been carried over to that venue. The result has been the creep of non-neutral behaviour, and according to Geist (2007b), the major ISPs already have a "history of blocking access to contentious content (Telus), limiting bandwidth for alternative content delivery channels (Rogers), and raising the prospect of levying fees for priority content delivery."

The telephone and cable company ISPs defend their traffic management practices as fair and legal, and to a large part, the CRTC has agreed with them. In November 2008, the CRTC denied a request by the Canadian Association of Internet Providers (CAIP) that Bell stop throttling secondary (retail) ISPs that use its network, and it subsequently turned down CAIP's appeal a year later. Following a July 2009 hearing, however, though the CRTC upheld Bell Canada's traffic shaping measures, it did establish some important requirements and restrictions. Specifically, it outlined a new test to determine reasonable traffic management practices, while cautioning that ISPs could be investigated for targeting specific applications. The decision also further mandated full disclosure of traffic management practices and banned the use of personal information gathered through deep packet inspection (CRTC 2009d). A subsequent CRTC ruling ensured that the policy framework established by the net neutrality decision would apply to the use of mobile wireless data services that provide Internet access (CRTC 2010d).

This net neutrality decision sets a policy direction for regulating the Internet in keeping with the democratic rights of citizenship long associated with communication (Winseck 1997). This is significant in a corporate telecoms sector hostile to a neutral network and bolstered by a regulatory environment that has urged greater reliance on market forces. The favoured policy direction has been one that enables "market forces to continue to shape the evolution of the Internet infrastructure, investment and innovation to the greatest extent feasible" (Goodman, quoted in Barratt and Shade 2007, 297). However, with the recent CRTC ruling, the Internet could well develop along broad public interest principles rather than as "a gift to the major industrial interests" (Barney 2004, 102).

An increasingly commercialized telecoms sector and policy arena is not the only threat to democratic (non-commercial, public) communication on the Internet, however. Digital copyright law portends a restrictive and punitive environment for cultural and political expression in cyberspace. The shift from transmission of content to the use and ownership of content reshapes the digital mediascape from a neutral and non-discriminatory network to corporate information highway controlled by toll charges and surveillance points.

Copyright Law: Balancing Act or Corporate Payday?

Rooted in both natural law and utilitarianism, Canadian copyright law has a dual objective: to ensure fair compensation for authors so as to encourage their creative labour and to promote social utility through limiting creators' exclusive rights (Scassa 2005). In other words, copyright enshrines the right of creators to be paid for their work as well as their obligation to share it. This view of copyright as a property right has emerged as the dominant rationale and the reigning view in policy circles. It regards the free market as the most effective way to allocate information "products" derived from the legislation. This interpretation prioritizes exchange value (rather than use value) so that financial incentives from the market appear to stimulate the generation of such products (Murray and Trosow 2007). It further recognizes a trade-off between promoting creation and providing access to creative works and is sometimes described as a balancing act between creators' and users' rights. Raab (1999, 69) has critiqued this "doctrine of balance," suggesting that regulators' activities must be understood in the context of wider frameworks of control wherein balancing often "constitutes steering towards a preferred ... outcome." Applied to copyright, the concept of balance can obfuscate real differences among various stakeholders in resources and political power, limiting its usefulness as a baseline criterion (Murray and Trosow 2007). On this account, the copyright regime is inherently conflict-ridden, a classically modern struggle between public and private: ideas must be shared (public) in order for cultural creation and innovation to occur; yet the capitalist drive to monetize ideas leads to their enclosure (privatization).

The contest over copyright is further complicated by the fact that the Department of Canadian Heritage and Industry Canada share jurisdiction for copyright but do not have corresponding views of its role in cyberspace. For Heritage, copyright is the economic stimulus behind the creation and dissemination of cultural content (Murray 2005). From this vantage point, the Internet, with its capacity for the infinite reproducibility of perfect and inexpensive copies, appears to jeopardize creators' economic compensation, therefore requiring a strict copyright regime in cyberspace. From Industry's utilitarian perspective, however, copyright is an important tool for promoting innovation. Here the Internet appears not as a threat (or massive illegal photocopying machine) but as an aid to economic prosperity, one that Industry Canada sees as stimulus to the economy (albeit concentrated in businesses and corporations) and innovation (creators and educators). As such, the Internet requires a more inclusive intellectual property regime (ibid.).

Canada's initial attempts to adapt copyright policy to the digital era came with the signing of the World Intellectual Property Organization (WIPO) Internet treaties in 1996. The WIPO treaties were conceived to address copyright concerns as applied to cyberspace, and they served as the inspiration for the highly restrictive Digital Millennium Copyright Act (DMC Act) established in the US. The DMC Act implemented digital rights management (DRM) and made it illegal to circumvent anti-copying technologies, regardless of whether copyright is being infringed. It also makes unlawful the production and dissemination of devices intended to circumvent DRM. Although Canada has not yet ratified the WIPO treaties, it has come under much pressure, particularly from the United States, to do so (Tawfik 2005). The policy trend suggests a limited interpretation of copyright law based on the economic remuneration to rights holders – increasingly, large corporations, as they buy up copyrights and privatize information like any other resource. Canada's last effort to modernize the Copyright Act, the now dead Bill C-62, prompted comparisons to the DMC Act (Geist 2008); however, as the DMC Act undergoes reforms in the US, Canada's newest legislation, Bill C-32, emerges as even more restrictive (Geist 2010).

While the government contemplated the intersection of the Internet and the Copyright Act, the courts weighed in on the issue, moving away from expansive interpretations of copyright and re-establishing the importance of users' rights. According to a 2002 Supreme Court of Canada majority ruling, copyright law should recognize creators' rights while acknowledging the limited nature of these rights (*Théberge v. Galérie d'Art du Petit Champlain Inc.* 2002). Further, the court affirmed users' rights: "Once an authorized copy of a work is sold to a member of the public, it is generally for the purchaser, not the author, to determine what happens to it" (ibid., para. 34). Users' rights earned similar recognition in three subsequent Supreme Court rulings, indicating the multiple interests in Canadian copyright law (Murray and Trosow 2007; Scassa 2005).

Adding further complexity to the debate is the unacknowledged but crucial difference between material property and intellectual property. Unlike material goods but similar to utilities and media content, information can be considered a public good in that it is non-rivalrous and essentially non-excludable. A non-rival good is a good whose consumption by one person does not reduce its availability for consumption by others: a person can read a newspaper, see by the light of a street lamp, or download a music file without limiting another's use. Non-excludability means that no one can be effectively excluded from using the good (Baker 2002); prior to encryption technology, there was no effective way to prevent the sharing and exchange of digital information. Consequently, though information is considered property, it does not have the same political economic characteristics that make it scarce and easily monetized.

These special characteristics of information – that it is non-rivalrous and non-excludable – confound its interpretation as property. Information's porous nature means that its exchange cannot be controlled in the same ways as material goods in a market economy. The proliferation of alternative news websites and social software, such as blogs, vlogs, wikis, and open publishing, has compounded the difficulties of control and undermined distinctions between creators and users, further complicating the application of copyright law (Geist 2005). The demand for free and open access to information on the

Internet has been met with an increasingly strident campaign by "rights hold-ers" for total control of creative works through the expansion of exclusive intel-lectual property rights (Glass 2009). The government has been receptive to this attitude in recent attempts at copyright modernization: Bills C-60, C-61, C-32, and the current Bill C-11 have all been criticized as being biased toward cor-porate interests while ignoring users' rights, sparking widespread opposition among Canadians (Shade 2008).[1] Such a narrowly economistic interpretation of copyright fails to address the wider implications for the right to communi-cate, freedom of speech, fair use, and other cultural practices that are founda-tional for alternative and independent media.

Digital Copyright

With increasing Internet connectivity in North America, the debate over copy-right in the digital arena has heated up. The ability to make perfect copies in-stantly and cheaply, and to share those copies with millions of people on-line, has rights holders – usually large corporations – worried about revenue losses and eager to expand their control over copyrighted material. While these cor-porate interests rail against piracy and other peer-to-peer file sharing, they fail to mention that digital rights management technology has enabled more con-trol over works "past the point of sale" than ever before (Murray 2005).

Net neutrality intersects with digital copyright over the issue of media con-vergence and the radical departure this signals from the practice of common carriage. The self-regulatory approach to the tiering of the Internet (fast and slow lanes) meshes seamlessly with restrictive digital copyright regimes pro-moted vigorously by corporate interests. In both cases, the public interest is subjugated to those of private profit. The objective, via technical and legal means, is to secure the Internet as a commercial medium for the exchange of information commodities while curbing or eliminating historical user free-doms. This dramatically contrasts with the hacker ethic, which states that infor-mation wants to be free. The ethic originated with graduate students working on the Internet's forebear, ARPANET, at the Massachusetts Institute of Tech-nology's Artificial Intelligence Lab. These original hackers eschewed locks of any kind – digital or physical – and shared computer source code in the col-laborative spirit of advancing knowledge and promoting innovation. The no-tion that information could be owned, much less bought or sold, was utterly foreign to these Internet pioneers (Levy 1984).

Information has been free – in the sense of the hacker ethic – since the Internet's inception, contributing to a commons-based ethos in cyberspace. The proliferation of information over the Internet – its creation, exchange, and dissemination – has been a boon to cultural creators and consumers, and the source of much angst for owners of copyright. The Internet, aided by the World Wide Web, made it possible to share creative works with mass audiences and allow people to access and make multiple copies perfectly, cheaply, and easily. Many artists saw this as a way to directly and inexpensively share the fruits of their labour with the public, but the large copyright owners in the music and film businesses feared revenue losses. This prompted a shift in copyright legislation in North America, starting with the DMC Act, from promoting innovation and cultural production to defending the property rights of copyright owners. The result has been a transition from the North American tradition of "free culture" to a "permission culture" wherein "creators get to create only with the permission of the powerful, or of creators from the past" (Lessig 2004, xiv). A free culture supports and protects creators and innovators by giving them certain rights over their work but also limits those rights in order that subsequent creators may benefit from a shared culture.

In the on-line environment, where people are both users and creators, and consumers and producers, the notion of free culture or information has become ingrained, an extension of the commons-based ethos of sharing that developed along with the Internet. The copyright revision process is thus a more relevant and, indeed, a more pressing concern to the public. The public's interest in copyright, according to Geist (2005, 2), "is the result of the remarkable confluence of computing power, the Internet, and a plethora of new software programs, all of which has not only enabled millions to create their own songs, movies, photos, art and software but has also allowed them to efficiently distribute their creations electronically without the need for traditional distribution systems." The demand for public policy to defend people's ability to interact with and create information, rather than just consume it, is growing (Murray and Trosow 2007). However, the perspective of corporate rights holders, that "the Internet has changed everything, that copyright reform must happen quickly and that the Internet is a lawless place" (Murray 2005, 25), has been influential, causing the copyright revision process in Canada to be more reactionary than reformist. Calls for the expansion of copyright have largely emanated from corporate rights holders, not creators. This explains why major copyright stakeholders, such as the Canadian Recording Industry Association, support copyright legislation that favours corporate interests, whereas independent artists, along with a large and vocal public, do not. "We have seen that creators, artists, cultural organizations and the publishing community do not support this bill," commented Carole Lavallée (2010), Bloc Québécois member of Parliament during the first reading of Bill C-32. "Only businesses support it." The Alliance of Canadian Cinema, Television and Radio Artists (2010) said Canadian performers were "alarmed that artists are being left out," and the Songwriters Association of Canada criticized the bill for following "other nations down the copyright rabbit hole into a netherworld that makes less and less sense" (Schwartz 2010).

The public face of the corporate efforts to tighten copyright legislation is largely focused on a scaremongering campaign over peer-to-peer file sharing (Longford 2007). Since 2003, the Recording Industry Association of America has opened legal proceedings against more than thirty-five thousand people; the Major Motion Picture Association continues to sue peer-to-peer websites while embarking on an aggressive "educational" campaign (McBride and Smith 2008). According to the Electronic Freedom Frontier, however, this "irrational war on P2P" is not generating a single penny for artists. In fact, despite lawsuits against many P2P providers and over twenty thousand music and movie fans, file sharing is "more popular than ever" (Electronic Frontier Foundation 2009). The main motivation for this aggressive campaign against music and movie fans is a perceived loss of revenue (not to be confused with creators' remuneration).

"Unauthorized use" and "illegal downloading" are the catchphrases of this campaign, drawing powerfully on capitalist society's deep identification with property and ownership rights. Misleading slogans such as "Piracy is theft" and "Artists/creators must be paid" serve to confuse the issue more. The effect has been a narrowing of the copyright revision debate to P2P file sharing, helping to normalize a ban on "all uses of copyrighted materials not expressly authorized by the copyright owner" (Murray 2005, 30). This challenges not only the spirit, but the letter of copyright law: the Copyright Act deals only with acts of making copies, so though rights holders are guaranteed a limited set of exclusive rights with regard to the copying of their work, they have little control over how their work is used. The expansive notion of copyright – that rights holders have unlimited control over all uses of their copyrighted materials beyond the point of sale – is unprecedented and contradicts the promotion of innovation that has been a cornerstone of copyright law.

It has been widely noted that access to the common stock of cultural creation and scientific discovery is necessary for human innovation and development (Benkler 2006; Geist 2005; Gutstein 1999; Lessig 2004; Vaidhyanathan

2004; Wu 2003). Because creativity is incremental, each increment requires reference to some element or elements of previous work. Thus, the Copyright Act's fair dealing exception preserves access to copyrighted works for research, private study, criticism, review, and news reporting. In this way, fair dealing acknowledges the "transformative or value-added uses that go beyond mere consumption" (Scassa 2005, 60). Canada's Supreme Court has interpreted fair dealing as a user's right, with a substantial role to play in maintaining balance between owners' exclusive rights and the public interest in access to cultural works (Murray and Trosow 2007).

Indeed, the creation of a fair copyright regime will require expanding fair dealing, a move the Conservative government appeared to make in its last copyright legislation. Bill C-32 extended fair dealing to education, parody, and satire; however, these new exemptions were subservient to technological protection measures. The legislation also provided for a "notice and notice" system for ISPs dealing with alleged digital copyright infringement – another step toward fair copyright. But where fair copyright advocates caution against regulating copyright through technology, Bill C-32 supported technological protection measures that were stronger than what international agreements such as the Anti-Counterfeiting Trade Agreement (ACTA) required (Geist 2010). In this regard, the bill looked more like an implementation of the WIPO treaties and of the most controversial aspect of the DMC Act than a "made in Canada" solution, as the government promised. The Conservatives' most recent rendition of copyright reform is Bill C-11, which is little more than a reintroduction of Bill C-32.

Freedom Fighters for Fair Use and Net Neutrality

Despite the corporate siege of the community model of the Internet, an array of civil society groups have mounted a vigorous defence of net neutrality and fair copyright on-line. Indeed, what actions have been taken to defend net neutrality and hold back new copyright legislation appear to have been, at least in part, the product of public pressure mounted by concerned citizens. The Internet served as the main organizational tool and platform in this defence, and mobilization occurred on several, often overlapping, virtual fronts.

On one of these, media activists have worked to "save" the Internet, recognizing its centrality to a democratic mediascape as well as political expression on-line. OpenMedia.ca, formerly called the Campaign for Democratic Media, has acted as a hub for media activism in Canada and has emerged as a clearing house for action around net neutrality and fair copyright. It has made net neutrality one of its main campaigns, called SaveOurNet. In May 2008, SaveOurNet organized a public rally at Parliament Hill in Ottawa to draw attention to ISP throttling practices and put net neutrality on the political agenda. The campaign went into high gear around the 2008 federal election, documenting and publicizing the different parties' policies on net neutrality. Another web-based effort in February 2009 encouraged Canadians to participate in the CRTC's public consultation on traffic shaping. The campaign used Facebook and YouTube to raise awareness, generate interest, and help almost thirty-five hundred Canadians submit comments to the CRTC. Both the OpenMedia and SaveOurNet websites offer a variety of resources, including press releases, media coverage, blogs, and educational videos. They show people how to get involved, either by signing a petition, joining an on-line advocacy group, registering for a news feed, making a donation, or contacting government agencies directly on policy matters. Interactivity is the key to such websites, which aim to draw people in with information and on-line "action items" before pushing them out again into cyberspace and additional forms of political engagement.

Other stakeholders in the fight for net neutrality include non-governmental organizations, researchers, and industry associations. The Council of Canadians issued an action alert calling on the government to protect net neutrality. The Canadian Centre for Policy Alternatives, a progressive research institute, has shown its support by publishing a timely book featuring Canada's leading experts on telecommunication policy (Moll and Shade 2008). Academic research projects have also been indispensable, such as the Canadian Internet Policy and Public Interest Clinic. Operating out of the University of Ottawa, the clinic is intended "to ensure balance in policy and law-making processes on issues that arise as a result of new technologies" (Canadian Internet Policy and Public Interest Clinic, n.d.). It has closely tracked the erosion of net neutrality and in 2008, filed privacy complaints against Rogers, Shaw, and Bell for using deep packet inspection technology to shape network traffic. The Canadian Research Alliance for Community Innovation and Networking has worked actively to preserve the open Internet, launching an educational website, www.whatisnetneutrality.ca, and hosting the Alternative Telecommunications Policy Forum in 2006. The forum's objective was the amendment of the Telecommunications Act to "confirm the right of Canadian consumers to access publicly available Internet applications and content of their choice" (Barratt and Shade 2007, 302). Some industry associations have also become active on behalf of their members, joining coalitions and initiating their own campaigns. As previously mentioned, the Canadian Association of Internet Providers, which represents the independent ISPs, asked the CRTC to instruct Bell Canada to stop its throttling practices.

As noted above, these efforts appear to have motivated the CRTC to hold hearings in 2009 that revisited its 2008 decision on Internet throttling. The resulting net neutrality decision is considered a partial victory for advocates of an open Internet, although discriminatory throttling practices by primary ISPs can continue. But the traffic management framework the decision outlined, although currently not binding, does mark a policy shift toward regulating the Internet a decade after the CRTC announced its hands-off approach. Net neutrality advocates continue to push for more regulation, calling on the CRTC to reinforce the traffic management framework by conducting regular compliance audits of ISP traffic management practices.

On the copyright front, Fair Copyright for Canada is perhaps one of the most important citizen-led coalitions to form in response to the last round of copyright revisions. It was launched by University of Ottawa professor Michael Geist through Facebook in December 2007. The intention was to use Facebook, a popular social networking platform, to draw public attention to an important issue that was likely to fall under the radar of most Canadians. It was a humble effort, with invitations sent to about a hundred of Geist's Facebook "friends." However, within hours, the group started to grow; two weeks later there were more than twenty-five thousand members and as of this writing, membership stands at over eighty-six thousand. What is remarkable about Fair Copyright for Canada is not only that so many people joined; one might question the efficacy of a strictly on-line group in any case (Wilson 2002). But it provided a portal into what might have otherwise been too complex or dry an issue, especially for the young people who typically use Facebook. It offered a starting point, as well as a forum for discussion and debate, as the numerous wall postings indicate.

The group also pushed people off the Facebook platform via links to key related websites, including its own. It further provided the incentive for "local" chapters to form, and for those chapters to organize off-line, in their communities. For example, the Vancouver chapter, with over twelve hundred members at the time of writing, uses its Facebook group to give updates, report on meetings with politicians, and post letters to and from government members and agencies. The group, like many other local chapters, holds face-to-face meetings, where it develops strategies for moving the proposed legislation in a more user-friendly direction. People were also inspired to organize real world actions, using Facebook to promote their event. For example, a Calgary blogger named Kempton – a professed non-activist – became interested in fair copyright through Geist's blog. He joined the Fair Copyright Facebook group and used the social networking site to organize a rally to meet with then-Minister of Industry Jim Prentice, who was responsible for drafting Bill C-61. Kempton generated mainstream media interest and mobilized about fifty people who gathered to confront Prentice on the proposed copyright amendments. Members of the Fair Copyright Facebook group have organized similar interventions, scheduling meetings with local politicians and dropping in on their public appearances.

Canadian artists have also been vocal about their opposition to restrictive digital copyright and their unwillingness to punish fans for downloading their work through on-line peer-to-peer networks. The Songwriters Association of Canada has called for the legalization of P2P file sharing, and the Canadian Music Creators Coalition (CCMC) (2008) decried proposed legislation as "an American-style approach to copyright. It's all locks and lawsuits." The CCMC formed in 2006, when six independent labels pulled out of the Canadian Recording Industry Association over fundamental differences with that organization's stance on copyright: "Until now, a group of multinational record labels has done most of the talking about what Canadian artists need out of copyright ... Legislative proposals that would facilitate lawsuits against our fans or increase the labels' control over the enjoyment of music are made not in our names, but on behalf of the labels' foreign parent companies" (Canadian Music Creators Coalition, n.d.). Similarly, the Documentary Organization of Canada (DOC) opposed Bill C-61, criticizing it for failing to protect fair dealing in the digital realm. Access to copyrighted work for the purposes of critique or discourse is at the "heart of free speech," noted DOC chair Michael McNamara (2008).

Policy for an Open Internet

A broad spectrum of Canadian society has become involved in the fight to preserve an accessible and open Internet. From academics and media activists to artists, computer geeks, and "regular" Internet users, people have grappled with the issues and converted their outrage and dismay into productive political engagement, both on-line and off. They have used the Internet in creative ways to educate, to inform, and perhaps most importantly, to connect Canadians to each other and the political process. But activism has not remained a

strictly on-line phenomenon: the flow of information and action from the virtual to the material world (and back again) demonstrates the integration of
the Internet into daily life and reinforces its importance as a public utility – a
communication medium accessible to all Canadians. The campaign to defend
the Internet has enlivened the democratic process, particularly around communication technology, forcing the federal government to defend its policy
positions. The public outcry has also gained the attention of opposition parties: all of them have expressed concerns with the proposed copyright legislation repackaged in Bill C-11. As far back as 2007, the Green Party had
incorporated net neutrality into its policy platform, and in 2008 and again in
2009, New Democratic Party MP Charlie Angus introduced a private member's
bill to protect a neutral network. In response to a questionnaire sent out by
Campaign for Democratic Media (now OpenMedia), the NDP, Green Party, and
Bloc Québécois explicitly supported legislation to prevent ISPs from traffic
shaping (Pinto et al. 2010). Liberal Industry critic Marc Garneau stated that "all
internet networks, including wireless networks, must treat all lawful content,
applications and services in a non-discriminatory manner" (Liberal Party of
Canada 2009).

   The diverse group of Canadians fighting for net neutrality has a simple goal:
non-discriminatory access to the Internet. In other words, digital information
should be delivered regardless of its content and at the same speed to any
user. User travel or activity in cyberspace should not be controlled or censored;
nor should a tiered system be imposed requiring double payments for this service (once for standard Internet connection and again on a "pay-per-use" basis
determined by content providers) (Mosco 1989). Regarding net neutrality, the
solutions offered are variations on the same theme. Some, such as SaveOurNet,
seek only government enforcement of the historic practice of common carriage, establishing the Internet as a common carrier like the telephone system.
Geist (2007a) and other advocates hold that regulatory reform granting legal
protection of the principle is necessary to ensure corporate compliance with
non-discriminatory practices. Lawson (2007) recommends legislative change to
enable the Telecommunications Act to deal adequately with the phenomena
of convergence and competition in the telecoms market. The public interest
group Canadian Research Alliance for Community Innovation and Networking
(2005) wants the government to enforce existing provisions within the act that
"ensure affordable access to high quality telecommunications networks for all
Canadians and that safeguard, enrich and strengthen the social and economic
fabric of Canada." Smaller content providers warned the CRTC to ensure "that

undue preferential treatment is not given to distributor-owned content or that the gate-keeping activities by the distributor are not permitted to influence accessibility and ultimately the diversity of Canadian voices available to the public" (Geist 2007a, 79).

On another front, the recommendations for copyright reform have taken an urgent tone as Bill C-11 makes its way through Parliament. Craig (2008) states that legislative change is needed to allow the Copyright Act to catch up to recent court decisions highlighting users' rights. Fair dealing is one of the most important components of an equitable copyright regime, and yet in the new legislation, fair dealing provisions are subservient to technological protection measures. Kerr (2010) proposes a "copy duty" that obliges those who use digital locks to provide a key when access is lawful in order to protect fair dealing exemptions. Tying anti-circumvention or technological protection measures directly to copyright infringement would further protect fair dealing (Craig 2010).

The historic connection between information, effective citizenship, and democracy is enshrined in telecommunication policy initiatives such as universal access and common carriage, and is maintained and championed by alternative media. In an era of ubiquitous computing and always-on connectivity, the Internet is a major conduit for information. It further promotes the participatory dimensions of democracy by enabling citizens to communicate, organize, and produce on-line, bypassing corporate and state media. An open Internet is thus an essential component of our media system. However, caught in the grip of debates over net neutrality and digital copyright, the future direction of the Internet is uncertain. It is not clear whether the Internet will become a cybermall dedicated to consumption or a virtual public sphere capable of being used to support and enhance democracy.

NOTE

1 Bill C-61 was the federal Conservative government's last effort to revamp Canadian copyright law prior to Bills C-32 and C-11. The bill was touted as fulfilling Canada's obligations under the WIPO Internet treaties, which in any case the government said it was already doing (Chung 2009). Bill C-61 faced much criticism for its bias toward large corporate rights holders as well as its restrictive approach to users. It died with an election call in 2008.

Regressive Social Relations, Activism, and Media

PATRICIA MAZEPA

Understanding media as the articulation of social relations suggests that progressive alternative media constitute activism working to alleviate or eliminate social relations of oppression and domination, as distinct from regressive media as activism that facilitates or entrenches these relations. Identifying what is progressive or regressive is, however, becoming increasingly challenging, since racist and anti-gay groups attack civil rights as special rights, conservative religious groups lay full claim to what is moral, and corporations identify themselves as ethical and socially responsible. It is further complicated when politically left-leaning groups can be divisive in their practices, whereas politically right-wing groups can appear to be inclusive and democratic, as the following quotation from the Canada Family Action Coalition (n.d.) suggests: "[We are] ... a grassroots citizens' action organization that provides strategies, networking, training and tools to enable ordinary Canadians to influence their government ... [We] provide a voice for Canadians with common-sense principles, citizens who believe in direct democracy ... We believe in the mutual responsibility of all citizens to be active in community life and participate in the democratic political practice."

Since alternative media can be similar at the level of structure (organized as non-profit), of participation (self-defined communities), and of activism (in working to affect government policy making or law), it is understandable when alternatives are reduced to a matter of perspective, between left and right, or us and them, particularly since competition, debate, and choice are constructed hallmarks of liberal democracy. Such framing is evident in policy making (appearing as a competition between interest groups, or stakeholders), in journalism (defining objectivity as a provision of opposing sides), or in law (as individual rights, as "my" rights versus "your" rights) (Miceli 2005). In the process, however, political economic and social relations are obfuscated, as the fixation is on the competition or the debate, not on the underlying power relations that give rise to them. In 1979, Golding and Elliott (2000, 642) pointed out this shift in politics as framed in news: "Power is reduced to areas of negotiation compromise, and politics to a recurrent series of discussions, debates and personalities. It is removed from the institutions of production. Thus news bears witness to the institutional separation of economics and politics, a precondition for the evacuation of power from its account of the world. Power is thus absent from news by virtue of this severance of politics from economics; power is located in authority not in control, in the office-holder not the property owner."

Given the increasing control of the property owner through the concentration of ownership of media and other resources, it is important to identify how power is also articulated in and through structured alternatives. In particular, we must consider the social relations that are manifest and invigorated in media and activism that, although appearing alternative, do not challenge power, but feed on it, cultivating it at the margins. This chapter thus begins by providing a conceptual overview of these social relations to consider how power is exercised via a series of regressions that facilitate control. It identifies how these relations are articulated through a number of organizations in Canada that advance them, from the group level to the larger organized networks that concentrate political and economic power. The chapter notes where commercial media lend themselves to regression and where alternatives are constructed, produced (in print, broadcasting, and on-line), and contained through state regulation. This chapter attempts to remedy the relative lack of in-depth studies that focus on this range of regressive media in general (Downing et al. 2001; Atton 2006) and particularly in Canada. It includes a representative number of examples from the far right through to religious, neoconservative, and market-libertarian variations, identifying what may be considered as a reinforced New Right, whose activism draws strength from existing social divisions, inequalities, and experiences thereof, and thereby further entrenches and extends them.

Regressive Social Relations

Underpinned by an epistemology and ontology that identify and separate phenomena on the basis of difference, a regressive understanding of social relations begins by viewing the social as if *naturally* divided into distinct, immutable categories. Although the politics of difference and identity have been advanced as a method of critique and a means of progressive social change, shared foundations can also be used to provide teleological evidence that people are *inherently* distinct in order to valorize difference in discrete categories. These range from the individual unit to social divisions of race, ethnicity, gender, or class, hierarchically arranged and operationalized in politics, policies, and practices. Although these distinctions exist both socially and analytically, and the meanings that fill these categories are negotiated (what it means to be black, white, male, or female, for example), once such categories are historically established and institutionalized via a whole range of religious dogma, cultural traditions, media representations, business practices, and government policies, they can appear to be permanent structures that are self-evident, unchanging, and therefore irrefutable. A categorical understanding of social relations is part of the process of what Mosco (1996) refers to as structuration, by identifying how social categories and relations are articulated (expressed and joined together) as a social formation in reaction to, and in defence against, social change. Structuration thus distinguishes how media and social movements can be regressive in struggles for hegemony.

Steps toward regression are taken when social categories are used to *legitimate and maintain* hierarchical order in dominant pairings such as man over nature, rich over poor, white over black, men over women, or Canadians over immigrants. Difference can be categorized by biological or visual signifiers (skin or hair colour, body or eye shape), cultural signifiers (speech, language, or clothing), or economic signifiers (income or employment). Berlet and Lyons (2000) identify this step as one in a series of regressions whereby people who are distinguished as different, whether self-identified or not, are subject to the following processes. They are *marginalized* (separated as abnormal or inferior in some way and labelled as "them" or as "the other"), *stereotyped* (assigned common signifiers, characteristics, specific social traits, or habits that are deemed inferior or disdained), or *objectified* (identified primarily by body parts, such as breasts, or clothing, such as a veil) of which one (or all) is used to entrench or advance dominant power relations. The exercise of power as fundamental to morality is key here, as Dyer (2000, 246) underscores: "It is not stereotypes, as an aspect of human thought and representation, that are wrong, but who controls and defines them, what interests they serve." How this process has worked is evident in the history of colonialism. As S. Hall (2000, 275) explains, hierarchies of inferiority and superiority are "displaced from the 'language' of history into the language of Nature. Natural physical signs and racial characteristics became the unalterable signifiers of inferiority. Subordinate ethnic groups and classes appeared, not as the objects of particular historical relations (the slave trade, European colonization, the active underdevelopment of the 'underdeveloped' societies) but as the given qualities of an inferior breed. Relations, secured by economic, social, political and military domination[,] were transformed and 'naturalized' into an order of *rank*, ascribed by Nature."

Further along a regressive continuum, people so differentiated are used (or invoked) as *scapegoats* (targeted or blamed for any political economic or social problem), *demonized* (identified as untrustworthy, irrational, conspiratorial, sinful, and evil), or *dehumanized* (as foreigners, enemies, and aliens) (ibid.). Once such categories gain hegemonic momentum, physical and social segregation, violence, or imprisonment – as reaction or as a means of social control – can ultimately establish a basis for justifying internment and extermination. In the last century this has been exercised in variants of fascism and Nazism, the latter when people were segregated and exterminated on the basis of politics (communism), gender (homosexuality), or religion and ethnicity (Jews, Russians, and Poles). The kind of media that articulate and facilitate this understanding of the social have been historically identified as authoritarian or totalitarian due to the concentrated control over their structures and content such that communication is reduced to propaganda, whether directly by the state or indirectly via corporate ownership (Mazepa 2011b).

Such regressions are not always so extreme or relegated to history, however. Policies and practices that underpin and legitimize regressive social relations are evident in seemingly benign commercial media (whether in news, music videos, or sitcoms), such that people marginalized in poverty are associated with moral failure (Kendall 2005; Swanson 2005; Parlette 2010); stereotyped black males are represented as threatening criminals (hooks 1996; Welch 2007); objectified women are reduced to tools for sex or procreation (Abrams 1996); violence is condoned as the de facto method of effective communication; and war is entertainment (Schubart 2009).

Linked to an ideology of populism, power is interpreted as operating linearly – up or down hierarchical categories. Experiences of oppression can thus be

understood as the result of the actions of a particular group and directed upward to, for example, "elites," "bureaucrats," or "bankers," who are blamed for
social oppression – as *exceptions* to capitalism, patriarchy, or racism rather
than endemic to them. Causes of social oppression can also be directed downward as complemented by ideologies of racism (for example, blame the
blacks), nationalism or nativism (blame the immigrants), patriarchy (blame
women or feminists), classism (blame welfare bums or labour unions), sexism
(blame homosexuals), or Orientalism (blame the Other) (Said 1979). Wright
(2009, 191) identifies this as a process of "strategic framing," which can be rhet-
orical, symbolic, or mediated, that invigorates the formation of regressive social movements whereby "causality or blame" for political economic or social
conditions is attached to particular subjects and assigned a specific response.

As with any social movement, these formations may range from small, locally concentrated groups (or "gangs") to national networks, as is evident in the
current Tea Party movement in the United States (Burghart and Zeskind 2010),
to formal political organizations as variously manifest in the current far right
parties elected to parliaments in Britain, the Netherlands, and the European
Union (Berezin 2009; Saunders 2009). Such articulations are not unique to the
US or Europe, however. As the rest of this chapter shows, Canada has its own
homegrown variants that span the range of far right, religious right, and neo-
liberal alternatives. Their membership, organizational base, and goals differ
widely, and the extent to which they can coalesce into a political movement
(like the Tea Party) is a matter of debate (Delacourt 2010), yet they share several common denominators such that the regressive social relations that they
invigorate are not contradicted but valorized and reinforced. It is important to
identify differences in these various ideologies as discussed below; but recognize that their commonalities are more significant, the progeny of power without which, despite denial, the current neo-liberal hegemony cannot survive.

Activism and Media of the Far Right

In Canada, no far right political party is currently elected at any governmental
level, but this does not mean that they do not exist; nor does it mean that the
regressive social relations they stimulate cannot be mobilized. Indeed, as
Wright (2009, 191) suggests, a "burgeoning transnational network" of far right
groups in North America and Europe is linked by what he calls a "trajectory of
contention." Aiming to be a registered political party at the federal level in
Canada, the National-Socialist Party of Canada (NSPC), for example, suggests

that it lies waiting for an impending crisis when its interpretation of social relations may be more acceptable as both explanation and solution, since it observes that "the current regime in Canada has failed to act in the interests of the white population of Canada and hence is rapidly losing legitimacy" (National-Socialist Party of Canada 2008). The party's campaign platform has included an emphasis on Canadian sovereignty, particularly in terms of national control of resources and public health care, as well as withdrawal of the Canadian military from Afghanistan. Although these positions may not be easily distinguishable from those held by the range of federally elected political parties, membership eligibility differs sharply: it is based on "100% White racial ancestry" and is opposed to "racial mixing," multiculturalism, homosexuality, and anything that can be identified as Jewish, particularly what is described as the "Jewish controlled media" (ibid.).

Since the NSPC's establishment in 2006, its emphasis on white nationalism has become more pronounced, and its website has become more sophisticated. It links to other neo-Nazi or white nationalist groups and websites from the United States, Great Britain, and Australia, providing a whole gamut of media offerings, including 24/7 live streaming radio, CDs, DVDs, pamphlets, posters, and other merchandise such as flags, T-shirts, jewellery, and gift certificates. The site links to commercial record producers and distributors such as Stormfront ("white pride worldwide") and National Socialist Movement (NSM) 88 Records, which promotes and sells hate rock and hate metal as a major method of recruitment and promotion of far right ideas (Jipson 2007; Beste and Kugelberg 2008).

Common terms indicate negotiated views of social relations fashioned to deflect criticism. The slogan of NSM's music website is "To provide the racialist public the best in original Internet media" (NSM Radio-Television Online, n.d.). Using the term "racialist" rather than "racist," and "white pride" rather than "white supremacy," suggests that there is no inherent hatred toward "non-whites" (views differ as to the degree of violence condoned), yet the term supports a regressive view of the social as naturally and hierarchically divided. Segregation or separatism (physically, socially, and spatially) are argued to be the necessary solution to social and political economic problems. Any racial mixing is perceived as a crime against nature, and offenders, particularly women, are considered race traitors, as studies of such groups in the United States have indicated (Fluri and Dowler 2004; Blee 2002).

The NSPC shares its white nationalist ideology with an umbrella organization, the Canadian Heritage Alliance, though the two are not directly linked.

Sporting the slogan "Fighting for freedom, fighting for Canada," the alliance's website was an articulation of anti-immigrant (xenophobic), nationalist, and populist ideology (anti-elitist, particularly against federal political leaders). In its own publicity, the Alliance identified itself as a "collection of dissident writers and concerned Canadians who have united to act as a political lobby group. We seek to revive the civil liberties of the Canadian citizen, which have been smothered by the voice of the minority" (Hack Canada 2010). The alliance website was removed by the federal government in the fall of 2008 due to (as proclaimed by the single web page that still exists) "soviet-style censoring ... under pressure by the corrupt Canadian 'human rights' Commission" (Canadian Heritage Alliance 2010). At the time, operating on a web page called Freedomsite, the Canadian Heritage Alliance was linked to similar organizations in Canada, such as the Heritage Front (white nationalism), Canada First Immigration Reform Committee (opposed to "special rights" for immigrants), the Citizens for Foreign Aid Reform (C-FAR, which aims to eliminate aid to other countries), and the Canadian Association for Freedom of Expression (CAFE), as variants on the same theme.

The emphasis on "voice of the minority" and "special rights" is intended to suggest that human rights and anti-discrimination policies are misnomers and that they discriminate against the white, particularly male, subject. In this view, real experiences of oppressive social conditions (such as poverty or unemployment), or inequality of access (to decision making or material resources), are explained as the direct consequence of liberal governments and progressive policies rather than of capitalism or individualism, for example. Blame for social conditions, such as crime or homelessness, is directed downward to the Other (fill in the blank) as the cause of the problem, and solutions typically consist of eliminating or "reforming" immigration (Canada First Immigration Reform Committee and Western Canada Concept are examples of groups that take this stance).

Although membership in the groups mentioned above is minor in actual numbers, policy activism can be significant, particularly in legal battles, when a wide range of ideological differences can converge over a specific issue. CAFE links, for example, to the American Electronic Frontier Foundation, which advocates for free speech on the Internet. The battle for free speech is one of many controversies in policy and law making; though free speech is intended to mitigate the legitimization of social relations of domination and oppression, it can also be used to facilitate them (Downing 1999).

Canada does have anti-hate provisions, identifying both hate crimes and hate propaganda with stipulations under the Criminal Code of Canada (sections 318, 319, and 430.4.1) and the Canadian Human Rights Act (section 13). The public expression of "hate" is legally recognized in Canada, and, subject to juridical review, offending web content can be deleted via the Criminal Code or removed via the Human Rights Act (section 320.1; Department of Justice 2008). Provincial codes contain similar provisions, particularly against racism (Ontario Human Rights Commission 2009), yet all are subject to ongoing criticism ranging from being too vague in language to being biased in application and rulings. Section 13 of the Canadian Human Rights Act in particular has garnered a wide variety of opponents, including the Canadian Civil Liberties Association (2009).

Since absolute free speech is necessary for the promulgation and propagation of regressive views, however, both federal and provincial institutions are subject to permanent and aggressive lobbying, to not only remove the provisions, but to abolish the institutions altogether as a "tyrannical reign of censorship" (National Citizens Coalition, n.d.; Canadian Human Rights Commission Exposed, n.d.). Similar criticism was voiced in certain mainstream media editorials, particularly in the newspapers of the former CanWest Global Communications Corporation – now owned by Postmedia Network – including the *Montreal Gazette* (2009), the *Ottawa Citizen* (2009), and the *National Post* (Brean 2009). These editorials reacted negatively to the Canadian Human Rights Commission's (2009, 40) report to Parliament, entitled *Freedom of Expression and Freedom from Hate in the Internet Age*, which reaffirmed that both "the *Criminal Code of Canada* and the *Canadian Human Rights Act* continue to contain provisions to deal with hate on the Internet." The commission (ibid., 15) reiterated that free speech can be socially (and legally) regressive whether published in a newspaper or electronically transmitted over the Internet: "Words and ideas have power. That power, which is overwhelmingly positive, can also be used to undermine democracy and freedom ... Hateful words have the power to harm. They can isolate, marginalize our fellow citizens, not because of what people have said or done, but solely because of their personal characteristics, such as ethnicity, religion, race or sexual orientation. The target [sic] of hateful words are seldom the powerful and secure."

After releasing this report, however, the Canadian Human Rights Commission decided to disallow a complaint launched under section 13, which was brought against Marc Lemire, webmaster of the site hosting the Canadian Heritage Alliance, indicating in its ruling that "the federal law governing hate speech violates Canadians' *Charter* rights to freedom of expression" (Krashinsky 2009). Although the ruling centres on eliminating the commission's ability to impose fines, many editorials and columns (across the former CanWest news chain in particular) explicitly heralded it as the tipping point toward abolishing the federal and provincial commissions entirely. In celebrating its victory, the Heritage Alliance website listed these media links as evidence of legitimacy.

Activism and Media of the Religious Right

In the media and activism of the religious right in Canada, regression is identified as a result of immorality, associated with any person, group, policy, law, organization, or institution that does not prioritize Christianity. Absolute perspectives, or "God-given rights," are considered eternal and unerring as linked with Christian fundamentalism elsewhere (Thomas 2005). Again, a categorical and relational perspective of social relations underpins understandings of gender (as either male or female) and sex and marriage (as between a man and a woman), with social relations hierarchically ordained. In this view, media constitute a tool used to propagate Christianity, and members of the Christian right have both a duty and a responsibility to contribute to, produce, and/or own media, whether on a local or global level.[1]

On the global level, for-profit Christian media conglomerates include the Christian Broadcasting Network (CBN) and Trinity Broadcasting Network; the latter also broadcasts to Latin America, India, Asia, and the Middle East. CBN utilizes the entire range of media technology, with 24/7 news programs, letter mail, telephone and on-line prayer counselling, daily radio and television shows (Pat Robertson's *700 Club*), RSS feeds, podcasts, blogs, and more recently, *700 Club Interactive,* for personal interaction with the hosts though e-mail, chat networks, and Skype (Domanick 2010). In the US, Christian broadcasters are organized and represented by the National Religious Broadcasters (2009), whose declaration of principles boldly asserts "a long standing commitment to use every electronic medium available to proclaim the Gospel of our Lord and Saviour Jesus Christ [and] ... to faithfully obey the command of Christ to preach the Gospel, even if human governments and institutions attempt to oppose, constrain, or prohibit it." In Canada, the political expression of the religious right is small in comparison to that in the US, but its influence on government is thought to be disproportionately significant, as Canadian journalist Marci McDonald (2010) argues in her book *The Armageddon Factor: The Rise of*

Christian Nationalism in Canada. The religious right encompasses a wide variety of organizations, including a federally registered political party called the Christian Heritage Party (n.d.), which considers itself a party of *permanent opposition* to what it defines as "the secularist minority in Canada that dominates four powerful institutions that shape all our lives: government, courts, the public education establishment and the major news and entertainment media." The Christian Heritage Party (CHP) has a minor web presence and produces a small newsletter (the *Communiqué*), focusing its activism on opposing (or supporting) government policies that intersect with its priorities and principles. The party also seeks to eliminate the CBC, which is viewed as biased and criticized for "us[ing] our hard-earned taxes to undermine the very Christian worldview responsible for our civilization, and for the very concept of freedom of speech." Additional criticism is directed toward the goal of reforming the Canadian Radio-television and Telecommunications Commission (CRTC) accordingly or eliminating it altogether (Hnatiuk 2009).

The CHP is fond of quoting the preamble to the Canadian Charter of Rights and Freedoms, in which "the supremacy of God" is recognized (Walkom 1981). This inclusion in the preamble is claimed to be a result of the Christian right's activism, particularly the self-identified key lobbying by the Evangelical Fellowship of Canada (EFC) with its own media presence. The EFC media range is minor in comparison to that of its US equivalents but is similarly organized to include resources such as a monthly magazine *(Faith Today)*, issue videos, short on-line radio programs by its president *(Canada Watch)*, and its on-line ministry, Christianity.ca, which includes links to Christian ministries and media worldwide. The EFC's activism is directed toward eliminating secularism in public policy and public institutions, and advancing religion as a public matter, to the extent that evangelicals are defined by their "social engagement," which is considered "a matter of obedience to God and is itself a form of worship" (Clemenger 2009; Benson 2007, 2008).

As the EFC is a registered charity, it reports to Canada Revenue Agency that "religious publishing and broadcasting," which constitute approximately 15 percent of its activities, are classified as part of its "programs to achieve its charitable purpose" (Canada Revenue Agency 2008). In its 2008 submission to the CRTC supporting its own broadcasting channel, the EFC criticized the CBC for not providing "representative" or "balanced" broadcasting "in the area of religion" (CRTC 2008a, 8287), and it has identified this as media bias in a published refereed journal article (Haskell 2007a; 2007b), which was retitled and published in book form by an evangelical publishing house in Toronto (Haskell 2009).

The EFC is affiliated with Crossroads Christian Communications, which describes itself as "life changing media" and is also a registered charity. It produces the program *100 Huntley Street* on both radio and television, complete with an on-line social media suite. It owns the Crossroads Television System (CTS), licensed to the city of Hamilton (see McDonald 2010, 246-76), and has recently become a financial and broadcasting partner with the US faith-based ComStar Media, owner of FamilyNet and AmericanLife Network, which "never compromis[e] conventional family values" (ComStar Media 2009). This gives Crossroads "exclusive rights" to its programming and its developing multi-platform and social media technology, which FamilyNet's CEO dubbed "GodTube on steroids" (Cartt.ca 2011a; Domanick 2010).

Under current CRTC regulations, religious broadcasting is considered a distinct form of broadcasting rather than an opportunity for one religion to disseminate its views (CRTC 1993).[2] However, the EFC is working to change this. In successive CRTC public hearings, it presented briefs arguing that government policies on religious broadcasting were discriminatory because the commission required "that each religious broadcaster ... provide opportunity for a diversity of religions to express themselves through programming" (CRTC 2007d, 8294). In the 2007 CRTC hearings on diversity in media, for example, the EFC argued that such a policy hindered its ability to attract advertisers because "advertisers who are targeting a Christian audience on Christian stations are not willing to pay for advertising during programming of other faiths" (ibid., 8296). The EFC noted an increase in Christian artists, music, and bookstores in Canada, as well as Christian broadcasting stations in general, as indicators of economic viability. One need only look to the commodification of religion in the US for evidence of a developing billion-dollar industry (Kintz and Lesage 1998; *BusinessWeek* 2005; Thomas 2005; Clark 2007b).

As televangelism exemplifies, the process of commodification is well suited to Christianity and evangelicalism specifically, since ways of propagating the faith can be indistinguishable from corporate branding and marketing strategies, which are used to promote a Christian identity, particularly among youth (Ward 2003; Clark 2007a).[3] This potential economic growth is recognized by Canadian media entrepreneurs such as Moses Znaimer, who purchased "certain assets" of the "multi-faith" VisionTV for $25 million, reportedly seeking to make its 1.6 million weekly audience of mostly senior-aged wealthy viewers "attractive to advertisers" (Flavelle 2009). In Canada, English and French radio stations primarily broadcasting religious content (music and/or spoken word) have increased from fifty-five in 2003 to seventy-five in 2010 (there are now more religious stations licensed than campus radio stations), whereas television stations have increased from five to seven over the same period (CRTC 2010c).

The goal of the EFC is to have the CRTC allow "single faith" broadcasting and to change the policy so that each religious group can purportedly have its own station and be considered for licensing just like any private broadcaster. In the Diversity of Voices hearings, CRTC commissioners were quick to observe that the EFC's argument sounded "discriminatory." In this instance, the CRTC adhered to the fundamental basis of the airwaves as public and the broadcasting of religion – all religions – as a public service, as both evidence and articulation of diversity rather than an opportunity for one religion to dominate and profit from it. Thus for Christian broadcasters (and any religious broadcasters which are, coincidentally, considered to be a charity for general tax purposes), the obligation of a religious broadcasting licence ensuring religious diversity should also be considered "charity." However, this ruling was dismissed by the EFC as injurious to its bottom line (CRTC 2007d, 8345), and the proceedings ended at that. Although there have been no significant changes to the CRTC's policy on religious broadcasting, the CRTC will be subject to increasing pressure to reconsider, as religion – particularly the Christian religion – is further developed into its own market globally and in Canada. As the EFC's submission indicates, it can use both the Canadian and American industries' financial growth as evidence of commercial viability, especially if the CRTC continues to advance policy making that favours private industry rather than public service. On the other hand, the EFC can secure its own niche and deflect its evangelical component by emphasizing the Canadian identity of the artists, thus appealing to the CRTC on the basis of the Broadcasting Act, rather than their specific religion. As these are early times in the battle for private religious broadcasting, it is more important that religion in general is accepted as mainstream and is thus marketed as such.

Indeed, the importance of the "electronic pulpit" should not be underestimated. As McDonald (2010, 248) emphasizes, the current CRTC regulation is "the single most important reason why Canadian evangelicals have lagged behind their American brethren in both numbers and political clout," and hence it "puts the CRTC on the top of the Christian Right's hit list." Since the majority of religious groups have charitable status for their properties and donations, their organizations have an advantage over the alternative media that do not enjoy this status, particularly as the range of what is considered political is so malleable. For example, after a lengthy court battle, the anti-poverty

magazine *Briarpatch* had its charitable status removed by the federal government because it was deemed too political. Although *Briarpatch* survives, the
Atlantic-based alternative magazine *New Maritimes* (1981-1997) was forced to
shut down when its Canada Council grant was cancelled; the council changed
the wording in its definition of "culture," and the editor was told that "politics is
not culture." Canada Revenue Agency (2008) does stipulate that "a charity may
pursue political activities that are non-partisan, related to its charitable purposes, and limited in extent." Yet, for the religious right, these purposes are not
limited in extent but include fundamental positions on gender, life, marriage,
and the family. Moreover, these positions are shared with federal political parties such as the Christian Heritage Party, the EFC, and other religious organizations including Focus on the Family Canada, the Canada Family Action Coalition,
the Institute for Canadian Values, and National House of Prayer, as well as
regional and local groups (see McDonald 2010).

Religious associations that are registered charities are somewhat limited as
to the extent of resources and degree of engagement they may invest in activities that are deemed political; depending on revenue earned, they may apply
10 to 20 percent of revenues to such work. As a result, some conservative religious groups choose not to register as charities, as their mandates are explicitly political and activist. For example, the aims of Equipping Christians for the
Public Square Centre (2007) included training and education to "motivate with
a new media alternative, one that tells our side of the story – the right side of
the story – NoApologies.ca; defend the free expression of Christianity everywhere and anywhere; and advocate on behalf of Christians who are facing the
Human Rights Commissions and other legal challenges simply because they
refuse to be 'politically correct.'"

The activism of the religious right is not always identified as religious per se;
instead, it is presented as *issue*-focused (on child care, education, crime, health
care), thereby deflecting attention from the power of patriarchy or racism. Such
activism is further supported through professional lobbying activities. Even
though the EFC is a registered charity, it employs professional lobbyists, as
does the Canada Family Action Coalition (CFAC), which is not a registered charity (Office of the Commissioner of Lobbying of Canada 2011b). CFAC also supports its own research institute, called the Institute of Marriage and Family
Canada (IMFC), with links to other research resources in what it calls the Family
Index (2005), which "catalogues social science findings on family matters obtained from journals, books and government surveys." The IMFC is "partnered"

with the American neo-conservative Heritage Foundation's Family and Society database, and it shares information with the National Family and Parenting Institute in the United Kingdom. These organizations collect and correlate research linking marriage and family to data on poverty, crime, sex, and violence. The research gathers evidence to argue that social problems result from changes to the traditional family and gender relations, and thus can be solved by strengthening, or returning to, the conservative model of the traditional family unit. Here, marriage is defined as solely between a man and a woman, the married male is head of the household and primary breadwinner, and the model is underpinned by an explicit anti-feminism (Dobson 2004; Reed 2004; Lukas 2006). More extreme versions attack education and science itself as a matter of faith and opinion, as exemplified in the construct of the debate between creationism and evolutionism (see McDonald 2010, 175-206).

Avoiding the hardline divisions that mobilize categorical views of social relations, the relatively new Canadian evangelical think-tank called Cardus softens its approach by using progressive language that aims to integrate religion into "the public sphere" as necessary and natural for the "common good" (Cardus, n.d.; see also Gruending 2007). Cardus was formerly the Work Research Foundation, as linked to the Christian Labour Association of Canada (Gruending 2007), which essentially advocates for corporatism as contextualized within the religious right's worldview (Neatby 2007; Canadian Labour Congress 2008). Calling itself a "think tank dedicated to the renewal of Canada's social architecture" (Cardus 2009), Cardus proclaims that its "thought, research and policy weaves through the integrity of the biblical story – which is not a private, but a public story, a public truth changing everything it touches" (Cardus, n.d.). It publishes the *Comment,* complete with a "manifesto," and regularly issues its own news releases reviewing public policy. Its current campaign is directed at the federal government "to increase charitable tax credits from 29% to 42% as part of its stimulus package" (Cardus 2009, 2010). As its director of research proclaimed, "Adopting this proposal will be a sound investment in Canada's social architecture ... The charitable sector is critical to the rich fabric of Canadian society, and provides taxpayers exceptional return on investment" (Cardus 2009).

Increasing tax credits or government funding to charitable institutions will complement the federal cancellation of "the capital gains tax on the transfer of publicly traded securities to public charities in Canada" (Flaherty 2006) and may facilitate further privatization, already bolstered by corporate tax credits, government deficits, and reductions in government services. Governments can thus increasingly cut back on services and download them to the established charities, as they did during the 1930s Depression, making access to assistance filtered through – and dependent on – Christian religious teachings and affiliation (Maurotto 2000).

Backed by doctorate- and master's-level university degrees, members of the religious right are present as sources and commentators in a range of Canadian media. This includes the CBC, the *Toronto Globe and Mail,* news talk radio in Ottawa, and frequent op-ed contributions (for example, see Institute of Marriage and Family in Canada, n.d.). The religious right's activism includes networking over particular issues; for instance, members of the Canada Family Action Coalition include related organizations such as the Campaign Life Coalition and the Defend Marriage Coalition, among others, which have promoted and supported the federal Conservatives' child care policy to forward government funding directly to the individual family rather than to public daycare facilities (Valiani 2006). CFAC also employs registered lobbyists to communicate directly with ministers and their branches on its targeted issues (Office of the Commissioner of Lobbying of Canada 2011b). At the provincial level, organizations of the religious right focus on policies that are provincial responsibilities such as those applying to education. They supported Alberta's Bill 44, which proposed that schools be required to notify parents in advance if a class intended to deal with "religion, sexuality or sexual orientation" so that parents could choose to "remove their children from the lessons" (CTV.ca 2009; Vanderklippe 2009). Activism and support for such initiatives can also come from similar groups that do not explicitly identify with a particular religion but espouse comparable views of social relations, as expressed in neo-conservative or market-libertarian ideologies.

Neo-Conservative, Neo-Liberal, and Market-Libertarian Variations

Sharing a categorical and relational view of social relations with the religious right but not explicitly identifying itself as religious, REAL Women of Canada calls itself the "alternative women's movement." Established in 1983, it provides an increasingly detailed website offering its current and archived position papers, newsletters, and evidence of its extensive activism. This includes, for example, support for the abolishment of the CRTC as "an unaccountable group of bureaucrats who are attempting to retain power over a broadcasting system, which has long outgrown its control and which Canadians do not want" (Landolt 2009). REAL Women has been successful in lobbying for several of the federal Conservative government's decisions involving gender in particular, whether through policy changes or direct funding cuts (see Chapter 4 in this volume; Public Service Alliance of Canada 2010).

REAL Women considers government programs, policy, or forums that deviate from or question its principles as concrete demonstrations of what it calls the "Silencing of the Conservative Voice in Canada" (Public Service Alliance of Canada 2010). Like the far right, it identifies a number of targets, which encompass "most of the major institutions" in Canada, including media. It argues that a powerful left-wing movement exists (in extreme forms, a conspiracy), a stance that is used to portray conservatives as victims or underdogs and to legitimize and justify their activism. Employing the language of progressive social change – of rights and social justice – thus appears as subjective and subject to interpretation rather than an explicit claim on public resources. As Kozolanka (2007a) suggests, this is a recurring tactic of the New Right: its continual demand for reiteration and rationales of policies that, over time, have become integrated into society forces progressives on the defensive, constantly drawing on (and exhausting) valuable resources. The stratagem has the added impact of stalling, undermining, and impeding any progressive gains.

Common to the arguments of neo-conservatives on both sides of the US-Canada border is that this dynamic is part and parcel of what is termed a cultural war in which the mainstream media are set up as the enemy (REAL Women of Canada 2003). The Canada Family Action Coalition (n.d.) suggests, for example, that the war is "being waged between traditional families and religious communities, on the one hand, and radical statists and secular 'liberation' movements, on the other. And traditional faith and family advocates must be prepared to approach the media in the role of combatants."

The war is thus being approached on a number of organizational levels that can be integrated into a series of overlapping networks in Canada to build on what Brownlee (2005) identifies as the "corporate cohesion" integrating a social movement. These include personal networking through groups that link Christian faith with business; one of these, an association called Intriciti, identifies five core values as "authentic faith, innovation, excellence, servant leadership and strategic partnership" (Intriciti, n.d.). The networking of corporate executives with politicians and journalists is advanced through another organization called Civitas, where "people interested in conservative, classical liberal and libertarian ideas can not only exchange ideas, but meet others who share an interest in these rich intellectual traditions" (Civitas, n.d.). These ideas are operationalized in business practices and researched and extended by think-tanks whose publications are promulgated via opinion leaders and major media sources (Abelson 2002; Brownlee 2005; Gutstein 2009). Further political lobbying of government and grassroots advocacy (as demonstrated by the EFC and REAL Women) reinforces regressive views of social relations and can influence public policy accordingly. The networks also advance a particular view of religion as both a social requirement and essential to public health.

The link between faith and business mixes both neo- and religious conservatism with neo-liberalism and market-libertarianism, and can legitimize and reinforce ideas that are held in common. These ideas are strengthened, as they do not criticize or contradict each other, particularly when it comes to accepting capitalism as synonymous with (or at least inseparable from) freedom and democracy. Although such combinations can be volatile in reconciling the range of views represented, common grounds include activism for free speech and against Human Rights Commissions, and for freedom of the marketplace and correspondingly for less government, while reinforcing conservative ideas of social relations that intersect gender and social class in particular. Currently on REAL Women's to-do list, for example, is the elimination of women's equity and labour unions, which it describes as tyrannous and "undemocratic." REAL Women identifies union dues as funding particular "left wing causes such as abortion, homosexual rights, promotion of feminism," and it criticizes them for being income-tax deductible, citing American examples of "right to work legislation" as ways to attack what it calls the Supreme Court of Canada's persistent backing of unions (REAL Women of Canada 2008). This complements the activities of the Christian Labour Association of Canada, as mentioned earlier, and the consistent view of the National Citizens Coalition (NCC), which was established in 1975 as an "advocacy group ... for more freedom and less government in Canada" (National Citizens Coalition, n.d.).

The NCC was formerly headed by the current Canadian prime minister, Stephen Harper, an evangelical Christian (and also a member of Civitas). It employs the discourses of populism to bolster support for policies such as privatization, and it seeks to eliminate unions as the "greedy 'big brother' indistinguishable from 'big government,'" as contrasted with "the little guy" (gender specific) and "ordinary freedom-loving people," who are comparatively powerless (ibid.). Such ideas gain momentum and credence through several neo-liberal research institutes or think-tanks, including the Fraser Institute, the

Conference Board of Canada, and the C.D. Howe Institute, which are registered non-profit organizations whose research focuses on public policy under-pinned by neo-liberal principles, and is supported by corporate donors.

These think-tanks, which approach research topics and policy criticism through such principles as individualism, market-liberalism, and variants of libertarianism, have also garnered Canadian political and media attention as major sources for identifying issues and their solutions (Abelson 2002; Carroll and Hackett 2006) to the extent that their views become hegemonic (Kozo-lanka 2007a). Such increased influence led Carroll (2007, 276) to observe that the fact that, "by the late 1990s, the Fraser Institute was no longer represented in mainstream media as the voice of the far Right confirms how effectively neo-liberal business activism has managed to shift the terms of political dis-course." This shift became all the more secure as funding cuts by the Con-servative government resulted in the demise of two relatively independent research institutes: the Canadian Policy Research Networks and the Canada Council on Learning (CCL), which closed in October 2009 and January 2010 respectively. As an editorial in the *Toronto Globe and Mail* (2010, A16) marking the demise of the latter exclaimed, if the CCL "is essential, corporations or the charitable sector or both should flock to its rescue." The editorial suggested that the CCL – and any independent think-tank, for that matter – should "speak relevantly, and powerfully, and the private money should come rolling in."

Going beyond media releases and policy advocacy, the Fraser Institute con-tinues to develop its educational purview to provide free seminars focused on economics for journalists, students, and teachers (Fraser Institute, n.d.). Taking this one step further, the Manning Centre offers a program titled Navigating the Faith-Political Interface, and its School of Practical Politics offers a certifi-cate in political communication (Manning Centre, n.d.). It is rumoured to be negotiating sponsorship of an academic research chair in political communi-cation at Carleton University's School of Journalism and Communication in Ottawa. The Manning Centre's board of directors includes a relatively diverse but well-connected set of individuals who espouse its stated goal of "the re-vitalization of Canadian conservatism ... the regulation of the genetic revolu-tion, and the management of the interface between faith and politics" (ibid.). The centre's offerings continue to develop the relationship between activism and media as was evident in the fall 2009 Firearms Political Activism School, which aimed to "equip firearms owners and activists with the skills and know-ledge necessary to effectively influence public policy." This includes how to "network with like-minded individuals and build strength through numbers;

properly communicate your message, and use the Internet to spread your message more effectively" (ibid.; see also the Law-abiding Unregistered Firearms Association, n.d.).

Media Activism: Democracy and Social Relations

The relationship between media and activism is historically one that is fundamental to democracy. If we accept that all media are constituted by social relations, identifying how categories, relations, and formations are activated through media and organizational networking is essential, since the closer one gets to power, the more regressive social relations seem to disappear and become viewed as natural, legitimate, and immutable. These shifts include activism and media that appear to be less about power relations and more about issues – that is, seemingly less about racism and violence than about individual rights and free speech, less about patriarchy and sexism than about families and religious freedom, and less about social class and labour exploitation than about cultural identity and the market. The strength of these shifts increases when they are complemented and valorized, whether through media framing or the commodification of religion, or when social and religious fundamentalisms are ignored (or advanced) to facilitate capitalism. This hegemony deepens when research is privatized or becomes so bound up with religion that reasoned argument is discredited and descends into relativism. These are dangerous formations that feed and embed social relations of domination and oppression, skewing policy and law making and setting up either/or scenarios. When regressive worldviews are presented as matters of belief, opinion, debate, or *cultural* war, their claim on resources and (re)entrenchment of power is masked. The more that regressive policies result in problems such as increased poverty and crime, the more that regressive solutions may appear as the only logical and moral choice, a cycle that is particularly disconcerting. When the language of "justice," the "common good," and the "public sphere" is appropriated to obfuscate power relations, progressive alternative media and directed policy activism become all the more necessary and urgent.

NOTES

I would like to thank graduate students Stephanie Guthrie and Mary Higgins, as well as co-editor Kirsten Kozolanka, for assistance in this ongoing work.

1   The struggle for progressive religious variants is evident in alternative media in Canada (see, for example, *Geez* magazine, www.geezmagazine.org/) and internationally through the World Association for Christian Communication (www.waccglobal.org/).

2   The CRTC (1993) defines "religious" as "anything directly relating to, inspired by, or arising from an individual's relationship to divinity, including related moral or ethical issues." See Grant, Lafontaine, and Buchanan (2006) for the specific licences granted by the CRTC under this policy.

3   Ward (2003, 125) identifies a psychological dimension, noting that "the religious experience is inseparable from a consumer experience. The consumer experience (consumer therapy) and the religious experience are both desire driven and aim at immediate satisfaction" (quoted in Taylor 2008, 21).

13

DIY Zines and Direct-Action Activism

SANDRA JEPPESEN

We look for the events and people and stories that lead up to where we are now and will compel us to go forward. This is our air, our nourishment. This is what must be dug up, following the deepest roots of arts and language and collective efforts. When we actualize our principles, when we struggle with our notions of right and wrong, we contribute to the development of a real anarchist culture.

– Arsenal Collective (2000)

Anarchists live in cultural spaces sustained by a lived commitment to collective principles and values that differ from mainstream norms. These values are based on a different way of thinking about and living in the world, which challenges established ideas on every issue, discourse, institution, and social relation imaginable. The backbone principle of anarchism is a critique of relations of domination, so anarchist values and practices are against domination, be it in the form of hierarchies, unequal power relations, structural inequities, or authoritarian behaviours. Media practices derive from this principle as well. Whereas many alternative media theorists and practitioners work against mainstream media practices, anarchists have lived anti-authoritarian values as a point of departure. These values include direct democracy, participation, cooperation, collective self-determination, taking action to create change, mutual respect, long-term accountability, and lived social equality, among others. They are crucial to the creation of anarchist media, and therefore as anarchists we come to media production and theory with different objectives. Media activists ask: How can we challenge mainstream media to get our voices out and gain power? In contrast, anarchists ask: How can we tell stories of our communities in directly democratic, mutually respectful, collectively accountable, caring, and compassionate ways that will continue to create the social transformation toward which we are working in our activism? How can media be created and shared in ways that prefigure a non-hierarchical society?

In this context, I will critically analyze the process of implementing these principles in the production of zines (small self-produced magazines) by green anarchist activists (radical environmentalists). I will theorize the field of anarchist cultural production and take the *Elaho Valley Anarchist Horde (EVAH)* zine (see EVAH 2001) as a case study.[1] Using Bourdieu's *The Field of Cultural Production* (1993), I will examine how anarchist zines are legitimated through their adherence to a complex range of activated political commitments that I call *value-practices*. For Bourdieu, this recognition is produced in three ways: (1) avant-garde cultural products legitimated by other avant-garde artists, (2) cultural products legitimated by the cultural apparatus, and (3) cultural products legitimated by the mass marketplace of culture.

I have been making zines and engaging in direct action since the 1990s. The research I present here is a participatory analysis of the value-practices engaged by anarchist zinesters (zine-makers). I chose the *EVAH* zine as a case study because I was part of the horde (a loosely structured anarchist affinity group), although I was not involved in making the zine. My subject position as a zinester, and an activist within this horde, is key to my methodology. My research thus engages the value-practice of self-representation based on the values of participation and experience as knowledge. I have shown elsewhere (Jeppesen 2009) that the notion of value-practices functions as a sliding scale, where the zine-maker emphasizes some practices over others, often based on negotiations with the material conditions of a culture that does not share their values. Thus, an analysis of value-practices is not to be used as a measuring stick (how anarchist is this text?), but rather as a way of understanding the underlying values in the activism being documented and in the production of texts. Considering alternative media from a cultural studies perspective will reveal the deeper social and cultural relationships that are profoundly transformed through anti-authoritarian value-practices enacted in media production and dissemination.

Anarchist Zines and the Field of Cultural Production

Duncombe (1997, 6) defines zines as "noncommercial, nonprofessional, small-circulation magazines which their creators produce, publish, and distribute by themselves." They are usually photocopied (though e-zines do exist), often on letter-size paper, folded in half to 8½ x 5½ inches and stapled or hand sewn along the fold. Variations of this include folding lengthwise to 11 x 4¼ inches, folding in four to 5½ x 4¼ inches, or folding twice again and cutting along the top and bottom edges to produce a mini-zine. Sometimes legal paper is used for a zine that is 8½ x 7 inches or 14 x 4¼ inches. Variations are infinite. Some zines are assembled in box sets. Covers can consist of card stock or vellum, they can be silkscreened, stamped, or adorned with three-dimensional objects, and bindings can be sewn in complex patterns. Some zines are one-of-a-kind, whereas others are published serially. Collectively published zines are similar to edited anthologies, whereas perzines (personal zines) are published by individuals. Compzines (compilations) are edited by an individual who includes other people's submissions and/or found text, art, and graphics.

Zinesters reject the capitalist profit motive, preferring horizontal production and distribution processes (Atton 2002). But anarchists have additional commitments not shared by all zinesters. For social movement alternative media zine producers, among which anarchists might be found, the process of production engages prefigurative politics (Downing 2003), anti-oppressive social relationships, and intersectional political commitments including anti-racism, anti-sexism, anti-poverty, anti-colonialism, anti-heteronormativity, and anti-ableism. Anarchist zinesters cultivate close connections and accountability to readers and communities (Atton 1999), and to activism and direct action, encouraging others to become activists (Schmidt 2005).

The field of anarchist culture can be understood as the politics of production engaged in the production of politics. Within the field of cultural production, social relations affected by anarchist value-practices include complex relationships among writers, publishers, editors, book designers, distributors, readers, and critics. These positions, however, are not individuated in anarchist culture, but rather they are tasks shared among activists whose main focus is direct-action activism, not professional media production. For Bourdieu (1993,

30), "the structure of the field, i.e. of the space of positions, is nothing other than the structure of the distribution of the capital of specific properties which governs success in the field." In mainstream culture, the specific properties of a text will include the reputations of the author, editor, publisher, cover-blurb writer, reviewer, and review publications, and even the fact that the text is reviewed at all. In evaluating its success, these factors contribute to the legitimation process of the text. For anarchists, however, success cannot be evaluated by these specific properties. Rather, a zine may be legitimated in anarchist communities because it enacts and engages a series of anti-authoritarian principles, in both the activism described and the processes of production and distribution of the zine.

According to Bourdieu (ibid., 50), "three competing principles of legitimacy" in the field of culture reveal the process by which a text is accepted: legitimation by other cultural producers, by cultural experts, and by the mass marketplace of culture. As he (ibid., 50-51) argues, "First, there is the specific principle of legitimacy, i.e., the recognition granted by the set of producers who produce for other producers, their competitors, i.e. by the autonomous self-sufficient world of 'art for art's sake,' meaning art for artists." Like avant-garde artists, green anarchists write for autonomous communities that distinguish themselves from the mainstream. Anarchists may legitimate the zine by circulating it materially and symbolically. Because cooperation is valued, competition for success is replaced by an engagement with the zine through spoken and written dialogue. Legitimation might also include readers copying zines (anarchist zines tend to be anti-copyright or "copy-left"), sharing a zine with friends, or becoming inspired to produce their own zines, art, or other media.

Producing for people who share our politics is important – it is not just preaching to the converted. In the *Colours of Resistance* zine, for example, Helen Luu (2000, 3) notes that one of the goals of producing the zine was to provide a forum for "writing for us, about us" to create a space for dialogue among anarchists of colour. Similarly, in the *EVAH* zine, other anarchists are the presumed audience. According to Bourdieu, the shared connection of avant-garde literary production creates the appeal among other artists to produce and consume art engaged in a similar project. Among green anarchists, the inspiration of shared projects also comes from a shared commitment, not to art but to revolutionary eco-politics, in creating a space where participants are presumed to share goals such as the use of direct action to protect old-growth forests, and to share values such as community, cooperation, accountability, horizontalism, and direct democracy. The symbolic production of texts about green anarchism thus extends beyond the actions represented. These shared political commitments, which augment the shared role of artistic producer in Bourdieu's (1993, 74) formulation, are based on the "disavowal of the 'economic,'" which for anarchists is taken up explicitly in anti-capitalist cooperation.

The disavowal of the economic is accompanied by the accumulation of cultural or symbolic capital. Bourdieu (ibid., 75) argues, "'Symbolic capital' is to be understood as economic or political capital that is disavowed, misrecognized and thereby recognized, hence legitimate, a 'credit' which, under certain conditions, and always in the long run, guarantees 'economic' profits." Symbolic capital works differently in anarchist circles. Zines and zinesters can become well known not only because of their challenges to literary or media conventions (in terms of ownership, format, content, collective production, anti-copyrighting, self-distribution, and genre), but also because of political challenges to the state, capitalism, sexism, racism, environmental destruction, and liberal environmentalists. Furthermore, anarchist zines may document direct actions, producing insider knowledge of activism. Anarchist cultural capital is based therefore on the activists' engagement in the anti-authoritarian production process of the zine, their participation in the actions the zine documents, and most importantly, the inseparable combination of the two. The first principle of legitimation can thus be understood as anarchists producing zines for other anarchists. People creating the zine must also be active in anarchist social movements, creating a consistent synergy of media production politics with direct-action activism.

According to Bourdieu (ibid., 76), the accumulation of symbolic capital requires, not ignoring capitalist modes of cultural production, but rather "a practical mastery of the laws of the functioning of the field in which cultural goods are produced and circulate" in order for these laws to be disavowed and thus subverted. Bourdieu makes reference here to the Lacanian concept of disavowal, which includes both denial and recognition. Artists refuse to engage in capitalism by first acknowledging that they are implicated by it. In anarchist culture, the disavowal of the economic, rather than being a simple rejection of the commodification of the culture industry, is a way of life in which capitalist culture (and its intersectional oppressions) is first understood and then rejected through lived social relations. What is at stake here is much more than a refusal to sell out by converting cultural or symbolic capital to economic capital.

The legitimation of the zine as an anarchist text is based on the revolutionary potential or actualization of the activism represented in the writing and artwork. The politics of the actions and the modes of cultural production are inextricably linked: there can be no text without action, and neither text nor action can exist without discussions before, during, and after the action – thus, there can be no action without texts. In green anarchist zine production, modes of activism, theory, textual production, and legitimation all depend on anarchist value-practices. But where specifically, we might ask, are these values put into practice? Where do we find anarchist culture?

To answer this question, Bourdieu's concept of habitus, or the habitual behaviours of a group of artistic producers, is useful. There are specific anarchist habitus spaces that engage these principles. These include but are not limited to the following: skill-shares (such as Montréal's Ste-Emilie Skill-Share, run by queer women of colour who offer art and media workshops that include silk-screening, sound production, and zine making); anarchist bookfairs (such as the annual Victoria Anarchist Book and Freedom Fair); "distros" (distributors of material without a storefront, such as the now defunct Black Cat distro in BC or Kersplebedeb in Montréal); free schools (anti-authoritarian schools, such as the Toronto Anarchist Free University); mass convergences (activist gatherings leading up to protests, such as the Toronto anti-G20 mobilization in 2010); teach-ins (workshops where knowledge is shared non-hierarchically); infoshops (shops that give away informative pamphlets); popular education (free community-based classes); temporary autonomous zones (week-long or longer gatherings for shared activities in temporarily reclaimed space); and housing collectives (a commune-style house where all tasks, cooking, meals, and expenses are shared). These spaces enact the same values as anarchist textual production, whereby the texts contribute to the spaces, and the spaces contribute to the texts. As part of the anarchist habitus, zines both reflect and simultaneously produce anarchist value-practices, even as the same value-practices are used to produce and disseminate zines.

Green anarchist zines tend to be produced in non-hierarchical collectives comprising direct-action activists who create media related to the actions in which they have participated. There are several important values at work here. First, the zinesters are environmental activists rather than professional writers or media activists, which reflects the DIY (do-it-yourself) ethos and rejects the need for expert training. Second, related to non-professionalism is resource sharing: items as diverse as computers, paper, printers, money, food, art spaces, and long-reach zine staplers – supplies that might otherwise be provided in or by a work environment – are shared (Atton 2002). Third, zines are photocopied (for free if possible) and distributed personally in the anarchist milieu at bookfairs, skill-shares, and zine libraries. Sharing, or the politics of mutual aid, is important as the zine may be given away, bartered for other zines or sundry items, or sold for a nominal amount (in the range of ten cents to five dollars). Fourth, this transaction is horizontal, as it includes a dialogue between the people involved about the content of the zines being traded, the kinds of activism in which the individuals have participated, other zines they have produced or read, and personal details. We might contrast this to a mainstream book launch, where authors stand on a stage and read from their book, separated physically, socially, and emotionally from the audience. The book-buyer consumes the reading, the autograph, and the book in a hierarchical writer-over-reader social relationship. Anarchist writers and textual producers avoid this kind of social relation, preferring mutualist conversations, whereby people who receive and read the zine develop a personal relationship with the zine and the people who created it. This horizontal practice engages the values of sharing, active listening, and respecting personal experience as a source of knowledge, which are grounded in principles such as mutual aid, equality, non-professionalism, and the gift economy. Because many anarchists are involved in zine production, and book fairs are also attended by producers of books, T-shirts, patches, buttons, CDs, videos, artwork, events, and a range of other cultural artifacts, almost everyone present will have something to contribute. The circulation of zines thus forges social relationships among equals, and thereby strengthens the experience of lived equality among people. The fifth value-practice is that non-hierarchical communication incorporates anti-oppression relations (anti-racist, anti-sexist, anti-heterosexist, anti-ableist, and many other axes of oppression) through speaking and listening in anti-authoritarian ways (not interrupting, not telling people what to do or think, not devaluing their opinions, openly sharing and questioning ideas, and valuing personal experience). These five value-practices and the equalized social relationships they are committed to producing are crucial in the first principle of legitimation. Through anti-authoritarian social relations, zines and other aspects of anarchist culture are consecrated.

We can see therefore that a refusal of capitalist economics is only a small component of anarchist zine production and circulation. What Bourdieu (1993, 30) calls "the space of positions" – the social and cultural position in relation to other cultural producers, not just of the writer, but also of the reader – is always already important in anarchist culture. This is because self-expression is crucial to accurate representation; anarchy and other avant-garde movements promote DIY ethics and aesthetics; technology has made zines affordable and easy to produce; and some contemporary anarchists challenge the spectacularization of culture. But most importantly, it is because anarchist culture is much more than just a set of cultural objects. It is grounded within a radically anti-hierarchical, dynamic set of complex lived social relations, which can be loosely understood as the anarchist habitus that I have begun to sketch in this chapter.

Bourdieu's model, however, does not account for a text that produces neither economic nor cultural capital. DIY green anarchist zines actively avoid both, since the cultural values evident in cultural capital itself are challenged. As Bourdieu (1993, 101) asserts, the field of cultural production hides the relationship "between cultural power (associated with less economic wealth) and economic and political power (associated with less cultural wealth)." For Bourdieu, economic and cultural capital are accrued in inverse proportion – the more you have of one, the less you have of the other. This relationship is weak in anarchist culture, given that eco-anarchist zine producers have neither cultural power nor economic-political power in the conventional sense of both these concepts. These forms of power are neither sought nor valued. Rather than accruing cultural or economic capital, green anarchists attempt to subvert the structure of the entire cultural field. Bourdieu (ibid., 102) suggests that only artists can subvert the field of culture: "The challenging of the established artistic hierarchies and the heretical displacement of the socially accepted limit between what does and does not deserve to be preserved, admired and transmitted cannot achieve its specifically artistic effect of subversion unless it tacitly recognizes the fact and the legitimacy of such delimitation by making the shifting of that limit an artistic act and thereby claiming for the artist a monopoly in legitimate transgression of the boundary between the sacred and the profane, and therefore a monopoly in revolutions in artistic taxonomies." A book that challenges literary hierarchies inadvertently reinforces the hierarchy intrinsic to the book form as the sole legitimate site of literature. Zines fall outside of this structuralist dilemma. They are not invested in defining socially accepted limits, and even their boundary transgressions start from a space of positions exterior to the literary. Bourdieu's analysis, furthermore, presumes that writers – or, in our case, zinesters – want their text to be the only revolutionary voice in circulation. But from the perspective of anarchist zinesters, who see zines as social movement activators, the more people who are producing zines and any other form of political culture or cultural politics, including direct actions, the better. A sixth value, then, is that the anarchist ethos of success is that one person's success makes space for the success of others, in contrast to mainstream ideologies in which one person's success is seen as a marker of other people's failures. Success in zine production fosters more zine production, which both supports and reflects a healthy cultural community.

Similarly, some independent textual producers negotiate the margins of publishing in Canada, but closer examination reveals that their value systems echo those of the mainstream. For example, independent magazines such as *Broken Pencil, This Magazine,* or *Adbusters* are in positions of domination relative to green anarchist magazines or zines. These indie magazines are proto-capitalist or non-profit and do not necessarily engage the value-practices of anarchist culture. They accrue economic and cultural capital to varying degrees and for reasons that differ from those driving anarchist texts.

If anarchists were producing simply for other anarchists, disavowing both economic and cultural capital, their texts might be relevant to very few people. However, this is not the case. Bourdieu suggests two additional ways in which texts can be legitimated. The second principle, for Bourdieu (ibid., 51), is that of "legitimacy corresponding to 'bourgeois' taste and to the consecration bestowed by the dominant fractions of the dominant class and by private tribunals, such as *salons,* or public, state-guaranteed ones, such as academies, which sanction the inseparably ethical and aesthetic (and therefore political) taste of the dominant." Obviously, anarchist culture does not depend on consecration by ideological bourgeois tastes. Nonetheless, the notion of spaces of legitimation occupied by dominant groups bears further investigation. Certainly, there are established habitus spaces that cultivate anarchist tastes. These are very different from the public spaces (such as academic conferences and presses) and the private spaces (book launches, book clubs) controlled by the dominant fraction of the dominant class. Anarchist spaces may be run by an established group of anarchists. Although not dominant, they have some power to consecrate texts, productions, and events. There may also be spaces, such as a café, bar, or activist gathering, where both anarchist and non-anarchist events take place, with anarchists attending both. Many towns and cities in Canada have places that, though not explicitly anarchist in name, are frequented by anarchists, and where anarchist and activist values, as described above, and "tastes" such as vegetarian food, radical art, and the like, are explicitly cultivated and catered to. Also, anarchists might engage alongside non-anarchists in many kinds of activist gatherings that are also not explicitly anarchist. This might include radical gatherings such as Climate Camp (week- or month-long camps where predominantly youth participants engage in activism around issues of climate change). Moreover, Occupy Wall Street, and Canadian versions such as Occupy Vancouver, feature anarchist-style events and organizing. These are not anarchist spaces per se, but anarchist texts circulate at and are consecrated by broader activist milieus, largely because anarchists influence the organizing modes and action strategies through their participation.

We might therefore consider how anarchist zines are legitimated by dominant fractions of the broader left, including Marxists, socialists, liberals, reformists, radicals, anti-globalization activists, social justice activist groups, and even some left-leaning politicos. Some people who might so identify work alongside anarchists on various campaigns, and are anarchist allies, such that anarchists texts may be consumed and consecrated by them, possibly with critiques. This has the potential to shift the broader political debate. For instance, a talk by a green anarchist writer, such as Derrick Jensen, may be attended by mainstream environmentalists, including Green Party members. In the principle of legitimation through spaces that produce certain tastes, we can see how non-anarchists are involved in the consecration of anarchist texts. These are important spaces of cross-pollination, where people share ideas through texts and horizontal social relations.

Anarchist spaces, both in terms of the specifically anarchist habitus (anarchist book fairs, collective houses, free schools, skill-share spaces, and the like) and understood in relation to the broader networks in which we participate, are useful in understanding the field of anarchist culture, revealing how zines might be legitimated according to Bourdieu's first two principles. If these anarchist and activist networks are small, how do anarchist texts engage with the rest of society? For Bourdieu (1993, 51), there is an important third "principle of legitimacy which its advocates call 'popular,' i.e., the consecration bestowed by the choice of ordinary consumers, the 'mass audience.'" Most anarchist zines do not target a mass audience; in fact, this is often actively avoided. Even in the broader networks, zinesters will not share their zine with everyone. Trust must be established somehow. Anarchist actions, sometimes based in illegal activities, both demand and cultivate trust. In this sense, certain texts, such as *Ecodefense* (Abbey 1993) or the Earth Liberation Front's *Setting Fires with Electrical Timers* (2002), are produced for self-identified anarchists, as in the first principle of legitimacy – anarchists producing for other anarchists. Familiarity with these texts, or having produced a similarly themed zine, might be part of demonstrating a political commitment as an activist joins an anarchist affinity group. Some green anarchist zines play a role in creating insiders to the movement, and thus they tend intentionally to hide themselves from a mass audience.

However, an interesting contradiction occurs here. Within anarchist organizing, there is a need to "do outreach" (publicity and promotion of events) and find ways of involving others in the movement so that anarchists don't become a stagnant, isolated, discontinuous community. Indeed, some anarchist textual producers such as CrimethInc. – a loose-knit North American network of post-punk, post-Situationist writers, activists, and artists – intentionally embrace a mass audience, suggesting that it is possible for everyone to understand themselves as anti-authoritarian in some way (see CrimethInc. 2002).

It is not just the social position of the textual producers, but also the social position of those consecrating the texts that contributes to the process of legitimation. Collective producers are consecrated by other anarchists who are often the only ones in a position to evaluate anarchist value-practices. The requirement of awareness of anarchist social habitus means that evaluation of the anarchist properties of a text might be difficult for someone who has no experience of such a milieu. The third principle of legitimacy is further challenged by the anarchist emphasis on self-produced autonomous texts. A text published by a publisher and consecrated externally is seen not as more legitimate, as it would be by the mainstream, but as less so, as it has entered into the capitalist marketplace without the prefigurative anti-oppression politics, DIY aesthetics, non-professionalism, self-reflexivity, collective self-production, and other value-practices that make an anarchist text what it is.

Texts can move from the first specific principle of consecration to a wider mass audience legitimation during their lifetime. Vancouver-based *Adbusters* is a good example. An anti-advertising magazine with roots in anarchist content, advocating property destruction and quasi-legal activities such as culture jamming, billboard détournement, and subverting, it has recently become an interesting paradox: a major mainstream anti-media media source. *Adbusters* has never engaged anarchist value-practices, as evidenced by its proto-capitalist hierarchical structure (it is run by Kalle Lasn, not an editorial collective), its production process (the magazine employs professional graphic designers), and its capitalist distribution (it is distributed by Disticor, a corporate magazine distributor). *Adbusters* is anti-corporate rather than anti-capitalist, focusing on middle-class media literacy and anti-consumerism campaigns such as Buy Nothing Day. Gender, race, sexuality, disability, the state, class, and other aspects of anarchist politics are often absent from its pages and campaigns. For a person in a lower socio-economic class, buying nothing is not an empowered political statement, but a stressful fact of daily life. *Adbusters* does not practise prefigurative politics or self-critique; nor does it foster anti-hierarchical directly democratic social relations or envision readers as writers the way zines and zine fairs do – indeed, it practises few anti-authoritarian principles. Although *Adbusters* may have started in the underground, and although it sometimes produces anarchist content (for example, depicting a masked anarchist on its cover), it is not an anarchist magazine; nor does it claim to be. The movement from first to third principle of legitimation, however, tends to delegitimate a text as anarchist.

But the line can be somewhat blurry. When *Adbusters* prints a picture of an anarchist on its cover, how does this affect the magazine's relationship to anarchist culture? Clearly, the risk is misrepresentation. At the same time, if *Adbusters* popularizes the notion that illegalized direct actions demand the anonymity of a hidden face, does this strengthen anarchist politics? The answer may depend on the reader. If the reader takes action, anarchist politics are furthered, whereas if the reader remains inactive, capitalism wins. Either way, *Adbusters* sells its magazine, so capitalism is inherent in the magazine's very existence. Herein lies a critical difference: with an anarchist zine, capitalism can't win. Even if the reader remains inactive, the people who made the zine have already shifted the political and cultural fields through the process of zine production. Legitimation through habitus ensures the zinesters' involvement in direct action and non-hierarchical production. The third principle of legitimation through mass marketplace sales does not provide clear-cut answers. Some anarchist texts gain mass appeal, such as CrimethInc's *Days of War, Nights of Love* (2000), which has sold thousands of copies, but many, by choice, do not.

The *Elaho Valley Anarchist Horde* Zine

Published in Vancouver, *EVAH* (EVAH 2001) is an eponymous DIY green anarchist zine documenting four years (1997-2000) of anarchist anti-logging activity in the Elaho Valley near Squamish, British Columbia. It consists of sixty pages of writing, artwork, photographs, newspaper clippings, ecological information and plant drawings, technical diagrams, action communiqués, poetry, rants, how-tos, RCMP reports, and InterFor (logging company) reports, as well as theoretical anti-capitalist, anti-state, pro-indigenous, anti-colonialist, anti-racist, feminist, and Situationist analysis. These items are not separate from each other. Communiqués contain poetry; ecological information is presented from an anti-colonialist, pro-indigenous, feminist perspective; poetry and graphics expound anti-capitalist theory; how-tos assert a politics of sustainability; and so on. As EVAH (ibid., 5) notes, "The struggle has come to be far more than another battle to save forests, it is a site in the continued battle against colonialism, capitalism, the state, and globalization." A multiplicity of intersecting issues are embedded in the green anarchist actions represented.

It is predominantly the first principle of legitimacy that is at work here, which will be demonstrated through an analysis of the zine's depiction of illegalized activities. Legitimation based on the second principle, by broader activist networks, will also be examined. Although possibly more than a thousand copies of the zine have circulated, it never reached a mass market, but we will see that the third principle of legitimation nonetheless applies.

EVAH was produced in the winter of 2001, and 100 copies were made from the original master. It was created by a subset of the horde, with the initiative of an editor, and is a partial representation of the horde's actions. I participated in some actions of the horde during the summer of 2000 but did not contribute to the zine. My analysis is informed by my involvement, but I do not claim to speak for the horde as a collective or for any individual participant. The zine was produced using a computer and printer that were shared from the Victoria activist community, and photocopies were "scammed" (obtained without paying). *EVAH* was sent to *Broken Pencil* magazine, where it was excerpted in the zine review section, and a series of letters and articles engaging with this excerpt followed. The zine travelled down the west coast into the US, proliferating as people took advantage of the anti-copyright principle. EVAH (the horde itself) has lost count of how many copies have been made. The editor produced another print run of 100 later that year, which also sold out. For a time, *EVAH* was sold at Spartacus, Vancouver's radical bookstore, and at anarchist bookstores and infoshops across Canada. Members of EVAH travelled (by freight train) to Montréal for the Anarchist Bookfair in 2001, selling and trading copies there.

The "position-taking" of the EVAH collective within the field of anarchist culture is articulated in several ways, including: the zine's anti-oppression content, whereby, for example, the horde's anti-colonialist demand for the return of unceded indigenous land differentiates it from liberal environmentalists who wanted to make the Elaho Valley into a nature park; the "low-fi" cut-and-paste aesthetic of the zine which positions the horde outside and against professional writers and artists; and the horde's anti-capitalist disavowal of the economic in their chosen modes of production and circulation.

Documenting Illegalized Activities

Following the first principle of legitimation, the *EVAH* zine was produced for other anarchists, which is made clear in its representation of illegalized activities through creative narrative strategies that contribute to its space of positions. It begins with two disclaimers: "NOTE: this publication is intended for entertainment purposes only" and "No one is encouraged to violate the laws of any country based on the information herein. All people and events depicted are purely fictional. Any resemblance to people, dead or alive, is a coincidence" (EVAH 2001, inside front cover). These were intended to protect the horde from arrest. Despite its disclaimers, the zine encouraged readers to initiate actions as indicated in the title of one of its pieces: "Liberate the land, Clearcut Capitalism" (ibid., 47). Michelangelo's *Creation* from the ceiling of the Sistine Chapel is subject to détournement: one hand passes a monkey wrench to the other, with the caption, "Pass it on" (ibid., 41). A photo collage of a tree-sitter suggests "It could be you" (ibid., 22). These are calls to action that contradict and thereby justify the need for the disclaimers.

The monkey wrench in the *Creation* détournement is an allusion to Edward Abbey's novel *The Monkey Wrench Gang* (1975), in which four characters burn or bomb billboards, bridges, and dams that are destroying the natural environment. In this instance, Abbey's approach to describing illegal actions was to write fiction. He has also written the "Foreward!" to a 360-page book called *Ecodefense: A Field Guide to Monkeywrenching* (Abbey 1993), which provides instructions for sabotaging industrial equipment in defence of the environment. In a disclaimer, *Ecodefense* notes that it is intended "for entertainment purposes only. No one involved with the production of this book – the editors, contributors, artists, publisher, distributors, retailers, or anyone – encourages anyone to do any of the stupid, illegal things contained herein" (Foreman and Haywood 1993, i). As an instructional book, *Ecodefense* does not implicate anyone in having carried out illegal activities. Conversely, *EVAH* represents a specific set of identifiable actions, so the EVAH zinesters faced an interesting quandary – how to represent illegal activities without implicating anyone.

They took several approaches beyond the disclaimers. They included an article titled "Security Culture" (EVAH 2001, 12-17); they provided captioned photographs of members of "ProSec, InterFor's security in the woods" (ibid.,

11); and they parodied a local newspaper article, reprinting photos of RCMP officers (ibid., 11, 36-37). Using these publicly available photographs, the zinesters provided activist strategies for avoiding law enforcement.

Moreover, they detailed only those actions for which people had already been arrested. The main action covered was the Artemis tree sit at Mile 65, which lasted from 25 July to 2 August 2000 (ibid., 29-32). Four tree-sitters were arrested when the RCMP destroyed the tree sit while it was underway, endangering the lives of all four activists. Details were therefore known to the police and could be disclosed in the zine. Nonetheless, the names of those involved were excluded from the zine, except in rare circumstances. Participants in actions typically have an "action name" so the police cannot identify them, and they cannot identify each other to police. These names were not used in the zine either.

Names were, however, given in a piece taken from an InterFor report, a day-by-day outline of work stoppages caused by activists. The original InterFor title was "Lava Creek Illegal Actions," (ibid., 8) but the horde called the title into question by adding a sur-title, "Resistance to Ecocide" (ibid., 8), blurring the boundary between resistance and illegalization (the rendering illegal of legal tactics after a group engages in them). Using InterFor's text allowed the horde to enumerate monkey-wrenching actions and to include names of arrestees without providing the police any new information. The InterFor text also listed many actions for which nobody was arrested. For example, the excerpt from 23 August reads: "Drill rig vandalized overnight. Batteries ruined / grind wheel broken / grease in cab. Cayenne pepper spread around. Drilled holes filled. Right of way flagging removed, fallers cannot work. Two RCMP. Tree sitter stays overnight" (ibid., 9). This entry serves as a how-to and directly correlates the actions to logging stoppages. The effectiveness of direct action is one of the main motivations to undertake it; thus, this passage is crucial in both protecting identities and inspiring activists.

These strategies for narrating illegal activities legitimate the zine as an anarchist text through the principle of anarchists writing for other anarchists. In fact, a reader needs to be familiar with the context of green anarchism in order to understand some of the content. The second principle of legitimacy also applies as the zine may have an outreach effect, being read by non-anarchist activists. Interestingly, a third audience is explicitly addressed: the mass market, which includes officers of the law, loggers, and people who might not be receptive to the messages in the zine. The zinesters adhered to anarchist security culture to ensure that nobody risked arrest because of the zine's content. This has also been an important consideration as I write this article, as I have intentionally left out some important details for security purposes. Anarchists assume that their texts, like their persons, might be under surveillance. Each of these principles is thus at play in the zine's legitimation.

Anti-Oppression Politics and *The Revolution of Everyday Life*
The EVAH collective intentionally developed anti-oppressive social relationships by challenging sexism, racism, colonization, and other internalized behaviours of domination, often with very little time to reflect during the action. The zine provided time and space for extending this reflection. A long article in *EVAH* (2001, 41) articulated the complexities of anti-oppression politics in green anarchist organizing: "Working through all these issues of how we come together quickly becomes a monumental task, both social and personal. A task of decolonizing minds from a life in the spectacle-commodity. Systemic power replicates itself everywhere: within our speech, gestures, perception outwards, and self-image." The willingness to engage in self-critique is another important value-practice in anarchist culture. While engaged in environmental struggles, participants recognized intersections among multiple systemic oppressions, and the zine analyzed how resulting power dynamics were dealt with. This, it must be said, was not always successful. Men tended to be dominant, although there were many strong outspoken women in the horde. As is commonly the case in environmental organizing, few people of colour were involved in the action in which I participated. Heterosexism and ableism were rarely mentioned by the zine or the activists.

Following environmental destruction and indigenous self-determination, politics at the heart of the actions, the other axis of oppression primarily addressed was social class. There was a clear connection made between middle-class consumerism and destruction of the environment. Some disdain was expressed for middle-class "weekend activists" who came to the camp without participating in actions but who nonetheless critiqued the horde's rejection of non-violence (see Gelderloos 2007). Non-violence, according to Churchill (1998), is a luxury of white middle-class privilege. Class differences were revealed in terms of who attended university, who grew up poor, who had a vehicle, who was broke, who shoplifted to survive, who had an apartment in the city, who was living in the forest full-time, and who was on welfare.[2] These differences were discussed at the camp and in the zine. Most people espoused a post-

Situationist "revolution of everyday life": anti-capitalist anti-spectacle politics based on liberation and freedom. In the zine, this was captured in excerpts from *Society of the Spectacle* (Debord 1967) and *The Revolution of Everyday Life* (Vaneigem 1967).

Many segments of the anarchist milieu are committed to everyday engagement with the politics of living differently; therefore, aspects of the anarchist habitus, including anti-oppression politics, and many of the value-practices mentioned above, are key to legitimation of the *EVAH* zine by anarchists, whereas they may not be important to the broader left. *EVAH* is strong in many of these aspects, but a less comprehensive zine might be heavily critiqued by anarchists. At the same time, although people on the broader left might critique the zine for refusing to take a non-violent stance, this critique is a form of engagement with anarchist culture, that, despite its appearance to the contrary, plays a role in the zine's legitimation.

A Transformative Relationship to Culture in a Culture of Transformation

Zines produce the culture that they represent, which can be seen by paying close attention to who is reading and legitimating them. The cultural capital of *EVAH,* however, does not exactly follow Bourdieu's theory, in that it is unlikely to be worth a great deal of money in the future; nor will the cultural capital of having produced it translate into economic capital for horde members. Rather, the legitimation of the zine is based on the horde's actions and on how horde members enact anarchist value-practices through cultural production. According to the Arsenal Collective (2000, 4), "Simple slogans can be replicated, shouted and worn by anyone. Words, action, style and more can be co-opted and/or criminalized by our enemies. That can't stop us. The state, its agents and others will never adopt our revolutionary intent. They will never promote potent content that will reveal their own limits and contribute to the downfall of their agenda. Our words and actions have meaning and intention they can't imitate, profoundly different ways of seeing the world and living in it." Thus, the *Adbusters* cover with the picture of the masked anarchist replicates only the surface of anarchist culture, not necessarily the "revolutionary intent." Similarly, though anarchist symbols may be used in corporate ad campaigns (the Gap, Calvin Klein) and may reach a mass audience, they will lack the transformative relationships inherent in anti-authoritarian cultural production. Rather than consecrating anarchist cultural products, these corporate ads circulate empty signifiers. The signifier (a circle-A, a black flag) can signify its appropriately an-archist meaning only if the viewer already knows what the signifier means. Although an anarchist signifier may circulate outside of anarchist culture, the anarchist signification process does not always accompany it. When an an-archist sign or symbol, or indeed anarchist symbolic capital, is converted to economic capital by corporations or even by independent magazines, this constitutes the very defeat, not of anarchism, nor of the symbol, but of the no-tion of symbolic capital itself. Signs of the revolution can never stand in for the revolution itself.

What the corporate signifier-thieves do not portray, and what cannot be represented in mainstream media, is the alternative system of values that is signified by the masked anarchist, values based on radically transforming community, self, others, society, relationships, and politics through the pro-found fabric of our daily lives – a transformative relationship to culture within a culture of transformation. Green anarchist zines rhizomatically multiply these transformative spaces of the possible. The result is not just the creation of alternative or autonomous media, but the production of foundational ef-forts toward long-term social sustainability.

NOTES

1 Anarchists use many of our own words and expressions, such as the word "zine." I will provide brief parenthetical definitions of these terms throughout the text. These ex-pressions are cultural references that are part of the symbolic capital within the an-archist habitus.
2 In one conversation with an activist, I said, "Grad school is great because you have the whole summer off," and they replied, "Being unemployed is great because you have the whole year off." Graduate school was thus revealed to be a capitulation to an au-thoritarian non-free structure of labour and co-opted knowledge production, in ten-sion with anarchist value-practices, making it difficult to live in the forest on a tree-sit for a protracted period of time.

References

Abbey, E. 1975. *The Monkey Wrench Gang.* New York: Perennial.

–. 1993. Foreward! In *Ecodefense: A field guide to monkeywrenching,* edited by D. Foreman and B. Haywood, 3-4. Chico, CA: Abzug Press. (Orig. pub. 1985.)

Abbott, J. 2000. Contesting relations: Playing back video. In *Making video "in": The contested ground of alternative video on the west coast,* edited by J. Abbott, 9-32. Vancouver: Video In Studios.

Abelson, D.E. 2002. *Do think tanks matter? Assessing the impact of public policy institutes.* Montreal and Kingston: McGill-Queen's University Press.

Aboriginal Peoples Television Network. 2005. Factsheet. http://www.aptn.ca/.

Aboriginal Voices Radio. 2007. Community. http://www.aboriginalvoices.com/.

Abrams, P.L. 1996. Reservations about women: Population policy and reproductive rights. *Cornell International Law Journal* 29(1): 1-42.

Action Coalition for Media Education. n.d. ACME's mission. http://www.acmecoalition. org.

Adams, J. 2009. Tories announce details of reworked Canadian magazine fund. *Toronto Globe and Mail,* 17 February. http://www.theglobeandmail.com.

Adamson, N., L. Briskin, and M. McPhail. 1988. *Feminists organizing for change: The contemporary women's movement in Canada.* Toronto: Oxford University Press.

Adilman, S., and G. Kliewer. 2000. Pain and wasting on Main and Hastings: A perspective from the Vancouver Native Health Society Medical Clinic. *BC Medical Journal* 42(9): 422-25.

Albert, M. 1997. What makes alternative media alternative? Toward a federation of alternative media activists and supporters – FAMAS. *Z Magazine,* 1 October. http://www.zcommunications.org/.

Alia, V. 1999. *Un/covering the North: News, media and Aboriginal people.* Vancouver: UBC Press.

–. 2004. *Media ethics and social change.* New York: Routledge.

Alliance for Community Media. 2010. Federal cable law thwarts local job creation; CAP act offers solution. http://www.alliancecm.org/node/626.

Alliance of Canadian Cinema, Television and Radio Artists. 2010. Canada's new copyright bill a blow to artists: "Half the bill is missing." News release, June. http://www.actra.ca/.

AMARC (World Association of Community Broadcasters). 2010. AMARC welcomes community radio breakthrough in Nigeria. 19 October. http://wiki.amarc.org/?action=shownews&id=1155&lang=EN.

–. n.d. Community radio social impact evaluation process. http://www.amarc.org/index.php?p=Community_radio_evaluation.

Anderson, Benedict. 1983. *Imagined communities: Reflections on the origin and spread of nationalism.* London: Verso.

Anderson, Byron, ed. 2002. *Alternative publishers of books in North America.* Gainsville, FL: CRISES Press.

Anderson, C. 2007. The New York Independent Press Association survives. *Indypendent,* 10 January. http://www.indypendent.org/.

Anderson, R.D., A. Hollander, J. Monteiro, and W.T. Stanbury. 1998. Competition policy and regulatory reform in Canada, 1986-1997. *Review of Industrial Organization* 13: 177-204.

Anderson, S., and M. Lithgow. 2009. A new vision for community TV. *The Tyee,* 2 October. http://thetyee.ca/.

Angel, J. 2007. Seven years of *Clamor:* Challenges, successes, and reflections. http://clamormagazine.org/Clamor-Reflections.pdf.

Appadurai, A. 1996. *Modernity at large: Cultural dimensions of globalization.* Minneapolis: University of Minnesota Press.

Ardyche, M. 1987. Ask not what your [group] can do for you ... *Pandora,* September-December, 4.

Arsenal Collective. 2000. Untitled. *Arsenal* 3, Spring, 3-4.

Association for Tele-Education in Canada. n.d. Untitled video. http://www.atecinfo.ca/.

Atherton, T. 1995. TVO at 25: Despite successes, provincial network's future in doubt. *Ottawa Citizen,* 30 July, A1.

–. 2001. TVO makes big gain in primetime. *Ottawa Citizen,* 23 February, E1.

Atton, C. 1999. Green anarchist: A case study of collective action in the radical media. *Anarchist Studies* 7: 25-49.

–. 2002. *Alternative media.* London: Sage.

–. 2003. Organization and production in alternative media. In *Media organization and production,* edited by S. Cottle, 41-55. London: Sage.

–. 2004. *An alternative Internet: Radical media, politics and creativity.* Edinburgh: Edinburgh University Press.

–. 2006. Far-right media on the Internet: Culture, discourse and power. *New Media and Society* 8(4): 573-87.

–. 2007. Current issues in alternative media research. *Sociology Compass* 1(1): 17-27.

Atton, C., and J. Hamilton. 2008. *Alternative journalism.* London: Sage.

Atton, C., and E. Wickenden. 2005. Sourcing routines and representation in alternative journalism: A case study approach. *Journalism Studies* 6(3): 347-59.

Avison, S., and M. Meadows. 2000. Speaking and hearing: Aboriginal newspapers in the public sphere in Canada and Australia. *Canadian Journal of Communication* 24(3): 347-66.

Babe, R.E. 1990. *Telecommunications in Canada.* Toronto: University of Toronto Press.

Bagdikian, B. 2000. *The media monopoly,* 6th ed. Boston: Beacon Press.

Bailey, O.G., B. Cammaerts, and N. Carpentier. 2008. *Understanding alternative media.* New York: Open University Press.

Baker, C.E. 2002. *Media, markets and democracy.* Cambridge: Cambridge University Press.

Balka, E. 1992. Womentalk goes on-line: The use of computer networks in the context of feminist social change. PhD diss., Simon Fraser University.

Bangladesh NGOs Network for Radio and Communication. 2010. http://www.bnnrc.net.

Barbier-Bouvet, J.-F., P. Beaud, and P. Flichy. 1979. *Communication et pouvoir: Mass media et media communautaires au Québec.* Paris: Éditions anthropos.

Barney, D. 2004. The democratic deficit in Canadian ICT policy and regulation. In *Seeking convergence in policy and practice: Communications in the public interest.* Vol. 2, edited by M. Moll and L.R. Shade, 91-108. Ottawa: Canadian Centre for Policy Alternatives.

Barratt, N., and L.R. Shade. 2007. Net neutrality: Telecom policy and the public interest. *Canadian Journal of Communication* 32(2): 295-305.

Benhabib, S. 1992. Models of public space: Hannah Arendt, the liberal tradition, and Jürgen Habermas. In *Habermas and the public sphere,* edited by C. Calhoun, 73-98. Cambridge, MA: MIT Press.

Benkler, Y. 2006. *The wealth of networks: How social production transforms markets and freedom.* New Haven: Yale University Press.

Bennett, W.L. 2003. New media power: The Internet and global activism. In *Contesting media power: Alternative media in a networked world,* edited by N. Couldry and J. Curran, 17-37. Lanham, MD: Rowman and Littlefield.

–. 2008. *News: The politics of illusion,* 8th ed. New York: Pearson Longman.

Benson, I.T. 2007. The freedom of conscience and religion in Canada: Challenges and opportunities. *Emory International Law Review* 21: 111-66.

–. 2008. *Taking a fresh look at religion and public policy in Canada: The need for a paradigm shift.* http://www.millerthomson.com/en/our-people/iain-t-benson/publications.

Berezin, M. 2009. *Illiberal politics in neo-liberal times: Culture, security and populism in the new Europe.* Cambridge: Cambridge University Press.

Berfield, S. 1997. Global TV: Still local, after all. *World Press Review* (February), 31.

Berlet, C., and M.N. Lyons. 2000. *Right-wing populism in America: Too close for comfort.* New York: Guilford Press.

Bernard, M. 2008. Critical and global perspectives of multiculturalism: Contested identities of Toronto Sri Lankan Tamils. Master's thesis, Carleton University.

Beste, P., and J. Kugelberg. 2008. *True Norwegian black metal: We turn in the night consumed by fire.* Brooklyn: Vice Books.

Betts, G. n.d. The rise of the small press movement in Canada. *Historical Perspectives on Canadian Publishing.* http://hpcanpub.mcmaster.ca/.

Bhabha, H. 1994. *The location of culture.* London: Routledge.

Black Women's Collective. 1986. New paper links black sisters. *Pandora,* September, 19.

Blee, K.M. 2002. *Inside organized racism: Women in the hate movement.* Berkeley: University of California Press.

Blumler, J.G., ed. 1992. *Television and the public interest: Vulnerable values in Western European broadcasting.* London: Sage.

Blumler, J.G., and W. Hoffmann-Riem. 1992. Toward renewed accountability in broadcasting. In *Television and the public interest: Vulnerable values in Western European broadcasting,* edited by J.G. Blumler, 218-28. London: Sage.

Bolan, K. 2005. *Loss of faith: How the Air-India bombers got away with murder.* Toronto: McClelland and Stewart.

Boler, M., ed. 2008. *Digital media and democracy: Tactics in hard times.* Cambridge, MA: MIT Press.

Book Critics Circle. 2008. *Critical Mass.* http://bookcriticscircle.blogspot.com/2008/05/pw-cuts-costs-reviewers-pay.html.

Bourdieu, P. 1993. *The field of cultural production.* New York: Columbia University Press.

–. 2005. The political field, the social field, and the journalistic field. In *Bourdieu and the journalistic field,* edited by R. Benson and E. Neveu, 29-47. Malden, MA: Polity Press.

Bourrie, M. 2004. Yes means no for al-Jazeera in Canada. *Anti-War.com,* 23 July. http://www.antiwar.com/.

Boyer, J.-P., J. Desjardins, and D. Widgington. 2007. *Picture this! 659 posters of social movements in Québec (1966-2007).* Montreal: Cumulus Press.

Brean, Joseph. 2009. Canadians "misinformed" on hate speech. *National Post,* 22 June.

Broadside. 1979. Volley number one. May, 1.

–. 1980. *Broadside* bulletin. February, 2.

–. 1982a. *Broadside* bulletin. February, 2.

–. 1982b. Something newsworthy. March, 2.

–. 1983. Classified advertising form. February, 14.

–. 1985. Outside *Broadside.* June, 15.

–. 1986. Masthead. March, 2.

–. 1988. A masterful job. November, 4.

Broadside Papers. Canadian Women's Movement Archives, University of Ottawa, Finding aid X10-66.

Brooten, L., and G. Hadl. 2009. Gender and hierarchy: A case study of the Independent Media Center network. In *Making our media: Global initiatives toward a democratic public sphere.* Vol. 1, *Creating new communication spaces,* edited by C. Rodriguez, D. Kidd, and L. Stein, 203-22. Cresskill, NJ: Hampton Press.

Browne, D.R. 2005. *Ethnic minorities, electronic media and the public sphere: A comparative study.* Cresskill, NJ: Hampton Press.

Brownlee, J. 2005. *Ruling Canada: Corporate cohesion and democracy.* Winnipeg: Fernwood.

Buddle, K. 2005. Aboriginal cultural capital creation and radio production in urban Ontario. *Canadian Journal of Communication* 30(1): 7-40.

Buddle-Crowe, K. 2002. From birchbark talk to digital dreamspeaking: A history of Aboriginal media activism in Canada. PhD diss., McMaster University.

Bunt, G.R. 2003. *Islam in the digital age: E-Jihad, online fatwas and cyber Islamic environments.* London: Pluto Press.

Burghart, D., and L. Zeskind. 2010. *Tea Party nationalism: A critical examination of the Tea Party movement and the size, scope, and focus of its national factions.* Institute for Research and Education on Human Rights. http://www.irehr.org/issue-areas/tea-party-nationalism/.

BusinessWeek. 2005. Online extra: The fashion of the Christ. 23 May. http://www.businessweek.com/.

Byerly, C.M., and K. Ross. 2006. *Women and media: A critical introduction.* Malden, MA: Blackwell.

CACTUS. 2007. About CACTUS. http://cactus.independentmedia.ca/.

–. 2009. A new vision for community TV. http://cactus.independentmedia.ca/.

Canada. 1970. *Special Senate committee on the mass media.* Ottawa: Information Canada.

–. 1981. *Royal commission on newspapers.* Ottawa: Information Canada.

–. 1983. *Towards a new national broadcasting policy.* Ottawa: Department of Communications.

–. 1988. *Canadian multiculturalism act.* RSC, c. 31. http://laws.justice.gc.ca/PDF/Statute/C/C-18.7.pdf.

–. 1991. *Broadcasting act.* RSC, c. 11. http://laws.justice.gc.ca/en/B-9.01/.

–. 1993. *Telecommunications act.* SC, c. 38. http://laws.justice.gc.ca/.

–. 2003. *The Government of Canada's response to the report of the Standing Committee on Canadian Heritage: Our cultural sovereignty: The second century of Canadian broadcasting.* Gatineau, QC: Canadian Heritage.

–. 2006. *Final report on the Canadian news media.* Standing Committee on Transport and Communications. Ottawa: Parliament of Canada.

–. 2010. Speech from the throne. 3 March. http://www.speech.gc.ca/.

Canada, Department of Canadian Heritage. 2003. *Northern Native Broadcast Access Program (NNBAP) and Northern Distribution Program (NDP) evaluation.* Final report. Prepared for Department of Canadian Heritage by Whiteduck Resources Inc. and Consilium. http://publications.gc.ca/pub?id=303376&sl=0.

Canada Family Action Coalition. n.d. About. http://www.familyaction.org/.

Canada Revenue Agency. 2008. Registered charity information return for the Evangelical Fellowship of Canada Alliance. Available from www.cra-arc.gc.ca.

Canadian Association of Broadcasters. 2001. Submission in response to CRTC public notice 2001-19: Review of community channel policy and low-power radio broadcasting policy. 7 May.

Canadian Civil Liberties Association. 2009. Submissions to the Canadian Human Rights Commission. 15 January. http://ccla.org/2009/01/15/ccla-submission-to-the-canadian-human-rights-commission-re-moon-report-and-s-13/.

Canadian Heritage Alliance. 2010. http://www.canadianheritagealliance.com.

Canadian Human Rights Commission. 2009. *Freedom of expression and freedom from hate in the Internet age.* Minister of Public Works and Government, June. http://www.chrc-ccdp.ca/pdf/srp_rsp_eng.pdf.

Canadian Human Rights Commission Exposed. n.d. http://canadianhumanrights commission.blogspot.com.

Canadian Internet Policy and Public Interest Clinic. n.d. About us. http://www.cippic.ca/.

Canadian Internet Project. 2008. Canada online! The Internet and traditional media: Uses, attitudes, and trends. *Canadian Media Research Consortium.* http://www. cmrcccrm.ca/.

Canadian Jewish Congress. 2004. CJC welcomes conditions placed on Al Jazeera broadcast license. News release, 15 July. http://www.cjc.ca/2004/07/15/cjc-welcomes -conditions-placed-on-al-jazeera-broadcast-license/.

Canadian Labour Congress. 2008. The Christian Labour Association of Canada (CLAC): An overview of an "employer-accommodating" pseudo union. February. http://www. legassembly.sk.ca/Committees/HumanServices/Bill%2080/Canadian_Labour_ Congress_Appendix_1.pdf.

Canadian Learning Television. 2008. About CLT. Copy on file with author (Kozolanka).

Canadian Music Creators Coalition. 2008. CMCC: Copyright reform bill doesn't help Canadian artists. 12 June. http://www.musiccreators.ca/wp/?p=264.

–. n.d. A new voice. http://www.musiccreators.ca.

Canadian Research Alliance for Community Innovation and Networking. 2005. Follow-up letter to telecommunications policy review panel. http://archive.iprp.ischool. utoronto.ca/cracin/alttelecomcontent/.

Canadian Television Fund. 2008. *Adjust your set: Annual report 2007-2008.* Toronto. http://www.cmf-fmc.ca/publications/annual-report-rapport-annuel.html.

Canadian TV Forums. 2003. Italian channel battles for carriage. 23 December. http:// www.broadcastermagazine.com/news.

Canadian Women's Movement Archives. 1984. *Kinesis* Papers, Box 46, *Kinesis Reader* Survey 1984. Finding aid X10-1. University of Ottawa.

–. 1998. *Kinesis* Papers, Box 46, 1 April 1998, open letter from Agnes Huang. Finding aid X10-1. University of Ottawa.

Cardinal, H. 1977. *The rebirth of Canada's Indians.* Edmonton: M.G. Hurtig.

Cardus. 2009. Increase charitable credit as part of stimulus package. News release, 15 January. http://www.newswire.ca/.

–. 2010. 29to42. http://www.29to42.ca.

–. n.d. http://cardus.ca.

Carpentier, N., R. Lie, and J. Servaes. 2003. Community media: Muting the democratic media discourse? *Continuum: Journal of Media and Cultural Studies* 17(1): 51-68.

Carroll, W.K. 2007. From Canadian corporate elite to transnational capitalist class: Transitions in the organization of corporate power. *Canadian Review of Sociology and Anthropology* 44(3): 265-88.

Carroll, W.K., and R.A. Hackett. 2006. Democratic media activism through the lens of social movement theory. *Media, Culture and Society* 28(1): 83-104.

Cartt.ca. 2011a. Crossroads/CTS team up with ComStar on programming, distribution. 17 January. http://www.cartt.ca/.

–. 2011b. TV still top of the heap and going strong says report. 19 January. http:// www.cartt.ca/.

Cassin, M. 1992. *Pandora*'s hearings document women's exclusion from law. *Pandora,* September, 14.

Castells, M. 2009. *Communication power.* Oxford: Oxford University Press.

CBC (Canadian Broadcasting Corporation). 2002. *Street Cents,* Episode 11, 1 January.

–. 2007. Fund has $265m for Canadian TV in coming year. http://www.cbc.ca/news.

–. 2008a. *CBC/Radio-Canada annual report 2007-2008,* Vol. 2. http://www.cbc.radio-canada.ca/.

–. 2008b. CRTC has deregulation agenda in hearings on cable, satellite. 7 April. http://www.cbc.ca/.

–. 2008c. The CRTC's report on the CTF – A $150m hit to public sector programming. News release, 5 June. http://www.cnw.ca/.

–. 2009. Rogers axes public TV. 14 September. http://www.youtube.com/.

CBCEDA. 2007. *A 10 year strategic plan for Cape Breton County.* Sydney: Cape Breton County Economic Development Authority. http://www.cbceda.org/download.php?FileID=139.

CDÉNÉ. 2006. *Plan communautaire 2006-2009.* Petit-de-Grat, NS: Le Conseil de développement économique de la Nouvelle-Écosse.

Centre d'études sur les médias. 2008. *Portraits sectoriels: la radio.* Québec City. http://www.cem.ulaval.ca/.

Chakravartty, P., and Y. Zhao, eds. 2008. *Global communications: Towards a transcultural political economy.* Lanham, MD: Rowman and Littlefield.

Chandler, A., and N. Neumark, eds. 2005. *At a distance: Precursors to art and activism on the Internet.* Cambridge, MA: MIT Press.

CHOQ. 2008. À propos. http://www.choq.fm/.

Christian Heritage Party. n.d. www.chp.ca/party/about.

Chuck0. 2002. The sad decline of Indymedia. *Infoshop News.* http://news.infoshop.org/.

Chung, E. 2009. Copyright wish lists. CBC News, 30 July. http://www.cbc.ca/news/technology/story/2009/07/30/f-copyright-roundup.html.

Churchill, W. 1998. *Pacifism as pathology: Reflections on the role of armed struggle in North America.* Winnipeg: Arbeiter Ring.

Chyi, H.I. 2005. Willingness to pay for online news: An empirical study on the viability of the subscription model. *Journal of Media Economics* 18(2): 131-42.

City of Vancouver. 2005a. *Downtown East Side monitoring report 2005/6.* http://www.city.vancouver.bc.ca/commsvcs/planning/dtes/pdf/2006MR.pdf.

–. 2005b. *Housing plan for the Downtown East Side.* http://www.city.vancouver.bc.ca/commsvcs/housing/pdf/dteshousingplan.pdf.

–. 2008. *Community statistics.* http://vancouver.ca/.

Civitas. n.d. http://www.civitascanada.ca/.

CKUT. 2006. New collective blog. http://ckutnews.wordpress.com/.

–. 2007. Re-defining media conference. http://www.ckut.ca/.

–. 2010. National campus and community radio conference. http://www.ckut.ca/.

–. n.d. Homelessness marathon. http://www.ckut.ca/.

Clark, J., and T. van Slyke. 2006. Welcome to the media revolution. *In These Times,* 28 June. http://www.inthesetimes.com/.

Clark, L.S. 2007a. Introduction: Identity, belonging, and religious lifestyle branding (fashion bibles, bhangra parties, and Muslim pop). In *Religion, media, and the marketplace,* edited by L.S. Clark, 1-36. New Brunswick, NJ: Rutgers University Press.

–, ed. 2007b. *Religion, media, and the marketplace.* New Brunswick, NJ: Rutgers University Press.

Clemenger, B.J. 2009. Evangelicalism and the advancement of religion. *Church and Faith Trends* 2(2). http://files.efc-canada.net/min/rc/cft/V02I02/Evangelicalism_Advancement_of_Religion.pdf.

Coffey, M.A. 1991. Feminist print media in Canada. *Resources for Feminist Research/ Documentation sur la recherche féministe* 20(1-2): 25-26.

Cohen, B., and M. Glassman. 2007. Curiosity, driving trucks, and a dash of Roland Barthes: Lessons in the games of truth and dynamic television. *Point of View* 67: 4-11.

Cohen, N. 2006. What's the frequency, Gwyneth? Why more women's voices are being broadcast on community radio. *This Magazine* 40(2): 24-27.

–. 2007. Love's labour lost: Working for a sustainable alternative press. *Briarpatch* 36(4): 24-26.

–. 2010. Beyond the margins: A roundtable on radical publishing. *Upping the Anti* 10: 131-48.

Cole, S.G. 1985. Sexuality and its discontents. *Broadside,* April, 8-9.

Collins, R. 1986. Broadcasting policy in Canada. In *New communication technologies and the public interest,* edited by M. Ferguson, 150-63. London: Sage.

–. 1998. Public service and the media economy: European trends in the late 1990s. *Gazette* 60(5): 363-66.

Collins, R., A. Finn, S. McFadyen, and C. Hoskins. 2001. Public service broadcasting beyond 2000: Is there a future for public service broadcasting? *Canadian Journal of Communication* 26(1): 3-15.

Comedia. 1984. The alternative press: The development of underdevelopment. *Media, Culture and Society* 6(2): 95-102.

Community Media Education Society. 2008. Private correspondence and interviews with Richard Ward, former executive director of CMES, and Lynda Leonard, current executive director of CMES.

Community Radio Forum. 2010. Community Radio Forum – chronology. http://www.crforum.in/.

Comor, E., and E. Casella. 1987. *Challenge and innovation: A history of the Workers' Educational Association.* Toronto: Workers' Educational Association of Canada.

ComStar Media. 2009. Our brands. http://www.comstarmedia.com/.

Coté, M., and J. Pybus. 2007. Learning to immaterial labour 2.0: MySpace and social networks. *Ephemera* 7(1): 88-106.

Cottle, S. 2003. Media organization and production: Mapping the field. In *Media organization and production,* edited by S. Cottle, 3-24. London: Sage.

Couldry, N., and J. Curran. 2003. The paradox of media power. In *Contesting media power: Alternative media in a networked world,* edited by N. Couldry and J. Curran, 3-15. Lanham, MD: Rowman and Littlefield.

Coyer, K. 2005. If it leads it bleeds: The participatory newsmaking of the Independent Media Centre. In *Global activism, global media,* edited by W. de Jong, M. Shaw, and N. Stammers, 165-78. London: Pluto Press.

Coyer, K., T. Dowmunt, and A. Fountain. 2007. *The alternative media handbook.* London: Routledge.

Craig, C. 2008. The changing face of fair dealing in Canadian copyright law: A proposal for legislative reform. In *In the public interest: The future of Canadian copyright law*, edited by M. Geist, 437-61. Toronto: Irwin Law.

–. 2010. Locking out lawful users: Fair dealing and anti-circumvention in Bill C-32. In *From "radical extremism" to "balanced copyright": Canadian copyright and the digital agenda*, edited by M. Geist, 177-203. Toronto: Irwin Law.

CrimethInc. 2000. *Days of war, nights of love: Crimethink for beginners.* Olympia: CrimethInc. Free Press.

–. 2002. Dear Aunt Joyce: You may already be an anarchist. In *Fighting for our lives*. Olympia: CrimethInc.

Crow, B., and M. Langford. 2004. Digital activism in Canada. In *Seeking convergence in policy and practice: Communications in the public interest*. Vol. 2, edited by M. Moll and L.R. Shade, 349-62. Ottawa: Canadian Centre for Policy Alternatives.

CRTC (Canadian Radio-television and Telecommunications Commission). 1975. Policies respecting broadcasting receiving undertakings (cable television). 16 December.

–. 1976. A background paper on community broadcasting in Canada. http://www.crtc. gc.ca/.

–. 1985. Review of community radio. Public notice CRTC 1985-194. 26 August. http:// www.crtc.gc.ca/.

–. 1986. Regulations respecting broadcasting receiving undertakings. Public notice CRTC 1986-182. 1 August. http://www.crtc.gc.ca/eng/archive/1986/PB86-182.HTM.

–. 1990. Native broadcasting policy. Public notice CRTC 1990-89. 20 September. http:// www.crtc.gc.ca/.

–. 1991. Policy proposals for community radio. Public notice CRTC 1991-118. 20 November. http://www.crtc.gc.ca/eng/archive/1991/PB91-118.htm.

–. 1993. CRTC religious broadcasting policy. Public notice CRTC 1993-78. 3 June. http:// www.crtc.gc.ca/.

–. 1996. Public notice CRTC 1996-69: Call for comments on a proposed approach for the regulation of broadcasting distribution undertakings. 17 May. http://www.crtc. gc.ca/eng/archive/1996/PB96-69.HTM.

–. 1997. New regulatory framework for broadcasting distribution undertakings. Public notice CRTC 1997-25. 11 March. http://www.crtc.gc.ca/eng/archive/1997/PB97-25.HTM.

–. 1998. Exemption order respecting certain Native radio undertakings. Public notice CRTC 1998-62. 9 July. http://www.crtc.gc.ca/.

–. 1999a. Ethnic broadcasting policy. Public notice CRTC 1999-117. 28 August. http:// www.crtc.gc.ca/.

–. 1999b. A proposed policy for community radio. Public notice CRTC 1999-75. 5 May. http://www.crtc.gc.ca/eng/archive/1999/PB99-75.htm.

–. 2000a. Call for comments concerning Order in Council P.C. 2000-1464. Public notice CRTC 2000-144. 20 October. http://www.crtc.gc.ca/.

–. 2000b. Call for comments concerning over-the-air television services in Vancouver – Order in Council P.C. 2000-1551. Public notice CRTC 2000-1551. 20 October. http:// www.crtc.gc.ca/.

–. 2000c. Call for comments – Proposed regulatory amendments for the purpose of implementing certain aspects of the revised policies for campus radio and community radio, and incorporating revised content categories for radio. Public notice CRTC 2000-44. 21 March.

–. 2000d. Community radio policy. Public notice CRTC 2000-13. 28 January. http://www.crtc.gc.ca/.

–. 2001a. Changes to conditions of licence for certain Native radio undertakings. Public notice CRTC 2001-70. 15 June. http://www.crtc.gc.ca/eng/archive/2001/PB2001-70.htm.

–. 2001b. Decision 2001-457. Licence renewals for the television stations controlled by CTV. 2 August. http://www.crtc.gc.ca/eng/archive/2001/DB2001-457.htm.

–. 2002. Policy framework for community-based media. Broadcasting public notice CRTC 2002-61. 10 October. http://www.crtc.gc.ca/eng/archive/2002/pb2002-61.htm.

–. 2005. CINQ-FM Montréal – Licence renewal. Broadcasting decision CRTC 2005-184. 2 May. http://www.crtc.gc.ca/eng/archive/2005/db2005-184.htm.

–. 2006a. Community-based campus AM radio station in Montréal. Broadcasting decision CRTC 2006-58. 10 March. http://www.crtc.gc.ca/eng/archive/2006/db2006-58.htm.

–. 2006b. The future environment facing the Canadian broadcasting system: A report prepared pursuant to section 15 of the Broadcasting Act. 15 December. http://www.crtc.gc.ca/ENG/publications/reports/broadcast/rep061214.htm?Print=True.

–. 2007a. Broadcasting decision CRTC 2007-219. Community-based television service in Toronto.

–. 2007b. Broadcasting decision CRTC 2007-429. Transfer of effective control of Alliance Atlantis Broadcasting Inc.'s broadcasting companies to CanWest MediaWorks Inc. 20 December. http://www.crtc.gc.ca/eng/archive/2007/db2007-429.htm.

–. 2007c. *Broadcasting policy monitoring report.* Ottawa: CRTC. http://www.crtc.gc.ca/eng/publications/reports/PolicyMonitoring/2007/bpmr2007.htm.

–. 2007d. *Transcript of proceedings of the CRTC Diversity of Voices Proceeding,* 21 September. Broadcasting public hearing 2007-05. Vol. 5.

–. 2008a. Broadcasting decision CRTC 2008-222. Licensing of new radio stations to serve Ottawa and Gatineau. 26 August. http://www.crtc.gc.ca/eng/archive/2008/db2008-222.htm.

–. 2008b. Broadcasting public notice CRTC 2008-04. Diversity of voices. 15 January. http://www.crtc.gc.ca/eng/archive/2008/db2008-75.htm.

–. 2009a. Broadcasting notice of consultation CRTC 2009-661. 22 October. http://www.crtc.gc.ca/eng/archive/2009/2009-661.htm.

–. 2009b. Broadcasting regulatory policy CRTC 2009-725. 26 November. http://www.crtc.gc.ca/eng/archive/2009/2009-725.htm.

–. 2009c. Broadcasting regulatory policy CRTC 2009-329. Review of broadcasting in new media. 4 June. http://www.crtc.gc.ca/eng/archive/2009/2009-329.htm.

–. 2009d. CRTC opens on-line consultation on Internet traffic management practices. 31 March. http://www.crtc.gc.ca/eng/news/RELEASES/2009/r090331.htm.

–. 2009e. Notice of hearing. Public notice CRTC 2009-418. 13 July. http://www.crtc.gc.ca/eng/archive/2009/2009-418.htm.

–. 2009f. Policy determinations arising from the 27 April 2009 public hearing. CRTC 2009-406. 6 July. http://www.crtc.gc.ca/eng/archive/2009/2009-406.htm.

–. 2009g. Telecom regulatory policy CRTC 2009-657. Review of the Internet traffic management practices of Internet service providers. 21 October. http://www.crtc.gc.ca/eng/archive/2009/2009-657.htm.

–. 2010a. Broadcasting regulatory policy CRTC 2010-499. Campus and community radio policy. 22 July. http://www.crtc.gc.ca/eng/archive/2010/2010-499.htm.

–. 2010b. Broadcasting regulatory policy CRTC 2010-622. Community television policy. 26 August. http://www.crtc.gc.ca/eng/archive/2010/2010-622.htm.

–. 2010c. *Communications monitoring report.* http://www.crtc.gc.ca/eng/publications/reports/PolicyMonitoring/2010/cmr41.htm#n24.

–. 2010d. Telecom decision CRTC 2010-445. Modifications to forbearance framework for mobile wireless data services. 30 June. http://www.crtc.gc.ca/eng/archive/2010/2010-445.htm.

–. 2011. Consumers. http://www.crtc.gc.ca/eng/consmr.htm.

CTV.ca. 2006. Report recommends sweeping changes to CBC. 21 June. http://montreal.ctv.ca/servlet/an/local/CTVNews/20060621/repor_cbc_060621?hub=MontrealHome949.

–. 2009. Alberta teachers slam planned human rights changes. http://www.ctv.ca/servlet/ArticleNews/story/CTVNews/20090505/schools_090505?s_name=&no_ads=.

Cunningham, S., and T. Nguyen. 2003. Actually existing hybridity: Vietnamese diasporic music video. In *The media of diaspora,* edited by K.H. Karim, 119-32. London: Routledge.

Cunningham, S., and J. Sinclair. 2000. Diasporas and the media. In *Floating lives: The media and Asian diasporas,* edited by S. Cunningham and J. Sinclair, 1-34. Lanham, MD: Rowman and Littlefield.

Curran, J. 2002. *Media and power.* London: Routledge.

–. 2005. Mediations of democracy. In *Mass media and society,* 4th ed., edited by J. Curran and M. Gurevitch, 122-49. New York: Oxford University Press.

Dahlgren, P. 1995. *Television and the public sphere.* Thousand Oaks, CA: Sage.

Dalla Costa, M., and S. James. 1972. *The power of women and the subversion of the community.* Bristol: Falling Wall Press.

Dávila, A. 2001. *Latinos Inc.: The marketing and making of a people.* Berkeley: University of California Press.

Davis, M. 1986. Feminist editor acts in solidarity. *Pandora,* December, 3.

Day, R.J.F. 2005. *Gramsci is dead: Anarchist currents in the newest social movements.* London: Pluto Press.

De Rosa, S. 1988. Our feminist presses deserve our support. *Pandora,* June, 4.

De Santis, H. 2003. Mi programa es su programa: Tele/visions of a Spanish-language diaspora in North America. In *The media of diaspora,* edited by K.H. Karim, 63-75. London: Routledge.

Debord, G. 1967. *Society of the spectacle.* Detroit: Black and Red.

Delacourt, S. 2010. The rise of the Tea Party in Canada? *Toronto Star,* 4 October. http://www.thestar.com/news/canada/article/870697.

Demay, J. 1993. The persistence and creativity of Canadian Aboriginal newspapers. *Canadian Journal of Communication* 18(1): 89-100.

Department of Justice. 2008. Parliamentary review of the Anti-terrorism Act. http://www.justice.gc.ca/antiter/home-accueil-eng.asp.

Descarriers-Belanger, F., and S. Roy. 1991. *The women's movement and its currents of thought.* Trans. J. Beeman. CRIAW papers 26. Ottawa: Canadian Research Institute for the Advancement of Women.

Deuze, M. 2007. *Media work.* Cambridge: Polity Press.

Deuze, M., A. Bruns, and C. Neuberger. 2007. Preparing for an age of participatory news. *Journalism Practice* 1(3): 322-38.

Dobson, J.C. 2004. Marriage is the foundation of the family. *Notre Dame Journal of Ethics, Law and Public Policy* 18(1): 1-6.

Domanick, A. 2010. Faith-based networks preach the multi-platform gospel. *Broadcasting and Cable,* 4 October. http://www.broadcastingcable.com/.

Dominion Newspaper Cooperative. n.d. Bylaws of the Dominion Newspaper Cooperative. http://www.mediacoop.ca/join/bylaws.

Downing, J. 1984. *Radical media: The political experience of alternative communication.* Cambridge, MA: South End Press.

–. 1999. "Hate speech" and "First Amendment absolutism" discourses in the US. *Discourse and Society* 10(2): 175-89.

–. 2003. The Independent Media Center movement and the anarchist tradition. In *Contesting media power: Alternative media in a networked world,* edited by N. Couldry and J. Curran, 243-57. Lanham, MD: Rowman and Littlefield.

Downing, J., and N. Fenton. 2003. New media, counter publicity and the public sphere. *New Media and Society* 5(2): 185-202.

Downing, J., T.V. Ford, G. Gil, and L. Stein. 2001. *Radical media: Rebellious communication and social movements.* Thousand Oaks, CA: Sage.

Downing, J., and C. Husband. 2005. *Representing "race": Racisms, ethnicities and media.* London: Sage.

Doyle, J. 2002. *Progressive heritage: The evolution of a politically radical literary tradition in Canada.* Waterloo: Wilfrid Laurier University Press.

Druick, Z. 2007. *Projecting Canada: Government policy and documentary film at the National Film Board.* Montreal and Kingston: McGill-Queen's University Press.

Duncombe, S. 1997. *Notes from the underground: Zines and the politics of alternative culture.* London: Verso.

Dyer, R. 2000. The role of stereotypes. In *Media studies: A reader,* edited by P. Marris and S. Thornham, 245-51. New York: New York University Press.

Dyer-Witheford, N. 1999. *Cyber-Marx: Cycles and circuits of struggle in high-technology capitalism.* Chicago: University of Illinois Press.

Dykstra, R. 1999. The hometown paper viability of news in the community press. Master's thesis, Carleton University.

Earth Liberation Front. 2002. *Setting fires with electrical timers.* Portland: North American ELF Press Office.

Edwards, Cathy. 2009. *Community television policies and practices around the world.* Report prepared on behalf of Timescape Productions for the Canadian Radio-television and Telecommunications Commission. http://www.vcn.bc.ca/cmes/1pages/Community-Television-Around-the-World.htm.

–. 2010. A new vision for community TV. http://cactus.independentmedia.ca/node/401.

Electronic Frontier Foundation. 2009. *File sharing.* http://www.eff.org/issues/file-sharing.

Enzensberger, H.M. 1974. *The consciousness industry: On literature, politics, and the media.* New York: Seabury Press.

Equipping Christians for the Public Square Centre. 2007. Our philosophy of engagement. http://www.ecpcentre.com/philosophy.php.

European Union Parliament. 2008. European Parliament resolution of 25 September 2008 on community media in Europe. http://www.europarl.europa.eu/sides/getDoc.do?type=TA&reference=P6-TA-2008-0456&language=EN&ring=A6-2008-0263.

EVAH (Elaho Valley Anarchist Horde). 2001. *EVAH: Elaho Valley Anarchist Horde.* Vancouver: Self-published.

Fairchild, C. 1993. The producers and the produced: Community radio in Toronto. Master's thesis, York University.

Fairley, M., ed. 1945. *Spirit of Canadian democracy: A collection of Canadian writings from the beginnings to the present day.* Toronto: Progress.

Falconer, S. 2004. Yours in solidarity: Alternative media projects with North American political prisoners. Master's thesis, Concordia University.

Family Index. 2005. http://www.familyindex.net.

Faris, R. 1975. *The passionate educators: Voluntary associations and the struggle for control of adult educational broadcasting in Canada, 1919-1952.* Toronto: Peter Martin.

Faulhaber, G.R. 2007. Network neutrality: The debate evolves. *International Journal of Communication* 1: 680-700.

Felski, R. 1989a. *Beyond feminist aesthetics: Feminist literature and social change.* Cambridge, MA: Harvard University Press.

–. 1989b. Feminism, postmodernism and the critique of modernity. *Cultural Critique* 13: 33-56.

Ferreira, G.A. 2007. Participatory video for policy development in remote Aboriginal communities. PhD diss., University of Guelph.

Flaherty, J. 2006. Address by the Honourable James M. Flaherty, P.C., MP, Minister of Finance, to the Toronto Board of Trade. 29 May. http://www.fin.gc.ca/n06/06-022_1-eng.asp.

Flavelle, D. 2009. Former youth media mogul Znaimer gets religion, takes over Vision TV with senior viewers in mind. *Toronto Star,* 16 June. http://www.thestar.com/printArticle651361.

Fleisher, F. 1995. Between postage stamps and digitization: The changing roles of educational broadcasting. *Educational Media International* 32(1): 18-20.

Fluri, J., and L. Dowler. 2004. House bound: Women's agency in white separatist movements. In *Spaces of hate: Geographies of discrimination and intolerance in the USA,* edited by C. Flint, 69-85. New York: Routledge.

Foreman, D., and B. Haywood, eds. 1993. *Ecodefense: A field guide to monkeywrenching.* Chico, CA: Abzug Press. (Orig. pub. 1985.)

Foucault, M. 1988. The ethic of care for the self as a practice of freedom. In *The final Foucault,* edited by J. Bernauer and D. Rasmussen, 1-20. Cambridge, MA: MIT Press.

–. 2002. The subject and power. In *Power: Essential works of Foucault 1954-1984,* edited by J.D. Faubion, 326-48. London: Penguin Books.

Fraser, N. 1989. *Unruly practices: Power, discourse and gender in contemporary social theory.* Minneapolis: University of Minnesota Press.

–. 1992. Rethinking the public sphere: A contribution to the critique of actually existing democracy. In *Habermas and the public sphere,* edited by C. Calhoun, 109-42. Cambridge, MA: MIT Press.

Fraser, S. 1985. The case for an editorial policy: *Pandora* should help others make connections. *Pandora,* December, 8.

–. 1987. Local journalist condemns sexist bias in media. *Pandora,* December, 3.

Fraser Institute. n.d. Education programs. http://www.fraserinstitute.org/education_ programs.

Free Press. 2010. *Annual report 2009.* http://www.freepress.net/about_us/annual_ reports.

–. n.d. Free Press and the Free Press Action Fund. http://www.freepress.net/about_us.

Freeman, B.M. 2001. *The satellite sex: The media and women's issues in English Canada, 1966-1971.* Waterloo: Wilfrid Laurier University Press.

–. 2006. From no go to no logo: Lesbian rights in *Chatelaine* magazine, 1966-2004. *Canadian Journal of Communication* 4(31): 815-41.

–. 2011. *Beyond bylines: Media workers and women's rights in Canada.* Waterloo: Wilfrid Laurier University Press.

Frey, L.R., and K.M. Carragee. 2007a. *Communication activism.* Vol. 1, *Communication for social change.* Cresskill, NJ: Hampton Press.

–. 2007b. *Communication activism.* Vol. 2, *Media and performance activism.* Cresskill, NJ: Hampton Press.

Fuchs, Christian. 2009. Some reflections on Manuel Castells' book "Communication power." *tripleC: cognition, communication, co-operation* 7(1): 94-108.

Garcia, D. 2007. Tactical media. In *The alternative media handbook,* edited by K. Coyer, T. Dowmunt, and A. Fountain, 6-7. New York: Routledge.

Garnham, N. 1986. The media and the public sphere. In *Communicating politics,* edited by P. Golding, G. Murdock, and P. Schlesinger, 37-53. Leicester: Leicester University Press.

–. 2003. A response to Elizabeth Jacka's "Democracy as defeat." *Television and New Media* 4(2): 193-200.

Gasher, M. 1997. From sacred cows to white elephants: Cultural policy under siege. In *Canadian cultures and globalization,* edited by J. Cohnstaedt and Y. Frenette, 13-30. Montreal: Association for Canadian Studies.

–. 2007. Redefining journalism education in Canada. *Our Schools, Our Selves* 17(1): 125-36.

Geist, M. 2005. Copyright's convergence. *Toronto Star,* 4 April. http://www.michael geist.ca/resc/html_bkup/april42005.html.

–. 2007a. Net neutrality in Canada. In *For sale to the highest bidder: Telecom policy in Canada,* edited by M. Moll and L. R. Shade, 73-81. Ottawa: Canadian Centre for Policy Alternatives.

–. 2007b. Putting up Internet borders. *Toronto Star,* 5 November. http://www.thestar. com/comment/columnists/article/273475.

–. 2008. The Canadian DMCA: Check the fine print. http://www.michaelgeist.ca/ content/view/3025/125/.

–. 2010. The U.S. DMCA vs. Bill C-32: Comparing the digital lock exceptions. http:// www.michaelgeist.ca/content/view/5229/125/.

Gelderloos, P. 2007. *How non-violence protects the state.* Boston: South End Press.

Gibbs, P., and J. Hamilton. 2001. Introduction: Alternative media in media history. *Media History* 7(2): 117-18.

Gilbert, J. 2008. *Anti-capitalism and culture: Radical theory and popular politics.* Oxford: Berg.

Gillespie, M. 1995. *Television, ethnicity and cultural change.* London: Routledge.

Gillett, J. 1999. Informed survival: Media activism by people with HIV/AIDS. PhD diss., McMaster University.

Ginsburg, F. 2002. Mediating culture: Indigenous media, ethnographic film, and the production of identity. In *The anthropology of media: A reader,* edited by K.M. Askew and R.R. Wilk, 210-36. Malden, MA: Blackwell.

Girard, B. 1992. *A passion for radio.* Montreal: Black Rose Books.

Gitlin, T. 1998. Public sphere or public sphericules? In *Media, ritual and identity,* edited by T. Liebes and J. Curran, 168-74. London: Routledge.

Glass, G. 2009. Art and culture create the spaces we live in. *Georgia Straight,* 5 November. http://www.straight.com/article-269247/geof-glass-art-and-culture-create -spaces-we-live.

Godard, B. 2002. Feminist periodicals and the production of cultural value: The Canadian context. *Women's Studies International Forum* 25(2): 209-23.

Goldberg, D.T. 1994. Introduction: Multicultural conditions. In *Multiculturalism: A critical reader,* edited by D.T. Goldberg, 1-41. Cambridge, MA: Basil Blackwell.

Goldberg, K. 1990. *The barefoot channel: Community television as a tool for social change.* Vancouver: New Star Books.

Golding, P., and P. Elliott. 2000. News values and news production. In *Media studies: A reader,* edited by P. Marris and S. Thornham, 632-44. New York: New York University Press.

Gollmitzer, M., and Catherine Murray. 2008. *From economy to ecology: A policy framework for creative labour.* Canadian Conference of the Arts. http://www.ifacca.org/ publications/2008/03/11/economy-ecology-policy-framework-creative-labour/.

Gómez, G. 2007. *Radio and television in the digital era.* Montevideo, Uruguay: AMARC-America Latina y Caribe and Friedrich Ebert Foundation Centro de Competencias en Comunicación.

Gordon, K. 2004. Feminist mags in trouble in Canada. *Ryerson Review of Journalism.* March. http://www.rrj.ca/online/462/.

Gottlieb, A. 1980. Movement comment. *Broadside,* February, 19.

GPI. 2003. Genuine progress index for Atlantic Canada: Measuring community wellbeing and development. GPI Atlantic. http://www.gpiatlantic.org.

Grant, P.S., M.T. Lafontaine, and G. Buchanan. 2006. *Canadian broadcasting regulatory handbook,* 8th ed. Toronto: McCarthy Tetrault LLP.

Gruending, D. 2007. Right-wing think tanks multiplying in Canada. *Straight Goods,* 4 September. http://www.dennisgruending.ca/pulpitandpolitics/?cat=1.

–. 2008. Pulpit and politics: The religious right and its growing influence on Canadian public life. Paper presented at "Sacred and Secular in a Global Canada," Huron College, University of Western Ontario, London, Ontario. http://www.dennis gruending.ca/pulpitandpolitics/?cat=1.

Guenette, F. 1986. Second Début [A new beginning]. *La vie en rose* 40, November, 4-5.

Guenette, F., and F. Pelletier. 1986a. La bonne et la mauvaise [Good news and bad news]. *La vie en rose* 36, May, 4-5.

–. 1986b. Des femmes de coeur [Women with big hearts]. *La vie en rose* 37, July-August, 4-5.

Gutstein, D. 1999. *E.con: How the Internet undermines democracy.* Toronto: Stoddart.

–. 2009. *Not a conspiracy theory: How business propaganda hijacks democracy.* Toronto: Key Porter Books.

Haas, T. 2004. Research note: Alternative media, public journalism and the pursuit of democratization. *Journalism Studies* 5(1): 115-21.

Habermas, J. 1987. *The theory of communicative action.* Vol. 2, trans. T. McCarthy. Boston: Beacon Press.

–. 1989. *The structural transformation of the public sphere.* Trans. T. Burger. Cambridge, MA: MIT Press.

Hack Canada. 2010. Canadian links. http://www.hackcanada.com/canadian/links.html.

Hackett, R.A., and W.K. Carroll. 2006. *Remaking media: The struggle to democratize public communication.* New York: Routledge.

Hackett, R.A., and R. Gruneau. 2000. *The missing news: Filters and blind spots in Canada's press.* Ottawa: Canadian Centre for Policy Alternatives and Garamond Press.

Hackett, R.A., and Y. Zhao. 1996. Are ethics enough? Objective journalism versus sustainable democracy. In *Deadlines and diversity: Journalism ethics in a changing world,* edited by V. Alia, B. Brennan, and B. Hoffmaster, 44-58. Halifax: Fernwood.

–. 1998. *Sustaining democracy: Journalism and the politics of objectivity.* Toronto: Garamond Press.

Hadl, G., and J. Dongwon. 2008. New approaches to our media: General challenges and the Korean case. In *Alternative media and the politics of resistance: Perspectives and challenges,* edited by M. Pajnik and J.D.H. Downing, 81-109. Ljubljana, Slovenia: Peace Institute, Institute for Contemporary Social and Political Studies.

Hafsteinsson, S.B. 2008. Unmasking deep democracy: Aboriginal Peoples Television Network (APTN) and cultural production. PhD diss., Temple University.

Hall, A. 2010. Ont. firm to purchase SCN. *Regina Leader-Post,* 22 July, A3.

Hall, S. 1997. The local and the global: Globalization and ethnicity. In *Dangerous liaisons: Gender, nation, and postcolonial perspectives,* edited by A. McClintock, A. Mufti, and E. Shohat, 173-87. Minneapolis: University of Minnesota Press.

–. 2000. Racist ideologies and the media. In *Media studies: A reader,* edited by P. Marris and S. Thornham, 271-82. New York: New York University Press.

Halleck, D. 2002. *Hand-held visions: The impossible possibilities of community media.* New York: Fordham University Press.

Hamilton, J. 2000. Alternative media: Conceptual difficulties, critical possibilities. *Journal of Communication Inquiry* 24(4): 357-78.

–. 2008. *Democratic communications: Formations, projects, possibilities.* Lanham, MD: Lexington Books.

Hargreaves, A.G., and D. Mahdjoub. 1997. Satellite television viewing among ethnic minorities in France. *European Journal of Communication* 12(4): 459-77.

Harris, C., and C. Dafoe. 1995. ACCESS waiting for CRTC green light: Privatized educational broadcaster would run publicly funded programs and commercials. *Toronto Globe and Mail,* 18 July, C2.

Harris, E.M. 1992. Dreaming reality: Small media in community development as critical education practice: A case study of community narrowcasting in the town on Buchans, Newfoundland, Canada. PhD diss., University of Toronto.

Hartley, J. 2000. Communicative democracy in a redactional society: The future of journalism studies. *Journalism: Theory, Practice and Criticism* 1(1): 39-48.

Harvey, D. 2000. *Spaces of hope.* Edinburgh: Edinburgh University Press.

Haskell, D. 2007a. Evangelical Christians in Canadian national television news, 1994-2004: A frame analysis. *Journal of Communication and Religion* 50(1): 118-52.

–. 2007b. News media influence on nonevangelical coders' perceptions of evangelical Christians: A case study. *Journal of Media and Religion* 6(3): 153-79.

–. 2009. *Through a lens darkly: How the news media perceive and portray evangelicals.* Toronto: Clements Academic.

Hassanpour, A. 2003. Diaspora, homeland and communication technologies. In *The media of diaspora,* edited by K.H. Karim, 76-88. London: Routledge.

Henry, F., and C. Tator. 2002. *Discourses of domination: Racial bias in the Canadian English language press.* Toronto: University of Toronto Press.

Herman, E.S., and N. Chomsky. 2002. *Manufacturing consent: The political economy of the mass media,* updated ed. New York: Pantheon Books.

Hesmondhalgh, D. 2007. *The cultural industries,* 2nd ed. London: Sage.

Hnatiuk, J. 2009. CRTC is the real culprit. *Communiqué* 16(12) (7 April). www.chp.ca.

Hoerder, D., ed. 1984. *Labor newspaper preservation project: Essays on the Scandinavian-North American radical press, 1880s-1930s.* Bremen: Publications of the Labor Newspaper Preservation Project.

–. 1987a. *The immigrant labor press in North America, 1840s-1970s.* Vol. 1, *Migrants from Northern Europe.* New York: Greenwood Press.

–. 1987b. *The immigrant labor press in North America, 1840s-1970s.* Vol. 2, *Migrants from Eastern and Southeastern Europe.* New York: Greenwood Press.

Hoerder, D., and C. Harzig, eds. 1985. *The press of labor migrants in Europe and North America, 1880s to 1930s.* Bremen: Publications of the Labor Newspaper Preservation Project.

hooks, b. 1996. *Reel to real: Race, sex and class at the movies.* London: Routledge.

Hoskins, C., S. McFadyen, and A. Finn. 1993. Canadian participation in international co-productions and co-ventures in television programming. *Canadian Journal of Communication* 18(2): 219-33.

Howley, K. 2005a. *Community media: People, places, and communication technologies.* New York: Cambridge University Press.

–. 2005b. Manhattan neighbourhood network: Community access television and the public sphere in the 1990s. *Historical Journal of Film, Radio and Television* 25(1): 119-38.

–, ed. 2010. *Understanding community media.* Thousand Oaks, CA: Sage.

Hoynes, W. 2003. Branding public service: The "new PBS" and the privatization of public television. *Television and New Media* 4(2): 117-30.

Huang, A. 1991. In Nova Scotia: *Pandora* boxed by complaint. *Kinesis,* September, 3.

–. 1991-1992. Feminist paper harassed: *Pandora* pressed by threats. *Kinesis,* December-January, 4.

Huesca, R., and B. Dervin. 1994. Theory and practice in Latin America alternative communication research. *Journal of Communication* 44(4): 53-73.

Husband, C., ed. 1994. *A richer vision: The development of ethnic minority media in Western democracies.* Paris: UNESCO and John Libbey.

IndependentMedia.ca. n.d. A directory of non-corporate journalism. http://www.independentmedia.ca/.

Industry Canada – Telecommunications Policy Branch. 2002. *Industry framework of Internet service providers.* Ottawa: Pollara.

Institute of Marriage and Family in Canada. n.d. Media room. http://www.imfcanada.org/default.aspx?cat=5.

International Media Support. 2010. A push for community radio in Jordan. 16 September. http://www.i-m-s.dk/article/push-community-radio-jordan.

Intriciti. n.d. http://www.intriciti.ca/.

Inuit Broadcasting Corporation. 1982. *Position on northern broadcasting.* Ottawa: Inuit Broadcasting Corporation.

Ipsos-Reid. 2002. *Broadcasting issues and Canadian public opinion.* Ottawa: Friends of Canadian Broadcasting.

Isenberg, D.S. 2003. End-to-end is a BIG political statement. *Isen.blog.* http://isen.com/blog/2003/11/end-to-end-is-big-political-statement.html.

Isuma. 2008. About us. http://www.isuma.ca/about.

Jacques, M. 1991. Martin Jacques bids a fond farewell to *Marxism Today.* http://www.amielandmelburn.org.uk/collections/mt/index_frame.htm.

Jakubowicz, K. 1999. Public service broadcasting in the information society. *Media Development* 2: 45-49.

Jankowski, N.W. 2003. Community media research: A quest for theoretically grounded models. *Public* 10(1): 5-14.

Jefferson, J. 1987. Abortion, lesbian, growth issues not to be funded by sec state. *Pandora,* September-December, 18.

Jeppesen, S. 2009. Creating guerrilla texts in rhizomatic value-practices on the sliding scale of autonomy: Toward an anti-authoritarian cultural logic. In *New perspectives on anarchism,* edited by N. Jun and S. Wahl, 473-94. Lanham, MD: Lexington Books.

Jipson, A. 2007. Introduction to the special issue: Influence of hate rock. *Popular Music and Society* 30(4): 449-51.

Jiwani, Y. 2010a. Doubling discourses and the veiled other: Mediations of race and gender in Canadian media. In *States of race: Critical race feminism for the 21st century,* edited by S. Razack, M. Smith, and S. Thobani, 59-86. Toronto: Between the Lines.

–. 2010b. Race(ing) the nation: Media and minorities. In *Mediascapes: New patterns in Canadian communication,* 3rd ed., edited by L.R. Shade, 302-15. Toronto: Nelson.

Jiwani, Y., and M.L. Young. 2006. Missing and murdered women: Reproducing marginality in news discourse. *Canadian Journal of Communication* 31(4): 895-917.

Johnston, D.E.B. 2005. Television outside the box: The case of PrideVision TV. PhD diss., University of Calgary.

Johnston, J. 2008. Gifts that keep on giving. *This Magazine* 41(6): 4.

Jones, F. 1987. Feminist publishing: A question of design. *Kinesis,* June, 20.

–. 1994. Feminist publishing in Canada: *Pandora* folds. *Kinesis,* July-August, 3.

Jones, J., and R. Martin. 2010. Crypto-hierarchies and technocrats: An Indymedia UK case study. In *Making our media: Global initiatives toward a democratic public sphere.* Vol. 1, *Creating new communication spaces,* edited by C. Rodriguez, D. Kidd, and L. Stein, 223-41. Cresskill, NJ: Hampton Press.

Jones, J.P. 2006. A cultural approach to the study of mediated citizenship. Paper presented at the annual meeting of the International Communication Association, Dresden, Germany, 16 June. http://www.allacademic.com/meta/p90744_index.html.

Juniper, D.K. 2002. The moccasin telegraph goes digital: First Nations and the political usage of the Internet. In *Seeking convergence in policy and practice: Communications in the public interest.* Vol. 2, edited by M. Moll and L.R. Shade, 142-51. Ottawa: Canadian Centre for Policy Alternatives.

Kalantzis, M. 1995. Civic pluralism: Renewing Australia's social contract. Paper presented at "Global Cultural Diversity," Sydney, Australia, 12 April.

Kanayama, T. 2007. Community ties and revitalization: The role of community radio in Japan. *Keio Communication Review* 29: 5-24.

Karim, K.H. 1993. Reconstructing the multicultural community: Discursive strategies of inclusion and exclusion. *International Journal of Politics, Culture and Society* 7(2): 189-207.

–. 2002. Public sphere and public sphericules: Civic discourse in ethnic media. In *Civic discourse and cultural politics in Canada: A cacophony of voices,* edited by S. Ferguson and L.R. Shade, 230-42. Westport, CT: Ablex.

–. 2003. Commentary from Canada's minority ethnic communities to Bill C-36: A review of ethnic and mainstream media. Report prepared for Justice Canada. Ottawa.

Karim, K.H., M. Eid, and B.E. de B'béri. 2007. *Settlement programming through the media.* Settlement and Intergovernmental Affairs Directorate, Ontario Region, Citizenship and Immigration Canada. Ottawa. http://atwork.settlement.org/downloads/atwork/Settlement_Programming_Through_Media1.pdf.

Karlin, M. 2007. Paul Jay and the Real News mean to bring us video-based news without the government or corporate spin. *BuzzFlash.com,* 24 July. http://blog.buzzflash.com/interviews/070.

Keane, J. 1991. *The media and democracy.* Cambridge: Polity Press.

Keast, R. 1986. Educational broadcasting in Canada: A brief overview. http://www.clt.ca/pdf/EBC03.pdf.

Kendall, D. 2005. *Framing class: Media representations of wealth and poverty in America.* Lanham, MD: Rowman and Littlefield.

Kerr, I. 2010. Digital locks and the automation of virtue. In *From "Radical extremism" to "balanced copyright": Canadian copyright in the digital age,* edited by M. Geist, 247-303. Toronto: Irwin Law.

Keung, N. 2004. Minorities fare poorly on TV. *Toronto Star,* 16 July, A2.

Khouri, M. 2007. *Filming politics: Communism and the portrayal of the working class at the National Film Board of Canada, 1939-45.* Calgary: University of Calgary Press.

Kidd, D. 1998. Talking the walk: The communication commons amidst the media enclosures. PhD diss., Simon Fraser University.

–. 1999. The value of alternative media. *Peace Review* 11(1): 113-19.

–. 2002. Indymedia.org: The development of the communications commons. *Democratic Communiqué* 18 (Summer): 65-86.

–. 2003. Indymedia.org: A new communications commons. In *Cyberactivism: Online activism in theory and practice,* edited by M. McCaughey and M.D. Ayers, 47-69. New York: Routledge.

Kiefl, B. 2003. *International TV programming and audience trends 1996-2001: A report prepared for the CRTC.* Canadian Media Research Inc. May. http://www.crtc.gc.ca/eng/publications/reports/drama/drama3.htm?Print=True.

–. 2004. Measuring TV audiences: How should it be done? *Playback Online,* 19 January. http://www.playbackonline.ca/articles/magazine/20040119/testing.html?page=1.

Kierans, K. 2008. CRTC reins in media ownership. *Journalism ethics for the global citizen.* 23 January. http://ethics.journalism.wisc.edu/.

Kinesis. 1975. Masthead. October, 19.

–. 1979. *Broadside* wants to be read outside the movement. August, 16.

–. 1984a. Socreds dump VSW. May, 1, 3.

–. 1984b. Update on *Kinesis* and VSW. September, 1.

–. 1984c. Reader survey. October, 2.

–. 1986. *Kinesis* price to go up to $1.75. February, 2.

–. 1987. Movement matters. February, 2.

–. 1988. *Kinesis* survey results now in. October, 3, 6.

–. 1990a. Inside *Kinesis.* March, 2.

–. 1990b. A small price to play. June, 21.

–. 1991-1992. Concentrating on women. December-January, 4.

–. 1992a. As *Kinesis* goes to press. October, 2.

–. 1992b. Victory bitter-sweet for *Pandora.* May, 3-4.

–. 1994a. Distribution list. April, 2.

–. 1994b. The survey: What you think of us. February, 15.

–. 1998a. Inside *Kinesis.* March, 2.

–. 1998b. Inside *Kinesis.* November, 2.

–. 1999-2000. Special 25th anniversary supplement. December-January.

–. 2001. Inside *Kinesis.* March, 2.

King, D., and C. Mele. 1999. Making public access television: Community participation, media literacy and the public sphere. *Journal of Broadcasting and Electronic Media* 43(4): 603-23.

Kintz, L., and J. Lesage, eds. 1998. *Media, culture, and the religious right.* Minneapolis: University of Minnesota Press.

Kivisild, E. 1985a. Feminist periodical conference a first. *Kinesis,* July-August, 1.

–. 1985b. Media under attack. *Kinesis,* July-August, 4.

Klee, M. 1995. "Hands-off the Labour Forum": The making and unmaking of national working-class radio broadcasting in Canada, 1935-1944. *Labour/Le travail* 35: 107-32.

Knowledge Network. 2006. Knowledge Network's new board of directors announced. News release, 25 July. Copy on file with author (Kozolanka).

–. 2008. Knowledge Network "rethinks" brand. News release, 17 April. http://knowledge.ca/press/corporate/2008-04-17.

Kozolanka, K. 2001. The new TVOntario: Salvation or suicide for public educational broadcasting. *Canadian Journal of Communication* 26(1): 53-88.

–. 2007a. *The power of persuasion: The politics of the new right in Ontario.* Montreal: Black Rose Books.

–. 2007b. Reading between the lines and crossing borders: Critical media literacy, good citizenship and democratic media. *Our Schools, Our Selves* 17(1): 17-25.

–. 2009. The politics of media literacy and the struggle for democratic citizenship and media: Lessons from Ontario, Canada. In *Issues in information and media literacy: Criticism, history and policy,* edited by M. Leaning, 71-91. Santa Rosa, CA: Informing Science Press.

Krashinsky, S. 2009. Hate-speech violates Charter rights, tribunal rules. *Toronto Globe and Mail,* 2 September. http://www.theglobeandmail.com/news/national/.

–. 2010. Sun TV gears down licence application. *Toronto Globe and Mail,* 5 October. http://www.theglobeandmail.com/.

Kristmanson, M., and N. McLaren. 1998. Love your neighbour: The Royal Canadian Mounted Police and the National Film Board, 1948-53. *Film History* 10(3): 254-74.

La vie en rose. 1986. Pour en finir avec les hommes! [To be done with men!] 33, February, 5. http://bibnum2.bnquebec.ca/bna/vierose/.

Laclau, E., and C. Mouffe. 2001. *Hegemony and socialist strategy: Towards a radical democratic politics,* 2nd ed. London: Verso.

Landolt, G.C. 2009. Feminists funded by the Canadian taxpayers still sow dissent. http://www.realwomenca.com/page/newsljf0901/html.

Langlois, A. 2005. How open is open? The politics of open publishing. In *Autonomous media: Activating resistance and dissent,* edited by A. Langlois and F. Dubois, 46-59. Montreal: Cumulus Press.

Langlois, A., and F. Dubois, eds. 2005. *Autonomous media: Activating resistance and dissent.* Montreal: Cumulus Press.

Lavallée, C. 2010. Carole Lavallée on Federal Sustainable Development Act. http://openparliament.ca/hansards/2283/246/only/.

Law-abiding Unregistered Firearms Association. n.d. http://www.lufa.ca.

Lawson, P. 2007. Gutting the Telecom Act. In *For sale to the highest bidder: Telecom policy in Canada,* edited by M. Moll and L.R. Shade, 17-26. Ottawa: Canadian Centre for Policy Alternatives.

Lazenby, J. 1975-1976. *Kinesis report.* In *Annual report of the Vancouver Status of Women,* 1 June-31 May. Vancouver Status of Women Papers, Canadian Women's Movement Archives, University of Ottawa, Finding aid X10-1, box 124, file 1, 16-17.

Lee, E. 1997. *The labour movement and the Internet: The new internationalism.* London: Pluto Press.

Lee, K. 2000. *Urban poverty in Canada: A statistical profile.* Ottawa: Canadian Council on Social Development. http://www.ccsd.ca/pubs/2000/up.

Lejtenyi, P. 2005. Dodging the dogma. *Montreal Mirror* 21(18). http://www.montrealmirror.com/2005/102005/watn5.html.

Lessig, L. 2004. *Free culture.* New York: Penguin Press.

Levendel, L. 1989. *A century of the Canadian Jewish press, 1880s-1980s.* Ottawa: Borealis Press.

Levy, S. 1984. *Hackers: Heroes of the computer revolution.* London: Penguin Books.

Lewis, P., ed. 1993. *Alternative media: Linking global and local.* New York: Oxford University Press.

Liberal Party of Canada. 2009. Liberals push for better competition and service for cell phone and Internet use. News release, 30 October. http://www.liberal.ca/en/newsroom/media-releases/16801_liberals-push-for-better-competition-and-service-for-cell-phone-and-Internet-use.

Light, E. 2007. A media of citizens: A comparative study of community radio in Montréal (Québec) and Montevideo (Uruguay). PhD diss., Université du Québec à Montréal.

Lin, J., C. Owen, T. Pringle, and R. Soucy. 1999. Vancouver's Downtown Eastside: Gentrification and developing housing for low-income persons. Real Estate Foundation of British Columbia.

Lindstrom-Best, V. 1985. *Toveritar* and Finnish Canadian women 1900-1930. In *The press of labor migrants in Europe and North America, 1880s to 1930s,* edited by C. Harzig and D. Hoerder, 243-64. Bremen: Publications of the Labor Newspaper Preservation Project.

Lithgow, M. 2008. Articulating counterpublics with community capital: A framework for evaluating community television. Master's thesis, Concordia University.

Little, M., and C. Chan. 2008. Tibetans ask Canada to boot Chinese TV channel: Say slanted broadcasts are hate-incitement. *Epoch Times,* 1 April. http://www.theepochtimes.com/news/8-4-1/68384.html.

Littlebear, L., M. Boldt, and J.A. Long. 1984. *Pathways to self-determination.* Toronto: University of Toronto Press.

Lloyd, B.-A. 1985a. We just couldn't keep the lid on *Pandora! Pandora,* September, 4.

–. 1985b. We need an ad policy. *Pandora,* September, 4.

–. 1986. Those 2 a.m. panic attacks will be held in committee. *Pandora,* December, 4.

–. 1987. "Hearing women into speech": The feminist press and the women's community. *Canadian Women's Studies/Les cahiers de la femme* 8(1): 29-32.

Longford, G. 2007. Download this! Contesting digital rights in a global era: The case of music downloading in Canada. In *How Canadians communicate.* Vol. 2, edited by D. Tara, M. Bakardjieva, and F. Pannekoek, 195-216. Calgary: University of Calgary Press.

Lukas, C.L. 2006. *The politically incorrect guide to women, sex, and feminism.* Washington: Regnery.

Luu, H. 2000. Redefining radical. *Colours of resistance: Multiracial, anti-racist revolt against global capitalism,* 3-7. Toronto: Self-published.

MacDonald, I. 1986. Publishing priorities. *Broadside,* June, 7.

MacLennan, A.F. 2005. American network broadcasting, the CBC, and Canadian radio stations during the 1930s: A content analysis. *Journal of Radio Studies* 12(1): 85-103.

Mahtani, M. 2008. Racializing the audience: Immigrant perceptions of mainstream Canadian English-language television news. *Canadian Journal of Communication* 33(4): 639-60.

Mandaville, P. 2003. Communication and diasporic Islam: A virtual Ummah? In *The media of diaspora,* edited by K.H. Karim, 135-47. London: Routledge.

Manning Centre. n.d. http://www.manningcentre.ca.

Marlow, I. 2010. CRTC chair urges telecom overhaul. *Toronto Globe and Mail,* 14 April. http://www.theglobeandmail.com/.

Marshall, B. 1995. Communication as politics: Feminist print media in English Canada. *Women's Studies International Forum* 18(4): 463-74.

Marx, K. 1978. Economic and philosophic manuscripts of 1844. In *The Marx and Engels reader,* 2nd ed., edited by R.C. Tucker, 66-125. New York: Norton.

–. 1990. *Capital.* Vol. 1. London: Penguin Books.

Masters, P. 1983. Feminist press: Front page challenge. *Broadside,* June, 8-9.

–. 1989. *Broadside* and beyond. *Broadside,* August-September, 3.

–. 1991. A word from the press: A brief survey of feminist publishing. *Resources for Feminist Research/Documentation sur la recherche féministe* 20(1-2): 27-35.

Mathers, D., and M. Ardyche. 1987. Why does "that word" have so much power? *Pandora,* December, 4.

Mattelart, A. 1980. *Mass media, ideologies and the revolutionary movement.* Trans. M. Coad. Brighton, UK: Harvester Press.

Maurotto, P. 2000. Private policing and surveillance of Catholics: Anti-communism in the Roman Catholic archdiocese of Toronto, 1920-60. In *Whose national security? Canadian state surveillance and the creation of enemies,* edited by G. Kinsman, D.K. Buse, and M. Steedman, 37-54. Toronto: Between the Lines.

Mazepa, P. 1997. The Solidarity Network in formation: A search for democratic alternative communication. Master's thesis, Carleton University.

–. 2003. Battles on the cultural front: The (de)labouring of culture in Canada, 1914-1944. PhD diss., Carleton University.

–. 2007. Democracy of, in and through communication: Struggles around public service in Canada in the first half of the twentieth century. *Info: The Journal of Policy, Regulation and Strategy for Telecommunications, Information and Media* 9(2): 45-56.

–. 2011a. Canada: The interwar cultural front. In *Encyclopedia of social movement media,* edited by J. Downing. Thousand Oaks, CA: Sage.

–. 2011b. Direct from the source: Canada's integrated system of state propaganda. In *The propaganda society: Promotional culture and politics in global context,* edited by G. Sussman, 297-313. New York: Peter Lang.

McBride, S., and E. Smith. 2008. Music industry to abandon mass suits. *Wall Street Journal,* 19 December. http://on-line.wsj.com/article/SB122966038836021137.html.

McChesney, R. 1999. *Rich media, poor democracy.* New York: New Press.

–. 2008a. *Communication revolution.* New York: New Press.

–. 2008b. *The political economy of media: Enduring issues, emerging dilemmas.* New York: Monthly Review Press.

McDonald, M. 2010. *The Armageddon factor: The rise of Christian nationalism in Canada.* Toronto: Random House.

McLellan, D. 1969. Marx's view of the unalienated society. *Review of Politics* 31(4): 459-65.

McNamara, M. 2008. Fodder for a good documentary. *Toronto Star,* 19 June. http://www.thestar.com/comment/article/445681.

McQuail, D. 2005. *McQuail's mass communication theory*. London: Sage.

McRobbie, A. 2002. Clubs to companies: Notes on the decline of political culture in speeded up creative worlds. *Cultural Studies* 16(4): 516-31.

Media Consortium. n.d. About the Media Consortium. http://www.themediaconsortium.org/about/.

Media Co-op. n.d. Questions and answers. http://www.mediacoop.ca/join/questions.

Mezei, J.-F. 2008. RE: Network interference (throttling of certain TCPIP packets by Bell). Bell Canada General Tariff Item 5410 – Gateway Access Service (GAS). www.vaxination.ca/crtc/jfmezei_crtc.pdf.

–. 2009. An analysis of telecom decision CRTC 2008-108. http://www.vaxination.ca/crtc/2008_108_analysis1.pdf.

Miceli, M. 2005. Morality politics vs. identity politics: Framing processes and competition among Christian right and gay social movement organizations. *Sociological Forum* 20(4): 599-612.

Milberry, K. 2005. Indymedia as a social movement? Theorizing the new global justice movements. Master's thesis, University of Windsor.

Ministère de la Culture et des Communications. 2004. *Rapport annuel, 2003-2004*. Québec City: Gouvernement du Québec.

–. 2005. *Rapport annuel, 2004-2005*. Québec City: Gouvernement du Québec.

–. 2006. *Rapport annuel, 2005-2006*. Québec City: Gouvernement du Québec.

–. 2007. *Rapport annuel, 2006-2007*. Québec City: Gouvernement du Québec.

Mitchell, D. 1988. Culture as political discourse in Canada. In *Communication Canada: Issues in broadcasting and new technologies,* edited by R. Lorimer and D.C. Wilson, 157-74. Toronto: Kagan and Woo.

Moll, M., and L.R. Shade, eds. 2004. *Seeking convergence in policy and practice: Communications in the public interest*. Vol. 2. Ottawa: Canadian Centre for Policy Alternatives.

–. 2008. *For sale to the highest bidder: Telecom policy in Canada*. Ottawa: Canadian Centre for Policy Alternatives.

Montreal Gazette. 2009. Rights commission threatens our liberty. 29 June. http://www2.canada.com/montrealgazette/features/viewpoints/story.html?id=b084ee2b-ed22-4e08-a689-f1c7dc989a51.

Morgan, J. 2001. Network launches digital vehicle: BC's public educational broadcaster celebrates its 20th anniversary with ambitious Knowledge Network Interactive. *Vancouver Sun,* 13 January, C2.

Morrow, F. 2009. A site for sore journalists. *Toronto Globe and Mail,* 22 August, R7.

Mosco, V. 1989. *The pay-per society: Computers and communication in the information age, essays in critical theory and public policy*. Toronto: Garamond Press.

–. 1996. *The political economy of communication: Rethinking and renewal*. London: Sage.

–. 1997. Marketable commodity or public good: The conflict between domestic and foreign communications policy. In *How Ottawa spends, 1997-98: Seeing red: A Liberal report card,* edited by G. Swimmer, 159-78. Ottawa: Carleton University Press.

Mosco, V., and P. Mazepa. 2003. High tech hegemony: Transforming Canada's capital into Silicon Valley north. In *Globalization, media hegemony, and social class,* edited by L. Artz and Y. Kamalipour, 93-112. New York: State University of New York Press.

Mosco, V., and C. McKercher. 2008. *The laboring of communication: Will knowledge workers of the world unite?* Lanham, MD: Lexington Books.

Murdock, G. 2003. Back to work: Cultural labor in altered times. In *Cultural work: Understanding the cultural industries,* edited by A. Beck, 15-36. London: Routledge.

Murdock, G., and P. Golding. 1989. Information poverty and political inequality: Citizenship in the age of privatized communication. *Journal of Communication* 39(3): 180-95.

Murphy, B.M. 2002. A critical history of the Internet. In *Critical perspectives on the Internet,* edited by G. Elmer, 27-45. Lanham, MD: Rowman and Littlefield.

Murray, C., S. Yu, and D. Ahadi. 2007. *Cultural diversity and ethnic media in BC.* Burnaby, BC: Centre for Policy Studies on Culture and Communities, Simon Fraser University.

Murray, L.J. 2005. Copyright talk: Patterns and pitfalls in Canadian policy discourses. In *In the public interest: The future of Canadian copyright law,* edited by M. Geist, 15-40. Toronto: Irwin Law.

Murray, L.J., and S.E. Trosow. 2007. *Canadian copyright: A citizen's guide.* Toronto: Between the Lines.

Nancoo, R.S., and S.E. Nancoo, eds. 1996. *The mass media and Canadian diversity.* Mississauga, ON: Canadian Educators' Press.

Napoli, P. 2007. Public interest media activism and advocacy as a social movement: A review of the literature. Report prepared for the Media, Arts and Culture Unit of the Ford Foundation. fordham.bepress.com/mcgannon_working_papers/21/.

National Campus and Community Radio Association. 1987. The NCRA statement of principles. http://www.ncra.ca/business/NCRAStatement.html.

–. 2008. Community Radio Fund of Canada launched to support local grassroots media. News release, 6 May. http://www.friends.ca/news-item/2734.

National Citizens Coalition. n.d. http://nationalcitizens.ca.

National Religious Broadcasters. 2009. Declaration of unity. http://nrb.org/about/declaration_of_unity/.

National-Socialist Party of Canada. 2008. http://nspcanada.nfshost.com.

Neatby, S. 2007. The Christian Labour Association of Canada. *Dominion,* 30 December. http://www.dominionpaper.ca/articles/1464.

Newspaper Association of America. 2007. Daily newspaper readership trends. http://www.naa.org/TrendsandNumbers.aspx.

–. 2008. Advertising expenditures. http://www.naa.org/TrendsandNumbers.aspx.

Niblock, S., and D. Machin. 2007. News values for consumer groups: The case of Independent Radio News, London, UK. *Journalism* 8(2): 184-204.

Nova Scotia Advisory Council on the Status of Women. 1992. Decision misses significance of lesbian oppression. *Pandora,* September, 14.

NSM Radio-Television Online. n.d. www.nsm88.org.

NYCMA. 2009. About NYCMA. http://www.indypressny.org/nycma/about/.

O'Connor, K. 2000. CRTC responded to public demand. *Regina Leader-Post,* 7 January, A2.

Office of the Commissioner of Lobbying of Canada. 2011a. Registry of lobbyists. http://www.ocl-cal.gc.ca/eic/site/lobbyist-lobbyiste1.nsf/eng/h_nx00274.html.

–. 2011b. Registry of lobbyists. http://www.ocl-cal.gc.ca/eic/site/lobbyist-lobbyiste1.nsf/eng/home.

Ogilvie, J. 1983. Community radio in Québec – Perspectives in conflict. Master's thesis, McGill University.

Ontario Human Rights Commission. 2009. Human rights code R.S.O. 1990, chapter H.19. www.e-laws.gov.on.ca/html/statutes/english/elaws_statutes_90h19_e.htm.

O'Reilly, T. 2005. What is Web 2.0? Design patterns and business models for the next generation of software. *O'Reilly Media.* http://www.oreillynet.com/pub/a/oreilly/tim/news/2005/09/30/what-is-web-20.html.

Organisation for Economic Co-operation and Development. 2008. Total broadband subscribers by country. http://www.oecd.org/document/54/0,3343,en_2649_34225_38690102_1_1_1_1,00.html.

Ottawa Citizen. 2006. TVO sends mixed signals. 6 July, C4.

–. 2009. Rights revisited. 17 June, A16.

Padovani, C., and M. Tracey. 2003. Report on the conditions of public service broadcasting. *Television and New Media* 4(2): 131-53.

Palmer, V. 2005. Partisan teachers' union finds itself noticed in Liberal election platform. *Vancouver Sun*, 26 April, A3.

Pandora. 1985a. Masthead. September, 4.

–. 1985b. Who are *Pandora* women? September, 5.

–. 1986a. Issue in article of obvious concern. June, 4.

–. 1986b. Lesbians, abortion rights activists question their deliberate exclusion. Spring, 13.

–. 1988. *Pandora*, too, needs support. June, 4.

–. 1989. Why is it that women do not let us know what they're doing? Can we change? Can they change? March, 4.

–. 1990. Notices/calendar. January, 12.

–. 1994a. *Pandora* women have a dream. March, back page.

–. 1994b. Righting the debt – Thanks to all. March, 2.

–. 1994c. We've been here before and we're back here ... AGAIN. March, 1, 4.

Pandora Collective. 1994. An open letter to *Pandora* supporters. March.

Pandora Collective Member. 1992. Victory for *Pandora* ... and all of us. *Womanist,* Spring, 32.

Pandora Coordinating Committee. 1987. Transitions make room for challenge and unity. *Pandora*, March, 4.

Parlette, V. 2010. *Toronto Street News* as a counterpublic sphere. In *Understanding community media,* edited by K. Howley, 96-105. London: Sage.

Peters, D. 2006. Independently yours: Paul Jay has a plan to make TV what it was meant to be. But is bias so easily banished? *This Magazine* 39(4): 40-41.

Pew Project for Excellence in Journalism. 2009. *The state of the news media: An annual report on American journalism.* http://www.stateofthemedia.org/2009/index.htm.

Pfanner, E. 2009. Google and News Corp. do need each other. *New York Times,* 30 November. http://www.nytimes.com/2009/11/30/business/media/30iht-cache30.html?_r=1.

Pickard, V.W. 2006. United yet autonomous: Indymedia and the struggle to sustain a radical democratic network. *Media, Culture and Society* 28(3): 315-36.

Pickerill, J. 2007. "Autonomy online": Indymedia and practices of alter-globalisation. *Environment and Planning A* 39(11): 2668-84.

Pilli, A. 1982. *The Finnish-language press in Canada: A study in the history of ethnic journalism.* Helsinki: Suomalainen Tiedeakatemia.

Pinto, L., S. Anderson, R. Yeo, and J. Cusack McDonald. 2010. Internet openness: Where do the parties stand? OpenMedia. http://openmedia.ca/saveournet/report.

Pitt, L. 2003. Masculinities@work: Gender inequalities and the new media industries. *Feminist Media Studies* 3(3): 378-82.

Pollak, N. 1989a. Inside *Kinesis. Kinesis,* July-August, 2.

–. 1989b. Inside *Kinesis. Kinesis,* September, 2.

–. 1989c. Services in peril. *Kinesis,* June, 3.

–. 1990. No centres, no staff, no service. *Kinesis,* March, 3.

–. 1993. Sec state funding cuts: Death of a thousand cuts. *Kinesis,* March, 3.

Pollak Private Collection. *Kinesis* Papers, 1988-1992.

Polster, C. 2000. The future of the liberal university in the era of the global knowledge grab. *Higher Education* 39: 19-41.

Powell, A. 2009. Co-productions of technology, culture, and policy in North America's community wireless networking movement. PhD diss., Concordia University.

Principe, A. 1999. *The darkest side of the fascist years: The Italian-Canadian press, 1920-1942.* Toronto: Guernica.

Professional Writers Association of Canada. 2006. *Canadian professional writers survey: A profile of the freelance writing sector in Canada.* http://www.pwac.ca/files/PDF/PWACsurvey.pdf.

Public Service Alliance of Canada. 2010. Harper government steps up attacks against women's human rights. http://www.newswire.ca/en/releases/archive/May2010/06/c9236.html.

Qiu, H. 2003. Communication among knowledge diasporas: Online magazines of expatriate Chinese students. In *The media of diaspora,* edited by K.H. Karim, 148-61. London: Routledge.

Raab, C. 1999. From balancing to steering: New directions for data protection. In *Visions of privacy,* edited by C.J. Bennett and R. Grant, 68-93. Toronto: University of Toronto Press.

rabble.ca. 2009. *Annual report.* http://rabble.ca/sites/rabble/files/Annualpercent20Report percent2008percent20draftpercent20v4.pdf.

Raboy, M. 1981. *Media alternatives and social movements: Québec 1960-1980.* Working papers in communications, Graduate Programme in Communications. Montreal: McGill University.

–. 1984. *Movements and messages: Media and radical politics in Quebec.* Toronto: Between the Lines.

–. 1990. *Missed opportunities: The story of Canada's broadcasting policy.* Montreal and Kingston: McGill-Queen's University Press.

Raboy, M., and J. Shtern. 2010. *Media divides: Communication rights and the right to communicate in Canada.* Vancouver: UBC Press.

Raboy, M., and D. Taras. 2005. The trial by fire of the Canadian Broadcasting Corporation: Lessons for public broadcasting. In *Cultural dilemmas in public service broadcasting,* edited by G.F. Lowe and P. Jauert, 251-69. Göteborg, Sweden: Nordicom.

Radio Centre-Ville. 2005. *Manuel d'accueil à Radio Centre-Ville.* Montreal: Radio Centre-Ville.

Radio Enfant. 2009. http://www.radiocentreville.com/pages/rae4.htm.

Ralph, D., A. Régimbald, and N. St-Amand, eds. 1997. *Mike Harris's Ontario: Open for business, closed to people.* Halifax: Fernwood.

Read, J. 2003. *The micro-politics of capital: Marx and the pre-history of the present.* Albany: State University of New York Press.

REAL Women of Canada. 2003. The courts and the culture war. *REALity.* November -December. http://www.realwomenca.com/archives/newsletter/2003_nov_dec/article_ 10.html.

–. 2008. The tyranny of labour unions in Canada. http://www.realwomenca.com/page/ pubanalys12.html.

Reed, R. 2004. A religious conservative vision for America. In *Ideas and ideologies: A reader,* 5th ed., edited by T. Ball and R. Dagger, 184-93. Toronto: Pearson Longman.

Reid, G. 1976-1977. Report on *Kinesis.* In *Annual report of the Vancouver Status of Women.* Vancouver Status of Women Papers, Canadian Women's Movement Archives, University of Ottawa, Finding aid X10-1, box 124, file 1, 16-17.

–. 1981. A diverse movement demands eclectic newspaper, open debate. *Kinesis,* July-August, 21-23.

Renan, E. 1990. What is nation? In *Nation and Narration,* edited by H. Bhabha, 8-22. London: Routledge.

Rennie, E. 2006. *Community media: A global introduction.* Lanham, MD: Rowman and Littlefield.

Resist.ca. n.d. About us. http://resist.ca/about.

Riaño, P., ed. 1994. *Women in grassroots communication: Furthering social change.* Thousand Oaks, CA: Sage.

Rideout, V. 2003. *Continentalizing Canadian telecommunications: The politics of regulatory reform.* Montreal and Kingston: McGill-Queen's University Press.

Riggins, S.H., ed. 1992. *Ethnic minority media: An international perspective.* Newbury Park, CA: Sage.

Riggs, J. 1987. REALW rumblings ... doors creak open again. *Pandora,* March, 6.

Riismandel, P. 2002. Radio by and for the public: The death and resurrection of low-power. In *Radio reader: Essays in the cultural history of radio,* edited by M. Hilmes and J. Loviglio, 423-50. New York: Routledge.

Robertson, G. 2008. TV networks losing ground to rival services. *Toronto Globe and Mail,* 9 July, B4.

Rodriguez, A. 2000. *Making Latino news: Race, language, and class.* Thousand Oaks, CA: Sage.

Rodriguez, C. 1996. Shedding useless notions of alternative. *Peace Review* 8(1): 63-68.

–. 2001. *Fissures in the mediascape: An international study of citizens' media.* Cresskill, NJ: Hampton Press.

Rodriguez, C., D. Kidd, and L. Stein, eds. 2010a. *Making our media: Global initiatives toward a democratic public sphere.* Vol. 1, *Creating new communication spaces.* Cresskill, NJ: Hampton Press.

–, eds. 2010b. *Making our media: Global initiatives toward a democratic public sphere.* Vol. 2, *National and global movements for democratic communication.* Cresskill, NJ: Hampton Press.

Rogers. 2001. Submission to the CRTC in response to CRTC public notice 2001-19: Review of community channel policy.

Romanow, P. 2005. "The picture of democracy we are seeking": CBC Radio forums and the search for Canadian identity, 1930-1950. *Journal of Radio Studies* 12(1): 104-19.

Roth, L. 2005. *Something new in the air: The story of First Peoples television broadcasting in Canada.* Montreal and Kingston: McGill-Queen's University Press.

Ruggles, M.A. 2005. Continentalizing Canadian telecommunications: The politics of regulatory reform. *Canadian Journal of Communication* 30(4): 707-8.

Said, E.W. 1979. *Orientalism.* New York: Random House.

Salter, L. 1981. Community radio in Canada. Canadian Broadcasting Corporation, Office of Community Radio.

–. 1988. Reconceptualizing public broadcasting. In *Communication Canada: Issues in broadcasting and new technologies,* edited by R. Lorimer and D.C. Wilson, 232-48. Toronto: Kagan and Woo.

Salter, L., and F.N.L. Odartey-Wellington. 2008. *The CRTC and broadcasting regulation in Canada.* Toronto: Thomson Carswell.

Sand, C. 1985. Periodicals in review. *Kinesis,* April, 34.

Sandborn, T. 2007. Work outsourced from *Sun, Province* newsrooms. *The Tyee,* 5 November. http://thetyee.ca/Mediacheck/2007/11/05/CanwestSynergies/.

Sangster, J., and M. Hobbs, eds. 1999. *The woman worker, 1926-1929.* St. John's: Canadian Committee on Labour History.

Santianni, M. 2003. The movement for a free Tibet: Cyberspace and the ambivalence of cultural translation. In *The media of diaspora,* edited by K.H. Karim, 189-202. London: Routledge.

Santo, A. 2004. Nunavut: Inuit television and cultural citizenship. *International Journal of Cultural Studies* 7(4): 379-97.

Sassen, S. 1996. *Losing control? Sovereignty in an age of globalization.* New York: Columbia University Press.

Saunders, D. 1988. Cabinet allocates stations. *Toronto Globe and Mail,* 17 March, D2.

–. 2009. Angry Europe embraces the fringe. *Toronto Globe and Mail,* 9 June, A1, A13.

Savage, P.D. 1985. Doing community radio: The practices of information programming at a community radio station in comparison to a commercial radio station. PhD diss., Simon Fraser University.

Sayers, S. 2005. Why work? Marx and human nature. *Science and Society* 69(4): 606-16.

Scassa, T. 2005. Interests in the balance. In *In the public interest: The future of Canadian copyright law,* edited by M. Geist, 41-65. Toronto: Irwin Law.

Schechter, D. 2005. Million-word march for media reform. *MediaChannel.org.* http://www.alternet.org/media/.

Schiller, H. 1989. *Culture, Inc.* New York: Oxford University Press.

Schmidt, A. 2005. Independent reporting: A tool for international solidarity building. In *Autonomous media: Activating resistance and dissent,* edited by A. Langlois and F. Dubois, 74-87. Montreal: Cumulus Press.

Schubart, R. 2009. *War isn't hell: It's entertainment.* Jefferson, NC: McFarland.

Schudson, M. 2000. The sociology of news production revisited (again). In *Mass media and society,* edited by J. Curran and M. Gurevitch, 175-200. New York: Oxford University Press.

Schwartz, E. 2010. Canadian copyright reform must be fair to music creators and consumers. Songwriters Association of Canada. http://www.songwriters.ca/Article/37/details.aspx.

Senate of Canada. 2006. *Standing Committee on Transport and Communications. Final report on Canadian news media.* Vol. 1. http://www.parl.gc.ca/39/1/parlbus/commbus/senate/com-e/tran-e/rep-e/repfinjun06vol1-e.htm.

Shade, L.R. 2008. Public interest activism in Canadian ICT policy: Blowin' in the policy winds. *Global Media Journal – Canadian Edition* 1(1): 107-21.

Shanahan, N. 1989a. Bye bye *Broadside. Kinesis,* April, 7.

–. 1989b. Inside *Kinesis. Kinesis,* June, 2.

Shandel, T. 1994. TV worth knowing: Engaging programming is available – From the BC government's TV station. *Vancouver Sun,* 17 November, A19.

Shannon, E. 1994. Commentary on feminist journalism and *Kinesis:* Influences and inspiration. *Kinesis,* June, 18-19.

Shragge, E. 2003. *Activism and social change: Lessons for community and local organizing.* Peterborough, ON: Broadview Press.

Simons, J. 1995. *Foucault and the political.* New York: Routledge.

Skinner, D. 2005. Divided loyalties: The early development of Canada's "single" broadcasting system. *Journal of Radio Studies* 12(1): 136-55.

–. 2010. Minding the gaps: Alternative media in Canada. In *Mediascapes: New patterns in Canadian communication,* 3rd ed., edited by L.R. Shade, 221-36. Toronto: Thomson Nelson.

Skinner, D., J.R. Compton, and M. Gasher, eds. 2005. *Converging media, diverging politics: A political economy of news media in the United States and Canada.* Lanham, MD: Lexington Books.

Skinner, D., and M. Gasher. 2005. So much by so few: Media policy and ownership in Canada. In *Converging media, diverging politics: A political economy of news media in the United States and Canada,* edited by D. Skinner, J.R. Compton, and M. Gasher, 51-76. Lanham, MD: Lexington Books.

Skinner, D., S. Uzelman, A. Langlois, and F. Dubois. 2009. Indymedia in Canada: Experiments in developing glocal media commons. In *Making our media: Global initiatives toward a democratic public sphere.* Vol. 1, *Creating new communication spaces,* edited by C. Rodriguez, D. Kidd, and L. Stein, 183-201. Cresskill, NJ: Hampton Press.

Smith, A.D. 1989. The origins of nations. *Ethnic and Racial Studies* 12(3): 340-67.

Smyth, D.E. 1987. R.E.A.L. Women claim discrimination by sec state. *Pandora,* June, 2.

Soron, D., and G. Laxer. 2006. Thematic introduction: Decommodification, democracy and the battle for the commons. In *Not for sale: Decommodifying public life,* edited by G. Laxer and D. Soron, 15-38. Peterborough, ON: Broadview Press.

Sparks, C. 1993. Raymond Williams and the theory of democratic communication. In *Communication and democracy,* edited by S. Splichal and J. Wasko, 69-86. Norwood, NJ: Ablex.

Spencer, M. 2003. *Hollywood north: Creating the Canadian motion picture industry.* Montreal: Cantos International.

Squires, C.R. 2002. Rethinking the black public sphere: An alternative vocabulary for multiple public spheres. *Communication Theory* 12(4): 446-48.

Sreberny, A. 2005. Globalization, communication, democratization: Toward gender equality. In *Democratizing global media: One world, many struggles,* edited by R.A. Hackett and Y. Zhao, 245-67. Lanham, MD: Rowman and Littlefield.

Stanley, D. 2006. The social effects of culture. *Canadian Journal of Communication* 31(1): 7-15.

Statistics Canada. 1999. *Service bulletin: Communications* 28(3). Catalogue no. 56-001-XIB.

–. 2004. *Broadcasting and telecommunications service bulletin* 34(4). Catalogue no. 56-001-XIE.

–. 2006a. *2006 census.* http://www12.statcan.ca/.

–. 2006b. *2006 community profiles.* http://www12.statcan.ca/.

–. 2007. *Service bulletin: Broadcasting and telecommunications* 37(2). Catalogue no. 56-001-XIE.

–. 2008. *Canada's ethnocultural mosaic, 2006 census.* Ottawa: Minister of Industry.

Stein, L. 2001. Access television and grassroots political communication in the United States. In *Radical media: Rebellious communication and social movements,* edited by J. Downing, T.V. Ford, G. Gil, and L. Stein, 299-324. Thousand Oaks, CA: Sage.

Stephen, L. 2007. "We are brown, we are short, we are fat ... we are the face of Oaxaca": Women leaders in the Oaxaca rebellion. *Socialism and Democracy* 21(2): 97-112.

Stevenson, J. 2007. *Community radio support in other jurisdictions.* Ottawa: National Campus and Community Radio Association.

Strachan, A. 1998. Knowledge Network grows by sticking to what it does best. *Vancouver Sun,* 29 April, C8.

Strangelove, M. 2005. *The empire of mind: Digital piracy and the anti-capitalist movement.* Toronto: University of Toronto Press.

Straubhaar, J.D. 2007. *World television: From global to local.* London: Sage.

Sullivan, B. 1970. The student press in Canada. In *Good, bad, or simply inevitable? Selected Research Studies.* Special Senate committee on the mass media. Vol. 3, 241-69. Ottawa: Queen's Printer.

Sumner, J. 2006. From the knowledge economy to the knowledge commons. In *Not for sale: Decommodifying public life,* edited by G. Laxer and D. Soron, 203-17. Peterborough, ON: Broadview Press.

Sun, W. 2002. *Leaving China: Media, migration, and transnational imagination.* New York: Rowman and Littlefield.

Surman, M. 1994. *The electronic commons: Community television and Canada's information highway.* Written comments in accordance with CRTC public notice 1994-130. http://www.ifla.org.sg/documents/infopol/canada/surman01.txt.

Surveillance Camera Players. 2006. *We know you are watching: Surveillance Camera Players 1996-2006.* San Diego: Factory School.

Swanson, J. 2005. *Poor bashing: The politics of exclusion.* Toronto: Between the Lines.

Tatla, D.S. 1991. The Punjabi ethnic press of North America. *Ethnic Forum* 11: 29-49.

Tawfik, M. 2005. *International copyright law: W[h]ither user rights?* In *In the public interest: The future of Canadian copyright law,* edited by M. Geist, 66-85. Toronto: Irwin Law.

Taylor, B. 2008. *Entertainment theology: New-edge spirituality in a digital democracy.* Grand Rapids: Baker Academic.

Terranova, T. 2004. *Network culture: Politics for the information age.* London: Pluto Press.

Théberge v. Galérie d'Art du Petit Champlain Inc. 2002. SCC 34. http://www.canlii.org/ca/cas/scc/2002/2002scc34.html.

Thomas, P. 2005. Christian fundamentalism and the media. *Media Development* 2. http://www.org.uk/wacc/publications/media_development/2005_2.

Thussu, D. 2000. *International communication: Continuity and change.* London: Arnold.

Toronto Globe and Mail. 1999. A sense of purpose for public broadcasting. 11 August, A8.

–. 2010. A think-tank should sink or swim. 12 January, A16.

Trepanier, R.J. 1991. Towards an alternative media strategy: Gramsci's theory in practice. Master's thesis, Simon Fraser University.

TRNN (The Real News Network). 2008. Opening the "gates of public consciousness." Document on file with author (Sonja Macdonald).

–. 2009. The plan 2009-2012: A new model for daily broadcast news. http://therealnews.com/t2/about-us/business-plan-2009.

Tsaliki, L. 2003. Globalisation and hybridity: The maintenance of a national and cultural identity. In *The media of diaspora,* edited by K.H. Karim, 163-76. London: Routledge.

Turk, J.L., ed. 2000. *The corporate campus: Commercialization and the dangers to Canada's colleges and universities.* Toronto: Lorimer.

TVOntario. 2006. *Annual report 2005-06.* http://www.tvo.org/about/AnnualReports/AR_TVO_05_06_EN/pdf.

–. 2008a. *The Ontario Educational Communications Authority 2007-08 annual report.* http://www.tvo.org/about/AnnualReports/TVO_AR_07-08_English.pdf.

–. 2008b. The role of public media: Content – packaging and context. Notes for presentation to Commonwealth Broadcasting Association, 26 January.

–. 2008c. What is TVO? http://www.tvo.org/cfmx/tvoorg/about/index.cfm?page_id=886#subSection_2.

–. 2010. *Strategic agenda 2010.* http://www.tvo.org/about/StrategicAgenda/TVO_StrategicAgenda2010.pdf.

Tyee, The. n.d. How to apply for a Tyee fellowship. http://thetyee.ca/About/FellowshipApplication/.

Uzelman, S. 2002. Catalyzing participatory communication: Independent Media Centre and the politics of direct action. Master's thesis, Simon Fraser University.

–. 2005. Hard at work in the bamboo garden: Media activists and social movements. In *Autonomous media: Activating resistance and dissent,* edited by A. Langlois and F. Dubois, 16-29. Montreal: Cumulus Press.

Vaidhyanathan, S. 2004. *The anarchist in the library.* New York: Basic Books.

Valaskakis, G.G. 1993. Parallel voices: Indians and others – Narratives of cultural struggle. *Canadian Journal of Communication* 18(3): 283-94.

Valentine, L.P. 1994. *Making it their own: Severn Ojibwe communicative practices.* Toronto: University of Toronto Press.

Valiani, S. 2006. Social conservatism in Canada: Examining the rise of the far right through the issue of childcare. Social and Economic Policy, Canadian Labour Congress. http://childcarecanada.org/documents/research-policy-practice/06/10/social-conservatism-canada-examining-rise-far-right-through.

Valiquette, M. 1989. Triple whammy for feminists. *Kinesis*, November, 19.

Vallantin, C. 2008. Fade to black: How cable companies and the CRTC's lenience are killing what's left of community TV. *Fast Forward Weekly*, 19 June. http://www.ffwd weekly.com/article/life-style/television/fade-black.

Van Dijk, T.A. 1993. *Elite discourses and racism*. Newbury Park, CA: Sage.

Vanderklippe, N. 2009. Bill under attack for catering to right-wing parents. *Toronto Globe and Mail*, 18 May, A4.

Vaneigem, R. 1967. *The revolution of everyday life*. London: Rebel Press.

Vaughn, K., J. Tobin, and E. Legault. 1999. Educational television in Canada: "Television that matters." Toronto: Leto Consulting.

Verzuh, R. 1986. Alternatives: Moving uptown? *Content*, March-April, 2-6.

–. 1988. *Radical rag: The pioneer labour press in Canada*. Ottawa: Steel Rail.

–. 1989. *Underground times: Canada's flower-child revolutionaries*. Toronto: Deneau.

Ville d'Acton Vale. 2008. Acton Vale en chiffres. http://www.ville.actonvale.qc.ca/opter/chiffres.html.

Vipond, M. 2002. *The mass media in Canada*, 3rd ed. Toronto: Lorimer.

Virno, P., and M. Hardt, eds. 1996. *Radical thought in Italy: A potential politics*. Minneapolis: University of Minnesota Press.

W2. n.d. Community media arts. http://www.creativetechnology.org/.

Wachtel, E. 1982. *Feminist print media*. Ottawa: Government of Canada, Secretary of State.

–. 1985. *Update on feminist periodicals*. Ottawa: Government of Canada, Secretary of State.

Waddell, C. 2009. The future for the Canadian media. *Policy Options/Options politiques*, June, 16-20.

Walkom, T. 1981. Tory plan would put God, family in preamble. *Toronto Globe and Mail*, 22 January, A15.

Waltz, M. 2005. *Alternative and activist media*. Edinburgh: Edinburgh University Press.

Ward, G. 2003. *True religion*. Oxford: Blackwell.

Waring, M. 1999. *Counting for nothing: What men value and what women are worth*, 2nd ed. Toronto: University of Toronto Press.

Watkins, M. 1977. *Dene Nation: The colony within*. Toronto: University of Toronto Press.

Waugh, T., M. Baker, and E. Winton, eds. 2010. *Challenge for change: Activist documentary and the National Film Board of Canada*. Montreal and Kingston: McGill-Queen's University Press.

Wawatay Native Communications Society. 2008. *Language survey*. http://wawataynews.ca/files/Wawatay%20Language%20Survey.pdf.

Weaver, D., ed. 1998. *The global journalist: News people around the world*. Cresskill, NJ: Hampton Press.

Weber, M. 1978. *Economy and society*, edited by G. Roth and C. Wittich. Berkeley: University of California Press. (Orig. pub. 1922.)

Webster, J.G. 2009. The role of structure in media choice. In *Media choice: A theoretical and empirical overview*, edited by T. Hartmann and P. Vordere, 221-34. London: Routledge.

Weinrich, P. 1982. *Social protest from the left in Canada, 1870-1970*. Toronto: University of Toronto Press.

Welch, K. 2007. Black criminal stereotypes and racial profiling. *Journal of Contemporary Criminal Justice* 23(3): 276-88.

Wennerlind, C. 2002. The labor theory of value and the strategic role of alienation. *Capital and Class* 77: 1-21.

Weston, J. 1997. Old freedoms and new technologies: The evolution of community networking. *Information Society* 13: 195-201.

Whitney, J. 2005. What's the matter with Indymedia? *AlterNet*. http://www.alternet.org/mediaculture/23741.

Wilkinson and Associates. 1988. *Community radio in Ontario*. Toronto: Ministry of Culture and Communications.

Williams, R. 1966. *Communications*. London: Chatto and Windus.

–. 1977. *Marxism and literature*. Oxford: Oxford University Press.

–. 1989. *Culture*. London: Fontana Press.

–. 2005. Means of communication as means of production. In *Culture and materialism*, 50-63. London: Verso.

Wilson, J., B. Bell, and W. Powell. 1984. *The provincial educational communications organizations in Canada*. New technologies in Canadian education, paper 7. Toronto: Ontario Educational Communications Authority.

Wilson, M. 2002. Does a networked society foster participatory democracy or is commitment to place-based community still a necessity for civic engagement? In *Citizenship and participation in the information age*, edited by M. Pendakur and R. Harris, 372-87. Aurora, ON: Garamond Press.

Wilson, P.M., and M. Stewart, eds. 2008. *Global indigenous media: Cultures, poetics, politics*. Durham, NC: Duke University Press.

Winseck, D. 1997. Canadian telecommunications: A history and political economy of media reconvergence. *Canadian Journal of Communication* 22(2): 217-60.

–. 2002. Netscapes of power: Convergence, consolidation and power in the Canadian mediascape. *Media, Culture and Society* 24(6): 795-819.

–. 2010. Financialization and the "crisis of the media": The rise and fall of (some) media conglomerates in Canada. *Canadian Journal of Communication* 35(3): 365-93.

Winter, R. 1998. Changes in the field of education – Challenges for public service broadcasters. *Educational Media International* 35(2): 122-24.

Winton, E. 2007. The spaces between: Grassroots documentary distribution and exhibition as counterpublics. Master's thesis, Concordia University.

Woodsworth, A. 1972. *The "alternative" press in Canada: A checklist of underground, revolutionary, radical, and other alternative serials from 1960*. Toronto: University of Toronto Press.

Wright, S.A. 2009. Strategic framing of racial-nationalism in North America and Europe: An analysis of a burgeoning transnational network. *Terrorism and Political Violence* 21(2): 189-210.

Wu, T. 2003. Network neutrality, broadband discrimination. *Journal of Telecommunications and High Technology Law* 2: 141-79.

Wu, T., and L. Lessig. 2003. Letter re: Ex parte submission in CS Docket No. 02-52. http://www.freepress.net/files/wu_lessig_fcc.pdf.

Yu, S.S., and C.A. Murray. 2007. Media under a multicultural policy: The case of the Korean media in British Columbia. *Canadian Ethnic Studies* 39(3): 99-124.

Zaremba, E. 1986. Movement comment – Periodical process. *Broadside,* February, 7.

Zeleke, E.C. 2004. *The status of women in community-based radio in Canada.* Women's Hands and Voices and the National Campus and Community Radio Association/ L'association nationale des radios étudiantes et communautaires. http://www.ncra.ca/women/stratplan/report.pdf.

Contributors

Marian Bredin is an associate professor in the Department of Communication, Popular Culture and Film, and director of the Centre for Canadian Studies at Brock University. She has participated in the Popular Culture Niagara Research Group, and her main research interests include Aboriginal and indigenous media, communications policy and cultural politics, and Canadian television. She co-edited *Indigenous Screen Cultures in Canada* (2010) and is co-editing *Text and Context: Critical Perspectives on English-Canadian Television* (2011).

Nicole S. Cohen is a PhD candidate in communication and culture at York University, where she researches labour in the communication and cultural industries. Her work has been published in *Democratic Communiqué*, the *Canadian Journal of Communication*, *Stream*, and *Feminist Media Studies*. Nicole has contributed to various alternative and activist media projects, including *Upping the Anti*, *Canadian Dimension*, *This Magazine*, and *Briarpatch*, and is a co-founder and former co-editor of *Shameless*, a feminist magazine for teenage girls and trans youth. She remains involved in the project in various capacities.

Barbara M. Freeman is a media historian and adjunct research professor in the School of Journalism and Communication at Carleton University, Ottawa. Her historical research centres on gender and diversity in the mainstream and alternative news media of the nineteenth and twentieth centuries. She is the author of *Beyond Bylines: Media Workers and Women's Rights in Canada* (2011), *The Satellite Sex: The Media and Women's Issues in English Canada, 1966-71* (2001), and *Kit's Kingdom: The Journalism of Kathleen Blake Coleman* (1989). She supports and occasionally writes for the feminist magazine *Herizons*.

Sandra Jeppesen is an assistant professor of media studies in the Department of Interdisciplinary Studies at Lakehead University–Orillia, Ontario. She has been an activist, zine-maker, and writer for many years. Her academic work on alternative media and direct-action activism has appeared in journals such as *Sexualities, Anarchist Developments in Cultural Studies,* and the *Canadian Journal of Communication,* as well as book chapters in *Post-Anarchism* (2011), *New Perspectives on Anarchism* (2009), and *Constituent Imagination* (2007).

Karim H. Karim is a professor at Carleton University's School of Journalism and Communication, where he was formerly the director. He has also served as co-director of the Institute of Ismaili Studies in London, UK. His publications include *The Media of Diaspora* (2003) and *Islamic Peril: Media and Global Violence* (2000, updated edition 2003). He has also worked as a correspondent for Inter Press Service (Rome) and Compass News Features (Luxembourg), with whom he also explored alternative ways to report on issues on international development. Karim received the inaugural Robinson Book Prize in 2001 for excellence in communication studies and has delivered several distinguished lectures. He attended Columbia and McGill Universities.

Kirsten Kozolanka is an associate professor in the School of Journalism and Communication at Carleton University. She is the author of *The Power of Persuasion: The Politics of the New Right in Ontario* (2007). She has published several times in the *Canadian Journal of Communication,* has written about poverty and the media in *Studies in Political Economy,* and is editing a book collection on publicity practices in politics. She is the founder of the Canadian Alternative Media Archive. Her first formal experience with alternative media was as co-editor of a human rights magazine titled *Rights and Freedoms/Droits et libertés.*

Evan Light is a PhD candidate in communication at Université du Québec à Montréal. A community radio activist since 1993 at WLFR (New Jersey) and

CKUT (Montréal), Evan was a board member of the National Campus and Community Radio Association, member of the AMARC Principles for a Democratic Legislation on Community Broadcasting research team, and member of the steering committee of a Canadian Heritage study on Canadian community broadcasting. His thesis concerns radio spectrum and water policy and participatory governance in Uruguay and Canada.

Michael Lithgow is a PhD candidate at Carleton University. His dissertation research is on aesthetics, dissent, and power in Canadian culture. He worked for many years as a community radio producer at CFRO (Vancouver) and later as a community television advocate with ICTV (Independent Community Television Cooperative). He is a co-founder of CACTUS (Canadian Association of Community Television Users and Stations) and is currently a research associate and member of the board at OpenMedia.ca, a national public interest policy group. He is also a research associate with the Canadian Alternative Media Archive.

Sonja Macdonald has been active in the Canadian communication policy field for the past fifteen years, with experience in the public, private, and non-profit sectors. She is co-founder and director of the Centre for Community Study, a Canadian research organization with a focus on urban and media issues. Sonja holds an MA and a BA in communication from Carleton University and a BA in political science from the University of British Columbia. Currently, she is a PhD candidate in communication and culture at York University. Her dissertation investigates local broadcasting policy in Canada.

Patricia Mazepa is an associate professor in the Department of Communication Studies at York University. She has been contributing to the development of alternative media since 1997 when she completed her master's thesis on the history and development of Solinet, and from 1999 through courses she designed on alternative media at Carleton and York Universities. Her published articles seek to build a history of alternative media in Canada, and her scholarship and activism are dedicated to the advancement of democratic, progressive media while seeking to understand the constitution and exercise of power in all its forms.

Kate Milberry is a post-doctoral fellow in the Faculty of Information at the University of Toronto. She is co-founder of *ROOM Magazine,* an alternative newsweekly that published from 1994 to 2001 in Windsor, Ontario. She has been researching radical media making in the global justice movement since 1999, writing her master's thesis on Indymedia and focusing on how the Internet has altered activist and media practice. She is a technology commentator for CBC Radio, helped organize the Alternative Media Centre for the Toronto G20 in 2010, and blogs on media and technology at www.geeksand globaljustice.com. She is @KateMilberry on Twitter.

David Skinner is an associate professor and chair of the Department of Communication Studies at York University. Previously, he was the founding chair of the bachelor of journalism at Thompson Rivers University in Kamloops, British Columbia. He is active in the media reform movement and has written a number of articles on alternative media, traditional media, and media reform in Canada and the United States. Most recently, he is co-author of the seventh edition of *Mass Communication in Canada* (2012).

Scott Uzelman is a lecturer and former Social Sciences and Humanities Research Council post-doctoral fellow in the Department of Sociology at Queen's University. He has been involved in the media democracy movement for many years as a researcher and activist. In 2002, he completed a master's thesis at Simon Fraser University on participatory research he conducted with fellow media activists in establishing and developing the Vancouver Independent Media Centre. His current research focuses on struggles against capitalist enclosure and subordination via collective attempts at preserving or creating commons or other autonomous forms of social life.

Index

Songwriters Association of Canada, 237, 241
South America community television situation, 142-43
South Asian Voice, 176
South Korea community television situation, 142
Sreberny, A., 139
Standing Committee on Canadian Heritage, 133, 140-41, 144n7
Star TV, 178
Stein, Laura, 10
Stewart, M., 185
Stormfront, 249
Straubhaar, Joseph, 107, 108
structuration, 246
structure: in Aboriginal media, 184-86, 186-89, 192-94, 195-98; autonomous media, 76-82; collective or prefigurative organization of alternative media, 26, 28; community radio (*see* community radio); community television (*see* community television); corporate media's concentration of ownership, 7-8, 21, 25, 26; definition, 15; diversity of organization, 27; educasters (*see* public service educational broadcasters [educasting]); of ethnic media, 173-77, 179-81; feminist media (*see* feminist media); funding and organizational structure in US, 32, 34-36; hybrid media, 104-5, 119-20, 202; labour (*see* labour in alternative media); participatory organizational form (*see* participation); regulatory structure in Canada (*see* Canadian Radio-television and Telecommunications Commission [CRTC]); zines, 21, 269-70. *See also* The Real News Network (TRNN) as hybrid media
Sumner, J., 50
Supreme Court of Canada, 234, 238, 260
sustainability: challenges for alternative media, 25-26, 44, 56; definition, 26-27; fundraising to pay for labour, 222-23; importance increasing, 43; literature

review of perspectives on alternative media sustainability, 28-30; membership in alliance or collaborative group to share costs, 221-22; strong social infrastructure, importance of, 17, 27, 30; "tactical media," 29; union membership for alternative media staff, 219-21. *See also* sustainability in Canada; sustainability in United States
sustainability in Canada: lack of call for media reform or support for alternative media, 37, 38; level of trade organization support, 40; media educational activities, 42-43, 44; media environment in US vs Canada, 37-38, 43; media policy, responsibilities and characteristics, 37-39; organizations supporting alternative media, 39-40; self-support initiatives of alternative media, 40-42, 43-44
sustainability in United States: capacity-building efforts, 31; Free Press' focus on policy issues, 32-33, 34; funding by philanthropic foundations, 36, 43; Grand Rapids Community Media Center, 36; Independent Press Association (IPA), 34, 36; media activism for media reform, 30-31; Media and Democracy Coalition to support media reform, 33-34; Media Consortium, 35-36; media environment vs that in Canada, 37-38, 43; New York Community Media Alliance, 34-35, 36; public education for more diverse media system, 32; support programs for community and public media, 30

T
Tamil ethnic media, 176, 180
Tan, Sid, 135, 136-37
Tea Party (US), 248
technology and alternative media, 10
Télé-Québec, 50, 53, 60. *See also* public service educational broadcasters (educasting)